Votes for Women!

VOTES FOR WOMEN!

The Woman Suffrage Movement in Tennessee, the South, and the Nation

Edited by Marjorie Spruill Wheeler

THE UNIVERSITY OF TENNESSEE PRESS / KNOXVILLE

First Edition.

The paper in this book meets the minimum requirements of the American National Standard for Permanence of Paper for Printed Library Materials. ♾ The binding materials have been chosen for strength and durability.

Library of Congress Cataloging-in-Publication Data

Votes for women! : the woman suffrage movement in Tennessee, the South, and the nation / edited by Marjorie Spruill Wheeler. — 1st ed.

p. cm.

Includes bibliographical references and index.

ISBN 0-87049-836-3 (cloth: alk. paper).

ISBN 0-87049-837-1 (pbk.: alk. paper)

1. Women—Suffrage—Tennessee—History. 2. Women—Suffrage—Southern States—History. 3. Women—Suffrage—United States—History. I. Wheeler, Marjorie Spruill.

JK1911.T2V68 1995

324.6'23'0973—dc20 94-18768

CIP

To the memory of
Dr. A. Elizabeth Taylor

Contents

Illustrations

Acknowledgments

Votes for Women! The Woman Suffrage Movement in Tennessee, the South, and the Nation grew out of a symposium that took place in Nashville, Tennessee, in August 1990 to celebrate the seventieth anniversary of the Nineteenth Amendment and Tennessee's pivotal role in the suffrage victory. The Tennessee Historical Society, with Don H. Doyle of Vanderbilt University as president, invited the six scholars whose essays appear in this volume to give lectures on various aspects of the suffrage struggle. Thus, Ann Toplovich, executive director of the Tennessee Historical Society and Sheila Riley, former special programs director (now with the Indianapolis Children's Museum), along with Don Doyle, deserve much credit for this volume. James Summerville, executive director through 1989, also played an important role in the symposium in its early stages. Credit is also due to the Tennessee Humanities Council, which provided financial support for the symposium.

The Tennessee Historical Society has continued to support the publication by locating and reproducing many of the photographs and broadsides herein. Susan Gordon, currently special projects director, and June Dorman, a professional photographer and a member of the Tennessee Historical Society, spent countless hours on these tasks, with Dorman generously donating her services. I am also grateful to Anastatia Sims of Georgia Southern University, so very knowledgeable concerning the Tennessee suffrage movement, who has played a major role in this project from the very beginning as a consultant as well as a contributing author.

Wayne C. Moore, archivist at the Tennessee State Library and Archives, has also been extraordinarily helpful while I prepared this book. In addition, I would like to thank Ralph Carlson and Maud Andrew of Carlson Publishing, Inc.; Jennifer McDade and Carolyn S. Parsons, Virginia State Library and Archives; William Marshall and Claire McCann, Margaret I. King Library, University of Kentucky; Sylvia McDowell and Marie Helen Gold, Schlesinger Library, Radcliffe College; Alice R. Cotten, University of North Carolina Library, Chapel Hill; Paula West Chavoya, Wyoming State Museum; Gentry Trotter and Scott Mandrell of the *Crisis*; Ellen L. Sulser, State Historical Society of Iowa—Des Moines; and Linda Zezulka, Austin History Center, Austin Public Library; Frank Sutherland of the Nashville *Tennessean*; and Lee Anderson of the *Chattanooga News-Free Press* (the father of my college roommate, Corinne Anderson Adams). Adele Logan Alexander has been most generous in furnishing photographs of her grandmother, Adella Hunt Logan.

I would also like to express my gratitude to the University of Southern Mississippi for its support for the project. A summer research grant, and the world's most capable and pleasant-to-work-with graduate assistants, Audra Odom and Donna Sedevie, played crucial roles in the completion of the project. Two colleagues (and friends), Theodore Feldman and Michael Salda, aided me in a last-minute search for particular broadsides and photographs.

Meredith Morris-Babb of the University of Tennessee Press has been a pleasure to work with, and I am grateful to her for her good ideas and enthusiasm for the project. I am also grateful for the aid of the copy editor Scot Danforth.

Finally, I'd like to thank my friend from childhood, Karen Edwards, her husband John Rieser, and their children, Kate and Michael, for their hospitality while I was in Nashville conducting research for *Votes for Women!* And, as always, I am truly grateful to my husband, David M. Wheeler, and our two sons, Scott and Jesse, for their encouragement and supportiveness.

As the dedication indicates, all of us involved are profoundly grateful to the late Dr. A. Elizabeth Taylor, who provided inspiration to everyone who has tried to understand the southern woman suffrage movement. Often called "a pioneer scholar" in women's history, she was the first to focus attention upon the suffrage movement in the region; she continued to labor alone in this neglected field, state by state, article by article, until she published a body of scholarship that has served as a virtual encyclopedia for those of us who have attempted to follow in her footsteps. On a personal level, she was extremely supportive of younger scholars and keenly interested in our findings on southern suffrage; you could always count on her for both advice and an encouraging word.

Dr. Taylor was profoundly interested in the woman suffrage movement in Tennessee and, indeed, began and ended her career with publications on the subject. Her dissertation (Vanderbilt, 1943), was published as *The Woman Suffrage Movement in Tennessee* by Bookman Associates of New York in 1957. And her essay herein, "The Thirty-Sixth State," was completed shortly before her death in October 1993. Thus, in many respects *Votes for Women!* which highlights the woman suffrage movement in Tennessee and demonstrates its crucial role in the history of the women's rights movement in America, is a fitting tribute to this exemplary historian who will be greatly missed by us all.

Marjorie Spruill Wheeler
Hattiesburg, Mississippi

Introduction

The year 1995 marks the seventy-fifth anniversary of the enfranchisement of American women. On August 26, 1920, the Nineteenth Amendment to the Constitution of the United States of America, also known as the Susan B. Anthony Amendment, became the law of the land. Ratification by Tennessee, the thirty-sixth state, brought to a conclusion the long struggle for woman suffrage that began seventy-two years earlier (1848) at the Seneca Falls Convention in New York.

The struggle ended, however, only after a mighty battle was fought in Nashville during the long, hot summer of 1920. The battle was seen by both sides as Armageddon, a holy war between the forces of good and evil: during and after the fateful summer, suffragists and antisuffragists alike accused politicians and one another of bribery and treachery. Edwin Mims, author of *The Advancing South: Stories of Progress and Reaction* (1926), insisted that "the Battle of Nashville in 1864 was a five o'clock tea in comparison with this one."[1]

The suffrage movement's Armageddon (also known as "The War of the Roses" owing to the yellow roses worn by suffrage supporters and the red roses worn by the antis) was marked by southern symbolism and rhetorical flourish. The national press and suffrage supporters portrayed Tennessee legislators as southern gentlemen with an opportunity to "chivalrously" enfranchise the ladies of the nation. But Tennessee antis, including their leader, Josephine Pearson, insisted that in opposing the amendment they were defending the South, and that "we in Tennessee could not fail in this most crucial test of Southern rights and honor, when Tennessee became the pivotal battle-ground of the Nation!"[2]

Antisuffragists warned that "*Woman Suffrage* means a reopening of the entire *Negro Suffrage* question; loss of State rights; and another period of reconstruction horrors, which will introduce a set of female carpetbaggers as bad as their male prototypes of the sixties."[3]

Those on both sides of the issue were convinced that much was at stake. Suffragists declared that female enfranchisement would *clean up* American politics while antisuffragists insisted it would *ruin* American politics—together with American women. Everyone was sure that *something* dramatic would come of it. In the November 1920 election looming on the horizon, women voters could prove to be the decisive factor, *if* they were enfranchised in time. With ratification a distinct possibility, both national parties were eager to win credit for the victory and the loyalty of the new voters. Suffragists were determined to clinch their victory; antisuffragists were equally determined to prevent ratification before the 1920 election, thus allowing the nation to recover from this dangerous "fad" (promoted as a natural corollary to a war fought for democracy), and postponing the adoption of a federal amendment indefinitely.

Yet, after winning the approval of Congress and ratification by thirty-five states, the formidable woman suffrage movement appeared to be stalled. The suffragists, recalled Carrie Chapman Catt and Nettie Rogers Shuler in *Woman Suffrage and Politics* (1923), were extremely "tense" and frustrated by the fact that the thirty-sixth state appeared to be so elusive.[4] Success depended upon the willingness of a governor from one of the five states that had not yet taken action to call a special session. That three of the five were southern states added to the difficulty, as many regional leaders were calling for the South to stand "solid" against ratification of "another federal amendment" that they saw as a threat to the state sovereignty necessary to defend white supremacy. Yielding to pressure from the National Democratic Party, Governor Thomas W. Bickett of North Carolina and Governor Albert H. Roberts of Tennessee very reluctantly called special sessions. North Carolina legislators defeated the measure and urged the Tennessee solons to follow their example: "If this crime is perpetuated let it not be laid at the door of either North Carolina or her daughter Tennessee. Fight to the last ditch, and then some." North Carolina legislators were not, they said, going to "sacrifice their honor upon the fickle altar of supposed political expedience."[5]

A poll of the Tennessee legislature earlier in the summer suggested that ratification was a distinct possibility, which led the antis from Tennessee and throughout the nation to redouble their efforts. Though Tennessee suffragists, aided by National American Woman Suffrage Association president Carrie Chapman Catt, made a concerted effort to preserve their advantage, the antis—with the aid of their allies in the liquor, cotton, and railroad industries—were successful in dissuading many a suffrage supporter. Indeed, they came close to blocking ratification before a twenty-four-year-old legislator from the mountains, the famous or infamous Harry Burn, changed his vote and followed the instructions of his elderly mother, Febb King Ensminger Burn, to help Mrs. Catt if his vote was required for ratification. Even then, the antis would not concede defeat but resorted to extraordinary methods: after calling for a recount, the "Red Rose Brigade" of antis fled the state to prevent a quorum and a second vote until their allies could hold mass meetings to demonstrate antisuffrage sentiment and "persuade" prosuffrage legislators to reconsider their votes. The remaining legislators met without them and reconfirmed the vote, and the Nineteenth Amendment was declared to be in effect.[6]

Thus, Tennessee's ratification, one of the most crucial legislative acts in the history of the woman suffrage movement, was by the slimmest of margins. Had Tennessee followed the pattern of most southern states and refused to ratify, American women might not have been enfranchised in time for the 1920 presidential election. The federal woman suffrage amendment could have been long delayed, or it could have been circumvented by the gradual enfranchisement of women state by state—a method of enfranchisement that had already proven to be slow, costly, exasperating, and, in many instances, fruitless.

Votes for Women! The Woman Suffrage Movement in Tennessee, the South, and the Nation helps to explain how and why Tennessee came to occupy such a pivotal position in the history of the movement. In part 1, the first three essays gradually narrow our focus from a national to a regional and then to a state perspective on the suffrage movement, answering questions including the following: How did leaders of the national woman suffrage movement decide to concentrate their efforts upon a federal amendment as opposed to other methods of enfranchisement? Why were most white southerners so opposed to woman suffrage, especially by federal amendment, and why and how did some elite white women seek enfranchisement nonetheless? What role did the race issue play in the suffrage struggle, nationally and regionally? How did a suffrage movement develop in Tennessee and what exactly happened during that sweltering summer of 1920? The last three essays discuss the role that African-American women played in the woman suffrage movement—particularly in the South where there was such hostility among whites to the enfranchisement of *any* African Americans; the ideas and actions of the antisuffragists; and, finally, the political impact of woman suffrage.

In the first essay in part 1, "Woman Suffrage (Not Universal Suffrage) by Federal Amendment," Ann D. Gordon surveys the various strategies employed by suffragists in the long fight for enfranchisement. Frustrated by the failure of the Fifteenth Amendment to include women and by their early attempts at winning another constitutional amendment (the proposed "Sixteenth Amendment") that would enfranchise women, suffragists turned to the states, seeking state amendments and various forms of partial suffrage. After a spate of victories in the West between 1910 and 1912, and strongly influenced by Alice Paul, suffragists renewed the drive for the federal amendment and finally attained their goal.

As Gordon's title suggests, however, white suffragists had narrowed their goal along the way, betraying the hopes of African-American women for enfranchisement. Gravely disappointed and bitter at their own exclusion from the Fifteenth Amendment, white suffrage leaders embraced, or at least permitted, racist arguments and tactics, even excluding African Americans from their ranks. When victory came, it was not a victory for universal suffrage. The vast majority of African-American women in the South were excluded from voting, and white women refused to come to their aid. *All* the women of the United States would not be enfranchised until the 1960s.

The second essay, "The Woman Suffrage Movement in the Inhospitable South," explains why the South was so opposed to woman suffrage. Indeed, Tennessee was one of only four southern states that ratified the amendment. (The others were Kentucky, Texas, and Arkansas.) Southern suffragists ran into resistance even when seeking enfranchisement through state action; most began to campaign for the federal amendment only after their repeated efforts to win state suffrage amendments were rebuffed.

After analyzing the cultural, political, and economic factors that caused the South to be the region most hostile to woman suffrage, I describe how and why a cadre of elite, southern, white women nevertheless stepped forward to lead this controversial movement, what they hoped to gain through woman suffrage, and the methods they used to promote it. The South's so-called "negro problem" was at once a major obstacle to woman suffrage in the South and a political issue that was exploited by these southern suffragists of the 1890s badly in need of an "expediency argument." White suffragists who sought enfranchisement in order to help themselves and less fortunate women and children were nonetheless willing to use racist arguments. Though these suffragists were united (at least publicly) on the race issue, differences of opinion over the federal amendment and "states' rights" divided them into warring camps during the last decade of the movement. When the Nineteenth Amendment was ratified, those who had opposed it were bitter at this blow to state sovereignty, while those in the states that refused to ratify were disappointed that their states—and region—had failed to give the endorsement of female equality they so desired.

A. Elizabeth Taylor's article, "Tennessee: The Thirty-Sixth State," is a shortened and updated version of her book *The Woman Suffrage Movement in Tennessee*. It is valuable not only in understanding Tennessee's history but also as a case study of the cultivation of suffrage sentiment at the state level.

Taylor describes the growth and development of the suffrage movement in Tennessee from 1889 to 1920, including: the emergence of leaders; the creation of the various suffrage organizations; the interaction between Tennessee suffragists and national and regional suffrage organizations; the several attempts to win enfranchisement by state action—including the successful efforts to obtain municipal and presidential suffrage; and the response of Tennessee antisuffragists to the suffragists' efforts. Taylor concludes with an explanation of how Tennessee came to play such a crucial role in the history of the movement and a detailed description of the dramatic ratification struggle in 1920.

Adele Logan Alexander's essay, "Adella Hunt Logan, the Tuskegee Woman's Club, and African Americans in the Suffrage Movement," surveys the disheartening experiences of black women attempting to participate in the woman suffrage movement in both North and South and then focuses upon the suffragists of Tuskegee, Alabama, led by Alexander's grandmother. Adella Hunt Logan, a Tuskegee faculty member and an intrepid suffragist who lived next door to Booker T. Washington while maintaining a friendship with W. E .B. Du Bois and even writing for the *Crisis*, was an extraordinary individual. Discriminated against by many NAWSA leaders from both North and South (including, to an extent, her heroine Susan B. Anthony), Logan sometimes attended suffrage conventions by "passing" for white.

Led by Logan, the Tuskegee Woman's Club, a chapter of the National Association of Colored Women, openly advocated woman suffrage as well as engaging in a broad range of "social uplift" endeavors for the benefit of women in their community and the surrounding countryside. Logan was "unwavering" in her conviction that if white women with all their advantages needed the ballot, African-American women needed it all the more to protect their children and their "efforts for human betterment."

Anastatia Sims's "Beyond the Ballot: The Radical Vision of the Antisuffragists" is a revisionist study of the antis. While she supports the suffragists' contention that the antis were quite corrupt and concurs with most historians' portrait of southern antis as extreme conservatives devoted to white supremacy and states' rights, she insists that the antis should not be dismissed as "narrow-minded reactionaries unable to envision a role for women beyond the traditional boundaries of domesticity." Sims argues that, rather than underestimating woman's power (as is often thought), the antis believed that, if enfranchised, women would use the vote to bring about radical changes not only in politics but in gender roles as well.

Sims's essay is also valuable for its analysis of antisuffrage literature (including a number of documents that appear in part 3 of this volume). It is to be expected that the race issue played a major role in southern antisuffrage arguments, she writes, as in that region—more than anywhere else in the United States—"any change in women's status brought with it portents of social upheaval" and "ideas about gender were inextricably intertwined with ideas about race." In the South, she explains, the "exaltation of white women" and their exclusion from politics went "hand-in-hand" with the "degradation of African-American men" and their exclusion from politics. Sims then proceeds to describe the background and motives (economic and ideological) of the antisuffragists of Tennessee, and their relentless, no-holds-barred fight against ratification in 1920.

The sixth and final essay, "Woman Suffrage and the Gender Gap," by Jean Bethke Elshtain, looks backward from 1920 to the hopes and fears of suffragists and forward from the suffrage victory to the present, analyzing women's use of political power once they attained it. From Mary Wollstonecraft on, Elshtain writes, feminists have been divided in their assessment of woman's nature, the sources of their differences from men, and the implications of these differences for woman's political behavior. To a certain extent, feminists were compelled to defend the idea of innate gender differences in order to have an argument for female enfranchisement, though (as is evident in this volume) many embraced this notion wholeheartedly and insisted that woman suffrage would usher in a new era of peace, morality, and justice. Others rejected the idea of female distinctiveness, as well as the idea that woman suffrage was a panacea for the woes of woman and of society.

Elshtain argues that whatever their sources, differences *do* exist in the political assumptions of women and men, particularly in regard to peace and social welfare issues. And though the predictions of suffragists—and antisuffragists—that female enfranchisement would drastically affect politics initially proved to be unfounded, the phenomenon that today is called "the gender gap" emerged at last in 1980 and is a significant factor in politics today. According to Elshtain, a "womanist" ideology seems to have "taken hold": as voters, women are demonstrating greater concern than men about "quality of life" issues. A majority of voters (when polled in 1992) said that "government would be better if women held office." As more and more women seek elective office, feminist leaders find themselves divided between two conflicting positions: an urge to argue that "women will do better because they somehow are better" and a desire to "defeat stereotypes about gender, *including* to say that women are morally superior to men." Elshtain hopes that those with high expectations for women in politics prove to be right. For, as was the case following the suffrage victory in 1920, "the danger in proclaiming deliverance if women gain power is that cynicism will result when women do not effect miracles."

The documents in parts 2 and 3 illustrate the themes and topics discussed in part 1 while offering readers the opportunity to examine these very interesting primary sources directly and interpret them for themselves. Among the documents are four prosuffrage articles or speeches by a diverse group of southern suffragists: articles by African-American suffragists Adella Hunt Logan and Mary Church Terrell published in 1912 in the NAACP journal, the *Crisis*; an address to a national governors' conference by popular novelist Mary Johnston, a white suffrage leader from Virginia active at the state, regional, and national levels; and the "Dixie Night" address given by Tennessee Woman Suffrage Association leader Anne Dallas Dudley at the 1916 NAWSA Convention in Atlantic City.

Differences in style and tactics between the National Woman's Party and the National American Woman Suffrage Association and its affiliates become clear in the next three documents. The first two are excerpts from Inez Haynes Irwin's *The Story of the Woman's Party* (1921) describing the treatment of NWP orators touring Tennessee in 1917 and a NWP demonstration in Washington, D.C., in which the best-known southern "militant," Tennessee's Sue Shelton White, burned one of President Wilson's speeches. These are followed by a series of letters between Sue White and NAWSA President Catt, in which White describes her encounters with the NWP representatives in 1917 and how the hostile reaction to her involvement with the "militants" practically pushed her into the "bosom" of the NWP. The next document, a press release written by Kate Burch Warner, president of the Tennessee Woman Suffrage Association in which she "deplores" the demonstrations by the "militants," typifies the reaction of southern NAWSA loyalists to the NWP.

The antisuffrage point of view is also well represented in these documents in *Votes for Women!* First, there is an excerpt from an antisuffrage pamphlet, "An Address to the Men of Tennessee on Female Suffrage," written by one of the most active and visible male antis, Nashville attorney John J. Vertrees. It is followed by two previously unpublished documents written by Josephine Pearson, president of the Tennessee Division of the Southern Women's League for the Rejection of the Susan B. Anthony Amendment. In the first, a letter of resignation dated September 30, 1920 (when the antisuffragists were still engaged in legal maneuvers to overturn ratification), Pearson actually *celebrates the victory of the antisuffragists* in blocking ratification. In the second, written many years later, she explains the reasons she became a leader of the fight against woman suffrage and expresses her lingering bitterness and outrage at the "fraudulent" victory: "The whole thing [Tennessee's ratification] was an acknowledged National 'fake' that produced a Jubilee!"[7]

The antisuffrage documents are followed by the chapter on Tennessee from Carrie Chapman Catt and Nettie Rogers Shuler's *Woman Suffrage and Politics: The Inner Story of the Suffrage Movement,* first published in 1923.[8] This fascinating and often-cited document, filled with colorful anecdotes, gives Catt's firsthand account of the incredible events in Nashville: Catt came to Tennessee expecting to spend a few days and ended up spending weeks, embroiled in a fight unlike any other this seasoned politician had seen before. From her description of the Tennessee suffragists, "who laid aside their political differences and worked together in a manner worthy of imitation of the men of the State," tracking down legislators despite the heat of that "merciless" southern summer, "by train, by motor, by wagons and on foot, often in great discomfort, and frequently at considerable expense to themselves," to Catt's astonished account of the pro- and antisuffrage legislators, who left a certain "hospitality suite" at the Hermitage Hotel "reeling through the hall in a state of advanced intoxication—a sight no suffragist had before witnessed in the sixty years of suffrage struggle," it is a pleasure to read.

The last document, an excerpt from a 1923 speech by Sue Shelton White, makes it clear that the victory for woman suffrage did not end the struggle for women's rights. White acknowledges the debt owed to the pioneers of the suffrage movement while outlining the many obstacles women still faced. One of the authors of the Equal Rights Amendment—first introduced in Congress in 1923—White urges the members of her audience to dedicate themselves to "the climb ahead" and not give up until women are guaranteed "equal rights in the United States and every place subject to its jurisdiction." Women, she insisted, must be allowed to develop as individuals unhampered by legal and social barriers; no "higher honor" could be given to the pioneers of 1848, she said, than to make their vision come true.

Finally, part 3 contains a large collection of broadsides and political cartoons that vividly and clearly display the views and tactics of both suffragists and antisuffragists. These give the readers an opportunity to see for themselves many of the documents described and analyzed in the essays in part 1. Part 3 also contains a series of cartoons showing the nation's reaction to the ratification battle and the victory for woman suffrage.

The six essays, thirteen documents, and the broadsides and cartoons together offer a full and rich portrait of this exciting and important episode in American history that will be of value to students and teachers as well as to scholars writing on the suffrage movement. At a time when there is tremendous interest in the suffrage movement and a growing awareness of the role of race, class, and region in the movement's history, we hope that *Votes for Women!* will be a valuable addition to the scholarship. It reminds us that many suffragists struggled for many years and against great opposition before women were enfranchised. Moreover, it reminds us that winning suffrage via federal amendment was not a foregone conclusion and that when victory finally came in 1920 it was incomplete. *Votes for Women!* contributes to our understanding of the long-neglected African-American and southern suffragists and reminds us that—in very different ways—both black and many white women of the South were quite dissatisfied by what was, for their northern counterparts, a thrilling victory. *Votes for Women!* also offers new ideas about antisuffragists. And it provides food for thought concerning the impact of the enfranchisement of women: though we celebrate seventy-five years of woman suffrage, it may still be too early to assess the significance of the enfranchisement of American women—who have yet to realize their full power at the polls.

Notes

1. Edwin Mims, *The Advancing South: Stories of Progress and Reaction* (Port Washington, N.Y.; reprint of 1926 edition by Doubleday and Company, Garden City, N.J.), 238. I am grateful to Anastatia Sims for bringing this to my attention.

2. Josephine Pearson, "President's Message, Retiring from Anti-Suffrage Leadership of Tennessee," 3. Josephine Pearson Papers, Tennessee State Library and Archives. Reprinted in part 2 herein.

3. Broadside entitled "BEWARE!" in the Pearson Papers, reprinted in part 3.

4. Carrie Chapman Catt and Nettie Rogers Shuler, *Woman Suffrage and Politics: The Inner Story of the Suffrage Movement* (New York: Charles Scribner's Sons, 1923; reprint, University of Washington Press, 1970), 423. Chapter 30, "Tennessee," is reprinted in part 2.

5. Quotations from the *Raleigh News and Observer,* Aug. 13, 1920, and Aug.

6, 1920.

6. The Tennessee story has been told by many. In addition to the essays in this volume, see Anastatia Sims, "'Powers That Pray and Powers That Prey': Tennessee and the Fight for Woman Suffrage," *Tennessee Historical Quarterly* (Winter 1991): 203–25; A. Elizabeth Taylor, *The Woman Suffrage Movement in Tennessee* (New York: Bookman Associates, 1957); MariRose Arendale, "Tennessee and Women's Rights," *Tennessee Historical Quarterly* 39 (1980): 62–78; and Carol Lynn Yellin, "Countdown in Tennessee," *American Heritage* 30 (Dec. 1978): 12–35.

7. Josephine Pearson, "My Story," Pearson Papers, excerpt reprinted in part 2.

8. Catt and Shuler, *Woman Suffrage and Politics*, 422–61.

PART 1

Essays

1

Woman Suffrage (Not Universal Suffrage) by Federal Amendment

Ann D. Gordon

The Nineteenth (or woman suffrage) Amendment to the Constitution of the United States bears witness to political triumph for one of the country's longest reform movements. But the amendment also serves as a reminder of compromises struck by woman suffragists in order to establish a woman's right to vote—compromises that undercut goals of achieving universal suffrage and all women's political sovereignty. In the United States in 1920, woman suffrage in practice meant primarily suffrage for white women.

To understand the Nineteenth Amendment, it is necessary to understand how it became the centerpiece of woman suffrage strategy. Since most women ultimately gained the vote with passage of the federal constitutional amendment, that particular route to woman suffrage comes to dominate the movement's history as if it had been a foregone conclusion. Yet much of the history of women agitating for their right to vote concerns precisely their discussions about where to get that right, where to voice their demand and concentrate their political forces. Woman suffragists faced the complexity of American federalism and the intense national debate, and even war, over the relative authority of federal and state governments. They might struggle along converting state governments to their need for enfranchisement or seize as precedent the model created when Congress guaranteed voting rights to the freedmen after the Civil War.

How women hoped to get the vote reflected, among other things, their response to the nation's racial politics. Suffragists' political choices were inescapably delimited by the intimate connection that existed between acknowledging the rights of women and the rights of African Americans. The very claim of a right to vote touched one of the sorest points in American politics after the Civil War: the dispute over extending that right to African Americans. Critical turning points in the history of one movement coincided with moments of crisis in the other—from the women's movement's rise in the antislavery cause, through Civil War and Reconstruction, the restoration of white supremacy in the South and revival of states' rights doctrine as federal policy, Woodrow Wilson's success at returning the White House to a southerner, and decisions that allowed the South to disfranchise black men before 1920 and black women after.

The history of the woman suffrage movement presents a difficult heritage, where progress and racism are intertwined. Modern works on woman suffrage history reveal persistent discrimination and recurrent denial by white women of an equality with black women that they claimed to deserve with white men. Moreover, a growing literature about the Civil Rights movement of the 1950s and 1960s and federal Voting Rights Act of 1965 highlights both the Nineteenth Amendment's limitations and the suffrage movement's unwillingness to pursue its enforcement.[1] These findings are not mere sidelights to the history but fundamental challenges to how the past has been understood. They suggest that racism affected not only personal experience within the movement but strategy as well. Understanding how, after seventy years of political experience campaigning for their right to vote, the woman suffrage movement finally consolidated behind the demand for passage of the Nineteenth Amendment is one way to begin to understand how white woman suffragists veered away from the sweeping democratic vision of universal suffrage that at times defined their movement and always attracted black women to the cause.

Origins of a Federal Suffrage Amendment

The first declaration of woman's right to vote carried no instruction as to where women would turn to win that right. The resolutions passed at the Seneca Falls Woman's Rights Convention in 1848 included a simple directive: "*Resolved*, That it is the duty of the women of the country to secure to themselves their sacred right to the elective franchise."[2] In the political experience of the authors and their audience—in the expansion of voting rights associated with Jacksonian democracy, in conflicts over voting rights for free black men in the North—state constitutions and law were the targets of reform. There was no suggestion that women could or should follow any other route, and, within a short time, pioneers in the women's rights movement were presenting their demand to state legislatures and constitutional conventions from New England to Kansas.

Women like Lucy Stone, petitioning for woman suffrage in Wisconsin, Clarina Nichols, lobbying the 1859 constitutional convention in Kansas Territory, and Elizabeth Cady Stanton and Susan B. Anthony, petitioning New York State's legislature, claimed rights for women as individuals, entitled equally with men to a voice in government. Drawing on a republican tradition of equal rights and infusing it with abolitionist critiques of arbitrary authority over certain classes of persons, the original woman suffragists asserted that recognizing the sovereignty of each individual was the only true basis for a republican government. Stanton would later describe the demand for woman suffrage as emerging from "the school of anti-slavery" where, for thirty years, men and women had "discussed the whole question of human rights."[3]

At the end of the Civil War, the antebellum women's rights movement shifted its focus to demand universal suffrage guaranteed by the federal government. Along with northern Republicans, woman suffragists had come to recognize, through the experience of war and the emancipation of slaves, the enormous power of amendments to the Constitution. Debate over the political status of former slaves focused on constitutional issues, particularly on federal authority to protect the rights of citizens within states, and there emerged from that debate in Congress the idea of national protection for a right to vote. "I plead now for the ballot, as the great guarantee; and *the only sufficient guarantee*," Senator Charles Sumner proclaimed in one of his eloquent addresses on the need to proceed beyond emancipation and ensure political rights for the freed slaves. "Ay, sir," he continued, "the ballot is the Columbiad of our political life, and every citizen who has it is a full-armed monitor. . . . The ballot is the one thing needful, without which rights of testimony and all other rights will be no better than cobwebs, which the master will break through with impunity. To him who has the ballot all other things shall be given . . ."[4] It was this conviction that the vote was at the pinnacle of rights and thus at the foundation of republican government that argued for challenging the right of states to regulate for themselves who might vote. Sumner spoke of men explicitly, but women extended the argument to themselves. They hoped that in the rethinking of federal power Congress might be persuaded to realize the logical extension of concern for freedmen's rights. "The only tenable ground of representation is UNIVERSAL SUFFRAGE," the Eleventh National Woman's Rights Convention told Congress in 1866, "as it is only through Universal Suffrage that the principle of 'Equal Rights to All' can be realized. All prohibitions based on race, color, sex, property, or education, are violations of the republican idea; . . ." At the same meeting, Elizabeth Cady Stanton put the same point in the form of question: "Has not the time come . . . to bury the black man and the woman in the citizen . . . ?"[5] Writing a year later from Kansas, where she campaigned for black and woman suffrage, Lucy Stone proclaimed: "The problem for the American statesmen to-day is no narrow question of races, but how to embody in our institutions a guarantee for the rights of every citizen. The solution is easy. Base government on the consent of the governed, and each class will protect itself."[6] Congress stepped back from that brink, however, and amended the Constitution to protect the voting rights of freedmen, seizing federal authority, but leaving women out of the new equation.

At that moment, while states considered ratification of the Fifteenth Amendment, woman suffragists shifted to new ground, in hopes of winning a sixteenth amendment for their rights that would, in combination with the Fifteenth, effectively establish universal suffrage. On March 15, 1869, George W. Julian introduced in Congress the first woman suffrage amendment to the Constitution. Stronger than the Fifteenth Amendment because it linked voting rights (constitutionally the states' domain) to citizenship (a national right in the Fourteenth Amendment), Julian's resolution read: "The Right of Suffrage in the United States shall be based on citizenship, and shall be regulated by Congress; and all citizens of the United States, whether native or naturalized, shall enjoy this right equally without any distinction or discrimination whatever founded on sex."[7] Within the year, woman suffragists formed national associations to coordinate support for this amendment and to build a movement capable of winning suffrage for themselves.

Their new federal strategy for gaining suffrage evolved from constitutional changes designed to establish the national citizenship and guarantee the political representation of former slaves. Historically and logically, suffragists' use of the precedent in 1869 affirmed the new rights of African Americans and exploited an inconsistency that Congress introduced to the Constitution by limiting voting rights to men. In practice, the affirmation of racial justice got lost in resentment over the privileges accorded to freedmen before themselves. To take but one example from 1869, Elizabeth Cady Stanton denounced manhood suffrage as "an open, deliberate insult to American womanhood to be cast down under the iron-heeled peasantry of the Old World and the slaves of the New."[8] At its most virulent, this refrain of racial superiority appealed to white Americans' worst fears of a barbaric race that threatened white civilization. Toned down or used ironically to ask how a racist Congress could so fear women as to prefer the freedmen's vote, the refrain undermined suffragists' claim to stand on the tradition of equal rights, and it set the women's rights movement apart from the struggle still facing northern and southern blacks.

When Stanton, Susan B. Anthony, and others complained of being ruled by freedmen and opposed passage of the Fifteenth Amendment in 1869, they took for granted the sanctity or certainty of the rights black men had won; "Our protest is not that all men are lifted out of the degradation of disfranchisement, but that all women are left in," Anthony wrote.[9] But the refrain took on a life of its own. Resentment over passage of the Fifteenth Amendment persisted over the course of woman suffrage agitation even while blacks lost the rights promised in the amendment, so that, though a constant expression of a racial hierarchy, the refrain's particular political meaning changed over time.

Agitation for Woman Suffrage

Postwar suffrage agitation took place within at least three different movements, distinguished most of all by their decisions about where to seek the power of the vote. The first in time (and, often, in prominence) was centered in the National Woman Suffrage Association (NWSA) led by Elizabeth Cady Stanton and Susan B. Anthony. "National" in the name referred to this group's pursuit of federal action to attain suffrage nationwide. Close on its heels came the American Woman Suffrage Association (AWSA) headed by Lucy Stone and Henry Blackwell. Through state suffrage societies, the AWSA would pursue whatever gains could be had from state legislatures. And least coordinated but fastest growing were local struggles to increase women's political influence by winning a fragment of the franchise that fell indisputably within state control, such as "school suffrage" (votes on public education) or "home protection" (votes on liquor questions).[10]

The critical factor dividing the two associations from each other was their response to the nation's "retreat from Reconstruction." Within a year or two after the sixteenth amendment's introduction in Congress, the role of the federal government as guarantor of certain national rights that the states were bound to respect was a contested point. The political will and power to give federal protection to former slaves against attempts to restore white supremacy in the South waned and all but disappeared. Supreme Court decisions on the Fourteenth and Fifteenth Amendments reflected and legitimated this change in northern commitment to equal rights. Rulings on the Fourteenth Amendment narrowed rights that the federal government could legitimately protect against decisions of the states, and the Fifteenth Amendment was understood to preserve the right of states to regulate their electorates. By 1876 the Supreme Court deemed constitutional southern practices and laws that disfranchised blacks on grounds other than explicitly racial.

In such a political climate, the sixteenth amendment would not slip by as a final or additional act of Reconstruction. Federal action to override state laws denying *women* their right to vote ran counter to the political current. To pursue the amendment, suffragists would need to put themselves in direct opposition to the new direction in national politics, and only one group did so. Thus, despite a common starting point in the push for universal suffrage by constitutional amendment, the movement entered a period of rapid growth, from 1869 to 1900, without unity of purpose. By the end of the century, suffragists who favored the federal amendment lost the contest within the movement over strategy, and a greatly expanded suffrage movement approached the twentieth century wedded to the notion of winning the vote state by state.

The National Woman Suffrage Association, committed from 1869 to gaining national suffrage from the federal government, defined itself in the 1870s in opposition to the restoration of states' rights and as an advocate of a stronger federal role in protecting voting rights. The NWSA launched a second campaign for a sixteenth amendment in 1876. California's Senator Aaron A. Sargent introduced the measure on January 10, 1878, petitions flooded Congress annually, activists lobbied national political parties for a woman suffrage plank in their platforms of 1880, and the Senate finally brought the measure to a vote on January 25, 1887. The amendment was defeated.[11]

Elizabeth Cady Stanton's phrase, "National Protection for National Citizens," summed up the principal idea of the NWSA campaign. It combined the ideals of radical Reconstruction with attacks on the Supreme Court's denial of a federal interest in protecting voting rights. Crucial to the National's argument was a claim, made in the original sixteenth amendment (though omitted in Senator Sargent's resolution), that the right of suffrage derived from citizenship. National *citizenship* for African Americans and women alike had survived the Supreme Court's whittling away of federal powers. But the Court had declared that such citizenship implied nothing about a national right to vote. States still retained the right to decide who voted.

The NWSA asserted that the principle of self-government, realized in the right to vote, could not be left to states to uphold. "In asking for a sixteenth amendment to the United States Constitution, and the protection of Congress against the injustice of State law," Stanton explained to Senators in 1878,

Susan B. Anthony and Elizabeth Cady Stanton. Wyoming State Museum.

> we are fighting the same battle as Jefferson and Hamilton fought in 1776, as Calhoun and Clay in 1828, as Abraham Lincoln and Jefferson Davis in 1860, namely, the limit of State rights and Federal power.
>
> . . . Inasmuch as we are, first, citizens of the United States, and, second, of the State wherein we reside, the primal rights of all citizens should be regulated by national government, and complete equality in civil and political rights everywhere secured.

Linking her argument to reports from the South of attacks on blacks exercising their rights, Stanton condemned as evidence of "the imperfect development of our own nationality" the paralysis that kept the federal government from protecting the freedmen. "The kind of government the people of this country expect, and intend to have, State rights or no State rights, no matter how much blood and treasure it may cost, is a government to protect the humblest citizen in the exercise of all his rights."[12] The National's campaign as Stanton constructed it provided an example as stunning as that of the early Seneca Falls Convention in 1848 of how reasoning through their predicament as disfranchised citizens of a republic could lead women to rethink the fundamentals of American government and define an advanced position on the constitutional issues of democracy.

As a political stance, however, the National's position was virtually hopeless. Within the eleven years it took to bring the sixteenth amendment to a vote in the Senate, the South's power in national politics increased, and northern complicity with southern disfranchisement of black voters rendered serious debate of national protection an impossibility. Moreover, there is no evidence that the National even considered allying itself with blacks to match its theory of political equality with its practice. Though Stanton and Anthony dropped the theme of resentment over the Fifteenth Amendment from their speeches and writings in this period, it survived in the movement. A woman writing to Stanton from Tennessee in 1880 opened her letter with a remarkable claim for the women of both races: "It is my impression that our sex both white & black have an earnest desire for the right of self government." She reserved her sarcasm and disdain for white men in power, doubting they had logic enough to heed women's petitions for rights. But as her definitive example of men's illogical minds she recalled their decision to ratify the Fifteenth Amendment. "Why," she asked, "is woman to be dreaded more than the ignorant stupid downtrodden black man for whom so many & valuable lives have been sacrificed."[13] Though self-government was her central point, it seems unlikely she found common ground with the black woman suffragists she acknowledged.

The National's campaign, especially in its last years, drew a lot of attention to the strategy of seeking a sixteenth amendment. When the association polled suffragists for expressions of support in 1880, women with all kinds of values about rights and womanhood replied. The language of equal rights, self-sovereignty, and self-government was used by women everywhere. But in nearly equal numbers, respondents spoke of votes as acknowledging women's special mission and giving them the tools to make society moral.[14] Briefly, it seemed, fundamental differences among suffragists themselves could be overlooked to amass women's limited power behind the amendment. That forces were rising, even among friends, to distance woman suffrage from the National's sweeping claims for rights and federal power could be seen at its annual convention in 1886. As the association prepared to renew its support for the amendment, then in congressional committee, newly converted southern delegates "vigorously opposed" supporting the amendment "as contrary to States' Rights." At that date, the National had the conviction to vote them down and reaffirm support for federal action.[15]

Though individuals would carry on the tradition of this campaign for national protection after Congress defeated the amendment in 1887, no organized voice for woman suffrage revived it. Neither its clear grasp of obstacles to winning equal rights within American federalism nor its embrace of national protection would be heard again from white suffragists. Not until twentieth-century civil rights activists restored voting rights in the South did Stanton's vision become law.

The American Woman Suffrage Association (AWSA) swam *with* the political tide, rarely working directly for passage of the sixteenth amendment after 1871 when to do so required opposing the new respectability of states' rights. Founded at the instigation of Lucy Stone a few months later in 1869 than the National, the American pursued an idea that local and partial suffrage victories would build popular support for women's political participation and enable women to pyramid their power from school district to township to municipality to state and, eventually, to gain full voting rights. Political equality for women need not disturb constitutional relations or upset local political practice.[16]

As a federation of state suffrage societies committed to increasing their number into every state, the American helped to institutionalize suffrage activism. The preamble to its constitution promised it would "embody the deliberate action of State and local organizations," and in the absence of an overarching strategy, it attracted more of the movement's grass-roots variety to its banner than the National did. The potpourri of objectives listed in the

American's annual plans of work met two tests: they might be winnable in certain locations and they would, by some measure, diminish the ways that men and women were unequal in political participation. To the goals favored by state societies, Henry Blackwell added pet schemes for gaining a voice in some corner of the political process. In 1871 the association adopted his idea of asking state legislatures for woman suffrage in the selection of presidential electors, a scheme that remained on its agenda for decades and was selected as the most important goal to seek in the Centennial year 1876, while the National launched its amendment campaign. Federal law to enfranchise women in all the territories came to the fore in 1872. In 1876 the American took up another Blackwell brainstorm: to seek suffrage from state political parties so that women could vote in primary elections. And during the 1880s, the association embraced all the schemes for municipal, school, and liquor-related suffrage that were gaining popularity.[17]

Stone herself certainly believed in the justice and ultimate necessity of a constitutional amendment but was, at the same time, ambivalent about working for its passage. After the amendment's introduction in 1869, the American urged constituent societies to support the measure but concentrate on state action. "[P]ending the [amendment's] adoption . . . we urge friends of woman to work in their respective States for the establishment of this reform by State legislation, especially as the ratification of any Constitutional Amendment must finally depend upon the State Legislatures." In 1872 the amendment lost precedence on the plan of work to goals of partial suffrage.[18] The National's 1876 campaign elicited qualified support from Stone. She could not stand opposed to the amendment, but neither would she join Stanton and Anthony in criticism of federal policy. Subscribers to her *Woman's Journal* received two petitions in the fall of 1877, one to Congress and one to states, with Stone's explanation, "We consider State action the more important, but signatures to both petitions can be obtained at the same time." Her office subsequently transmitted petitions bearing six thousand signatures to Congress. Meeting in 1878, after Sargent had introduced the amendment and Stanton had spoken on "National Protection," the American's annual meeting resolved for "renewed effort upon the next and each following State Legislature," in light of the fact that federal courts had "affirmed that the regulation of suffrage belongs exclusively to the States" and that passage of a sixteenth amendment, "although just and necessary," would "be more easily obtained" if women had previously won suffrage in "several States."[19]

Stone's strategy proved no more successful in the nineteenth century than the National's. Though she would protect their right to do so, states were not willing to exercise that right to enfranchise women. Two territories granted women the right to vote immediately after the war, and one of them, Wyoming, won statehood in 1890 with a constitution that preserved woman suffrage. But every state campaign failed until Colorado voters approved an amendment to their constitution in 1893. Moreover, in no case did the power from partial suffrage within a state allow women to leverage themselves from one level of political activity to another.[20]

Stone did succeed in embracing as suffragists all people who sought to increase women's political power, and thus in disassociating the cause from its roots in the tradition of equal rights and racial justice. To be a woman suffragist in the American association one need not believe that the federal government should protect the rights of all its citizens. One need not even believe that women should be the full political equals of men.

Distance between the two suffrage associations and the third, amorphous grouping of suffragists did not result from disputes over Reconstruction, its demise, or the rights of blacks. Women in the third group looked to state government because by simple legislation states could provide the limited kinds of power they sought. As this group converged with the earlier suffrage movement near the end of the century, however, they helped tip the balance toward limiting suffrage agitation to the states. This third force in the movement was born of the convergence between a women's movement wedded to its differences from men and opposed to equal rights, on the one hand, and the idea of woman suffrage divorced from its roots in the equal rights tradition, on the other. In growing numbers after the Civil War, women who would not think of joining a suffrage society wanted to vote—usually for some specific cause—in order to enhance the power of womanhood and improve the world. Their argument for votes followed from their belief that "the world must be saved from much degradation" by women themselves. In a fit of pique, an Oregon suffragist once described theirs as a politics that posited "an arbitrary government over the inalienable rights of men, to which the average voter quite naturally objects." [21]

The largest and most coherent of these limited or partial suffrage movements grew up within the Woman's Christian Temperance Union. As members turned from prayer to politics in their search for the best way to end the traffic in liquor, they alighted first on a precise issue for which women should have the vote and asked only that laws about licensing the sale of liquor be rewritten to include women in the eligible electorate. These were not simply modest women making modest claims; they doubted they should have full suffrage. In Wausau, Wisconsin, for instance, the local Union split on the question of petitioning the Republican Party for woman suffrage in 1880. Fifty-eight wanted full woman suffrage; twenty-four declared an interest only in the temperance vote.[22]

Campaigns for "school suffrage" probably engaged the largest numbers of women across the country. The term school suffrage encompassed any revision of law that gave women a vote on matters of public education, and in most states women needed to change numerous laws governing school elections. Only in Kansas had they succeeded in guaranteeing school suffrage for themselves in the state constitution. States not only wrote their own unique laws but wrote different legislation for schools depending on the concentration of population, so that rural district schools, schools in towns, schools in medium-sized cities, and metropolitan schools fell under different laws, and women were fighting for reform law by law. By 1902 they had gained some variety of school suffrage in twenty-six states.[23]

The women in this third element of the movement had not approached suffrage through the "school of anti-slavery" and Reconstruction. Expressing reform in moral rather than legal terms, they seemed oblivious to constitutional questions or even to abstractions about the workings of government, preferring instead to balance the powers of men and women. As historian Paula Baker has suggested, these women "fused domesticity and politics" to extend their limited sphere of action to absorb the ballot box. Votes were tools to be used on questions they regarded as safely within women's realm. Liquor votes to protect the home, school votes to protect the children, and, in time, municipal votes to clean up the cities were not, Baker asserts, foundations for establishing equal citizenship.[24] Without necessarily believing in the abstraction of states' rights, they nonetheless weighted the movement in that direction because states indisputably controlled the aspects of society they sought to reform.

Suffragists from these varied traditions began to mingle in the 1890s and needed to resolve their differences over strategy about where to get the vote. Against the background of the South's decision to make disfranchisement a matter of law during the same decade, suffragists not only abandoned the federal amendment but also affirmed a belief in states' rights to determine who voted. The most conspicuous convergence of traditions and experience occurred in the merger of the American and National associations to form the National American Woman Suffrage Association (NAWSA) in 1890. With its campaign defeated in the Senate, women involved with the National were tempted to look for action in the states. Members of the American were moved by the amendment's defeat to resolve that no more issues of substance distinguished them from the National and the two groups should merge. Aging leaders believed the union necessary in order to have an organization in place that could direct the mounting interest in suffrage. Both associations found themselves drawing more southerners, women from the temperance movement, and women who used terms like "the mother's vote."[25] Elizabeth Cady Stanton, newly elected president of the NAWSA and speaking for a large segment of the old National's members, tried to hold the new organization to the traditional program of her association. Her own list of resolutions for the first joint meeting to consider underscored the divisions among nineteenth-century suffragists. It began:

> *Resolved*, That as the fathers violated the principles of justice in consenting to a three-fifths representation, and in recognizing slavery in the Constitution, thereby making a civil war inevitable; so our statesmen and Supreme Court Judges by their misinterpretations of the Fourteenth Amendment, declaring that the United States has no voters and that citizenship does not carry with it the right of suffrage, not only have prolonged woman's disfranchisement but have undermined the status of the freedmen and opened the way for another war of races.

She cut to the heart of her disagreement with the American, reaffirmed the importance of federal action for women, and tied both directly to the growing disfranchisement of African Americans in southern states. More figurehead than leader at this stage of her life, Stanton had neither the will nor the followers to win a fight on this point.[26]

For the next two and a half decades, the NAWSA poured its meager resources and considerable talents into state campaigns—encouraged by victories in Idaho and Utah in 1896 but undeterred by the subsequent resumption of failure until 1910. Only token resources were devoted to the federal amendment. After 1896 in the Senate and 1894 in the House, Congress did not even bother to report the measure out of committee until 1913. Thus, while the South undermined the Fifteenth Amendment, the woman suffrage movement stopped agitating about the question of federal responsibility for voting rights altogether. Their complicity went further. To gain ground in the white South, the NAWSA affirmed its belief in the South's prerogative to legislate white supremacy. Meeting in New Orleans in 1903, the executive board informed the public that the association "is seeking to do away with the requirement of a sex qualification for suffrage. What other qualifications shall be asked for it leaves to each State. The southern women most active in it have always in their own State emphasized the fact that granting suffrage to women who can read and write and who pay taxes would insure white supremacy without resorting to any methods of doubtful constitutionality."[27] The official position of woman suffragists no longer defined their principle to be the political equality of all citizens.

The old complaint, about freedmen winning votes before white women, took on more potent meaning in a nation accepting black men's disfranchisement. Charlotte Forten Grimké described in the *Washington Post,* while the National American Woman Suffrage Association met in the city in 1898, how a black woman reacted to the chorus of resentment from white suffragists. "We have felt the injustice done to the colored men of the South in those oft-repeated words . . . 'the inconsistency of giving the right of suffrage to ignorant negroes, and denying it to refined and intellectual white women.' These expressions . . . can only be characterized as contemptible; for their direct effect is to strengthen a most unjust and cruel prejudice; . . ." Taking a swipe at the new power of southerners in the movement, Grimké juxtaposed their past disloyalty to the nation and the contributions black men made to northern victory. More than a history lesson, Grimké's references made clear that the old refrain about the Fifteenth Amendment was nothing more than an expression of white superiority and an excuse for disfranchisement. "Some of us certainly cannot believe that it would have been just to deny the right of citizenship to the great majority of the loyal men of the South—as the negroes certainly were, and are—and confer it upon the disloyal women, who not only did not conceal, but gloried in their disloyalty, however intellectual and refined they may have been. . . . And while [the colored women] appreciate the value of woman's suffrage quite as keenly as other women do, . . . we would desire for ourselves no recognition that would involve injustice to such men."[28] In vain she called for woman suffragists to find a more universal basis for their cause.

Federal Amendment Again

When suffragists returned to the federal amendment strategy in 1914 and 1915, the old cause had lost virtually all connection to its origins. Federal action this time appealed to suffragists for its simplicity, not its principle. Concerted action for a federal amendment after 1915 transformed the woman suffrage movement's political possibilities. An intense campaign, aided by newfound help from President Wilson and other elected leaders, won congressional passage in 1919 and ratification in 1920.

Suffragists did not decide to follow the federal strategy again without a fuss. The chief instigator was Alice Paul, new to the American movement but a veteran of British suffrage campaigns who brought militancy and political savvy back to Washington. Reviving the NAWSA's moribund committee for congressional work, Paul managed to have the amendment reintroduced in 1913 and voted upon in 1914. Her success necessitated breaking with the National, whose president, Anna Howard Shaw, had no tolerance for independent initiative and whose leading members still favored state, not federal, action. Indeed, the National backed a rival amendment in 1914 that would protect states' rights to enfranchise women. Through 1915, the National carried on, as Shaw described it, in "the field in which such inspiring opportunities still confront us—campaign work in the various states."[29] With the return of Carrie Chapman Catt to the presidency of the National in 1916, the older association finally integrated its state plans with a strategy for pressing Congress to pass the amendment. By then Alice Paul's Congressional Union (renamed the Woman's Party) competed with the National for leadership of the movement.

Experience was pushing women to find a more efficient solution than winning the vote state by state. Across the country suffragists of all types were identifying political, legal, and constitutional obstacles that a federal amendment could surmount or bypass. First, each state campaign required enormous resources; few states passed full woman suffrage on the first try, if they passed it at all; some states proved to be intractable; and in many states, notably but not exclusively in the South, the effort to build public support in advance of an amendment campaign had only recently begun. Though anyone could have pointed out this weakness in the state strategy, and some did during the nineteenth century, accelerated campaigning after 1910 drove home the point.

Second, in some states women were simply blocked by constitutional provision from passing an amendment in favor of woman suffrage. In Minnesota and Nebraska, at least, amendments to the state constitutions could no longer be approved by a simple majority of those voting on the measure; an amendment needed a majority of all votes cast in the particular election. By design, this standard was virtually impossible to attain no matter what amendment went to the voters. From Minnesota woman suffragists reported their predicament by 1902: their "only hope for the full suffrage lies in the submission of an amendment to the Federal Constitution by Congress to the Legislatures of the various States." From Nebraska came similar news: "it is useless to ask the Legislature to submit [an amendment] conferring Full Suffrage upon women."[30]

Third, partial suffrage campaigns were meeting with all kinds of obstacles that underscored why women needed political power and rights, not just chances to vote on some issues. The very women who had earlier distanced themselves from talk of law and rights to seek a "mother's vote" and other modest gains were learning the vulnerability of partial suffrage. It could be lost more easily than won. Suffrage under a county school law would evaporate when the district grew and fell under a different law; votes allowed to women in one class or size of city would disappear when the city graduated to the next higher class. The examples were everywhere. Dakota Territory's equal school suffrage laws were not preserved under the state governments of North and South Dakota in 1889. Legislators took back the privilege of school suffrage in Kentucky's second-class cities in 1902 when more black women than white went to the polls. Courts in New Jersey and Michigan declared existing laws for women's school and municipal suffrage to be unconstitutional in the mid-nineties.[31]

The twentieth-century campaign for a federal woman suffrage amendment addressed practical difficulties that women understood from fifty years of experimenting with alternatives. Speaking to an emergency convention of the National in 1916, Carrie Chapman Catt described Congress as a kind of court of last resort in the case of women versus American federalism. Gone was any vision of shifting the center of American politics. "Our cause," she explained, "has been caught in a snarl of constitutional obstructions and inadequate election laws . . . and we have a right to appeal to our Congress to extricate it from this tangle." That new slant, the emphasis on practical politics, had the advantage, too, of winning greater support from politicians. Speaking to the same 1916 meeting, President Woodrow Wilson told the National's delegates, "I get a little impatient sometimes about the discussion of the channels and methods by which [woman suffrage] is to prevail." Not yet an advocate of federal action but ready to recognize woman suffrage as a legitimate objective, Wilson signaled his belief that suffrage should be separated from the controversial question of federal vs. states' rights: "we shall not quarrel in the long run as to the method of it, . . ."[32] Gone was any vision of federal suffrage as a more certain guarantee of republican government, but with it had gone the objection that federal action would compromise the rights of states.

Leaders of both the Congressional Union and the National described this new federal campaign as a continuation of the effort begun in 1869. It behooved them to do so. Justice was obviously due to women who had shown such patience and persistence. And endurance implied power; binding their complex history into a single story, the suffragists' demand appeared like an arrow, shot in 1848 or 1869 and now to find its mark. But history was selectively recalled. Elizabeth Cady Stanton disappeared from the movement's iconography, as if her memory would bring to mind such dangerous thoughts as "National Protection for National Citizens."[33] Outside the movement, W. E. B. Du Bois recalled the long history of cooperation between women and African Americans, while inside its circle, leaders distanced themselves from the growing numbers of African-American suffragists, lest the movement project an integrationist image.[34]

Times had changed beyond the reach of the movement as well, to transform the meaning of the amendment that now united them in their final campaign. Wording for the Nineteenth Amendment matched what Senator Sargent had introduced in 1878, and that in turn came from the Fifteenth Amendment, with "on account of sex" substituting for the earlier "on account of race, color, or previous condition of servitude." The Nineteenth reads in full: "Section 1: The right of citizens of the United States to vote shall not be denied or abridged by the United States or any State on account of sex. Section 2: Congress shall have power, by appropriate legislation, to enforce the provisions of this article." Despite the Fifteenth Amendment, by 1913 the South had successfully disfranchised black men without federal challenge. By the time it became the object of woman suffragists, this language had proved to be no obstacle to disfranchisement by states and to hold no promise that Congress would extend national protection for voting rights.

By continuing to deny the relationship between their demand and the rights of African Americans, woman suffragists moved their cause to the racist center of American politics. As it became clear that woman's demand would indeed be met, African-American leaders remained hopeful about the effects of the change on their own suffrage struggle. "[A]ny agitation, discussion or reopening of the problem of voting must inevitably be a discussion of the right of black folk to vote in America and Africa," W. E. B. Du Bois had written in the *Crisis* in 1912 to rouse African-American support for the woman suffrage demand. But white suffrage leaders were bent on reassuring the South that their demand posed no threat to white supremacy. Echoing the National's 1903 position on states' rights, Alice Paul, in 1919, described her goal as "removing the sex qualification from the franchise regulations . . . to see to it that the franchise conditions for every state were the same for women as for men." States could impose any restrictions allowed by the Constitution that they desired. Carrie Chapman Catt distinguished between "qualifications" of the voter—reserved to the states—and what the National sought—"removal of the sex restriction, nothing more, nothing less."[35]

If there were any doubts in 1919 as to the intent of the code words that Paul and Catt used to indicate they would not tamper with the right of states to disfranchise black women, they soon vanished when the woman suffrage movement turned its back on African-American women. Within months of the amendment's ratification in 1920, additional needs of black women became evident. At the November elections of 1920, there were reports from the South of harassment and rights denied. A year later the situation had worsened, and more women met resistance at the polls. The next phase of woman suffrage history had begun. African-American leaders sought the support of white suffragists for investigations into compliance with the Nineteenth Amendment. If earlier refusals to oppose the disfranchisement of blacks in the South could be understood (but not forgiven) as efforts to ensure congressional support for the amendment's passage or state ratification, surely by 1921 white suffragists might find a way to use their new political power to undo the earlier damage. Both Paul's National Woman's Party and Catt's League of Women Voters met in 1921, and both refused to back an investigation. In the League, the debate prompted southern delegates to walk out, and the needs of black women were sacrificed to hold the South within the new organization. The measure met defeat at the Woman's Party convention as well, and the party refused to include black women's disfranchisement on its list of unfinished business of woman's emancipation.[36]

Affirming their political judgment that the fight for woman suffrage had been won, suffragists closed their histories at 1920 as well, shunting into a separate history the subsequent suffrage movement embedded within the Civil Rights movement. Carrie Chapman Catt closed her own historical contribution, published first in 1923, with the old resentful refrain about the privileges accorded black men. Describing the political consciousness "American women" would now bring to the voting booth, she wrote: "American women who know the history of their country will always resent the fact that American men chose to enfranchise Negroes fresh from slavery before enfranchising American wives and mothers, . . ."[37] With black women excluded from the categories "American women" *and* "Negroes" and with the reality of disfranchisement ignored, Catt chose to close the movement's history on a divisive and vicious note. The significant part played by African-American women in the ongoing struggle to gain the universal suffrage that had once been the objective of the woman suffrage movement would thereafter come in separate historical packages. National protection of voting rights would be, not the achievement of the woman suffrage movement, but the twentieth-century Civil Rights movement.

Notes

1. See, for example, Aileen S. Kraditor, *The Ideas of the Woman Suffrage Movement, 1890–1920* (New York: Columbia University Press, 1965), chap. 7; Rosalyn Terborg-Penn, "Discrimination Against Afro-American Women in the Woman's Movement, 1830–1920," in *The Afro-American Woman: Struggles and Images*, ed. Sharon Harley and Rosalyn Terborg-Penn (Port Washington, N.Y.: National University Publications, 1978), 17–27; Bettina Aptheker, *Woman's Legacy: Essays on Race, Sex, and Class in American History* (Amherst: University of Massachusetts Press, 1982); Paula Giddings, *When and Where I Enter: The Impact of Black Women on Race and Sex in America* (New York: Bantam Books, 1984); Barbara Hilkert Andolsen, *"Daughters of Jefferson, Daughters of Bootblacks": Racism and American Feminism* (Macon, Ga.: Mercer University Press, 1986); Jean Fagan Yellin, *Women & Sisters: The Antislavery Feminists in American Culture* (New Haven: Yale University Press, 1989); Steven F. Lawson, *Running for Freedom: Civil Rights and Black Politics in America Since 1941* (Philadelphia: Temple University Press, 1991); Armstead L. Robinson and Patricia Sullivan, eds. *New Directions in Civil Rights Studies* (Charlottesville: University Press of Virginia, 1991).

2. In Mari Jo Buhle and Paul Buhle, eds., *Concise History of Woman Suffrage: Selections from the Classic Work of Stanton, Anthony, Gage, and Harper* (Urbana: University of Illinois Press, 1978), 96. Where possible I have cited this source in preference to the six volumes from which it excerpts sources because of its greater availability.

3. Early state campaigns are best described in volumes one and three of Elizabeth Cady Stanton, Susan B. Anthony, and Matilda Joslyn Gage, eds., *History of Woman Suffrage* (1881, 1886; reprint, New York: Arno Press, 1969). Quotations from Stanton's address to the Eleventh National Woman's Rights Convention, 1866, Buhle and Buhle, *Concise History of Woman Suffrage*, 230.

4. Cited within "Address to Congress, Adopted by the Eleventh National Woman's Rights Convention, held in New York City, Thursday, May 10, 1866," *Concise History of Woman Suffrage*, 226.

5. "Address to Congress" and Elizabeth Cady Stanton's address, Eleventh National Woman's Rights Convention, 1866, *Concise History of Woman Suffrage*, 228, 230.

6. Lucy Stone to Susan B. Anthony and the American Equal Rights Association, Lawrence, Kansas, May 6, 1867, Stanton, Anthony, and Gage, *History of Woman Suffrage* (1882; reprint, New York: Arno Press, 1968), 2: 919–20.

7. Ibid., 333. Amendments proposed for woman suffrage were referred to as the sixteenth until 1913 when the amendment authorizing federal income tax was ratified as the Sixteenth Amendment. Thereafter, amendments for direct election of senators and prohibition were incorporated into the Constitution before passage of the woman suffrage amendment—making it the Nineteenth Amendment. When writing about the nineteenth century, I refer to the sixteenth amendment.

8. Stanton's address to the National Woman Suffrage Convention, Washington, D.C., Jan. 19, 1869, Buhle and Buhle, *Concise History of Woman Suffrage*, 255.

9. *Revolution* (New York) Oct. 7, 1869, in *The Papers of Elizabeth Cady Stanton and Susan B. Anthony*, ed. Patricia G. Holland and Ann D. Gordon (Wilmington, Del.: Scholarly Resources Inc., 1991), microfilm edition, reel 2, frame 108.

10. Historians have paid little attention to the differences among late nineteenth-century suffragists and how the movement spread after the Civil War. No history exists of the American Woman Suffrage Association. The most significant interpretation of the National's position in the seventies is Ellen Carol DuBois, "Outgrowing the Compact of the Fathers: Equal Rights, Woman Suffrage, and the United States Constitution, 1820–1878," *Journal of American History* 74 (Dec. 1987): 836–62. Steven Buechler, *The Transformation of the Woman Suffrage Movement: The Case of Illinois, 1850–1920* (New Brunswick, N.J.: Rutgers University Press, 1986), though specific to one state, offers one of the best accounts of this "middle period."

11. Volumes two and three of Stanton, Anthony, and Gage, *History of Woman Suffrage*, detail the National's campaigns of this era, though a fuller collection of documents is now available in *Papers of Stanton and Anthony*.

12. Testimony of Elizabeth Cady Stanton, *Arguments Before the Committee on Privileges and Elections of the United States Senate, in Behalf of a Sixteenth Amendment to the Constitution of the United States, . . . January 11 and 12, 1878, . . .* (Washington: Government Printing Office, 1878), 4–17; Stanton titled this address "National Protection for National Citizens." See *Papers of Stanton and Anthony*, reel 19, frames 1017–19, 1029–86, and reel 20, frames 38–114.

13. Mrs. E. W. McMillan to Elizabeth Cady Stanton, Memphis, May 2, 1880, National Woman Suffrage Association Collection, Chicago Historical Society, in *Papers of Stanton and Anthony*, reel 5, frame 463.

14. An appeal for expressions of support went out from the National's leadership under the heading "A Mass Meeting For All Women Who Want to Vote," in *National Citizen and Ballot Box* (Syracuse), Apr. 1880. Nearly two thousand replies make up the manuscript collection cited in note 13, also available on reels 4 and 5 of the *Papers of Stanton and Anthony*.

15. Susan B. Anthony and Ida Husted Harper, eds., *History of Woman Suffrage* (1902; reprint, New York: Arno Press, 1969), 4: 78.

16. A history of the American is sorely needed. Stone and Blackwell published the weekly *Woman's Journal* as its organ, with the official accounts of annual conventions. Additional, often fuller, reports are available in local newspapers of the cities where the American met. I have relied on the short summaries prepared for volumes two and four of the *History of Woman Suffrage*. On early strategy, see also Richard E. Welch, Jr., *George Frisbie Hoar and the Half-Breed Republicans* (Cambridge: Harvard University Press, 1971), 29.

17. Stanton, Anthony, and Gage, *History of Woman Suffrage*, 2: 763, 809, 810, 826, 843, 849; Anthony and Harper, *History of Woman Suffrage*, 4: 410, 416–17.

18. Stanton, Anthony, and Gage, *History of Woman Suffrage*, 2: 780, 826.

19. Ibid., 851 and 851n. For different wording of Stone's directions about petitions, see Buhle and Buhle, *Concise History of Woman Suffrage*, 308.

20. On state campaigns see Eleanor Flexner, *Century of Struggle: The Woman's Rights Movement in the United States*, rev. ed. (Cambridge: Belknap Press, 1975); and Carrie Chapman Catt and Nettie Rogers Shuler, *Woman Suffrage and Politics: The Inner Story of the Suffrage Movement* (1926; reprint, Seattle: University of Washington Press, 1970). Chapters on individual states in *History of Woman Suffrage* are also useful.

21. Mrs. Schuyler Bundy to Elizabeth Cady Stanton, Fox River, Wisconsin, May 30, 1880, National Woman Suffrage Association Collection, Chicago Historical Society, in *Papers of Stanton and Anthony*, reel 5, frames 543–44; Abigail Scott Duniway, *Path Breaking: An Autobiographical History of the Equal Suffrage Movement in Pacific Coast States* (1914; reprint, New York: Schocken Books, 1971), 106.

22. Ruth Bordin, *Woman and Temperance: The Quest for Power and Liberty, 1873–1900* (Philadelphia: Temple University Press, 1981); Petition from Wausau Woman's Christian Temperance Union to meeting of Wisconsin Woman Suffrage Association [June 1880], National Woman Suffrage Association Collection, Chicago Historical Society, in *Papers of Stanton and Anthony*, reel 21, frames 275–78.

23. There is no history of the school suffrage movement. Most state chapters in the *History of Woman Suffrage* report on its progress, as do state reports published with the annual National-American Woman Suffrage Association *Proceedings* after 1893. On the totals, see Anthony and Harper, *History of Woman Suffrage*, 4: 461.

24. Paula Baker, "The Domestication of Politics: Women and American Political Society, 1780–1920," in *Women, the State, and Welfare*, ed. Linda Gordon (Madison: University of Wisconsin Press, 1990), 68–69. Baker's emphasis is on convergence between male and female politics, not convergence between different streams of female politics.

25. On the American's resolution for merger, see Anthony and Harper, *History of Woman Suffrage*, 4: 426; on disagreements over the term "mother's vote," see report of District of Columbia Woman Suffrage Association in National-American Woman Suffrage Association, *Proceedings for 1895*, 57, *Papers of Stanton and Anthony*, reel 33, frames 552ff.

26. Anthony and Harper, *History of Woman Suffrage*, 4: 165. Full coverage of the meeting can be found in *Papers of Stanton and Anthony*, reel 28, frames 50–142. For reaction to Stanton's resolutions, see especially coverage in the *Washington Post*, Feb. 19–22, 1890. Stanton reiterated these views to a special meeting of the National in 1893 in her address, "Suffrage a Natural Right," *Papers of Stanton and Anthony*, reel 32, frames 273–85. After 1894 she began to advocate educated suffrage.

27. "NAWSA Position on the Race Question, Letter to the *New Orleans Times-Democrat*, during March 1903 Convention," Buhle and Buhle, *Concise History of Woman Suffrage*, 350–51; also *Papers of Stanton and Anthony*, reel 43, frame 395.

28. "The Rights of the Negro," *Washington Post*, Feb. 24, 1898. Grimké's quotation comes from an earlier open letter by her friend Helen A. Cook to Susan B. Anthony, published by the *Post* on Feb. 19. Cook, in turn, quoted Anthony, who, ironically, used the argument to remind her audience of the importance of the federal amendment, though she clearly courted southern suffragists by this date.

29. Anna Howard Shaw, with Elizabeth Garver Jordan, *Story of a Pioneer* (New York: Harper and Bros., 1915), 316; on Paul, see Christine A. Lunardini, *From Equal Suffrage to Equal Rights: Alice Paul and the National Woman's Party, 1910–1928* (New York: New York University Press, 1986); on Shaw and Catt, see Robert Booth Fowler, *Carrie Catt: Feminist Politician* (Boston: Northeastern University Press, 1986).

30. Anthony and Harper, *History of Woman Suffrage*, 4: 779, 808.

31. Dakota Territory: Stanton, Anthony, and Gage, *History of Woman Suffrage*, 3: 663; Anthony and Harper, *History of Woman Suffrage*, 4: 550–51, 561. Kentucky: ibid., 674–75. New Jersey: ibid., 828, 830–32. Michigan: ibid., 761–63, 769.

32. "Carrie Chapman Catt, 'The Crisis,'" and "Woodrow Wilson's Address," NAWSA Emergency Convention, Atlantic City, New Jersey, Sept. 4–10, 1916, Buhle and Buhle, *Concise History of Woman Suffrage*, 430–34.

33. On Stanton's declining fame, see Ellen Carol DuBois, "Making Women's History: Activist Historians of Women's Rights, 1880–1940," *Radical History Review* 49 (Winter 1991): 61–84, though DuBois does not link the decline to racial justice.

34. Jean Fagan Yellin, "Du Bois' *Crisis* and Woman's Suffrage," *Massachusetts Review* 14 (Spring 1973): 365–75, traces the close attention Du Bois paid to the movement from 1910 forward.

35. Yellin, "Du Bois' *Crisis*," 368; Alice Paul to Mary White Ovington, Mar. 31, 1919, and Carrie Chapman Catt to John R. Shillady, May 6, 1919, both in National Association for the Advancement of Colored People Papers, Library of Congress, and quoted in Giddings, *When and Where I Enter*, 163.

36. Giddings, *When and Where I Enter*, 165–70; Yellin, "Du Bois' *Crisis*," 374–75; Nancy F. Cott, *The Grounding of Modern Feminism* (New Haven: Yale University Press, 1987), 68–70.

37. Catt and Shuler, *Woman Suffrage and Politics*, 491.

2

The Woman Suffrage Movement in the Inhospitable South

Marjorie Spruill Wheeler

In 1892, Laura Clay of Kentucky sent a warning to the leaders of the National American Woman Suffrage Association in a letter to *The Woman's Journal*: "Since we claim to be national let us never forget that the South cannot be left out of our calculations. You have worked for forty years and you will work for forty years more and do nothing unless you bring in the South."[1] Clay's letter was both insightful and prophetic. The woman suffrage movement, she realized, had begun in the Northeast in 1848 and had spread to a certain extent to other sections of the nation, but its leaders had made little effort to organize in the South. Yet the NAWSA, which hoped to enfranchise women throughout the United States, would have to "bring in" supporters in all regions if it wanted to achieve a "national" victory. After all, a federal suffrage amendment would have to be approved by three-fourths of the states; the suffragists would need some southern states in order for the amendment to be ratified. When victory finally came in 1920, it was won with the support of four southern states that broke ranks with the otherwise "Solid South" and ratified the Nineteenth Amendment: Kentucky, Texas, Arkansas, and the famous thirty-sixth state, Tennessee.[2]

"Bringing in" the South, however, was a difficult task that was never fully accomplished. In the 1890s, under Clay's leadership and with strong support from the NAWSA, a small but determined group of elite white women became suffragists and sought enfranchisement, primarily through the new state constitutions of that era. Between 1909 and 1916, a much larger contingent of southern suffragists sought the vote through amendments to their state constitutions. When these efforts failed, most but not all southern suffragists joined national leaders in supporting the federal amendment. Southern hostility to the suffrage movement frustrated southern suffragists in their efforts to become enfranchised through either state or federal action, however. Prior to the ratification of the Nineteenth Amendment in 1920, southern women gained full enfranchisement in *no* southern state and partial suffrage in only four. Southern politicians managed to block passage of the federal suffrage amendment in Congress for many years and, once it was submitted to the states, made a concerted effort to prevent ratification—despite the pleas of regional favorite son President Woodrow Wilson to support the amendment for the sake of the National Democratic Party. Of the ten states that failed to ratify, *nine* were south of the Mason-Dixon line. Several southern states passed "rejection resolutions" denouncing the federal amendment variously as "unwarranted," "unnecessary," "undemocratic," and "dangerous." Indeed, the South is notorious in the history of the woman suffrage movement as the region that afforded the movement the greatest resistance and the least success.[3]

The southern suffrage movement has long been neglected by historians, probably because it was so unsuccessful.[4] Yet the regional hostility to the movement, owing to the South's paternalistic, hierarchical social structure, which placed special value on the southern white woman remaining in her traditional sphere; the drive to restore and maintain white political supremacy; and the regional reverence for state sovereignty makes the history of the southern suffrage movement fascinating and instructive, as well as distinctive. This overview of the woman suffrage movement in the South examines the obstacles to the movement, its development despite these obstacles, and the profound impact of the race and states' rights issues. The primary focus is upon the ideas and actions of the movement's most prominent leaders and the strategies they devised in order to cope with the "peculiar institutions" of their region.

The fierce opposition of most white southerners to the woman suffrage movement resulted from several interrelated cultural, political, and economic factors. The southern suffrage movement took place in a period, from 1890 to 1920, in which white southerners were passionately devoted to the preservation of a distinct and, they believed, superior "Southern Civilization." As one leading minister put it, they were eager that the "victory over Southern arms" not be followed by "a victory over Southern opinions."[5] A key element of this Southern Civilization they wished to preserve was a dualistic conception of the natures and responsibilities of the sexes that precluded the participation of women in politics and cast "The Southern Lady" in the role of guardian and symbol of southern virtue. Charged with transmitting southern culture to future generations, as well as inspiring current statesmen to serve as their noble defenders, southern womanhood had a vital role to play in preserving the values of "the Lost Cause." A leading "Lost Cause" minister, Albert Bledsoe, urged southern women to shun the fruit offered by the women's rights movement and take as their "mission," not to "imitate a Washington, or a Lee, or a Jackson," but to "rear, and train, and educate, and mould the future Washingtons, and Lees, and Jacksons of the South, to protect and preserve the sacred rights of woman as well as of man."[6] That representatives of the burgeoning industries of the New South, particularly the textile industry, wished southern women to confine their beneficent influence to the home rather than vote for child labor legislation and other encumbrances was an additional and potent obstacle to the success of woman suffrage in the South.[7]

In the eyes of white southerners, the cornerstone of this Southern Civilization was white supremacy, and their determination to restore white supremacy in politics—and then defend the state sovereignty thought necessary to preserve it—also presented a tremendous obstacle to the southern suffrage movement.[8] In the late nineteenth and early twentieth centuries, white southerners were generally contemptuous of the women's rights movement as yet another unfortunate product of an inferior northern culture that they were trying to resist, as an offshoot of abolitionism led by northern women with the same "naive" and dangerous belief in equality that had characterized the abolitionists. Southern suffragists were scolded for playing into the hands of social "levelers" who had no understanding of the crucial social distinctions of gender and race that accounted for the superiority of Southern Civilization; moreover, suffragists were accused of unwittingly complicating the South's efforts to restore and protect white supremacy. The suffragists, charged the "antis," failed to recognize that the proposed federal woman suffrage amendment was nothing more than a "reaffirmation of the Fifteenth Amendment" and that its ratification by the South would signal acceptance of black suffrage and concede the right of the federal government to determine suffrage qualifications in the states.[9]

In 1919, during the ratification battle, a leading antisuffragist, James Callaway, editor of the *Macon (Georgia) Telegraph*, clearly articulated these sentiments, which virtually held southern women hostage to the Lost Cause.

> May our Southern women remain on the pedestal, forever preserve that distinctive deference which is theirs so long as they remain as they are—our highest ideals of the true, the beautiful and the good. . . . Deference to its womankind has always been a distinguished characteristic of the Southern people. Southern men would perpetuate it. But foreign forces have invaded us, established branches over the South of a huge National Woman's Association whose ideals are not our ideals; whose women are not like our Southern women. They are women of a different clay, and are of different mould. Should these foreign crusaders succeed, pervert the tastes of our women, persuade them to abandon their old ideals and descend into the arena of politics . . . woe is the day for Southern civilization.[10]

Even after President Wilson became convinced that woman suffrage was inevitable and that the Democrats must not allow the Republicans to claim credit for the victory, he could not convince most southern congressmen or state legislators to support woman suffrage. Surrender of principle in anticipation of defeat was not an acceptable alternative to these children of the Confederacy who had grown up amidst tales of the heroic sacrifices of their ancestors. The majority of southern politicians believed that their constituents—as well as their corporate sponsors—required them to fight to the last ditch, and then some.[11]

The southern women who were willing to embrace woman suffrage, indeed to become the leaders of such an unpopular cause, were formidable individuals. In their 1923 reflective, *Woman Suffrage and Politics*, Carrie Chapman Catt and Nettie Shuler observed, "No stronger characters did the long struggle produce than those great-souled southern suffragists. They had need to be great of soul."[12] Catt and Shuler meant, of course, that advocacy of woman suffrage in such an inhospitable climate was character-building; but the leaders of the woman suffrage movement in the southern states had to have unusual self-confidence and determination in order to take up this cause in the first place.

Certainly it was no coincidence that most of the leaders of the southern suffrage movement were descended from the South's social and political elite. These included Laura Clay, the so-called "Susan B. Anthony of the South," the crucial intermediary between northern and southern suffragists; the Gordon sisters, Kate and Jean, of New Orleans, "silk-stockinged reformers" who were leaders of the states' rights suffragists; Nellie Nugent Somerville of Mississippi, the impressive leader of the suffragists in her state whose father was revered by white Mississippians for his role in restoring "home rule" in the state and ending Reconstruction; FFV Lila Meade Valentine of Richmond, leader of the Virginia suffragists; her close friend and associate, the famous novelist and descendent of Confederate heroes, Mary Johnston; Rebecca Latimer Felton of Georgia, whose husband served several terms in the state legislature and in the United States Congress; Madeline McDowell Breckinridge of Kentucky, granddaughter of Henry Clay and wife of Desha Breckinridge (who was the great-grandson of Thomas Jefferson's attorney-general, the son of a congressman, and the editor of the *Lexington Herald*); Pattie Ruffner Jacobs of Alabama, a star among the younger suffragists and wife of a wealthy Birmingham industrialist; and Tennessee's socialite suffragist Anne Dallas Dudley, to name a few.[13]

Their privileged socioeconomic positions provided these suffrage leaders more opportunities for education than most southern women of their era enjoyed as well as opportunities for travel outside the region that contributed to the undermining of provincial attitudes concerning woman's role. Furthermore, economic security provided the leisure and the means that allowed them to assume leadership roles in the suffrage movement. A few southern leaders were members of families that were experiencing financial distress, including Mississippi's Belle Kearney, who wrote of taking in sewing for former slaves one day and dancing as a debutante in the governor's mansion the next, and Tennessee's Sue Shelton White, who supported herself as a court reporter. Most, however, were daughters of wealth and privilege who could hire maids, cooks, and baby tenders as well as personally finance most of the suffrage work in the South. Indeed, other southern suffragists sometimes expressed disdain for Kearney because she requested payment for some of her suffrage lectures.[14]

Exalted social position facilitated their suffrage work, giving them a certain familiarity and access to the political process and a degree of immunity from criticism—or at least social ostracism—not enjoyed by southern women of lesser social standing. Well aware of the particular importance of social position in the South, national suffrage leaders deliberately recruited southern suffrage leaders from prominent families, women who had, as Kate Gordon phrased it, "names to conjure with."[15] These women could demand and receive a respectful hearing, if not suffrage. Antisuffragists found it expedient to treat them decorously even while denouncing northern suffragists in no uncertain terms. Indeed, Desha Breckinridge once gave editorial chastisement to *Louisville Courier-Journal* editor Henry Watterson for daring to criticize the suffragists of Kentucky, led by the women of the Breckinridge and Clay families, "the hems of whose garments he was not fit to touch."[16]

The remarkable self-confidence of these women was owed in part to their social position. They were, after all, members of families that were accustomed to guiding, rather than simply being guided by, public opinion. Kate Gordon once wrote, "Review every advance, moral or other wise. Have the majority ever desired the advance? The great earnest minority always shapes thought and leads the van."[17] Nellie Nugent Somerville and her associates in Greenville, Mississippi, suggested their attitude toward public opinion when they named their literary society after Hypatia, a learned woman stoned to death by a mob in ancient Egypt.[18] Somerville also derived confidence from her religious convictions, and both Laura Clay and Belle Kearney felt that God had called them to serve the cause of women's rights. Still others revealed, through diaries and private correspondence, a mischievous desire to be different, deriving pleasure from going against the grain.[19]

Indeed, the decisions of these suffrage leaders to take up this unpopular cause resulted from a combination of personal characteristics and experiences that made them receptive to feminism. The attitudes and example of family members were very important in shaping the views of these women. For example, Laura Clay's family background—which would have converted almost anyone to feminism—certainly had that effect on Clay, her mother, and all her sisters: upon his appointment as Lincoln's ambassador to Russia, Laura's father, Cassius Marcellus Clay, took his family with him to St. Petersburg, but when living with six children and in the style expected of an ambassador proved too costly, he sent them back home. Mary Jane Clay managed to get her family back to Kentucky, despite the hazards of travel in the midst of the Civil War, and she managed "White Hall," the family plantation, and a multitude of children by herself for eight years—even remodeling and expanding their plantation and providing her daughters with formal education despite her husband's objections. Meanwhile, Cassius Clay became involved in a well-publicized scandal involving a notorious St. Petersburg courtesan and then returned to Kentucky with an illegitimate son whom he legally adopted. Advanced in his thinking when it suited his own purposes, Clay divorced his wife, who lost the plantation she had tended so carefully. Mary Jane Clay and her four daughters *all* became suffragists and advocates of expanded political and legal rights for women in Kentucky and the South.[20]

Positive attitudes toward women and feminism on the part of family members also played a role in the making of southern suffragists. Sue White and the Gordon sisters all had mothers who inspired them to adopt an expanded view of woman's role; Somerville's father saw to it that Nellie received the best education available to a woman and even invited her to read for the law in his office. (She declined.)[21] Several of the suffrage leaders had sisters who supported them in their work. NAWSA president Anna Howard Shaw once

Laura Clay. Courtesy of the State Historical Society of Iowa—Des Moines.

said, in reference to the Clays, the Gordons, the Johnstons, the Howards of Georgia, and the Finnegans of Texas, "If there was a failure to organize any state in the South . . . it must be due to the fact that no family there had three sisters to start the movement." Madeline Breckinridge, Pattie Jacobs, and Lila Meade Valentine all enjoyed the enthusiastic support of their husbands in their suffrage work.[22] Contacts with suffragists from the North, the West, from other countries, and with suffragists from other southern states were also crucial in the decisions of these women to become advocates of women's rights. And once recruited, they interested scores of other southern women in the cause. Like all reformers, southern suffragists came to feel themselves part of a supportive subculture and to judge themselves according to the precepts of that group rather than those of the larger society they were trying to reform.[23]

Nevertheless, these white southern suffragists identified strongly with their region and shared many of the attitudes of the men of their race and class. Though they were quite clearly "New Women" who sought expanded rights and privileges for themselves and their gender, they took pride in their heritage as Southern Ladies, accepting the traditional duties if not the restrictions that role entailed. Their opponents called them "unconscious agents" of northern saboteurs, but they fully understood what they were doing and why. For the most part, they considered their movement to be supportive rather than destructive of Southern Civilization. Yet they were clearly weary of their indirect, supportive role in politics, which, they had concluded, not only denied their individuality but also had proven to be inadequate for the protection of their interests or that of their "constituency," the "unprivileged" of the South—particularly women and children.

Drawn from the region's social and political elite, the women who led the southern suffrage movement fully supported the 1890s campaign led by the men of their race and class to return government to the so-called "best people." They took it for granted that it was the duty of the "most qualified" to guide and protect the rest, but they believed themselves to be among the best qualified. Indeed, their goal in fighting for suffrage was to add maternalism to paternalism, to carry the traditional role of the Southern Lady into politics, to offer their services and unique feminine insights to the governing of their region. They sought, in fact, to restore and preserve elements they believed had once been integral in southern politics but were missing in the politics of the New South: morality, integrity, and the tradition of noblesse oblige.[24]

Indeed, one important characteristic shared by all of these white southern suffrage leaders that inspired them to take up this unpopular cause and continue working for it despite so many defeats was their low opinion of the current management of the New South. All of the suffrage leaders had friends or relatives in public office. They believed, however, that southern politics since the Civil War had degenerated to the point that too few honest and intelligent men were willing to serve. Nellie Nugent Somerville, for example, contrasted the "boys" of the Confederacy, who "gave up prospects of material advancement to fight for principle," with the politicians of the present, who spoke of the rampant chaos and corruption in government as "practical politics," which if deplorable was nonetheless inevitable. And she insisted that if "good men" continued to say "no man can go into politics and maintain his integrity . . . and therefore hold themselves aloof and do not even vote," women would have to step in where men feared to tread. At the time of her conversion to the suffrage cause (1897), Somerville was furious over the overt bribery and coercion of voters employed by the "wets" in her county—with the knowledge and cooperation of local officials.[25]

A series of political murders in 1899 and 1900, including the shooting of a gubernatorial candidate by a member of a rival "gang" in the yard of the Kentucky state capitol, first prompted Madeline McDowell Breckinridge to become involved in politics. Shocked by what she considered a general atmosphere of lawlessness in her state, she organized a women's committee that pledged itself to "make every effort in our power for the overthrow of lawlessness and crime, and for the establishment of that social and political purity of righteousness which makes for good citizens and exalteth a nation."[26]

Rebecca Latimer Felton's long struggle for Prohibition and against the convict lease system convinced her that women must be enfranchised; she was well aware of the "Liquor Interest's" eagerness to contain woman's influence. When criticized for meddling in politics, she insisted that men's failure to give "sober homes to women and children" made it necessary for women to become involved. And though she was a member of the United Daughters of the Confederacy, she blasted Georgia politicians for invoking their war records and "waving the Bloody Shirt" to perpetuate their power and thereby extend their opportunities to fleece the public.[27]

Involvement in charitable work and reform societies led these women to a greater knowledge of social ills and a conviction that many of the social and economic problems that were formerly addressed by the private sector now required governmental attention. Yet it seemed clear to the suffragists that southern politicians either failed to understand the crucial need for reforms, such as improved public education and health care, temperance, and legislation to regulate child labor and to protect women and children, or they simply preferred to use public office to line their own pockets. Indeed, the suffragists believed that, in their eagerness to promote economic development, the leaders of the New South were willing to offer up the South's working class for northern exploitation. Breckinridge accused southern boosters of trading "ideals of the past" for material prosperity, and she expressed disgust at attempts to attract northern manufacturers by advertising "that we have not only the cotton and the fuel . . . but the cheap child labor as well."[28] To the suffragists, this failure to live up to their responsibilities in keeping with the concept of noblesse oblige meant that the legislators must be assisted in fulfilling their moral obligations by those citizens to whom such concerns were paramount—women.

Obviously, many southern women of the same race and class, including women who were also attempting to influence public policy through voluntary associations, chose to rely strictly upon the traditional "weapon" of the Southern Lady, the highly touted "indirect influence." Some lacked the courage to defy public opinion; others had no desire for the vote and thought it foolish for women to insult men by demanding it. The president of the Georgia Federation of Women's Clubs, for example, testified that the state's women's clubs had "no difficulty getting their measures passed by the legislature" using powers of persuasion, and that "we are the power behind the throne now, and would lose, not gain, by a change."[29]

And it was true that southern women, lobbying their legislators through voluntary associations, achieved some successes. Suffrage clubs often worked together with traditional women's clubs and succeeded in bringing about a number of significant changes in women's status and opportunities, including the admission of women to colleges and professional schools, the right to serve on governmental commissions and boards and as factory inspectors in some states, and legal reforms regarding inheritance and custody, to name a few. But the women who became suffragists grew more and more convinced that moral suasion was ineffective; even as Breckinridge applauded the accomplishments of the women's clubs of Kentucky, she observed ruefully, "When one remembers that it is the result of twenty-five years of work of a group of able and determined women, it is seen to be small."[30]

Their own indirect influence seemed negligible compared to that exercised by the brewers, the "cotton men," the railroad barons, and other industrialists. As they grew increasingly frustrated by legislative resistance to the reforms they supported, the suffragists grew increasingly cynical about the celebrated chivalry of southern men and denounced the southern woman's enforced reliance upon indirect influence as degrading as well as inefficient.

Many were converted to what Jean Gordon called "a belief in the potency of the ballot beyond that of 'woman's influence'" after the defeat of child labor legislation. Gordon recalled that the failure of a child labor bill heartily supported by New Orleans clubwomen—including the wives of many legislators—caused many of the women to question the efficacy of indirect influence. We learned, she said, "what we had suspected," that "the much-boasted influence of the wife over the husband in matters political was one of the many theories which melt before the sun of experience."[31]

The suffragists were disgusted by the way southern politicians insisted on "chivalrously" shouldering the burden of politics for women by invoking chivalry as a reason for denying women direct influence, while refusing to offer women and children genuine legal protection. They were frustrated by the slow pace of reform as they sought to open up educational institutions to women and revise outdated guardianship and inheritance laws. They were indignant that legislators who so celebrated the influence of the mother refused to change laws that gave the father full legal rights to their children, even the power to appoint a guardian for his unborn child. Breckinridge found it ironic that a society allegedly intent on protecting women clung to antiquated property and inheritance laws that left a married woman totally dependent on her husband's decency *and* his survival. "It was one of the anomalies of the old Common law," she said, "that it seemed to feel that a man left with children to support and without a wife, needed three times as much as a wife left with children and no husband."[32] After observing the effects of woman suffrage in Colorado, she pointed out that the "age of consent" laws in the states where women were already enfranchised ranged from eighteen to twenty-one, while in the South the "age of consent" ranged from ten to sixteen (with only Kentucky having it as high as sixteen), and she asked, "Do Southern men protect Southern women at all comparably to the way Western women, granted the right to do it, protect their own sex?"[33]

Considering that indirect influence was still their only weapon with which to pry suffrage from a reluctant South, the suffragists tried to make their demand for power as unthreatening as possible. They *did* invoke "natural rights" arguments, insisting that, as Rebecca Latimer Felton put it, "I pay taxes and obey the laws, and I know the right belongs to me to assist in selecting those who rule over me."[34] Somerville denied a statement by an editor who said that the suffragists' chief argument was that enfranchised womanhood would "bring about great reforms." "The orthodox suffragists," she wrote, "do not base their claims on any such argument. We stand upon the Declaration of Independence, 'governments derive their just powers from the consent of the governed.' Any argument based on results is merely incidental and not fundamental."[35]

Yet, like suffragists all over the nation, they argued for equal partnership in governing with the men of their race and class by emphasizing the differences in the interests and responsibilities of the sexes—a nice and less challenging way of saying that the interests of women and children would never be adequately represented as long as women were relying upon men to protect them. "Men have done remarkably well to battle so many foes of the human race and its progress," said Pattie Jacobs, but as some "for-sighted [*sic*] men" now realize, woman's "highly developed moral nature and intimate knowledge of conditions governing the welfare of women and children . . . would ultimately result in great good to the state, the nation, and the race."[36] Mary Johnston wrote in a similar vein: "Men have their minds too much fixed on the large political issues, and there are a multitude of details that slip through their fingers, so to speak, and which women can better attend to [including] . . . legislation concerning schools and children."[37]

The suffragists took care to look and act like ladies, avoided *additional* unpopular causes, issued press releases celebrating the beauty, femininity, and domesticity of their leaders, and sometimes addressed their legislators in such a fashion that northern co-workers were shocked and dismayed at their "honey-tongued charm." Most southern suffragists strenuously avoided association with the National Woman's Party, publicly denouncing their "unseemly," "fanatical," and "misguided" tactics including picketing the White House and burning Woodrow Wilson's speeches in Lafayette Square.[38] Lila Meade Valentine begged the public not to "condemn the suffrage cause as a whole because of the folly of a handful of women" and urged Virginia suffragists to avoid all "spectacular tactics."[39]

The suffragists greatly resented having to stoop to wheedling and coddling male egos, however. Mary Johnston deplored the fact that society still encouraged—indeed required—women to rely upon this "sinuous, indirect way of approaching and of obtaining the object or the end which they desire . . . just as when they were the cowering mates of savages half as strong again as they." Johnston, a friend and admirer of Charlotte Perkins Gilman who echoed Gilman's message that female dignity could only be won through economic independence and that marriage was somewhat akin to prostitution, predicted that the phrase "indirect influence" would in the near future become "most distasteful to a naturally self-respecting and straightforward woman. . . . *It means, make me comfortable, and I will see what I can do about it*."[40]

Clearly they recognized the contrast between rhetoric and reality when it came to discussions of woman's role in southern society. Said Nellie Nugent Somerville in a 1914 article:

> It is quite common for men to say . . . that women should not vote because they are too good and must not be degraded to the level of men. . . . Now the facts in the case are that there is not a word of truth in this proposition. It is exasperating because it is short-sighted, unreasonably and historically false. . . . Exclusion from the right to vote is a degradation—always has been, always will be, never was intended as anything else, can not be sugar-coated into anything else. The age-long cause of all of these things [discrimination against women in education, in industry, in property rights and political rights] has been the theory that women were too bad and too incompetent.[41]

Somerville and her associates in the movement were demanding that the men—southern men—who surpassed all others in extolling the goodness and virtue of woman, accept woman's help in governing southern society. These white suffragists gladly accepted their role as soul and conscience of the South, but wanted to be in a position to actually carry out that role. They did not object to the vote being restricted so much as they wanted to be among the elect. To them, the vote was a badge of honor as well as a tool. As Pattie Jacobs said, "We of all people understand the symbolism of the ballot . . . [as we live] in states where its use is restricted and professedly based upon virtue and intelligence."[42] Indeed, it was largely the perception that *they*—moral, God-fearing, intelligent, educated, women whose families had been largely responsible for settling and guiding the South—were being denied the right to vote, even as inferior men were not only voting but governing the region, that fueled their activism. They wanted, and believed that *they*, if not all women, deserved, in Mary Johnston's words, "the dignity of citizenship."[43]

White southern suffragists, who spoke eloquently of the inalienable right of women as citizens to self-government, nevertheless advocated or at least acquiesced in the restoration of white supremacy that took place contemporaneously with the southern woman suffrage movement. Rebecca Latimer Felton, an open racist, declared in a 1915 suffrage speech:

> Freedom belongs to the white woman as her inherent right. Whatever belongs to the freeman of these United States belongs to the white woman. Her Anglo-Saxon forefathers, fleeing from English tyranny won this country from savage tribes and again from English bayonets, by the expenditure of blood and treasure. Whatever was won by these noble men of the Revolution was inherited alike by sons and daughters. Fifty years from now this country will hold up hands in holy horror that . . . any man or set of men in America should assume to themselves the authority to deny to free-born white women of America the ballot which is the badge and synonym of freedom.[44]

Like most white southerners of their class, but also like a growing number of white, native-born Americans all over the nation in the late nineteenth century, the suffragists believed that voting was *not* a right of all citizens but the privilege and duty of those best qualified to exercise it. Indeed, the contemporary meaning of the phrase "the negro problem" to white southern suffragists was not the use of the race issue against their cause—though this concerned them greatly—but the enfranchisement after the Civil War of several million blacks considered by southern whites to be ignorant, purchasable, and unfit for political participation.[45]

The suffragists believed they were better qualified to participate in politics than most white men; they had no doubts that they and other white women were more desirable as voters than the African-American men who had been enfranchised by the Fifteenth Amendment. Like many other upper-class southerners, they saw themselves as advocates for and protectors of blacks, paternalistically (or maternalistically) defending African Americans' rights to public education and social services, and they deplored the mistreatment of blacks by lower-class whites. Political rights, however, were another matter. Indeed, these suffragists were highly indignant that black men had become the political superiors of "the best white women of the South."[46]

There was a range of opinion within this group of southern suffrage leaders, ranging from negrophobes such as Kate Gordon, Belle Kearney, and Rebecca Latimer Felton who spoke of African Americans as though speaking of another, inferior species,[47] to Mary Johnston, who denounced the use of racist tactics by suffragists, saying, "I think that as women we should be most prayerfully careful lest, in the future, that women—whether colored women or white women who are merely poor, should be able to say that we had betrayed their interests and excluded them from freedom."[48] The "liberal" position among white southern suffragists (most clearly articulated by Madeline Breckinridge) was that white supremacy in politics was only a temporary necessity until "undesirable" voters became "desirable" through education and gradual social progress—advancements that elite whites were morally obligated to guide and support (through noblesse oblige), and that, meanwhile, "qualified" blacks should be allowed to vote.[49] Still, most southern suffragists employed racist arguments to promote woman suffrage, some aggressively and enthusiastically and others defensively and reluctantly. African Americans were systematically excluded from all white-led suffrage organizations and meetings as the suffragists sought to distance their movement from its historic association with advocacy of the rights of black Americans.[50]

One of the most fascinating aspects of the relationship between the southern suffrage movement and the South's "negro problem" is the crucial role of the latter in determining the strategy, the rhetoric, and even the timing of the woman suffrage movement in the South. Though historians usually focus upon the race issue as a prime obstacle to the suffragists' success, there is considerable evidence to indicate that the race issue was also a major *causative* factor in the development of the southern suffrage movement in the 1890s—not in causing southern women to *want* suffrage, but in giving them a *reason to expect that they could win it*. An organized regional movement with strong national support came into existence in the 1890s because many leading suffragists—both southern and northern—believed the South's "negro problem" might be the key to female enfranchisement.[51]

It is one of history's many ironies that this idea was originally conceived by Lucy Stone's husband, Henry Blackwell, a former abolitionist. He began presenting this idea to southern politicians in 1867 and, by 1890, was able to persuade delegates to the Mississippi Constitutional Convention of 1890 to give it serious consideration. This impressed Laura Clay, whose pleas for woman suffrage as "justice" were falling upon deaf ears, as well as the leaders of the NAWSA, who launched a major campaign based on Blackwell's southern strategy. Indeed, many of them, including Carrie Chapman Catt, shared the indignation of these elite, white southern women that their social "inferiors," whether African Americans in the South or immigrants in the North, had become their political "superiors."[52]

Late-nineteenth-century suffragists found it quite difficult to believe that the federal government would, as it did, abandon the defense of black suffrage and allow the South to solve its "negro problem" by disfranchising African-American men. They believed that should southern states attempt to disfranchise voters protected by the Fifteenth Amendment, Congress would invoke the amendment's enforcement clause, or the Supreme Court would rule the disfranchisement provisions unconstitutional. However, solving "the negro problem" by *extending* the franchise to *women* (with property requirements that would ensure that the vast majority of new voters would be white) would, they predicted, be seen as a *liberalization*, rather than a restriction, of suffrage and provide the means to preserve white political supremacy without risking congressional retribution or an unfavorable ruling by the Supreme Court. Throughout the 1890s, many southern suffragists believed that as the men of their class cast about for a means of countering the effects of black suffrage, they might resort to enfranchising white women—just as conservatives in the West had made use of woman suffrage to consolidate their political position.[53]

The 1890s movement to restore white supremacy and Democratic hegemony, like the Progressive movement that came after it, gave white southern suffragists grounds to argue that the enfranchisement of women was expedient to society. But unlike the Progressive movement, which was relatively weak in the South and inspired no great hopes for success on the part of national suffrage leaders, the zealous campaign of the self-proclaimed best classes of whites to regain hegemony in southern society encouraged southern suffragists and their northern co-conspirators to believe the South would actually lead the nation in the adoption of woman suffrage.[54]

By 1910 it was clear, however, that the dominant southern politicians had managed to solve "the negro problem" without resorting to woman suffrage and that the federal government was going to allow them to get away with disfranchising African-American men. In the second stage of the suffrage movement in the South, southern suffragists rarely raised the race issue and were almost exclusively on the defensive in regard to the race issue against opponents who claimed that state or federal woman suffrage amendments would endanger the newly established white dominance in politics. Suffragists insisted that the race issue was now irrelevant to the woman suffrage issue; "negresses" would be disfranchised by the same provisions that applied to "negroes."[55]

On the race issue, white suffragists presented a united front. Those who questioned the use of racist tactics or disapproved of the wholesale exclusion of blacks from the electorate kept such sentiments to themselves or at least out of the public arena; they had no desire to confirm the widespread perception that suffragists were advocates of black political power.[56] But there was no such consensus or show of solidarity regarding the states' rights issue; and in the last decade of the suffrage movement, as the federal suffrage amendment gained momentum elsewhere in the nation, differences of opinion over the state sovereignty issue divided southern suffragists into warring camps as the National American Woman Suffrage Association, the newly formed National Woman's Party, and a new southern organization—the Southern States Woman Suffrage Conference—followed separate strategies and competed for the loyalty of southern suffragists. The controversy over strategy strained, and in some cases, severed long-standing friendships and added to the difficulties the woman suffrage movement faced in the South.[57]

All of the southern suffragists identified strongly with their region and with their states. This was true even of those suffragists most critical of the region and its institutions, such as Mary Johnston, who wrote in 1905: "In spite of all reason and [owing to] merely an ingrained and hereditary matter, . . . Virginia (and incidentally the entire South) is my country, and not the stars and stripes but the stars and bars is my flag."[58] Indeed, *because* these women so revered their states and the South they were determined to *reform* them.

Thus, winning the suffrage battle *at home* was paramount. Even the suffragists with no theoretical objection to a federal amendment—those who were not states' rights devotees—longed for suffrage victories on the state level, victories that would proclaim an acceptance of women's equality and the triumph of a new progressive spirit over southern conservatism. This filial attachment to their states and region combined with expediency (they were all well aware of the regional reverence for state sovereignty, particularly in regard to the franchise) led them to seek enfranchisement only through state action until all hope of such action was lost.

A minority of southern suffragists, of course, could not bring themselves to support a federal suffrage amendment. When in 1913 the National, prodded into action by Alice Paul and her associates, renewed its campaign for a federal suffrage amendment, Kate Gordon decided it was time that southern suffragists go their own way. A disgruntled former NAWSA officer and a committed states' rights advocate, Gordon led in the establishment of the Southern States Woman Suffrage Conference (SSWSC). She and her followers insisted that the southern states would never allow a federal amendment to be passed by Congress; even if it were passed, the SSWSC would remain solid against ratification and thus block any possibility of enfranchisement through federal action. The National, Gordon charged, was just wasting its time and money and making things even more difficult for southern suffragists to win state victories. And southern suffragists, who must gain their rights from southern Democrats, must never even *appear* to favor a federal amendment or to question the doctrine of state sovereignty. Gordon demanded the support of all other southern suffragists for the Southern Conference and insisted that the NAWSA turn over the South to her leadership before it misled any more southern suffragists into advocacy of a federal amendment.[59]

Most southern suffragists, however, did not follow Gordon's lead. Few were willing to renounce federal suffrage when it might be necessary to secure their enfranchisement. In fact, after one of her tirades against NAWSA leaders, Gordon achieved the notoriety of being formally reprimanded by not one but two southern state suffrage organizations. Led by Sue Shelton White and Pattie Ruffner Jacobs, respectively, the state suffrage organizations of Tennessee and Alabama rebuked Kate Gordon and her presumptuous claim to speak for southern suffragists. Tennessee's resolution, drafted by White, declared that "the Convention of the Tennessee Equal Suffrage Association go on record as

Kate Gordon. From the National Woman's Party Papers, Library of Congress.

disapproving the action of Miss Kate M. Gordon in undertaking to dictate to the NAWSA or its Congressional Committee in regard to its policy, methods, or plans . . . and in her presuming to speak for the women of the South; and that the Recording Secretary of this convention be instructed to immediately notify the National officers and the Chairman of the Congressional Committee of such action."[60]

As Gordon and her tactics alienated nearly all of the prominent southern suffrage leaders with the exception of her sister and her faithful friend Laura Clay, the Southern Conference ceased to exist except in name. And of the leading suffragists, only Laura Clay and the Gordons were so committed to the concept of state sovereignty that they ultimately refused to support and indeed opposed the federal amendment.[61]

After 1916, when many pleas for state suffrage amendments had been made and rejected throughout the South, and the National was fully committed to securing enfranchisement through federal action, the majority of southern suffragists campaigned actively for a federal woman suffrage amendment. Some, including Nellie Nugent Somerville, set aside reservations about federal intervention in the affairs of states and labored to convince fellow southerners that the federal amendment held "no menace for the institutions of any State or any group of States."[62] Others had no such reservations to overcome. Indeed, Anne Dallas Dudley insisted that "the spirit of the New South has been misunderstood by our representatives in Congress" who so long blocked the progress of the amendment, and she declared that, far from seeing themselves as separate entities with interests that conflicted with those of other Americans, southerners were "glad and proud to acclaim ourselves loyally an integral part of our nation today."[63] Sue White warned that rather than expecting suffragists to yield to the wisdom of the Democratic Party and uphold state sovereignty, the Democrats would be well advised to modify their doctrines in order to keep the loyalty of southern women: "Moss-backed traditions of political parties will no longer be accepted as an excuse for withholding democracy from women. There are suffragists born Democrats who have hoped to live and die in the political faith of their fathers who can no longer accept such an excuse."[64] Tennessee suffragists supported NAWSA President Catt in her "Winning Plan" designed to secure a final victory nationwide through a federal amendment.

Catt's plan, however, was not fully satisfactory to NAWSA supporters in the South, partly because it largely "wrote off" the region until time for ratification. The NAWSA fully supported and contributed generously to state suffrage campaigns in critical states such as New York—where there was a good chance of victory. But fearing that the failure of state suffrage campaigns might blunt the momentum of the suffrage cause, Catt demanded that NAWSA affiliates in states she considered poor prospects suspend efforts at winning full suffrage through state amendment and seek only partial suffrage—advice followed in many southern states including Tennessee, where suffragists sought and won municipal and presidential suffrage.[65] Yet, to the chagrin of many southern suffragists, especially Madeline McDowell Breckinridge of Kentucky, a state in which a victory was quite likely, Catt's poor prospects included *all* southern states.[66] Indeed, it is probable that the main reason Sue White embraced the National Woman's Party was that it began a bold new effort to recruit in the South in 1917, just as the National seemed to be conceding the region to the antis. That NAWSA loyalists in Tennessee and even President Catt demanded that White choose between the National and the Woman's Party—such was the enmity between the two organizations—also played a key role; when White came to the aid of an embattled NWP organizer, the "regular" suffragists reacted so negatively that, said White, they practically forced her "into the bosom of the National Woman's Party"—in which she rose rapidly to national prominence.[67]

When in June 1919 Congress finally submitted the proposed Nineteenth Amendment to the states for ratification, the leaders of the woman suffrage movement in the southern states found themselves fighting one another as well as the antis—a situation that did nothing to help the cause.[68] In Virginia, there was open hostility between the NAWSA loyalists led by Valentine and the state's chapter of the NWP.[69] In Mississippi, Somerville and her associates endured the bitter experience of sitting in the gallery while Kate Gordon, in Jackson at the invitation of the *Clarion-Ledger,* denounced the federal amendment as a threat to state sovereignty and the constitution.[70] In Louisiana, the Gordons and other advocates of woman suffrage through state action combated a coalition of federal amendment supporters *and* the antisuffragists, creating a three-way struggle in which no form of woman suffrage was adopted.[71] In Tennessee, both Gordon sisters and Laura Clay actually campaigned against ratification of "this hideous amendment" though Clay had "a great distaste" at being publicly associated with the despised antis.[72]

As the end of the long struggle for woman suffrage approached, those southern suffragists who opposed the Nineteenth Amendment were bitter, disappointed in their fellow suffragists, and dismayed that the success of woman suffrage for which they had worked for so many years helped undermine another cherished political ideal—state sovereignty. Most southern suffragists, however, were jubilant when ratification came at last and grateful to Tennessee for, in the words of Virginia suffragists, "redeeming the honor of the country."[73]

Still, their celebration was dampened by the fact that so many of them had to be enfranchised "courtesy of Uncle Sam." Madeline McDowell Breckinridge, from one of the four southern states that contributed to the victory of the Nineteenth Amendment, was joking when she told the NAWSA's "Jubilee Convention" assembled in Chicago in 1920:

> We'll get all our rights with the help of Uncle Sam,
> For the way that they come, we don't give a ———.[74]

For she fully understood the disappointment of those suffragists in the states that failed to ratify—or worse, adopted "rejection resolutions."

Pattie Ruffner Jacobs, speaking for the "defeated" suffragists at the Jubilee Convention, observed: "It only remains for the outward and visible sign of our freedom to be put in the hands of Southern women by the generous men of other states, a situation which hurts our pride and to which we submit with deep regret but not apology." Having hoped to win from their home states and region a public endorsement of woman's political equality, these women had instead been enfranchised—like African-American men had been—over the strenuous opposition of the political leaders of their states. And the analogy was not lost on the suffragists: said Jacobs, "It is acutely distasteful to Southern suffragists not to be enfranchised by Southern men, for we of all people understand the symbolism of the ballot."[75] Yet these white suffragists, at least, would be *allowed* to exercise this privilege granted them by the "generous men of other states." Most of the African-American women of the region would not be so fortunate.[76]

White southern suffragists, with their elite cadre of leaders who shared many of the ideas of other southerners of their race and class, offered no thoroughgoing indictment of their society. They did not challenge the idea that many within the region needed the "guardianship" of the more enlightened citizenry, but they objected to the idea that *they* needed such guidance and protection.[77] These suffragists were "radical" for their region only in their advocacy of women's rights—their support for important changes in the relations between the sexes and their insistence upon expanding and improving woman's lot in southern society.

None of these reforms, however, were as threatening to the social order as woman suffrage; reforms short of suffrage could still be seen as evidence of male protection of women and children, secured through "indirect influence." The request for the vote, on the other hand, was interpreted as a challenge to the fundamentally hierarchical and paternalistic political structure of the region as well as to the sovereignty of the states; and however nicely the suffragists tried to put it, demanding the power to represent their own interests constituted an indirect accusation of failure that southern politicians understood and did not appreciate.

The South was never, as Laura Clay hoped, fully "brought in" to the suffrage fold—even though sufficient numbers of southern states ratified for the Nineteenth Amendment to become law. And in rejecting woman suffrage, southern politicians made it clear that they still found much about the old pattern of relations between the sexes quite attractive. After 1920, southern women would still have far to go in their quest for equality in the South.

Notes

This essay is drawn largely from Marjorie Spruill Wheeler, *New Women of the New South: The Leaders of the Woman Suffrage Movement in the Southern States* (New York and Oxford: Oxford University Press, 1993), and is published with the permission of Oxford University Press.

1. *Woman's Journal* (Boston), Mar. 10, 1892, Laura Clay Scrapbook, Laura Clay Papers, Special Collections and Archives, Margaret I. King Library, University of Kentucky, Lexington.

2. For a fuller discussion of the southern suffrage movement and its role in the national movement, see Wheeler, *New Women of the New South*.

3. On Clay's role in the movement, see Paul E. Fuller, *Laura Clay and the Woman's Rights Movement* (Lexington: University Press of Kentucky, 1975). For information on all full and partial suffrage victories prior to 1919, see National American Woman Suffrage Association, *Victory: How Women Won It: A Centennial Symposium, 1840–1940* (New York: The H. W. Wilson Company, 1940), 161–66; on southern opposition to the federal amendment, see Carrie Chapman Catt and Nettie Rogers Shuler, *Woman Suffrage and Politics: The Inner Story of the Suffrage Movement* (1923; reprint, Seattle: University of Washington Press, 1970), especially 227–49, 316–42, 398–413, and 422–88; and David Morgan, *Suffragists and Democrats: The Politics of Woman Suffrage in America* (East Lansing: Michigan State University Press, 1972).

4. A. Elizabeth Taylor's numerous articles on the suffrage movement in most of the southern states, appearing in state historical journals, are an obvious exception to the pattern of neglect (see bibliography) as is Paul E. Fuller's *Laura Clay*. Aileen S. Kraditor's *The Ideas of the Woman Suffrage Movement: 1890–1920* (Garden City, N.Y.: Doubleday and Company, 1971), and Anne Firor Scott's *The Southern Lady: From Ped-*

estal to Politics, 1830–1930 (Chicago: University of Chicago Press, 1970) also include important chapters on the southern suffrage movement.

5. On the efforts of southern whites to preserve traditional southern culture in the late nineteenth and early twentieth centuries, see Charles Reagan Wilson, *Baptized in Blood: The Religion of the Lost Cause, 1865–1920* (Athens: University of Georgia Press, 1980), quotation, 7; see also Gaines M. Foster, *Ghosts of the Confederacy: Defeat, the Lost Cause, and the Emergence of the New South* (New York and Oxford: Oxford University Press, 1987).

6. Dr. Albert Bledsoe, "The Mission of Woman," *The Southern Review* (Oct. 1871): 923–42, quotations, 941–42.

7. Wheeler, *New Women of the New South*, 8–13; Anastatia Sims, "Beyond the Ballot: The Radical Vision of the Antisuffragists," below; and Elna C. Green, "Those Opposed: The Antisuffragists in North Carolina, 1900–1920," *North Carolina Historical Review* 67 (July 1990): 316–33, and her book on suffrage in the South, forthcoming from the University of North Carolina Press.

8. On the effort to restore white political supremacy, see J. Morgan Kousser, *The Shaping of Southern Politics: Suffrage Restriction and the Establishment of the One-Party South, 1880–1910* (New Haven: Yale University Press, 1974).

9. Wheeler, *New Women of the New South*, 13–19; See antisuffrage literature in the Clay Papers, the Pattie Ruffner Jacobs Papers, Birmingham Public Library, Birmingham, Ala., the NAWSA Papers, Manuscripts Division, Library of Congress, and the Josephine A. Pearson Papers, Tennessee State Library and Archives, Nashville.

10. Antisuffrage pamphlet quoting James Callaway, editor of *Macon (Ga.) Telegraph*, Clay Papers.

11. Wheeler, *New Women of the New South*, 29–37.

12. Catt and Shuler, *Woman Suffrage and Politics*, 88, 89.

13. Wheeler, *New Women of the New South*, chap. 2, 38–71.

14. Belle Kearney, *A Slaveholder's Daughter* (Abbey Press, 1900; reprint, Negro Universities Press, 1969); James P. Louis, "Sue Shelton White," in Edward T. James and Janet Wilson James, eds., *Notable American Women*, 3 vols. (Cambridge: Harvard University Press, 1971, hereafter cited as NAW), 590–92; Kate Gordon to Henry Blackwell, Oct. 1, 1907, Clay Papers.

15. Wheeler, *New Women of the New South*, 45–50; quotation from Kate Gordon to Catharine Waugh McCulloch, June 1, 1915, McCulloch Papers, Dillon Collection, Schlesinger Library, Radcliffe College.

16. Desha Breckinridge to Madeline McDowell Breckinridge, May 4, 1913, Madeline McDowell Breckinridge Papers in the Breckinridge Family Papers, Manuscript Division, Library of Congress, Washington, D.C. (hereafter cited as MMB Papers).

17. Kathryn W. Kemp, "Jean and Kate Gordon: New Orleans Social Reformers, 1898–1933," *Louisiana History* 24 (1983): 389–401, especially 389, 394.

18. Lucy Somerville Howorth, interview with Marjorie Spruill Wheeler, Mar. 15, 1983, Cleveland, Miss. Transcript, the Mississippi Oral History Program, The University of Southern Mississippi, vol. 297, pt. II, 1991: 1, 2.

19. Wheeler, *New Women of the New South,* 59, 60.

20. Fuller, *Laura Clay,* 1–29.

21. Sue Shelton White, "Mother's Daughter," in Elaine Showalter, ed., *These Modern Women: Autobiographical Essays from the Twenties* (Old Westbury: The Feminist Press, 1978), 45–52; Kemp, "Jean and Kate Gordon," 189; Constance Ashton Myers, interview with Judge Lucy Somerville Howorth, June 20, 22, and 23, 1975, Monteagle, Tenn. (#4007), Southern Oral History Collection, Southern Historical Collection, University of North Carolina, Chapel Hill, 7.

22. Anna Howard Shaw, *Story of a Pioneer* (New York: Harper and Bros., 1915), 309; Melba Porter Hay, "Madeline McDowell Breckinridge: Kentucky Suffragist and Progressive Reformer," (Ph.D. diss., University of Kentucky, 1980), esp. 177–78, and 217–18; Marie Stokes Jemison, "Ladies Become Voters," *Southern Exposure* 7 (Spring 1979): 51–52; Lloyd C. Taylor Jr., "Lila Meade Valentine: The FFV as Reformer," *Virginia Magazine of History and Biography* 70 (Oct. 1962): 486–87.

23. Wheeler, *New Women of the New South,* 63–65.

24. For example, in 1911, Breckinridge spoke of the Democratic Party's being led once again by "the best element" and hoped that would mean the party would be more receptive to allowing women to vote. "The Prospects for Woman Suffrage in the South," address to the NAWSA Convention of 1911, MMB Papers.

25. Nellie Nugent Somerville, "Christian Citizenship," 1898, quotations, 1, 2, see also Somerville, "Presidential Address to First Mississippi Woman Suffrage Association," Mar. 28, 1898, handwritten, Somerville–Howorth Family Papers, Schlesinger Library, Radcliffe College. Somerville's daughter believes that Frances Willard's endorsement of suffrage had a great deal to do with her mother's decision to work for suffrage. Wheeler interview, Mar. 1983.

26. Sophonisba P. Breckinridge, *Madeline McDowell Breckinridge: A Leader in the New South* (Chicago: University of Chicago Press, 1921), 34–42, quotation, 41, 42.

27. Rebecca Felton, "The Subjection of Women and the Enfranchisement of Women," No. 2, Rebecca Latimer Felton Papers, Special Collections Division, Hargrett Rare Book and Manuscript Library, University of Georgia, Athens (hereafter cited as RLF Papers); Josephine Bone Floyd, "Rebecca Latimer Felton: Champion of Women's Rights," *Georgia Historical Quarterly* 30 (June 1946): 81–104; Josephine Bone Floyd, "Rebecca Latimer Felton: Political Independent," *Georgia Historical Quarterly* 30 (Mar. 1946):14–34; Rebecca Latimer Felton, *Country Life in Georgia in the Days of My Youth* (Atlanta, 1919), 93.

28. M. Breckinridge, "Public Schools and Southern Development," handwritten speech, n.d., MMB Papers.

29. A. Elizabeth Taylor, "Last Phase of the Woman Suffrage Movement in Georgia," *Georgia Historical Quarterly* 43 (Mar. 1959): 11–28, quotation, 14.

30. M. Breckinridge, "Direct Versus Indirect Influence in Kentucky." written for the *New York Evening Post*, Feb. 3, 1914, MMB Papers.

31. Jean Gordon, "New Louisiana Child Labor Law," *Charities* 21 (Jan. 26, 1908): 481.

32. M. Breckinridge, "Direct Versus Indirect Influence in Kentucky."

33. Hay, "Madeline McDowell Breckinridge," 139–40.

34. Floyd, "Rebecca Latimer Felton: Champion of Women's Rights," 86.

35. Nellie Nugent Somerville to the editor of a Greenville, Miss., newspaper, 16 May ?, Scrapbook, Somerville-Howorth Family Papers.

36. Pattie Ruffner Jacobs to the editor, Feb. 12, 1912, *Birmingham Ledger*, Jacobs Scrapbook, Jacobs Papers.

37. Mary Johnston, "Sentimental Idea Hurts Suffrage," *Woman's Journal*, Apr. 12, 1913, Johnston Papers.

38. Otelia Cuningham, president of the North Carolina suffragists, denounced the NWP as "unseemly," "misguided," and "fanatical" and appealed to the press to stop giving them the publicity they were seeking. Otelia Cuningham Connor Papers, Southern Historical Collection, Wilson Library, University of North Carolina, Chapel Hill; see also Tennessee Woman Suffrage Association President Kate Burch Warner's denunciation of the Woman's Party representatives working in her state, printed in full in part 2 of this volume. Clipping, Josephine A. Pearson Papers.

39. Northern suffragists' reaction to the "honey-tongued charm" is described in Scott, *The Southern Lady*, 183, 184; Lila Meade Valentine, press release of the Equal Suffrage League of Virginia, July 2, 1917; "Resolutions Adopted by the Equal Suffrage League of Virginia," Nov. 14, 1917; Lila Meade Valentine to Mrs. Townsend, Apr. 7, 1914, Virginia Suffrage Papers, Virginia State Library, Richmond.

40. Mary Johnston, "Speech, Woman's Club Alumnae, May 31," 1910–11 suffrage speeches, Johnston Papers.

41. Somerville, "Are Women Too Good to Vote?" clipping, c. 1914, Somerville-Howorth Family Papers.

42. Pattie Ruffner Jacobs, "Tradition Vs. Justice," speech at the 1920 NAWSA "Jubilee Convention" in Chicago, reprinted in the *Southern Review* (Asheville, N.C.), May 1920, under the title "The Pulse of the South, How the South Really Feels About Woman Suffrage," clipping, Clay Papers.

43. Mary Johnston, draft of a speech to be given in Philadelphia, 1910–11 suffrage speeches, Johnston Papers.

44. Rebecca Latimer Felton, "The Subjection of Women and the Enfranchisement of Women," May 15, 1915, RLF Papers.

45. On southern suffragists' racial attitudes, see Wheeler, *New Women of the New South*, 100–112.

46. This was a common theme as suffrage leaders pushed their cause in the South. Even northern suffrage leaders, including Anna Howard Shaw, chided southern men for making black men the "political superiors of your white women" (though they had

obviously had little choice). "Never before in the history of the world," she said, "have men made former slaves the political masters of their former mistresses!" Shaw, *Story of a Pioneer,* 310–11.

47. For example, see Kearney, *Slaveholder's Daughter,* 62–64, 92, and 97.

48. Mary Johnston to Lila Meade Valentine, Jan. 5, 1913, and Oct. ? 1915, Lila Hardaway Meade Valentine Papers, Virginia Historical Society, Richmond (hereafter cited as LHMV Papers).

49. M. Breckinridge to Miss Mary Winser, Jan. 1, 1912, Clay Papers; see also Suzanne Lebsock, "Woman Suffrage and White Supremacy: A Virginia Case Study," in Nancy A. Hewitt and Suzanne Lebsock, eds., *Visible Women: New Essays on American Activism* (Urbana: University of Illinois Press, 1993), 62–100. Lebsock argues the racism exhibited by southern white suffragists must be considered in light of the extreme racism of the antisuffragists, and that in Virginia white suffragists "negotiated a middling course," neither "disavowing white supremacy" nor engaging in the "poisonous polemics" of the antisuffragists.

50. Wheeler, *New Women of the New South,* chap. 4, 100–132. Second-generation suffragists, active after the disfranchisement of African Americans, had the most to gain by denying, as they did, any relationship between their movement and the race issue and insisting that whatever restrictions applied to black men would also apply to black women.

51. Ibid.

52. For the text of Blackwell's letter to southern legislatures, see Aileen S. Kraditor, ed., *Up from the Pedestal: Selected Writings in the History of American Feminism* (New York: Quadrangle, 1968), 253–57; Lois Bannister Merk, "Massachusetts in the Woman Suffrage Movement," (Ph.D. diss., Harvard University, 1961), 232–34; Henry Blackwell to Laura Clay, Nov. 21, 1885, Clay Papers; Fuller, *Laura Clay,* 54–56; on the Mississippi convention, see A. Elizabeth Taylor, "The Woman Suffrage Movement in Mississippi," *Journal of Mississippi History* 30 (Feb. 1968): 1–34; for evidence that consideration of woman suffrage by the 1890 Mississippi convention inspired the national leaders to organize in the South, see Nellie Nugent Somerville, "President's Address, 1898 MWSA (Mississippi Woman Suffrage Association) Convention," Somerville-Howorth Family Papers.

53. See Blackwell, "What the South Can Do (1867)" in Kraditor, *Up from the Pedestal,* 253–57; Fuller, *Laura Clay,* 66–70; Belle Kearney, "Address to the 1903 NAWSA Convention," Belle Kearney Papers, Mississippi Department of Archives and History, Jackson, Miss.; on the West, see Alan P. Grimes, *The Puritan Ethic and Woman Suffrage* (New York and Oxford: Oxford University Press, 1967).

54. Wheeler, *New Women of the New South,* 113–20.

55. Ibid., 125–32; for examples, see Nellie Somerville, "Arguments to be Met: MWSA," "Report of Legislative Work, 1914," and letter to the editor, *Greenville Times-Democrat,* clipping, n.d., in Scrapbook, Somerville-Howorth Papers; see also quotation from Pattie Ruffner Jacobs's testimony to Congress that the federal woman suffrage

amendment would not "involve the race problem or any other complication" (Kraditor, *Ideas of the Woman Suffrage Movement,* 156). Suzanne Lebsock, examining literature of the Virginia suffragists during this period, also found that white suffragists rarely employed white supremacist arguments and that the race issue, when it was raised, was raised by the antisuffragists. The suffragists insisted it was irrelevant, as white supremacy was not in danger. Lebsock, "Woman Suffrage and White Supremacy."

56. For example, correspondence between Lila Meade Valentine and Mary Johnston reveal that both women were disgusted by Kate Gordon's racist "utterings." Johnston resigned as an honorary vice-president of the Southern States Woman Suffrage Conference that Gordon led in order to avoid public association with Gordon's racism. But Johnston did this quietly, making no public issue of her resignation. Mary Johnston to Lila Meade Valentine, Jan. 5, 1913, LHMV Papers.

57. Wheeler, *New Women of the New South,* 133–86.

58. Johnston quoted in Anne Goodwyn Jones, *Tomorrow Is Another Day: The Woman Writer in the South, 1859–1936* (Baton Rouge: Louisiana State University Press, 1981), 186.

59. Kenneth R. Johnston, "Kate Gordon and the Woman Suffrage Movement in the South," *Journal of Southern History* 38 (Aug. 1972): 365–92; Wheeler, *New Women of the New South,* 133–70.

60. Ibid., 154–57; on Tennessee, see "Resolution adopted by the 1915 state convention of Tennessee suffragists, Jackson," Sue Shelton White Papers, Schlesinger Library, Radcliffe College; the Alabama resolution appears in Wayne Flynt and Marlene Hunt Rikard, "Pattie Ruffner Jacobs: Alabama Suffragist, 1900–1930," paper presented at the Southern Association for Women Historians' Conference on Women's History, Converse College, June 1988.

61. Wheeler, *New Women of the New South,* 156–80.

62. Somerville quoted in Johnston, "Kate Gordon and Woman Suffrage," 381.

63. Anne Dallas Dudley to Mrs. John South, KERA president, Jan. 2, 1919, Clay Papers.

64. "Democratic Party May Lose Support," clipping, n.d., White Papers.

65. On Catt's "Winning Plan," see NAWSA, *Victory,* 123, 124, 129, 134, 162, 163; Carrie Chapman Catt to Laura Clay, Nov. 27, 1916; Carrie Chapman Catt to southern presidents, Jan. 11, 1916, Clay Papers.

66. Breckinridge's disappointment in not being allowed to proceed with state suffrage campaigns is revealed in Madeline McDowell Breckinridge, "Kentucky Chapter Woman Suffrage History: 1900–1920," MMB Papers.

67. White explained to Catt that her initial sympathy for embattled NWP workers who were trying to speak for suffrage grew into strong interest in the NWP only "after it developed that the southern states could not expect any assistance from the National." Sue Shelton White to Carrie Chapman Catt, Apr. 27, 1918; Carrie Chapman Catt to Sue Shelton White, May 6, 1918; Sue Shelton White to Carrie Chapman Catt, May 9, 1918, White Papers, reprinted in part 2 of this volume.

68. Wheeler, *New Women of the New South*, 172–80.

69. Adele Clark to Carrie Chapman Catt, Aug. 13, 1919; Carrie Chapman Catt to Adele Clark, Aug. 29, 1919, Virginia Suffrage Papers; Sheldon, "Woman Suffrage and Virginia Politics, 1909–1920" (M.A. thesis, University of Virginia, 1969), 56–64.

70. Kate Gordon to Laura Clay, Mar. 19, 1920; most of Gordon's speech appears in a clipping from the *Jackson (Miss.) Clarion-Ledger*, n.d., Clay Papers.

71. Loretta Ellen Zimmerman, "Alice Paul and the National Woman's Party, 1912–1920," (Ph.D. diss., Tulane University, 1964), 317, 318; Patricia L. Spiers, "Woman Suffrage Movement in New Orleans," (M.A. thesis, Southeastern Louisiana College, 1965), 60–64.

72. Laura Clay to Kate Gordon, July 31, 1920, Clay Papers; Fuller, *Laura Clay*, 160; Morgan, *Suffragists and Democrats*, 150.

73. *Richmond Times-Dispatch*, Aug. 19, 1920.

74. S. Breckinridge, *Madeline McDowell Breckinridge*, 236, 237.

75. Pattie Ruffner Jacobs, "Tradition Vs. Justice," speech at the 1920 NAWSA "Jubilee Convention" in Chicago, Clay Papers.

76. The suffragists were quite right when they predicted that the same restrictions that had been used to prevent black men from voting would be applied to black women. Not until the late 1960s would they be fully enfranchised. On discrimination against black women trying to register to vote and the failure of former suffragists to assist them, see Paula Giddings, *When and Where I Enter: The Impact of Black Women on Race and Sex in America* (New York: William Morrow and Company, 1984), 164–69, and Glenda Elizabeth Gilmore, "Gender and Jim Crow: Women and the Politics of White Supremacy in North Carolina, 1896–1920," (Ph.D. diss., University of North Carolina, Chapel Hill, 1992); see also Morgan, *Suffragists and Democrats*, 152, 153.

77. See, for example, Pattie Ruffner Jacobs, "Tradition Vs. Justice," Clay Papers.

3

Tennessee: The Thirty-Sixth State

A. Elizabeth Taylor

Almost two centuries ago, in 1796, Tennessee became the sixteenth state to enter the federal Union. The state constitution under which it was admitted made little provision for the rights of woman. The same was true of the subsequent constitutions of 1834 and 1870. When evaluating the traditional status of Tennessee women, legal historian Agnes Thornton Bird called them "nonpersons" who had "neither place nor power in government."[1] Their lack of place and power was evidenced by the fact that they were disfranchised and had no voice in affairs of state.

During the century that followed Tennessee's admission to statehood, there was little change in their status. In the 1870s, a few individual women began expressing an interest in voting.[2] Woman suffrage as an organized movement, however, began with the formation of a suffrage league in Memphis in May 1889. The league had forty-five members, and its president was Lide A. Meriwether.[3]

For four years, the Memphis group was the only woman's rights association in the state. In 1893, however, a league was formed in Maryville, and in 1894 one was organized in Nashville.[4]

Lide Meriwether traveled throughout the state lecturing and organizing. By 1897, there were ten suffrage societies in Tennessee.[5] Through her initiative, a statewide gathering of women was held in Nashville in May 1897. Many prominent southern suffragists, including National American Woman Suffrage Association officer Laura Clay of Kentucky, addressed the convention. During this meeting, the Tennessee Equal Rights Association was organized with Lide Meriwether as president.

As was generally the case with NAWSA affiliates, the association's announced purpose was to "advance the industrial, educational, and legal rights of women" and to secure suffrage for them by "appropriate state and national legislation."[6] The inclusion of the word "national" indicated that Tennessee women would not object to receiving the ballot through a federal amendment. This was true of southern suffragists generally, although some said that they would prefer to be enfranchised by the men of their own state. [Editor's note: during this period some southern suffragists regarded a federal woman suffrage amendment as a distant if not impossible goal, but believed that endorsement of a federal amendment might help them win state victories, as state legislators would want to avoid federal action. All NAWSA affiliates included the goal of obtaining suffrage by "appropriate state and national legislation" in their constitutions.]

The Tennessee Equal Rights Association held its next convention in Memphis in April 1900. The chief speaker of the occasion was Carrie Chapman Catt, president of the National American Woman Suffrage Association. She stressed the modesty of women's demands and pointed out that they asked only "for the liberty to vote, for the privilege of acting and voicing," and for the right to enter the political realm, if they chose.[7] At the organization's business session, Meriwether refused to continue as president and was succeeded by Elise M. Seldon of Memphis.[8]

Following the 1900 convention, suffrage activity declined, and for several years the issue was dormant in Tennessee as in most southern states. Interest revived as a result of a December 1906 conference of southern suffragists called by Belle Kearney of Mississippi, which formed the Southern Woman Suffrage Conference with Laura Clay as president. Though this organization proved to be short-lived, the Memphis conference resulted in the formation of a permanent statewide suffrage organization, the Tennessee Equal Suffrage Association. Martha Allen was its president.[9] Four years later, in 1910, a suffrage society was formed in Knoxville with Lizzie Crozier French as president. Another was organized in Nashville in 1911 with Anne Dallas Dudley as president.[10] Also in 1911, suffrage societies were organized in Morristown and Chattanooga, making a total of five in the state.

A sixth suffrage society was formed in Jackson in 1912. Clarksville, Franklin, Gallatin, and Murfreesboro organized in 1914, making a total of ten. Organizational work continued, and, by the end of 1917, there were more than seventy suffrage societies in Tennessee. This was an unusually large number, and, with the exception of Texas, no other southern state was so well organized.[11]

Much of the success of the Tennessee movement was due to the local societies. They were chiefly responsible for the work on the grass-roots level. Suffrage was an emotional issue, and there was much misunderstanding about it among the general public. The local leagues were able to gain the confidence of the people of their respective communities and to convince many of them that women's enfranchisement would be beneficial to the existing social order.

The local societies conducted their work in a variety of ways. They held parlor meetings. They conducted house-to-house canvasses. They sponsored public lectures and distributed large quantities of literature. They sent suffrage information to newspapers and endeavored to win their editorial support. They sponsored debates and essay contests. They entertained likely prospects with teas, luncheons, and balls. They conducted suffrage schools to make more effective workers of their members. During the First World War, they participated in activities relative to winning the war. They did this both as a matter of patriotism and as an answer to the charge that women should not vote because they did not serve in the armed forces.

The Tennessee Equal Suffrage Association was the umbrella organization for the local societies. It aided, abetted, and assisted them in their work. It arranged state conventions and handled relations with the National American Woman Suffrage Association. In November 1914, the annual convention of the NAWSA was held in Nashville. The convention lasted several days and was attended by prominent people from many parts of the nation. The publicity it generated aroused the interest of many who had previously been indifferent toward the issue. In the opinion of Anne Dallas Dudley, president of the Nashville league, the convention marked a turning point in the suffrage movement in Tennessee.[12]

A byproduct of the national convention was a split in the ranks of the Tennessee suffragists. The divisive issue was the choice of the convention city. A group led by Lizzie Crozier French favored Nashville, but another under the leadership of Mrs. James M. (Eleanore O'Nonell) McCormack favored Chattanooga. The French group prevailed, and the convention was held in Nashville. The two factions then became separate organizations. Those favoring Nashville formed a corporation and became the Tennessee Equal Suffrage Association, Incorporated. Those favoring Chattanooga did not incorporate and were known simply as the Tennessee Equal Suffrage Association. Both associations functioned as state organizations. Both were recognized by the NAWSA. In March 1918, they united to form the Tennessee Woman Suffrage Association with Kate B. Warner of Nashville as president.[13]

Chattanooga did host another suffrage convention in 1914, however. The week before the NAWSA convention in Nashville, the newly organized Southern States Woman Suffrage Conference, a NAWSA affiliate, held a two-day gathering of prominent southern suffragists in Chattanooga. At the conference, the SSWSC president, Kate Gordon of New Orleans, tried in vain to get the organization to declare itself for woman suffrage by state action only.[14] A year later, Gordon's opposition to the federal amendment and efforts to get the NAWSA to leave southern suffrage work to southern women and the SSWSC prompted the Tennessee Equal Suffrage Association to issue Gordon an official rebuke. Though vigorously seeking suffrage through state action [at this time], most Tennessee suffragists, like the NAWSA, were willing to work for suffrage by either state or national legislation.[15]

Another state-level society was the Tennessee division of the Congressional Union for Woman Suffrage or the National Woman's Party. [Editor's note: the Congressional Union and its western affiliate, the National Woman's Party, merged under the latter title in April 1917.] The Tennessee division was organized by Alice Paul at a meeting in Knoxville in 1916. Mrs. Hugh L. White of Johnson City was state chairman.[16] The National Woman's Party was the so-called militant branch of the suffrage movement. The Tennessee division engaged in no militant agitation, but supported the national organization in its work in behalf of the federal woman suffrage amendment. Its most outstanding member was Sue Shelton White of Jackson, who became state chairman in 1918. On February 9, 1919, she was one of a group of women who burned an effigy of President Wilson in front of the White House. For so doing, she was arrested and imprisoned for five days in a District of Columbia jail.[17] Apparently, she was the only Tennessee woman to be jailed for suffrage activities.

From its beginning, the Tennessee movement encountered the disapproval of many of the general public to whom suffrage was a dangerous and radical idea. The opposition did not become organized until 1916, however. In April of that year, a chapter of the National Association Opposed to Woman Suffrage was formed in Nashville. Its president was Virginia Vertrees, wife of John J. Vertrees, a staunch opponent of the enfranchisement of women. After a few months, she was succeeded by Josephine A. Pearson of Monteagle, who filled the office during the next several years. The antisuffrage organization engaged in little routine activity, but energetically opposed the ratification of the Nineteenth Amendment when it was before the legislature in 1920.[18]

In 1915, the Tennessee suffragists made their first serious attempt to win concessions from the state legislature. By that time, women had full voting rights in eleven states, and pro-suffrage sentiment was increasing in Tennessee. A legislative committee, headed by Anne Dallas Dudley, directed the lobbying. In a message to the legislature on January 6, Governor Ben W. Hooper recommended that Tennessee women be enfranchised through an amendment to the state constitution.[19]

Resolutions for such an amendment were introduced in both houses. There was little opposition. The proposal passed the house by a vote of seventy to fourteen and the senate by a vote of twenty-five to two.[20] Perhaps the resolution's easy passage was due to the fact that the legislators knew that the victory was a hollow one. It was merely the first step toward enfranchisement through a state constitutional amendment. Before the proposition could become part of the constitution, it had to pass the next legislature by a two-thirds majority and then be voted on by the men of the state in a referendum. The fact that this was a lengthy and difficult procedure caused the suffragists to alter their strategy.

During the 1917 legislative session, Governor Tom C. Rye recommended that women be enfranchised by an amendment to the state constitution. When making this resolution, he noted that they were taxpayers and, as such, should have a voice in governmental affairs.[21]

In spite of the governor's recommendation, the suffragists did not seek a state constitutional amendment. Instead, they directed their efforts toward a form of limited but more easily obtainable enfranchisement—the right to vote in municipal elections and the right to vote for presidential electors. The legislature had the authority to grant this limited suffrage. No constitutional amendment or referendum was necessary. This strategy was in keeping with NAWSA President Carrie Chapman Catt's "Winning Plan," which urged southern suffragists to seek partial suffrage rather than risk losses in state amendment campaigns.[22]

On January 4, 1917, a presidential and municipal suffrage bill was introduced in the house. It was referred to the Judiciary Committee, which recommended that it be passed. On January 19, the house debated the bill and approved it by a vote of fifty-nine to twenty-four.[23] The measure fared less well in the senate, where it was defeated by a vote of twenty-one to twelve.[24] The suffragists were disappointed but not disheartened. Anne Dallas Dudley's reaction was: "We are not cry babies. . . . We will simply work harder for suffrage in Tennessee."[25]

The presidential and municipal suffrage issue was raised during the 1919 legislative session. It was introduced in the house on March 19, and debated on April 3. At the close of the debate, the house passed the bill by a vote of fifty-four to thirty-two.[26] On April 14, the senate approved by a vote of seventeen to fourteen.[27] It was then signed by Governor A. H. Roberts, and Tennessee thereby became the only southern state to confer presidential and municipal suffrage on women.

On June 4, 1919, a few weeks after the passage of the presidential and municipal suffrage act, the federal woman suffrage amendment was submitted to the state legislatures. This proposed amendment had been before Congress continuously since it was first introduced in January 1878. It had attracted little support, however, until the second decade of the twentieth century when, after several defeats, it received the required two-thirds majority in the U.S. House on May 21, 1919, and in the Senate on June 4, 1919.

Before becoming part of the United States Constitution, however, it had to receive the approval of the legislatures in thirty-six of the forty-eight states. To many it seemed that this would be a matter of routine. Fifteen states had already given women full voting rights through state amendment. Many foreign nations were conferring suffrage on their women citizens. Woman suffrage appeared to be an issue whose time had come. Knowledgeable observers, however, realized that a struggle lay ahead.

Ratification began auspiciously. On June 10, six days after the amendment's submission, Wisconsin, Michigan, and Illinois ratified. On June 16, they were joined by Kansas, Ohio, and New York. Then came Pennsylvania on June 24 and Massachusetts on June 25.

On June 28, the Texas legislature ratified in a special session called by Governor William P. Hobby for the purpose of amending the election laws. Texas was the first state in the South and the ninth in the Union to ratify what was now being called the Susan B. Anthony Amendment.[28]

The second southern state to ratify was Arkansas. Governor Charles H. Brough called a special session for the sole purpose of acting on the amendment. The legislature convened on July 28, and, on that day, both houses approved.[29]

The next southern state was Kentucky. For several decades, there had been an active movement in the state, but its success had been limited to school suffrage. By the time that the federal amendment was submitted, however, Kentucky's political leaders were coming to realize that the suffrage issue was no longer to be taken lightly. The legislature met in regular session on January 6, 1920. On the first day of the session, both houses approved ratification. Kentucky, thereby, became the third state in the South and the twenty-third in the Union to ratify the amendment.[30]

Other ratifications followed. Three additional states ratified during January, 1920, six during February, and two in March. On March 22, Washington became the thirty-fifth state to ratify.

The approval of only one more was needed to make the amendment part of the United States Constitution. The suffragists were realists, however, and knew that the antis would increase their opposition and that the last state would be difficult to win.

Which state would be the thirty-sixth? Georgia, Alabama, South Carolina, Virginia, Maryland, Mississippi, Louisiana, and Delaware had refused to ratify, making a total of eight states on record as opposed to the amendment. Five states had, as yet, taken no action, including the New England states of Connecticut and Vermont and the southern states of Florida, North Carolina, and Tennessee.

When the Anthony amendment had been submitted on June 4, 1919, the Florida legislature was nearing the end of a regular session. A group of its supporters hastened to Tallahassee to urge ratification. Unfortunately, the legislature adjourned on June 6 without acting. The suffragists urged Governor Sidney J. Catts to call a special session immediately, but he refused to do so. Florida, thereby, took no action on the amendment during the 1919–20 ratification campaign.[31]

Special sessions were also needed for Connecticut and Vermont to be able to act on the amendment, but the governors of both states were reluctant to call such sessions. The suffragists insisted that public opinion favored ratification and demanded that calls be issued. Both governors remained firm, however.

The fate of the amendment now rested with two states—North Carolina and Tennessee. In both states, special sessions would be necessary.

In March 1920, Governor Thomas W. Bickett of North Carolina announced that he would call a special session. Several months passed before the formal call was issued, however, and the legislature did not convene until August 10. On August 13, Bickett sent a message in which he stated that he doubted the "wisdom of" and the "necessity for" woman suffrage. He felt that the amendment's eventual ratification was inevitable, however, and recommended that the legislature "accept the inevitable and ratify."[32] Antisuffrage sentiment was strong in the legislature, however, and its members did not follow the governor's advice. On August 17, the senate voted to postpone action until the next regular session, which would be in 1921. Two days later, on August 19, the house defeated a resolution to ratify. Thus, North Carolina lost its opportunity to become the thirty-sixth state.[33]

In Tennessee, Governor Albert H. Roberts hesitated to call a special session because of a restriction in the Tennessee constitution. Article II, Section 32 stated that no legislature should act upon any proposed federal amendment unless it had been elected after the amendment had been submitted. Since the current legislature had been elected before the submission of the Anthony amendment, it would be ineligible to act.

In June, however, the constitutionality of this requirement was placed in doubt by a decision of the United States Supreme Court in a case concerning the state of Ohio. The Ohio constitution contained a provision that stated that a referendum should be held on any proposed federal amendment before it could be acted upon by the legislature. George S. Hawke of Cincinnati challenged this provision, and in the case of *Hawke* v. *Smith*, the United States Supreme Court ruled the referendum requirement unconstitutional. The Court stated that the federal Constitution provided the method for its own amendment and that the states had no authority to designate a different procedure.[34]

Many people reasoned that this decision invalidated the restriction in the Tennessee constitution. The governor was uncertain, however. On June 23, Assistant Attorney General W. L. Frierson issued an opinion in which he stated that the power of a legislature to ratify was derived from the federal Constitution and could not be "taken away, limited or restrained" by the constitution of a state.[35] The next day, June 24, the attorney general of Tennessee issued an opinion in which he advised that ratification by a special session would be legal. President Wilson sent a telegram to Governor Roberts in which he stated: "It would be a real service to the party and to the nation . . . having in mind the recent decision of the Supreme Court in the Ohio case [for you] to call a special session of the legislature of Tennessee to consider the suffrage amendment. Allow me to urge this very earnestly."[36] Many prominent persons throughout the nation urged Roberts to call the session, and, by the end of June, he had decided to do so. Because of his preoccupation with his campaign for reelection, however, he delayed the formal call until August 7, at which time he announced that the legislature would convene on August 9.

During the campaign for ratification, several committees worked in support of the amendment. One was the League of Women Voters committee led by Catherine T. Kenny. Another was a Democratic ratification committee appointed by Governor Roberts and chaired by Mrs. James S. (Minnie Edwards) Beasley. A third was a Men's Ratification Committee with ex-governor Tom C. Rye as chairman. The Men's Ratification Committee had more than two hundred members and had been organized at the suggestion of Carrie Chapman Catt.[37]

On July 17, Carrie Chapman Catt arrived in Nashville expecting to stay only a few days. She remained more than a month, however. Assisted by Marjorie Shuler and Harriet Taylor Upton, she played a leading and essential role in the campaign.

Governor Albert H. Roberts (seated), Kate Burch Warner (seated), Anne Dallas Dudley (standing behind Mrs. Warner), and a group of suffragists, as pictured in the Nashville Tennessean, *Sept. 5, 1920. From a clipping in the Josephine Pearson Papers, Tennessee State Library and Archives. Courtesy of the Tennessee Historical Society.*

Alice Paul did not come to Nashville. During the campaign, the National Woman's Party was represented by Sue Shelton White, formerly of Jackson, Tennessee, but currently living in Washington. She came to Nashville in June, established headquarters in the Tulane Hotel, and began working actively for ratification. She was assisted by Anita Politzer, Betty Gram, and Florence Bayard.[38]

Meanwhile, the antisuffragists were marshaling their forces. The Tennessee Chapter of the National Association Opposed to Woman Suffrage had been dormant for several years. It was activated as the Tennessee Division of the Southern Women's League for the Rejection of the Susan B. Anthony Amendment.[39] The Southern Women's Rejection League had been organized in Montgomery, Alabama, in December 1919 for the purpose of opposing the Anthony Amendment.[40] Its president, Mrs. James S. (Nina Winter) Pinckard of Alabama, came to Nashville to work against ratification. Others who came from out of state were Mary G. Kilbreth of New York, president of the National Association Opposed to Woman Suffrage; Anne Pleasant, wife of the immediate past governor of Louisiana, Ruffin G. Pleasant (the Pleasants favored woman suffrage but by state action only); and Charlotte Rowe, a New York attorney and active crusader against suffrage.[41] The Southern Women's Rejection League led the opposition. It sent letters and other appeals to members of the legislature. It sponsored public speeches. It placed advertisements in newspapers and distributed large numbers of leaflets.

The antis considered the federal amendment a grave threat to the states. They thought that it would lead to federal interference in state elections and, in turn, to federal control of state politics. This fear was augmented by the amendment's enforcement clause, which stated that Congress would have the power to enforce its provisions by appropriate legislation.

The antis distributed numerous leaflets. Among them was "THAT DEADLY PARALLEL," which pointed out that the Anthony amendment's wording was patterned after that of the Fifteenth Amendment of 1870. This similarity in wording aroused thoughts of the Reconstruction era, an era that the white South remembered with dismay.[42] Another leaflet was entitled "BEWARE." It warned that ratification would mean the "reopening of the entire Negro suffrage question, the loss of State rights, and another period of reconstruction horrors."[43]

It is ironic that so much emphasis was placed on the "Negro question" when it was, in fact, a false issue as southern blacks had now been disfranchised. The suffragists pointed out that the Fifteenth Amendment stated that the right to vote should not be denied because of race, color, or previous condition of servitude, but it did not apply to women. The Anthony amendment forbade disfranchisement because of sex. It would confer suffrage on all women, theoretically at least including black women; yet, since there were more white than black women in many parts of the South (certainly in Tennessee), and since white southerners had effectively disfranchised blacks in most southern states well before 1920, black political power would not be increased. Nevertheless, many whites were apprehensive. They feared that enfranchising black women would lead to a reconsideration of the place of blacks in both southern politics and southern society. They did not want to risk disturbing the status quo.

The antisuffragists maintained that enfranchisement would cause women to neglect their homes and families. One leaflet, "HOME," pictured a man coming home from work to find his children alone in the house. Pinned to a "VOTES FOR WOMEN" banner was a note saying, "Back some time this evening."[44] Another showed a hen wearing a "VOTES FOR WOMEN" ribbon and walking away from a nest of eggs. The rooster was saying: "Why Ma, these eggs will get all cold!" The hen answered "Set on them yourself, Old Man, my country calls me."[45] Still another stated that the Anthony Amendment was "A PERIL TO THE SOUTH" and a threat to "Womanhood, the Family and the State." It urged the "REAL MEN" of Tennessee to do "THEIR DUTY" and defeat it.[46]

When the legislature convened on August 9, Governor Roberts transmitted the question of the Anthony amendment. He stated that enfranchisement was a matter of justice to the women of America and noted that both the Democratic and Republican Parties favored it. Since thirty-five states had ratified, Tennessee occupied a pivotal position. Therefore, he "earnestly and urgently recommended" that Tennessee ratify.[47]

The following day, August 10, ratification resolutions were introduced in both houses. The senate resolution was introduced by Andrew L. Todd of Murfreesboro and the house resolution by the Shelby County delegation. The suffragists had expected house speaker Seth Walker of Lebanon to introduce the measure. Much to their disappointment, however, he joined the opposition and led the fight against ratification.[48]

On August 12, the Committees on Constitutional Amendments of both houses conducted a joint hearing. The next day, August 13, the senate committee returned a favorable report in which it stated: "National woman's suffrage by Federal Amendment is at hand; it may be delayed, but it cannot be defeated; and we covet for Tennessee the signal honor of being the thirty-sixth and last State necessary to consummate this great reform."[49] The senate then debated the issue. Only two of its members spoke in opposition, and the ratification resolution was approved by a vote of twenty-five to four.[50]

The fate of the amendment now rested with the house. On August 17, the House Committee on Constitutional Amendments "heartily recommended" approval.[51] The following day, August 18, the house debated the question. At the close of debate, Seth Walker moved that the pending ratification resolution be tabled. A roll call was then taken, and the motion to table failed to carry. The vote was forty-eight to forty-eight. The person responsible for this tie vote was Banks P. Turner of Yorkville. Turner had been counted against suffrage, and his vote was a shocking surprise. Seth Walker could hardly believe his ears. He then called for a second vote on the same question. The second was the same as the first—forty-eight to forty-eight against tabling.[52]

Then came the vote on the resolution to ratify the amendment. This resolution was approved by a vote of forty-nine to forty-seven. The winning vote was that of Harry T. Burn, a twenty-four-year-old freshman legislator from Niota. Burn had been wearing a red rose, the antisuffrage symbol, and had been counted among the opposition. After Burn voted aye, Seth Walker changed his vote to aye and entered a motion to reconsider. Thus, the final vote on August 18, 1920, was fifty to forty-six.[53]

Why had Harry Burn voted aye? The opposition charged that he had been bribed. There was no basis for this charge, however. In a formal statement of explanation, Burn said that he had promised his mother that he would vote for ratification should his vote be needed. He said that he believed in "full suffrage as a right," and he welcomed the opportunity "to free" millions of women from "political slavery."[54]

The ratification resolution had been approved by both houses of the Tennessee legislature. There was much rejoicing. The victory was not yet complete, however, because of Seth Walker's motion to reconsider.

According to the rules, Walker had three days to bring the motion before the house. During the three-day interlude, the antis worked unsuccessfully to break the suffrage majority. Fearing defeat, Walker let the time pass without calling for the reconsideration resolution.

At a Saturday morning session on August 21, R. K. Riddick moved that the house take up the question of reconsideration. Speaker Walker ruled Riddick's motion out of order. He said that no quorum existed. There were many vacant seats in the house chamber that morning. During the preceding night, thirty-six members had left Tennessee and gone to Alabama in an attempt to

Representative Harry Burn, holding a sheaf of congratulatory telegrams, as pictured in the Nashville Tennessean, Sept. 5, 1920. From a clipping in the Josephine Pearson Papers, Tennessee State Library and Archives. Courtesy of the Tennessee Historical Society.

prevent the presence of a quorum. The house then voted on Walker's out-of-order ruling and defeated it forty-nine to eight. Walker then demanded a roll call. The Chair, then occupied by Joe F. Odle, ruled that Riddick's motion should be disposed of before a roll call should be made. Walker continued to insist that no quorum existed. Odle stated that the business before the house was the motion to reconsider the ratification of the federal suffrage amendment. The house then voted on the reconsideration motion and defeated it forty-nine to zero. Thus, both houses of the Tennessee legislature had ratified the Nineteenth Amendment to the United States Constitution.[55]

The governor did not sign the certificate of ratification for several days, however. Before the house voted on Walker's motion to reconsider, the chancery court at Nashville issued an injunction restraining Governor Roberts, Secretary of State Ike B. Stevens, and the presiding officers of the house and senate from signing or issuing any proclamation declaring that Tennessee had "constitutionally and legally" ratified the Nineteenth Amendment. On August 23, however, the Tennessee Supreme Court dissolved this injunction.[56]

The following morning, August 24, Governor Roberts signed the certificate of ratification and mailed it to Secretary of State Bainbridge Colby in Washington. During the early morning of August 26, 1920, Secretary Colby signed it without ceremony.[57]

The Tennessee antis still refused to admit defeat, however. They held meetings of protest in several cities and once again brought the issue before the Tennessee House of Representatives. Due to the absence of some of the suffrage supporters on August 31, the antis had a majority. Taking advantage of this opportunity, F. S. Hall of Dickson moved that the house not concur in the ratification of the Nineteenth Amendment, a motion that carried by a vote of fifty-seven to twenty-four.[58] The antis then asked Governor Roberts to report this non-concurrence to the secretary of state in Washington, and Roberts complied.[59] This effort on the part of the antis was futile, however, since no state may withdraw its ratification after it has been accepted and approved.

The Nineteenth Amendment became part of the United States Constitution on August 26, 1920. For many years, however, August 26 passed unnoticed among American women. As a byproduct of the current women's rights movement, however, it came to the attention of the general public and was often called "Woman's Equality Day." That designation was a misnomer since the Nineteenth Amendment said nothing about equality. Its only provision was that citizens should not be denied the right to vote because of sex.

Tennessee's ratification made women eligible to participate in the general election in November 1920. Some states would not allow them to do so, however, because ratification had come too late to permit them to comply with state election laws. On the theory that the Nineteenth Amendment took precedence over state laws, Mary Latimer McLendon of Atlanta appealed to the secretary of state in Washington. He declined to become involved, and Georgia women who went to the polls were turned away.[60] Mississippi women experienced the same exclusion. Ironically, a state constitutional amendment to enfranchise women was before the Mississippi electorate in November 1920. In this referendum, in which only men voted, the proposed amendment was defeated at the polls.[61]

Tennessee's ratification was followed by that of two New England states. On September 14, 1920, Connecticut became the thirty-seventh state to ratify, and on February 8, 1921, Vermont became the thirty-eighth. Delaware followed on March 12, 1923, making a total of thirty-nine.

Almost twenty years were to pass before there would be another ratification. On May 2, 1941, Maryland became the fortieth state. The neighboring state of Virginia ratified on February 21, 1952. Alabama followed on September 8, 1953. In 1969 Florida (May 13) and South Carolina (July 1) ratified, making a total of forty-four states.

The next year, 1970, was the fiftieth anniversary of the Federal Suffrage Amendment. During that year, two states, Georgia (February 20) and Louisiana (June 11) ratified. They were joined by North Carolina on May 6, 1971. Finally, on March 22, 1984, Mississippi, the lone dissenter, ratified.

As originally written, the United States Constitution was a "gender neutral" document. The preamble referred to the citizenry simply as "the people." Members of the House, the Senate, and even the chief executive were designated only as "persons." Sex as a qualification was not written into the document until the ratification of the Fourteenth and Fifteenth Amendments during the Reconstruction era. These amendments indicated that the Constitution conferred no voting rights on women. To gain such rights, they would need their own amendment.

Tennessee's ratification of the Nineteenth Amendment in 1920 was, and remains today, a landmark in the history of women's rights. It removed any doubt about women's political status. No longer would American women find themselves disfranchised because of their sex. The supreme law of the land had recognized them as both citizens and voters. This victory was not achieved easily but was a result of years of crusading by individuals and organizations on national, state, and local levels.

Notes

1. Agnes Thornton Bird, "Legal Status of Women in Tennessee, the First Seventy-five Years," *Tennessee Bar Journal* 15 (Feb. 1979): 38.

2. A. Elizabeth Taylor, *The Woman Suffrage Movement in Tennessee* (New York: Bookman Associates, 1957), 15–17.

3. *Memphis Commercial*, May 19, 1889; Lide A. Meriwether, "Tennessee," in *The History of Woman Suffrage*, ed. Susan B. Anthony and Ida Husted Harper (Rochester, N.Y.: Susan B. Anthony, 1902), 4: 926.

4. NAWSA, *Proceedings of the Twenty-Seventh Annual Convention of the National American Woman Suffrage Association . . . Held in Atlanta, Georgia*, Jan. 31–Feb. 5, 1895 (Warren, Ohio: William R. Ritezel & Company, n.d.), 89.

5. NAWSA *Proceedings*, 1897, 112.

6. *Nashville American*, May 12, 13, 1897.

7. *Memphis Commercial Appeal*, Apr. 25, 1900.

8. Meriwether, "Tennessee," *History of Woman Suffrage* (1902), 4: 927.

9. *Memphis Commercial Appeal*, Dec. 21, 1906.

10. Taylor, *Woman Suffrage Movement in Tennessee*, 131.

11. For a list of towns having one or more equal suffrage organizations, see Taylor, *Woman Suffrage Movement in Tennessee*, 131.

12. A. Elizabeth Taylor, interview with Anne Dallas Dudley, Jan. 16, 1943.

13. Taylor, *Woman Suffrage Movement in Tennessee*, 61, 62, 67, 68. Kate B. Warner was Mrs. Leslie Warner, president of the Nashville Equal Suffrage League.

14. The Chattanooga women who hosted the conference were Frances Fort Brown, Margaret Ervin, Ernestine Nos, Catherine Wester, Mrs. C. H. Pyron, and Mrs. J. L. Hughes; see *Chattanooga News*, Nov. 10, 1914; SSWSC Press bulletin; and Laura Clay to A. C. Prive, Nov. 28, 1914, Laura Clay Papers, Special Collections and Archives, Margaret I. King Library, University of Kentucky, Lexington.

15. Resolution adopted by the 1915 State Convention of Tennessee suffragists, Jackson; Sue Shelton White Papers, Schlesinger Library, Radcliffe College.

16. *Suffragist* 4 (3) (Jan. 22, 1916): 8.

17. Doris Stevens, *Jailed for Freedom* (New York: Liveright, 1920), 370. In researching the movement, the author found no record of any woman's being jailed in Tennessee or in any southern state because of participation in suffrage activities.

18. *Woman's Protest* 9 (1) (May 1916): 13; Taylor, *Woman Suffrage Movement in Tennessee*, 80, 81.

19. Tennessee *House Journal*, 1915, 181, 182. Anne Dallas Dudley, director of lobbying, was Mrs. Guilford Dudley.

20. Ibid., 308; Tennessee *Senate Journal*, 1915, 318.

21. Ibid., 1917, 151.

22. NAWSA, *Victory: How Women Won It: A Centennial Symposium, 1840–1940* (New York: H. W. Wilson Company, 1940), 123, 124.

23. Tennessee *House Journal*, 1917, 189; *Nashville Tennessean*, Jan. 20, 1917.

24. Tennessee *Senate Journal*, 1917, 309.

25. *Nashville Tennessean*, Feb. 2, 1917.

26. Tennessee *House Journal*, 1919, 920.

27. Tennessee *Senate Journal*, 1919, 1271.

28. A. Elizabeth Taylor, "The Woman Suffrage Movement in Texas," *Journal of Southern History*, 27 (2) (May 1951): 215; Elizabeth Cady Stanton, Susan B. Anthony, et al., eds., *History of Woman Suffrage* 6 vols. (Rochester and New York, 1881–1922), 6: 642, 643.

29. A. Elizabeth Taylor, "The Woman Suffrage Movement in Arkansas," *Arkansas Historical Quarterly* 15 (1) (Spring 1956): 34; Stanton and Anthony, *History of Woman Suffrage*, 6: 21.

30. Paul E. Fuller, *Laura Clay and the Woman's Rights Movement* (Lexington: University Press of Kentucky, 1975), 159; Stanton and Anthony, *History of Woman Suffrage*, 6: 213, 214.

31. A. Elizabeth Taylor, "The Woman Suffrage Movement in Florida," *Florida Historical Quarterly* 36 (July 1957): 59–60.

32. A. Elizabeth Taylor, "The Woman Suffrage Movement in North Carolina," *North Carolina Historical Review* 38 (2) (Apr. 1961): 186, 187.

33. Ibid., 188.

34. *Hawke* v. *Smith*, 253, U.S. 221–39; Carrie Chapman Catt and Nettie Rogers Shuler, *Woman Suffrage and Politics: The Inner Story of the Suffrage Movement* (New York, 1923), 415–19.

35. *Ibid.*, 427.

36. Woodrow Wilson to A. H. Roberts, June 23, 1920, A. H. Roberts Papers, Tennessee State Library and Archives, Nashville.

37. Carrie Chapman Catt to Catherine T. Kenny, June 20, 1920, Carrie Chapman Catt Papers, Tennessee State Library and Archives, Nashville.

38. Taylor, *Woman Suffrage Movement in Tennessee*, 109.

39. *Nashville Banner*, July 24, 1920.

40. *Woman Patriot* 3 (35) (Dec. 13, 1919): 7.

41. *Nashville Tennessean*, Aug. 6, 1920.

42. "THAT DEADLY PARALLEL," Josephine A. Pearson Papers, Tennessee State Library and Archives, Nashville.

43. "BEWARE," Pearson Papers, reprinted in part 3.

44. "HOME," Pearson Papers, reprinted in part 3.

45. "America When Feminized," Pearson Papers, reprinted in part 3.

46. "CAN ANYBODY TERRORIZE TENNESSEE MANHOOD?" Pearson Papers.

47. Tennessee *House Journal*, Called Session, 1920, 16–18.

48. Catt and Shuler, *Woman Suffrage and Politics*, 440.

49. Tennessee *Senate Journal*, Called Session, 1920, 293.

50. Ibid., 295.

51. Tennessee *House Journal*, Called Session, 1920, 87.

52. Ibid., 91.

53. Ibid., 92–94.

54. Catt and Shuler, *Woman Suffrage and Politics*, 451.

55. Tennessee *House Journal*, Called Session, 1920, 119–21; Margaret Ervin Ford, "Tennessee, Part II.," *History of Woman Suffrage* (1922), 6: 624–25.

56. *Nashville Tennessean*, Aug. 25, 1920.

57. Catt and Shuler, *Woman Suffrage and Politics*, 455; *Nashville Tennessean*, Aug. 27, 1920.

58. Tennessee *House Journal*, Called Session, 1920, 130–135.

59. Ibid.

60. A. Elizabeth Taylor, "Woman Suffrage Activities in Atlanta," *Atlanta Historical Journal* 23 (4) (Winter 1979–80): 52.

61. A. Elizabeth Taylor, "The Woman Suffrage Movement in Mississippi," *Journal of Mississippi History* 30 (1) (Feb. 1968): 33, 34.

4

Adella Hunt Logan, the Tuskegee Woman's Club, and African Americans in the Suffrage Movement

Adele Logan Alexander

"The right of citizens to vote is denied and abridged in . . . one third of the states of the union . . . on account of race, color and previous condition of servitude," the ardent Ida B. Wells-Barnett asserted in a 1910 essay that addressed the many ways by which political disempowerment made members of her race so vulnerable to lynching and other forms of physical, economic, and political persecution in the early twentieth century. Wells-Barnett strongly believed that women (race notwithstanding) as well as all black men should not have the right to vote denied them, but she also somewhat cynically challenged one white leader of the woman suffrage movement by asking: "Do you really believe that the millennium is going to come when women get the ballot?" Mary Church Terrell, an African-American educator, suffragist, and dedicated clubwoman, on the other hand, expressed her own rather differently focused concerns about the injustice of denying women—all women—the vote when she queried: "How can anyone who is able to use reason, and who believes in dealing justice to all God's creatures, think it right to withhold from one-half the human race rights and privileges freely accorded to the other half, which is neither more deserving nor more capable of exercising them?" For a number of years before antiblack terrorism forced her to flee to Chicago, the Mississippi-born Wells-Barnett had toiled as a crusading journalist and political activist in Memphis, Tennessee, the same city where the indefatigable social feminist Terrell had been born and raised in a comfortable, middle-class household.[1]

Ida B. Wells-Barnett. From the Ida B. Wells-Barnett Papers, the University of Chicago Library.

On other occasions, still another black person with ties to Tennessee, Margaret Murray Washington, expressed her opinions about woman suffrage. During the 1880s the young Margaret Murray had been a student at Nashville's Fisk College, but then she moved to Tuskegee Institute in the neighboring state of Alabama where she became a school administrator and a perennial leader of the national "colored" women's club movement. She probably earned that leadership role on her own merits, but it also surely was bestowed on her, at least in part, because she married Booker T. Washington, who, even before 1900, had become the most renowned and influential black man in the United States. Like Terrell and Wells-Barnett, Margaret Murray Washington thought that women should be allowed to vote, but she tempered her position by stating that "personally, woman suffrage has never kept me awake at night." Her famous husband once declared, "I am in favor of woman suffrage" and then added, "I do not believe that any harm can be done, and I think on the other hand that much good might be accomplished." He concluded, however, with a seeming lack of concern about women's disempowered political status that closely paralleled his wife's views: "There are many other questions of far greater importance before the country."[2]

In 1899, however, Booker T. and Margaret Murray Washington's close friend, next-door neighbor, and professional associate, Adella Hunt Logan, sent a letter to a white friend in the North expressing her concerns about the critical political situation facing, especially, those Americans with whom she shared both race and gender. "The southern states seem determined to disfranchise the Negro," she wrote with obvious despair. She saw "little hope for women's claim, and none for the black woman." Six years later she completed a comprehensive essay about suffrage in which she asserted: "Government of the people, for the people, and by the people is but partially realized so long as woman has no vote." Then, in 1912, Logan, who was both a devoted educator and an avid reformer, further argued that "more and more colored women . . . are convinced . . . that their efforts would be more telling if [they] had the vote." More than eight decades later, these diverse pronouncements from four different African-American women—and one man—seem surprising and revealing only because not enough is yet known or understood about the many southerners, both black and white, who for so long involved themselves in the struggle for woman suffrage and equal political rights for all black people as well.[3]

Half a century prior to the time when Wells-Barnett, Terrell, the Washingtons, and Logan ever began to express their differing opinions about the franchise, a group of frustrated and articulate Americans, primarily women, gathered in Seneca Falls, New York, to address a number of concerns about their lack of political prerogatives and authority. From that time—1848—until 1920, the year that marked the passage and ratification of the Nineteenth Amendment, not only white women but also a limited number of African Americans as well involved themselves in efforts to gain political rights for women. They did so because they knew that black women often were doubly victimized by both sexism and racism, and acquiring the vote to provide at least some degree of influence on the affairs of government could help to reduce those two-pronged assaults. They also considered universal suffrage an integral part of the country's moral and social reform movements. Finally, and most importantly perhaps, they became convinced that women's political empowerment would benefit the black community in its entirety.[4]

Prior to the Civil War, all women and most black men could vote neither in the southern states, where most African Americans remained enslaved, nor in much of the North, where even the non-enslaved were denied many basic rights. This almost universal denial of the franchise notwithstanding, several black men and one black woman attended the woman's rights convention at Seneca Falls. During this same period, a small but vocal number of other African Americans also expressed their support for woman suffrage. The majority lived in and around northern cities such as Buffalo, Boston, and Philadelphia, which were centers for a variety of "radical" reform activities—especially abolitionism. Much like the modest circle of white people who supported woman suffrage prior to the Civil War, these men and women were involved primarily in the struggle to abolish slavery, but many of them also believed in equal political rights for all Americans regardless of gender. Frederick Douglass, the prominent journalist who often formed strategic alliances with white reformers, fit that description. Several black women, including Sojourner Truth, the forthright and provocative former slave, and New England's controversial political lecturer, Maria Stewart, also spoke out on behalf of both abolition and women's rights.[5]

When politicians who were bent on expanding and insuring black Americans' rights introduced the Fifteenth Amendment in the late 1860s, a controversy concerning its contents soon emerged within the ranks of prosuffragists. Many white female reformers, especially those who had supported abolition themselves, became incensed when they learned that the proposed national voting rights amendment was designed to guarantee the franchise for black men only—most of whom just recently had been freed from slavery—yet provided no benefits whatsoever for women. On the other hand, because they recognized the importance of obtaining even limited access to the ballot, many black activists who were proponents of universal suffrage raised few objections to shelving the gender issue, at least temporarily. In the spirit of America's Reconstruction period, the argument that it should be "the Negro's hour" prevailed. The exclusion of women from the Fifteenth Amendment, however, contributed to the creation of a philosophical and organizational rift within the woman suffrage movement that would not be healed for more than twenty years.[6]

Most African Americans who wanted to continue their support of woman suffrage during the 1870s and 1880s worked within the ranks of the American Woman Suffrage Association (AWSA), which took the position that it could both advocate and support the franchise for black men, and yet simultaneously and vigorously assert that the Fifteenth Amendment had unfairly slighted all women. By contrast, vocal members of the other faction, the National Woman Suffrage Association (NWSA)—Susan B. Anthony and Elizabeth Cady Stanton among them—sometimes openly expressed their resentment at black people, whom they considered ingrates who once had welcomed their support on behalf of abolition but then ultimately deserted women in their own time of political need. Stanton went so far as to write almost approvingly of the lynching of a black Tennessean accused of raping a white woman. She implied that granting African-American men the right to vote essentially gave them license to rape and even suggested that universal manhood suffrage (meaning, in this particular context, suffrage for *black* men) could "culminate in fearful outrages on womanhood, especially in the southern states." Understandably, the NWSA had few African-American members.[7]

Despite the barely veiled racist rhetoric that emerged during this period of angry internecine feuding within the woman suffrage movement, many black women and men, such as Frederick Douglass, maintained their working relationships with white reformers and remained vocal proponents of women's rights. They recognized and despaired over African-American women's absence of political power and spoke out about the need for universal suffrage, arguing that voters, regardless of race or gender, made better citizens, and that both the continued progress and overall empowerment of black people required their women's political participation.[8]

The two embattled contingents of the suffrage movement, the AWSA and the NWSA, finally settled many of their disagreements around 1890 and merged into the more powerful and effective National American Woman Suffrage Association (NAWSA). This reconciliation within the organized ranks of women's political activism, however, did nothing to alleviate the travails that African Americans endured. In many ways, in fact, they multiplied. Southern state legislatures began to adopt various franchise-limiting provisions, such as property requirements, literacy tests, and Tennessee's poll tax, which increasingly stripped black men of their recently granted voting rights. Because of these and other repressive Jim Crow developments and a widespread upsurge in race-related violence, historian Rayford Logan has characterized the late nineteenth and early twentieth century—ironically labeled the Progressive Era for most of America—as the "nadir" for Negroes.[9]

During that same period, a few black women also felt compelled to express their concerns that, even when and where black men maintained their hard-won and precious right to vote, they sometimes either ignored or abused it. In 1893, for example, the poet, essayist, and longtime woman's rights advocate, Frances Ellen Watkins Harper, wrote:

> Day after day did Milly Green
> Just follow after Joe,
> And told him if he voted wrong
> To take his rags and go.[10]

True to the spirit of Progressivism, the women's club movement expanded exponentially during these same years under the aegis of the almost exclusively white General Federation of Women's Clubs (GFWC). Many black women began to address their own concerns about critical local and national problems that, in many ways, were quite comparable to those that spurred white women to action. Much like their white counterparts, they too saw the need for social uplift and sought to tackle some of the most critical problems through reform clubs of their own. At least partially in response to their often contemptuous exclusion from the GFWC, concerned African-American women throughout the country started clubs and then began working within their own associations to address their communities' most pressing needs. Soon, however, they became aware—just as white women had—of the importance of creating some sort of national network, or at least a more centralized organizational structure. To this end, pioneering representatives of African-American women's clubs from dozens of far-flung towns and cities met in Washington, D.C., in 1896 to establish the National Association of Colored Women (NACW). This coalition of affiliated chapters eventually would expand its total individual membership to at least fifty thousand women, and for many years it served as the umbrella organization for a broad array of local clubs. The following summer many of the same women reconvened in Nashville to organize further, to form strategy, and to reinforce the solidarity of their recently founded alliance. Over the next twenty years, Tennessee's three activist daughters, Terrell, Washington, and even Wells-Barnett—whose outspoken militancy often put her at odds with the other two women—all became important policy makers and leaders of the NACW.[11]

Local NACW chapters addressed a wide variety of issues that particularly concerned women, and, through these clubs, a number of African Americans first became informed about and involved in the issues that were relevant to suffrage. Many members of "colored" women's clubs began to realize, especially, the ways that having the franchise might help them gain at least a few civil and economic rights for themselves and subsequently might result in improved conditions both for their families and their communities. Awareness of and sensitivity to both African-American and female disfranchisement began to develop more rapidly in the black community as Jim Crow regulations and legally sanctioned racial discrimination became increasingly entrenched, especially throughout the South. Around the turn of the century, activist southern leaders, including Fisk's registrar, Minnie L. Crosthwait, Atlanta University's Lugenia Burns Hope, Washington educator Anna Julia Cooper, the New Orleans clubwoman Sylvanie Williams, and others, advocated social and political reform in many arenas—including woman suffrage. Quite a few all-female alliances, such as temperance unions, church auxiliaries, sororities, and educational groups, emerged during this period, and some of them embraced the enfranchisement of women as one of many different issues they endorsed. Other African-American women around the country not only advocated suffrage from within those clubs, which addressed a broad range of reform interests, but they also started separate organizations exclusively dedicated to the question of votes for women. Among the latter were groups in Deep South and border cities such as Memphis, Washington, D.C., Charleston, St. Louis, and New Orleans. By the turn of the century, women from the black community who supported this cause were moving in the direction of more organized—and organizational—outlets for their advocacy.[12]

These African-American advocates of woman suffrage, however, must have speculated about and consequently been appalled by the motivations, words, and actions of some of their supposed "partners" in the movement. White spokeswomen—such as Louisiana's Kate Gordon, who called for state-by-state suffrage amendments that would enfranchise white women only and also spoke freely of "fool niggers" who exhibited their "coon nature," Mississippi's highly articulate Belle Kearney, and a number of others as well—had begun to develop and project a racist strategy and philosophy concerning female enfranchisement. These suffrage advocates hoped to acquire the ballot for white women at least in part as a counterbalance to what they perceived to be the threatening and corruptive impact of black male voters, particularly where there were high and potentially influential percentages of African Americans. Kearney, for one, frequently contended that the South was "compelled to look to its Anglo-Saxon women as the medium through which to retain the supremacy of the white race over the African."[13]

Many, if not most, members of the African-American community, on the other hand, viewed the situation quite differently. *Crisis*, the NAACP's widely read magazine, for instance, published a whimsical yet cogent couplet—in "Negro dialect"—which stressed the commonality of blacks' and women's political disempowerment:

> When it come ter de question er de female vote,
> Der ladies an' der cullud folk is in de same boat.[14]

That brief verse made a clearly valid comparison, yet few politically active white women either in the North or the South chose to acknowledge any solidarity whatsoever with African Americans, especially when the NAWSA began actively to pursue support for suffrage in the South, and when both racist rhetoric and deed had experienced a virulent resurgence, and unyielding segregation became common practice.

In the latter months of 1912, for example, the combined forces of the woman suffrage movement began planning a major demonstration in Washington, D.C., that was scheduled to coincide with President Woodrow Wilson's inaugural early the following year. The organizers of this massive effort hoped that a strong and visible female presence in the nation's capital might help to convince national legislators seriously to consider approving a voting rights amendment. A number of white women argued, however, that for reasons of so-called "political expediency," African Americans should be excluded from the march altogether. The NAWSA's newspaper, the *Woman's Journal*, reported that "a few white women said they would not march at all if any colored women did." Adella Hunt Logan, Alabama's outspoken African-American suffragist, for one, was taken aback by this resistance on the part of the suffragists. She promptly dispatched a letter to a sympathetic white colleague in upstate New York in which she stated, "I am writing Mrs. Terrell [Mary Church Terrell] and a few other friends there [Washington, D.C.] encouraging them to take part. . . . It would seem to me a travesty to have a float of Indians and no Negroes in that great demonstration." As an alternative to their total exclusion, other white demonstration strategists encouraged black women to segregate themselves voluntarily into a discrete assemblage at the tail end of the parade. Terrell, in fact, did decide to join a cadre of eager young women from Howard University, but the always assertive and uncompromising Ida B. Wells-Barnett refused to yield to any attempts at segregation or second-class participation: she slipped into the march to walk among a group of white colleagues from Chicago. Certain individual delegations were less prejudiced and less committed to the goal of maintaining a segregated march than others, and the *Woman's Journal* also noted that some black women—"three in the college section, and a number among the teachers"—had the opportunity to demonstrate their support for a constitutional amendment that would give women the right to vote by marching right alongside their white associates.[15]

In this and in other instances as well, these black female advocates of votes for women were determined not to be denied access to, or involvement in, any prosuffrage activities, nor did they shirk their civic responsibility in the isolated instances when the opportunity arose. During the late nineteenth and early twentieth century, a few states and local jurisdictions, especially in the far West, either passed legislation or amended their constitutions in ways that allowed women to take part in some elections. Wherever possible, African-American women as well as white women in those locales registered and began to vote.[16]

Although they marched for suffrage, educated themselves about the importance of the vote, and went to the polls when and where they could, black women, nonetheless, were widely discriminated against in their attempts to work for and acquire the vote throughout the entire period from the Seneca Falls convention up to, and even after, 1920. At the same time, and particularly, it seems, in the South, many antisuffragists argued that, regardless of race, all women should be satisfied to remain their spouses' "helpmates"—overlooking the fact that they often had no husbands or, at least, might have vehemently disagreed with them. These arguments also concluded that women did not either want or need the ballot and that political involvement inevitably would dirty their hands, corrupt their morals, and lead them to neglect their families. Because of their African ancestry, however, nonwhite women endured the added contentions that black male suffrage during and after Reconstruction had been a failure on many counts and that only the so-called "educated and deserving classes" should be granted the right to vote. Some white men, and many white women as well, including a number of advocates of woman suffrage, advanced this elitist line of reasoning. The prosuffragists (and, of course, antisuffragists as well) who put forth these arguments considered black people—who had few opportunities to secure either financial assets or an education—ignorant, derelict, easily corruptible, and otherwise unworthy of the franchise. As a result, many white suffragists continued to rebuff any involvement whatsoever in the suffrage movement by black female reformers.

A great deal of this resistance and rejection was grounded in persistent racist practices and traditions that were spawned in the legacy of slavery and then nourished by the impassioned white backlash that followed Reconstruction. Negative perceptions of black people among whites nationwide also perpetuated a strong belief in the alleged sexual immorality of all African Americans, both male and female. Some nonwhite women—especially, perhaps, those who were more privileged and educated—openly articulated their bitter outrage at the latter humiliating presumptions, which both fueled efforts to deny black people the franchise and concurrently perpetuated their vulnerability in a variety of other circumstances as well. In addition, and even though a plethora of late-nineteenth- and early-twentieth-century legislative endeavors already had severely curtailed the number of black male voters, many white southerners feared the possible political impact of a motivated black female electorate, especially in those states where African Americans constituted a substantial percentage of the population.[17]

A number of northerners who attempted to exclude African Americans from prosuffrage activities certainly harbored their own homegrown racial prejudices, but, in addition, they were highly aware of and responsive to intransigent southern "sensitivities" and practices in this arena. Many suffrage leaders argued that the national strategy they were developing—one that they believed was central to the success of the ongoing efforts to ratify a voting rights amendment—required backing from white male legislators in at least a few southern states. They worried that the open and visible involvement of nonwhite women would only exacerbate the latent antagonism of those politicians from Dixie and would thereby reinforce and guarantee their opposition to woman suffrage. As a result of these combined factors, African-American women—at best—enjoyed only intermittent and reluctant support from whites in national, regional, and state suffrage organizations. In some instances they were tolerated, but more often they were ignored, scorned, and even repulsed.[18]

Overall, therefore, African Americans who supported woman suffrage faced forbidding obstacles throughout the more than seven decades that the struggle for voting rights continued, but after 1900 the ongoing battle to pass a constitutional amendment that would give all women the right to vote became a truly national effort. Such an amendment required the support of white southerners who, by and large, were not only hostile to woman suffrage in general, but were also particularly, and fervently, opposed to an empowered black electorate of either sex. This became a further excuse for already reluctant and prejudiced white activists to shun the participation of African Americans in the movement. At the same time, however, and notwithstanding the bias and abuse they habitually encountered, opposition to the cause was only minimal within the black community, and African-American leaders of both sexes consistently showed less resistance to the idea of votes for women than did white leaders.[19]

The activities of a small circle of black Americans—most of them educators—who learned about and then worked on behalf of woman suffrage in the state of Alabama should be considered within this general context. Even during the painful era that Rayford Logan designated the "nadir" for Negro Americans, some of these women of the South tried especially to infuse the young people whom they encountered with the gravity of their civic responsibilities. They also developed tactics and strategies to mold public opinion and reached out beyond their home community at Tuskegee Institute—Booker T. Washington's influential and much-emulated school—to touch and activate an even larger circle of their peers. Thus, they began to build a solidly grounded foundation that could support and advocate an expanded franchise—one that finally might include black women.

About a dozen faculty women, plus the wives of some of Tuskegee Institute's top officials, first convened in 1895 to form the Tuskegee Woman's Club, an organization that would devote itself to numerous aspects of community uplift. The next year, that club formally affiliated itself with the newly established NACW. Members of the Tuskegee chapter immediately began to address their energies toward many urgent social, medical, educational, and economic needs in their predominantly black, rural, and financially disadvantaged community. They also started to inform themselves and those around them in preparation for acquiring the vote, even though most people, especially in the Deep South, thought that the enfranchisement of women really was only the most remote possibility and considered it both a threatening and an exceedingly radical proposition.[20]

In Alabama, Jim Crow laws passed in the late nineteenth century and then reinforced in 1901 by a revised state constitution successfully denied the vote to most black men in the state, and no woman of any race could exercise that fundamental democratic right even in local elections or referenda.[21] In the white community, the prevailing and idealized image of the "Southern Lady" as someone who was ever pure and unsullied, clingingly dependent, and always held herself aloof from the gritty political hurly-burly, still remained intact around 1900, even though that picture greatly distorted reality. Living with these debilitating assumptions, only a very few exceptionally determined and progressive white women in Alabama managed to defy tradition and address the issue of women's political disempowerment at all, and at least one of those who did described the possibility of votes for women—white women exclusively, she clearly anticipated—as "a way out of the Negro difficulty." In addition, well into the second decade of the twentieth century not one white male journalist or newspaper in the state openly promoted equal political rights for women. And yet, even in this notably hostile environment, the Tuskegee Woman's Club initiated and then continued to hold frequent, open exchanges about that very topic.[22]

Tuskegee Institute was located just outside the town of the same name in rural east-central Alabama. It lay within a fertile agricultural swath that cut across much of the South and was characterized by its distinctive black soil. "The badge worn by members of the Tuskegee Woman's Club," the NACW journal, *Woman's Era,* therefore noted in 1895, "is a gold pin in the unique form of the state of Alabama, having a 'Black Belt' of enamel across the center with initials of the club and a star to mark the situation of Tuskegee." In many ways, the acclaimed school at Tuskegee became Margaret Murray Washington's own personal dominion when she married the famed Booker T. Washington. She herself was a forceful, shrewd, and energetic woman who held sway in almost all local matters—social, cultural, and educational—and for many years she served as the president of the local club, whose membership included neither students nor women from the town or surrounding plantations. Although they would not grant local women membership in the Tuskegee Woman's Club itself, members of the institute's own "restricted" club nonetheless organized and then led affiliated groups comprised of female students, "town girls," ministers' wives, and farm women. With few exceptions, members of the institute's chapter were educated women who had attended Tuskegee, Fisk, Alabama State, Atlanta University, Howard, Hampton, and normal schools from as far away as Massachusetts. By most standards, these were a comparatively favored and successful group of African Americans.[23]

Much like other NACW chapters and a number of white women's clubs as well, many activities of the Tuskegee Woman's Club emanated from the domestic sphere. Some of its meetings were devoted to discussions of the family, literature, religion, and history. Members dealt with a broad range of social concerns within homes and schools, on nearby tenant farms, and in the community at large. The Tuskegee Woman's Club promoted prison reform, operated a small lending library, and its members worked with the less well-situated women from the surrounding countryside by offering expertise, volunteering their time, and dispensing clothing, medication, and household necessities while they advocated improved nutrition, hygiene, and child and maternal health. These endeavors often were broadly characterized as "social uplift," and they represented a successful coalescing of the moral, material, and cultural concerns of the institute's clubwomen. Their work reflected the goals of the NACW and echoed its motto, "Lifting as We Climb." The woman's club at Tuskegee Institute was a closely affiliated chapter that contributed to the financial support of its parent organization and regularly sent representatives to state, regional, and national conventions.[24]

Adella Hunt Logan was one of the Tuskegee Woman's Club's charter members. As Adella Hunt, she had been born free during the Civil War in a small plantation-belt Georgia town to a light-skinned African-American and Cherokee Indian mother and a financially well-situated white father who reportedly often "talked politics" with his always intense second daughter. Her mother, though only minimally educated herself, had vehemently insisted that her children acquire as much schooling as possible. During Adella's childhood, the Hunts lived in a comfortable though modest home in a section of Sparta, Georgia, known as "Hunt's Hill" where, largely because of family affiliations with prominent members of the local white community, she and her siblings enjoyed certain advantages usually denied others of their race. The girls in the family never steered a plow or chopped cotton, but they did learn classical music, gardening, and fine needlework. The three younger sisters, Adella included, also managed to complete at least some college-level education during the 1880s—a rarity even for white females in that era. "I got my education," she stated about that formative period of her life, "by no greater hardship than hard work which I regard as exceedingly healthful." Adella Hunt graduated from the "upper normal" school program at Atlanta University in 1881, worked for two years in southwest Georgia, then turned down an unusual opportunity to teach under the "well organized and pleasant conditions" at her more prestigious alma mater and instead committed herself to becoming an educator at the new Tuskegee Institute, in what she described as "one of the darkest regions of the South." She brought discipline and dedication to her vocations and avocations as a teacher, a member of the Tuskegee Woman's Club, and a committed suffragist.[25]

At Tuskegee Institute Logan was a dedicated clubwoman, but she saw herself, first and foremost, as an educator of young people. She wanted, especially, to inspire, inform, and stimulate her students on the importance of universal suffrage. With this goal in mind, she tried to put participatory educational exercises to their best possible use. In early November 1900, for example, coinciding with President William McKinley's bid for reelection, she dropped Booker T. Washington a note explaining that "my class in civics wanted to have a political parade tonight just after supper." Logan further asked whether "a few women teachers might be excused for a while from the faculty meeting [to] . . . chaperone the girls." "My plan is to make the meeting of an educative character and," she tactfully concluded, "we will try to keep reasonable order." She also worked with the institute's debate team, which competed against other nearby black schools on, among many subjects, the question of votes for women. When Tuskegee found itself assigned the *anti*suffragist position at one such event, its team (fortunately or unfortunately) lost the competition.[26]

Logan's interest and participation in informative civic activities extended beyond the classroom to her work with the Tuskegee Woman's Club. Active discussion about woman suffrage began within that group as early as 1897, when Adella, who had become the school's "second lady" as a result of her marriage to the institute's vice-president and treasurer, Warren Logan, started and then continued to conduct monthly meetings that focused on the significance and progress of the movement. Despite their leader Margaret Murray Washington's lukewarm endorsement, most members of the club seem to have agreed that all women should be able to vote. Officially, the group took the moderate position that "when the time comes for women to vote . . . the colored woman . . . will be educated along all lines enough to cast her vote wisely and intelligently."[27]

To supplement its customary monthly discussions the club also occasionally planned and presented somewhat more formal "suffrage nights." In early 1915, one such affair began with an exposition about the "origin, development, and influence of the Woman's Suffrage Movement." The "lantern show" that followed featured projected photographs of noted suffrage advocates, both black and white, and a different club member provided appropriate comments about each portrait. The institute's newspaper, *The Tuskegee Student*, enthusiastically reported that "the picture of Sojourner Truth was greeted with especial applause." The evening's mistress of ceremonies then reviewed the circumstances of Truth's appearance at a women's rights meeting in the early 1850s. "When all sentiment seemed to be going against suffrage," this account explained, Truth "rose to address the audience, [and] by her magnetic personality and most unusual speech, she turned the sentiment back toward suffrage." The commentator then directly quoted Truth, who, more than six decades earlier, had boldly asserted: "if de fust woman God ever made was strong enough to turn de whole world upside down, all dese togedder ought to be able to turn it back and get it right side up again; and now since dey is asking to do it, de men better let 'em." After that provocative passage, Adella Hunt Logan took

Adella Hunt Logan with her family. Photo by Arthur P. Bedou, New Orleans, 1913. Collection of Adele Logan Alexander.

the podium to deliver the keynote presentation, a paper entitled "The Present Status of Woman's Suffrage." The session finally closed with the distribution of festive yellow—the official color of the woman suffrage movement—sashes conspicuously emblazoned with the provocative slogan, "Votes for Women."[28]

Some members of the Tuskegee Woman's Club clearly took these continuing programs and other activities that described, explained, and promoted women's political empowerment quite seriously. Certainly Logan did. Margaret Murray Washington, on the other hand, while she never denounced the cause, on at least a few occasions deliberately downplayed the significance of black women's involvement in the quest for an expanded franchise. In 1912, for example, she wrote a letter to a white Kansas suffragist and clubwoman stating her personal conviction that "colored women . . . have done little or nothing . . . for the suffrage movement."[29]

In contrast to Washington's relative neutrality, Adella Hunt Logan had always been an enthusiastic proponent of and participant in all aspects of the suffrage movement, and she attempted to involve herself in as many forums as possible. When NAWSA decided to hold its annual convention in Atlanta, Georgia, in 1895, the organization categorically excluded all African Americans—even NAWSA president Susan B. Anthony's longtime friend and supporter, Frederick Douglass—from its activities on the grounds of "expediency" and in acquiescence to southern custom. Anthony, however, also spoke that same week at Atlanta University, Logan's alma mater. That speech was not Logan's initial exposure to the issue, but her interest was further aroused on that occasion when Anthony proclaimed to her predominantly black audience, "The people who feed and clothe you feel that they have a right to dictate to you. . . . Some men even say to their wives," she continued, "'If you vote, you have to go elsewhere to live!'" Those words seem to have challenged Logan and insured her ongoing commitment both to Anthony personally and especially to her political agenda.[30]

In that same period, Emily Howland, a white northern suffragist and Quaker who frequently visited Tuskegee Institute and made generous financial contributions to the school, became Logan's good friend and even was named godmother to one of her children. Howland, for one, helped to focus Logan's attention on the issues of women's continuing political impotence, and later Logan poignantly wrote her comrade, "So few people look deeply enough into the woman problem to see that it is herself that the suffragist wants to free."[31]

Because Adella Hunt Logan developed such a deep interest in woman suffrage and in the NAWSA as well, Emily Howland sponsored her life membership in the organization. But Logan's role as a nonwhite member often was problematical, contradictory, and sometimes puzzling. In one instance, Emily Howland's politically active niece proposed Logan, whom she had met at Tuskegee Institute, as a speaker for the NAWSA's 1898 national convention in Washington, D.C. In her response to that request, however—notwithstanding the fact that she had been a dedicated abolitionist who usually had supported full political rights for African Americans—Susan B. Anthony revealed both her own apparent biases about blacks' presumed inferiority, plus a reluctance or incapacity to deal forthrightly with issues concerning race. In rejecting Logan as a potential speaker, Anthony wrote: "I would not on any account bring on our platform a woman who had a ten thousandth part of a drop of African blood in her veins, who should prove to be an inferior speaker either as to matter or manner, because it would so militate against our cause. . . . I do not in the slightest shrink from having a colored woman on the platform but I do shrink from having an incompetent one, so unless you know that Miss Logan is one who would astonish the natives, just let her wait until she is more cultured and can do the colored race the greatest possible credit."[32]

The NAWSA's political strategies, which certainly in part were aimed at wooing support for woman suffrage in the southern states, combined with her own personal racial and class prejudice—or at the least, insensitivity—seem to have made Anthony disinclined to invite a little-known African-American woman to sit on the platform at her organization's widely publicized conference in the nation's capitol. On the other hand, the more renowned and always well-spoken Mary Church Terrell (whom Anthony must have considered more "cultured" than Logan, or possibly more likely to "astonish the natives") did attend that gathering. This personal slight notwithstanding, Logan was neither disheartened nor deterred. She made regular contributions to the organization, wrote articles about NACW activities for the NAWSA's newspaper, the *Woman's Journal,* which appeared under the deliberately enigmatic bylines "A. H. L." and "L. H. A.," and attended at least one other NAWSA convention—and that, ironically, in the segregated South. She met Susan B. Anthony on several occasions and retained an enduring and respectful admiration for her. When the famed suffrage leader died in 1906, Logan wrote their mutual friend Emily Howland: "The death of Miss Anthony goes to my heart. Nearly all my life I have regarded her as the most wonderful of American women. It was such a privilege for me to know her."[33]

Adella Hunt Logan never questioned her own identity as a "colored" woman and always lived and worked within the African-American community. Because of her predominantly Anglo-American ancestry, however, she looked white. Her brown hair was long and straight, her skin pale, her nose narrow and lips thin. On some occasions she used her rather misleading physical appearance in pursuing the political goals she advocated for all women. At the NAWSA's second convention in Atlanta in 1901, Logan somehow arranged to have an "off the record" private meeting with Carrie Chapman Catt, the organization's new president. Logan later reported to her friend Emily Howland that after her conversation with Catt, she entered the all-white general session, seating herself discreetly at the back of the meeting hall, where she "could not resist the temptation to stay . . . a while, observing how the 'superior sister' does things." She further (and somewhat sarcastically) wrote, "You know a number of colored women would have done it more intelligently, and yet if they [the white suffragists] had known me [had known, that is, that she was not white], I would have been ordered out in no very gracious manner." Her letter to Howland clearly reveals that Adella Hunt Logan engaged in the surreptitious, and often censured practice known as "passing." At the same time, however, her comments reveal both her pragmatic reasons for doing so and her skeptical views of the racist attitudes and behavior she observed within the country's most significant woman suffrage organization during her incognito attendance at that supposedly—and officially—"all white" event. That 1901 convention was not the only occasion on which Logan "passed" as a white woman. She did so to attend other segregated conferences, when she worked on behalf of woman suffrage in Ohio in 1908, and she patronized "whites' only" railroad cars during her travels as well. It is, however, difficult to evaluate the long-term emotional cost of this sort of deceptive behavior.[34]

Additional evidence reveals other ways that Adella Hunt Logan may have shuttled between the distinctly separate worlds of African Americans and whites. Her personal library included a highly prized four-volume set of *The History of Woman Suffrage*, which Susan B. Anthony herself had warmly and personally inscribed, "because," Anthony wrote, "of my admiration of you and your work." These autographed books are presently housed in the archives at Auburn University, just a few miles east of Tuskegee, but exactly how they got there is not clear. In the early years of the twentieth century, of course, Auburn University was a strictly segregated all-white institution. In that same period, Logan had collected, and then maintained at her home, a substantial collection of materials about suffrage that she distributed among club members, students, and other local colleagues. Since Auburn University has no acquisition records whatsoever for those four particular volumes from Anthony, it seems possible that—just as she always shared books and pamphlets about women's issues with her African-American friends at Tuskegee—Logan also might have loaned her very special treasures to some unidentified white colleague (possibly a faculty wife) who had joined the suffrage club that was organized in the nearby college town of Auburn in 1914. That anonymous woman either did not know that Logan was "colored" or may have been a willing conspirator in a subterfuge that masked the true identity of her outwardly racially ambiguous and politically progressive friend from Tuskegee.[35]

Although Logan dedicated much of her life to her family and her work as a teacher, her residence at Tuskegee Institute, per se, provided her, and others at the school as well, with unique opportunities to meet and interact with many of the nation's leading reformers and suffrage proponents. One of the earliest of these guests was the former abolitionist and renowned composer Julia Ward Howe, who visited the institute in 1894 as part of a wide swing through the South that she made in her capacity as leader of the Association for the Advancement of Women.[36] Almost a decade later, a group from the NAWSA came to the Alabama school, inspired by the prominence of Booker T. Washington and encouraged by Emily Howland, who was both Susan B. Anthony's colleague and a great booster of Tuskegee Institute. The institute's newspaper reported in early 1903 that "we are to be especially favored today with a visit by a number of the most prominent delegates in attendance at the National Suffrage Association which has been in session for a week at New Orleans." That conference in segregated Louisiana officially was restricted to whites only—the vigorous African-American club leader, Sylvanie Williams of New Orleans had especially protested her own exclusion—just as were the previous NAWSA conventions in Atlanta. The white suffragists who journeyed to Tuskegee Institute at that time included Carrie Chapman Catt, Anthony, Howland, and, the *Tuskegee Student* stated, "perhaps ten others." More than fifteen hundred individuals, including "officers, teachers, families, and the entire student body," assembled to welcome the visitors by waving a "sea of snowy handkerchiefs." A number of speakers addressed the crowd, and late that afternoon following an extended program, all of the institute's female students "passed in review before Miss Anthony and received each a hearty hand shake."[37]

In contrast to the supportive environment at Tuskegee Institute, Alabama's white population in the period around the turn of the century was far more than merely apathetic to the issue of woman suffrage. In truth, widespread resistance prevailed. After a brief and limited flurry of prosuffrage activity during the 1890s, attempts to gain the franchise for the state's women virtually disappeared for well over a decade. Furthermore, and certainly another indication of the almost endemic aversion to woman suffrage, for a number of years the NAWSA's widely circulated newspaper, the *Woman's Journal*, had just seven subscribers in the whole state, three of whom were associated with Tuskegee Institute. In addition, in 1900 Adella Hunt Logan became Alabama's first and only life member of the NAWSA. The next woman from the state who acquired a life membership did so well over a decade later.[38]

Notwithstanding the subject's widespread unpopularity among white Alabamans, efforts on behalf of woman suffrage continued in and around the country's most celebrated black educational institution. Representing her school and its woman's club, Adella Hunt Logan lectured widely about suffrage issues—especially as those issues pertained to black women—during the early 1900s. Between 1900 and 1914, she spoke often at conventions of the Alabama Federation of Colored Women's Clubs, the Southern Federation of Colored Women's Clubs, and the NACW. She even served for several years as head of the national organization's department of suffrage. Chairing the resolutions committee at the Alabama Federation's 1913 convention, Logan introduced a stirring proposal that endorsed unrestricted suffrage and optimistically anticipated the time when "our broad country woman shall share with man the responsibility of deciding questions—social, economic, and civic."[39]

She also wrote two significant articles about suffrage directed toward a national audience of her peers. *The Colored American* magazine published the first, "Woman Suffrage," in 1905. In that essay Logan argued that "all governments derive their just powers from the consent of the governed. . . . The power that coerces," she continued, "that controls without consent is unjust." Unwavering in her belief that suffrage was an issue that especially should concern African-American women, she rhetorically asked: "If white American women with all their natural and acquired advantages need the ballot, that right protective of all other rights; if Anglo-Saxons have been helped by it—and they have—how much more do black Americans, male and female, need the strong defense of a vote to secure their right to life, liberty, and the pursuit of happiness?"[40]

Logan's second article, "Colored Women as Voters," appeared in September 1912 as part of a group of essays (including one by Mary Church Terrell) collectively titled "A Woman's Suffrage Symposium" in *Crisis*, the NAACP's popular monthly magazine. W. E. B. Du Bois, that journal's editor, always had been a committed and vocal supporter of an expanded and broadly democratic franchise, and his initial published symposium on the subject was followed by a similar yet more inclusive presentation three years later. In 1912 Logan articulated her strong conviction that black women would be well prepared to vote once they had the chance because "more and more colored women are studying public questions and civics. . . . As they gain information and have experiences in their daily vocations and in their efforts for human betterment," she went on, "they are convinced . . . that their efforts would be more telling if [they] had the vote. . . . Without a vote," Logan continued, a woman "has no voice in educational legislation, and no power to see that her children secure their share of public school funds." She further suggested that African-American women were ready to prove themselves good citizens. In those western states where women already had the ballot, Logan argued, black women were "reported as using it for the uplift of society and the advancement of the State. . . . Women who see that they need the vote see also that the vote needs them," she concluded, "colored women feel keenly that they may help in civic betterment."[41]

Adella Hunt Logan had the opportunity to present her views to a national audience through these articles, but in addition, substantial numbers of educated black professionals frequently went down to Tuskegee, Alabama. In the summer of 1912, for example, a large group of influential African Americans traveled to the institute to attend a conference of the National Medical Association (NMA).[42] At that time, the NMA included not only physicians, but many African-American pharmacists and dentists as well. Alabama, of course, had a sizeable host delegation, and Drs. A. M. Townsend, C. V. Roman, and several others represented the neighboring state of Tennessee. Both Booker T. and Margaret Murray Washington, Adella's husband Warren Logan, and other Tuskegee officials welcomed the visitors, and the stimulating three-day agenda included clinics, lectures, discussions about surgical techniques, public health, infant and child care, and preventive medicine. These symposia, of course, directly reflected the NMA's purposes, goals, and interests. They were, therefore, predictable components of any such medical convention. Supplementing these activities, however, one unexpected and apparently unrelated event, which was planned and presented by the institute's Hospital Aid Society, highlighted the conference's festive welcoming pageant.[43]

Not coincidentally perhaps, the "directrix" of those opening ceremonies was Adella Hunt Logan's oldest daughter, Ruth, the new coordinator of Tuskegee's physical education programs for women. The gala spectacle that Ruth Logan organized featured first-aid demonstrations, folk dancing, and tableaux representing subjects such as "Education" and "Prevention of Disease." The afternoon's highlight, however, was a stirring "Suffragette Parade." A large and enthusiastic group of students marched, and every conference participant and visiting dignitary received program inserts printed with lyrics for a rousing sing-along titled "Just as Well as He." The words had been taken directly from the pages of the *Woman's Journal* and were provided, no doubt, by Adella Hunt Logan. The clever, though rather awkward, stanzas were intended to be sung to the familiar melody "Coming through the Rye":

If a body pays the taxes,
Surely you'll agree
That a body earns the franchise
Whether he or she. . . .

Every man now has the ballot;
None you know have we,
But we have brains and we can use them
Just as well as he.

If a home that has a father
Needs a mother too,
Then every state that has men voters
Needs its women too.[44]

The demonstration featured at that 1912 NMA convention, and other prosuffrage efforts which originated at Tuskegee Institute and concerned acquisition of the franchise for women, reverberated beyond the small group of Tuskegeeites who were members of the local woman's club. In the classroom and through participatory debates and other exercises, Adella Hunt Logan and her colleagues disseminated information about civic affairs generally, and woman suffrage specifically, to a new generation of young people who learned about the positive attributes and operations, as well as the shortcomings, of American democracy. Despite Margaret Murray Washington's limited enthusiasm for the suffrage issue, several Tuskegee Woman's Club members—Logan especially—lectured on the subject in many venues, primarily at gatherings of the NACW and its subsidiaries in the South. A number of influential and highly politicized women, both black and white, also visited Tuskegee. In addition, Logan wrote articles about the importance of votes for women, African-American women in particular, which reached a wide audience through national publications such as *The Colored American* and *Crisis* magazines. Finally, because Tuskegee Institute itself was such a magnet for national organizations, people from the school could advocate woman suffrage at gatherings of influential African Americans who hopefully might then generate even broader support for woman suffrage around the country.

In 1898 Logan had written a poignant letter to her friend Emily Howland in which she stated her intense desire to "see my daughter vote right here in the South," but she died at the age of fifty-two, five years prior to the time when the Tennessee legislature's support insured ratification of the Nineteenth Amendment.[45] In late 1915, Adella Hunt Logan suffered a severe emotional breakdown. Her friend, colleague, and neighbor—black America's most acclaimed leader—Booker T. Washington passed away that fall, throwing Tuskegee into a deep abyss of community mourning. Her own physical health was poor, she was experiencing a difficult menopause, and persistent rumors at the institute suggested that her husband had become romantically involved with a young teacher. In addition to all that, and further intensifying her depression, a woman suffrage referendum had gone down to defeat in Alabama's legislature. On the eve of—and at the very site of—an elaborate memorial service planned for Booker T. Washington, Adella Hunt Logan jumped to her death from a top floor window of the institute's tallest building. A decade earlier Logan had written with macabre foresight about woman's political impotence and other often agonizing frustrations: "She meanwhile stays at home to cry, to swear or to suicide—as she chooses."[46] Her tragic and premature death notwithstanding, some of the seeds that she helped to plant and then nurture managed to survive even in the politically barren soil of Alabama's black belt.

Because he was such a cunning, pragmatic, and opportunistic political operator, Booker T. Washington managed to establish and then maintain some tenuous agreements predicated on mutual self-interest between his famous institute and the white-controlled town of Tuskegee—which, otherwise, of course, was hardly a bastion of racial enlightenment. Washington (whose reputation has been characterized by the accommodationist spirit and content of his 1895 Atlanta Compromise speech, which downplayed the significance of black political rights) rarely has been considered a champion of suffrage of any sort, and on at least one occasion he characterized woman suffrage, specifically, as a "hornet's nest" that he hoped to avoid. Nevertheless, largely as a result of his continuing negotiations with local white officials, Tuskegee remained one of the few jurisdictions in rural Alabama where at least a few African-American men—although admittedly only those associated with the institute who retained unblemished reputations and acquired both property and an education—could vote even during the most repressive decades of Jim Crow rule. But access to the franchise for black men throughout the state deteriorated dramatically during the early decades of the twentieth century. In 1900 Alabama had more than 180,000 eligible black male voters. By 1908 a revised state constitution and further repressive legislative action combined with physical and economic intimidation precipitously slashed that number to fewer than 4,000, and it continued to decline over the ensuing years. At least prior to 1920, however, a disproportionate percentage of those very few African-American men who could and did still vote in the state lived at, and were associated with, Tuskegee Institute. When the opportunity arose, therefore, a small but determined cadre of women from the institute found themselves in a less disadvantaged position than many other black Alabama women, and they prepared themselves to act in accordance with their club's long-standing initiatives and also to follow their male colleagues' example.[47]

Over the years Adella Hunt Logan influenced many young women at Tuskegee, and one special protégée was a teacher named Bess Bolden Walcott, who arrived at the institute in 1907 from Oberlin College in Ohio, which she described many years later as a "hot bed of suffrage activity." Like her mentor, Walcott became actively involved in the Tuskegee Woman's Club. Logan and Walcott's common devotion to community uplift and gaining the franchise for women helped to forge strong bonds between them. Although Adella Hunt Logan died long before her oldest daughter could vote, her friend Walcott remembered her own experiences just after the Nineteenth Amendment became the law of the land and Alabama grudgingly complied with that national initiative and removed its legislative barriers to woman suffrage. One day during that autumn of 1920, she and three female associates at the school steeled their nerves and buggied the short distance into the town of Tuskegee. "When the four of us went in to register," she recalled, "the clerk said to me, 'Miz Walcott, I wish the white ladies here in town were as interested in voting as you women from out at the Institute'" as he completed the paperwork that was required to make them registered voters in Macon County, Alabama.[48] That determination to exercise the franchise may have been one of the lasting legacies of Adella Hunt Logan and the Tuskegee Woman's Club, which had helped to establish a foundation for suffrage among African-American women in the Deep South.

Tuskegee Institute's dowager queen, the widowed Margaret Murray Washington, however, seems to have remained both ambivalent and cautious about woman suffrage even as late as 1920. She, along with Jennie Dee Moton, the wife of the school's new principal, and six other prominent African-American women had the unique opportunity to attend what was probably the first openly interracial conference of southern female reformers, which had convened that summer in Memphis, Tennessee. Washington and Moton, however, declined to support the uncompromising language concerning votes for all women—especially black women—that the other African-American delegates to that gathering all rigorously advanced. Concerning the reluctance of the two conservative women from Tuskegee, Fisk's outspoken Minnie L. Crosthwait bluntly asserted: "I can not agree with them on this question . . . because I am so sick and tired of dodging and parleying over things I know to be right."[49]

Crosthwait's sentiments, rather than Washington's, most likely predominated in the black female community throughout the South. In addition, the statement made to Bess Bolden Walcott by that astonishingly accommodating white male courthouse clerk in Tuskegee, Alabama, further illustrates one problem that African-American women faced and, ironically, may have generated themselves in the period after 1920. A number of white people all over the South had correctly speculated that their women cared about voting far less than black women did. In fact, only a few years before, the ever astute Frances Ellen Watkins Harper had prophetically observed that many white southerners particularly feared "the colored vote in those states where it is likely to equal or exceed the white woman's vote." Several decades earlier, however, even Adella Hunt Logan had privately expressed her own apprehensions that black women were "a very needy class . . . who are slow to believe that they might get any help from the ballot." But when voting rights for women throughout the country became a reality, African-American women in one southern community after another went out and attempted to register and cast their votes in proportionately greater numbers than their white female counterparts. In Nashville, for example, twenty-five hundred black women registered in 1920, and others like them prepared to go to the polls all through the South. Apprehensions about being outnumbered as voters by black women even may have stimulated a retaliatory prosuffrage backlash among white women, and the white South did not hesitate to strike back.[50]

W. E. B. Du Bois, the NAACP leader, *Crisis* editor, and long-time supporter of both African-American and woman suffrage, once correctly predicted that "southern white women, who are one of the most repressed and enslaved groups of modern, civilized women will help willingly to disfranchise Negroes." He also commented that in response to the new and perceived challenge to white hegemony, "the South proposes to keep colored women from voting in exactly the same way in which it had disfranchised colored men." Indeed, after 1920 the white community eagerly endorsed, embraced, and then rigorously employed many sorts of "legal" and extralegal exclusionary tactics—such as physical and economic intimidation, poll taxes, property, educational, and "character" requirements, and, finally, the "white" Democratic primary—that were all designed to keep both black men *and* black women politically disempowered. Many white southerners never wanted to see any females whatsoever become enfranchised, black women least of all, but when gender alone no longer could be used to deny the franchise to American women as a whole, African-American women still encountered massive barriers to equality because of race. The deteriorating political climate during this period recalled the prescient sentiments and fears of the abolitionist and reformer Frederick Douglass, who, many years earlier, had argued that the black woman needed political power to avoid a wide variety of abuses, "not because she is a woman, but because she is black."[51]

The Nineteenth Amendment to the Constitution of the United States gave women the right to vote, but for many more decades most black women in Tuskegee, the entire state of Alabama, neighboring Tennessee, and elsewhere in the South as well rarely were able to take advantage of that hard-won privilege. The old obstacles to political participation that they once had faced because of sex finally had tumbled, but the almost insurmountable barriers they came up against simply because they were not white remained rigidly in place—often enforced by stringent and even brutal means—at least until the great changes brought about through the titanic efforts of African Americans (and certainly some whites as well) in the Civil Rights movement and passage of the historic federal Civil Rights Acts during the "second American revolution" of the 1960s. Dorothy Height, president of the National Council of Negro Women, for example, has pointed out that almost half a century after women acquired the vote, "it took lynching, bombing, the Civil Rights movement, and the Voting Rights Act . . . to get it for Black women."[52]

In state after southern state during the turbulent 1950s and 1960s, women such as Tuskegee's Jessie Guzman, Kathleen Neal Cleaver, and Gwen Patton; bus boycott leader Rosa Parks, and Jo Ann Robinson from the Montgomery Women's Political Council; Fisk's intrepid Diane Nash; and Septima Clark, who organized numerous voter registration efforts from the mountain campus of Tennessee's Highlander Folk School, all recognized the importance of both acquiring and then exercising the franchise. Whenever and wherever they could do so, these and other African-American women—rural and urban, young and old, lettered and unschooled, from all walks of life—stood up and sat-in, organized, marched, cooked, prayed, helped to educate the politically disempowered in their communities, ran for office, and braved the wrath of many vengeful and intransigent white southerners as they went unhesitatingly to the polls where they attempted to register and then vote in numbers that were proportionately higher than those of either white women or black men. Perhaps, even half a century later, they still could hear echoes of Adella Hunt Logan's voice, adamantly asserting that "our broad country woman shall share with man the responsibility of deciding questions—social, economic, and civic—which have to do not only with her own welfare, but with the deepest interests of those dearer to her even than herself."[53]

In some ways, Tennessee's daughters, Ida B. Wells-Barnett, Mary Church Terrell, and Minnie Crosthwait, plus Adella Hunt Logan, Bess Bolden Walcott, and other pioneering members of the Tuskegee Women's Club all helped to lead the way concerning black political activism and the significant, diverse, and expanding roles that black women soon would come to play in the American South. During the Civil Rights movement, however, numerous dauntless African-American women in that region may have worked more diligently, and surely they encountered even greater physical perils as they moved with unflinching determination toward their goal of creating a better world for their children by trying to eliminate at least some of the enduring, demeaning, and gross inequities of southern society.

Notes

The paper from which this chapter has evolved was first presented at a conference, "Afro-American Women and the Vote: 1837 to 1965," in 1987 at Amherst, Mass. A related essay appears in Mary Martha Thomas, ed., *Stepping Out of the Shadows: Women in Alabama from 1819 to 1990* (Tuscaloosa: University of Alabama Press, 1995).

1. Ida B. Wells-Barnett, "How Enfranchisement Stops Lynching," *Original Rights Magazine*, June 1910, 42–53, and Mary Church Terrell, "Woman Suffrage and the 15th Amendment," *Crisis* (Sept. 1915): 191. For more information on Terrell, see "Mary Eliza Church Terrell," *Black Women in America: An Historic Encyclopedia*, ed. Darlene Clark Hine (Brooklyn, N.Y.: Carlson Publishing Inc., 1993), 2: 1157–59, and on Wells-Barnett, see "Ida Bell Wells-Barnett," *Black Women in America*, 2: 1242–46. The brutal 1892 lynching of a Memphis postman and prominent black merchant, Thomas Moss—a close friend of both women—was the tragedy that first politicized both Terrell and Wells-Barnett. Paula Giddings, *When and Where I Enter: The Impact of Black Women on Race and Sex in America* (New York: William Morrow and Company, 1984), 19–20, 108.

2. Giddings, *When and Where I Enter*, 108. For more information about Washington, see "Margaret Murray Washington," *Black Women in America*, 2: 1233–35. Booker T. Washington to Washington Gladden, July 30, 1912, in Louis R. Harlan and Raymond W. Smock, eds., *The Booker T. Washington Papers* (Urbana: University of Illinois Press, 1981), 11: 566.

3. Dorothy C. Salem, *To Better Our World: Black Women in Organized Reform, 1890–1920*, in *Black Women in United States History*, ed. Darlene Clark Hine (Brooklyn, N.Y.: Carlson Publishing, Inc., 1990), 14: 39; Adella Hunt Logan to Emily Howland, Nov. 13, 1899, Emily Howland Papers, Cornell University, Ithaca, N.Y. (hereafter cited as EH Papers); Adella Hunt Logan, "Woman Suffrage," *The Colored American* (Sept. 1905): 487–89, and Logan, "Colored Women as Voters," *Crisis* (Sept. 1912): 212-13. For more information, see "Adella Hunt Logan," *Black Women in America*, 1: 729–31. Like Terrell, Wells-Barnett, Washington, and Logan, most early leaders of the "colored" woman's reform movement were born in the decade of the 1860s. Marjorie Spruill Wheeler, *New Women of the New South: The Leaders of the Woman Suffrage Movement in the Southern States* (New York: Oxford University Press, 1993), is immensely readable and insightful and provides the most complete information to date about white southern suffragists.

4. My essay owes a great deal to the work of Rosalyn Terborg-Penn, especially her remarkable study, "Afro-Americans in the Struggle for Woman Suffrage," (Ph.D. diss., Howard University, 1978), which remains the definitive work on this subject. Unless otherwise specified, general information about the involvement of African Americans in the suffrage movement has been gleaned from Terborg-Penn's dissertation. Terborg-Penn first introduced me to the suffrage activities of my paternal grandmother, Adella Hunt Logan of Tuskegee Institute. Terborg-Penn and a group of other historians—many of them female and many of them African American—are now addressing the critical roles that black women played as reformers and activists. Because of this new body of work, the profession can no longer legitimately address these issues and report only activities within the white community. See also Rosalyn Terborg-Penn, "Discrimination against Afro-American Women in the Woman's Movement, 1830–1920," in Sharon Harley and Rosalyn Terborg-Penn, eds., *The Afro-American Woman: Struggles and Images* (Port Washington, N.Y.: Kennikat Press, 1978), and Adele Logan Alexander, "How I Discovered My Grandmother, and the Truth about Black Women and the Suffrage Movement," *Ms.*, (Nov. 1983): 29–33.

5. Terborg-Penn, "Afro-Americans in Woman Suffrage," 31–39. Terborg-Penn, unfortunately, cannot identify the black woman who went to Seneca Falls. See also "Maria W. Stewart," *Black Women in America*, 2: 1113–14, and "Sojourner Truth," *Black Women in America*, 2: 1172–76.

6. Terborg-Penn, "Afro-Americans in Woman Suffrage," 71–75, 104–5.

7. Giddings, *When and Where I Enter*, 66.

8. Terborg-Penn, "Afro-Americans in Woman Suffrage," 80–90, 95–97.

9. Rayford Logan, *The Negro in American Life and Thought: The Nadir, 1877–1901* (New York: Dial Press, 1954). Rayford Logan was not related to Adella Hunt Logan.

10. Giddings, *When and Where I Enter*, 122. See "Frances Ellen Watkins Harper," *Black Women in America*, 1: 532–36.

11. There had been a number of women's clubs dedicated to social reform in the free black community even prior to the Civil War. The establishment and rise of the NACW paralleled the overall reform movement that swept the country in the 1890s. "National Association of Colored Women," in *Black Women in America*, 2: 842–51; Mary Martha Thomas, *The New Woman in Alabama: Social Reforms and Suffrage, 1890–1920* (Tuscaloosa: University of Alabama Press, 1992), 123; Ruby M. Kendrick, "'They Also Serve': The National Association of Colored Women, Inc., 1895–1954," in *Black Women in United States History*, 7: 817–24; Salem, *To Better Our World*, especially 26–27, 41–43, and Giddings, *When and Where I Enter*, 24, 29, 92, 108. Wells-Barnett became embroiled in conflicts with a number of the more conservative members of her own race, but her militancy and intensity especially outraged many whites. Giddings cites a *New York Times* article characterizing her as a "slanderous and nasty-minded mulatress," seeking "income" rather than "outcome." With large black populations in several nearby cities, Fisk's location in Nashville, plus other active "colored" women's clubs in both Memphis and Chat-

tanooga, Tennessee, was a natural choice for this 1897 NACW convention. Coincidentally, the first Tennessee woman suffrage convention—a segregated all-white event as far as can be determined—was also held in Nashville that same summer.

12. Salem, *To Better Our World*, 38–41, and Terborg-Penn, "Afro-Americans in Woman Suffrage," 21, 27. See also "Lugenia Burns Hope," *Black Women in America*, 1: 573–79, and "Anna Julia Haywood Cooper," *Black Women in America*, 1: 275–81.

13. Thomas, *New Woman in Alabama*, 123–31; *Woman's Journal*, Apr. 4, 1903, and Dec. 12, 1913. Wheeler, *New Women of the New South*, discusses the controversial and contradictory role of Henry Blackwell, the former abolitionist.

14. *Crisis* (Sept. 1912): 199. Most of this issue of *Crisis* was devoted to the topic of votes for women.

15. Giddings, *When and Where I Enter*, 127–28, and Salem, *To Better Our World*, 127–29; *Woman's Journal*, Mar. 15, 1913; Logan to Emily Howland, Feb. 10, 1913, EH Papers.

16. Terborg-Penn, "Afro-Americans in Woman Suffrage," 121–22.

17. This does not suggest that African-American women of the more privileged classes were any more vulnerable to sexual innuendo and abuse than less advantaged women, but only that they were more able to express their outrage. They had at least some outlets for their protests, and their words were more often recorded. Wheeler, *New Women of the New South*, chap. 4, "Southern Suffragists and 'the Negro Problem.'"

18. Ibid., 286–94.

19. Logan, "Colored Women as Voters," stated: "In all, the colored woman is taking part, not as fully as she will when the question is less of an experiment, not as heartily as she will when her horizon broadens, but she bears her part" (213). This discussion does not imply that prosuffragists were any more opposed to black enfranchisement than other white southerners; if anything, they were probably less intransigent.

20. "The Tuskegee Woman's Club, 1950–51" (including information about that group's early history), in Margaret Murray Washington Papers, Tuskegee Institute Library (hereafter cited as MMW Papers). Most information about the Tuskegee Woman's Club is found in this collection, much of it not clearly identified. Cynthia Neverdon-Morton has written extensively about women's activities at Tuskegee Institute in "Self-Help Programs as Educative Activities of Black Women in the South, 1895–1925: Focus on Four Key Areas," *Journal of Negro Education* 51 (3) (1982): 207–21, and in *Afro-American Women of the South and the Advancement of the Race, 1895–1925* (Knoxville: University of Tennessee Press, 1989).

21. Thomas, *New Woman in Alabama*, 123.

22. Ibid., 125–26. Thomas points out that several white-controlled newspapers in the state did, however, run separate columns written by white female suffragists that presented dissenting opinions. See also Lee N. Allen, "The Woman Suffrage Movement in Alabama, 1910–1920," *Alabama Review* 11 (Apr. 1958): 83–99. *Woman's Journal*, May 22, 1901.

23. *Woman's Era* (Oct. 1895), in Mary Church Terrell Papers, Library of Congress (hereafter cited as MCT Papers). Louis J. Harlan, *Booker T. Washington: The Making of a Black Leader, 1901–1915* (New York: Oxford University Press, 1983), includes information about the backgrounds of some of Tuskegee Institute's female faculty members and wives of the school's officials who were members of the Tuskegee Woman's Club.

24. *Woman's Era* (Oct. 1895), MCT Papers and MMW Papers. On a number of occasions, *Woman's Journal* carried notes about activities at Tuskegee Institute. On September 19, 1896, for example, it reported that the Tuskegee Woman's Club held "a weekly conference with over four hundred women, some of them walking sixteen miles to be present." Glenda Elizabeth Gilmore, "Gender and Jim Crow: Women and the Politics of White Supremacy in North Carolina, 1896–1920," (Ph.D. diss., University of North Carolina at Chapel Hill, 1992), argues persuasively that, at least in North Carolina, African-American clubwomen "tilted" the industrial education ideology, epitomized by "the Tuskegee model," turning it "into a self-help endeavor." For example, Gilmore says, "cooking courses became not vocational classes, but nutrition courses" (330).

25. Adele Logan Alexander, *Ambiguous Lives: Free Women of Color in Rural Georgia* (Fayetteville: University of Arkansas Press, 1991), see especially chap. 4, "On Hunt's Hill," which details the lives of members of the Hunt family during Reconstruction; *Bulletin of the Atlanta University*, Dec. 1895. In its earliest years, Atlanta University employed only white teachers from the North. Adella Hunt was one of the first African Americans offered employment there.

26. Adella Hunt Logan to Booker T. Washington, Nov. 3, 1900, Booker T. Washington Papers, Library of Congress (hereafter cited as BTW Papers), and *Woman's Journal*, Apr. 4, 1914.

27. In 1888, Adella Hunt married Warren Logan, whose close association with Booker T. Washington dated back to their boyhood days at Hampton Institute. Warren Logan, the school's treasurer and second-ranking official, served as "Acting Principal" during Washington's many absences from Tuskegee and became a member of the school's Board of Trustees. Salem, *To Better Our World*, 39. *Tuskegee Student*, June 5, 1909, and June 28, 1913; "Tenth Annual Report of the Tuskegee Woman's Club, 1905," BTW Papers.

28. *Tuskegee Student*, Apr. 3, 1915. Terborg-Penn, "Discrimination against Afro-American Women," 20, states that many white women opposed Truth's participation at that 1851 meeting, fearing that her presence would suggest that their cause—woman's rights—was "mixed with abolition and niggers." The modern-day equivalent of the "lantern show" would be a slide presentation. Photographic images were projected onto a screen or the wall of a meeting hall with illumination provided by a rudimentary electric projection device.

29. Margaret Murray Washington to Lucy Brown Johnston, May 21, 1912, in Harlan and Smock, eds., *Booker T. Washington Papers*, 11: 539. Washington's letter did not really oppose woman suffrage, but rather argued that most African Americans, male

and female, had other priorities. Black women, she continued, would "try hard" to "take our stand . . . when the country reaches the point of giving the women equal rights with all other citizens."

30. *Woman's Journal,* Mar. 2 and 16, 1895, reported that during the previous month the white Alabama suffragist Ellen Stephens Hildreth had visited Tuskegee Institute and reported that Booker T. Washington was "doing wonders for the race." There is no indication as to whether or not she might have met Adella Hunt Logan or discussed woman suffrage at that time. There are suspicions, but no hard proof of Logan's possible interaction with white Alabama suffragists. Atlanta University, where Logan graduated in 1881 and then received an honorary M.A. degree in 1905, was one of the first schools for African Americans established in the South following the Civil War. Thomas, *New Woman in Alabama,* 124; *Bulletin of Atlanta University,* Mar. 1895. Anthony's reference here to those "who clothe and feed you" referred to black men—fathers and husbands—rather than to white people who might have been employers.

31. Logan to Howland, Mar. 6, 1906, EH Papers. Emily Howland was a reformer and suffragist who may have been somewhat paternalistic, but was, nonetheless, a genuine friend to African Americans—especially African-American women—as evidenced, in part, by her extensive correspondence with Logan. Logan's second son was christened Paul Howland, and one of her letters refers to Emily Howland as "the fairy godmother." See also Judith Colucci Breault, *The World of Emily Howland: Odyssey of a Humanitarian* (Millbrae, Calif.: Les Femmes, 1974).

32. NAWSA Convention Proceedings, 1900, Schlesinger Library, Radcliffe College, and Susan B. Anthony to Isabel Howland, Oct. 5, 1897, Rachel Avery-Susan B. Anthony Papers, University of Rochester Archives. Ironically, Anthony herself, although an accomplished speaker, had less education and arguably less "culture" than did Logan. A member of a moderately privileged family who had been well educated at Atlanta University, Logan had been teaching English, debate, and rhetoric for almost two decades at the time of the exchange between Howland and Anthony. Anthony's views and actions concerning African Americans have been widely debated. See, for example, Kathleen Barry, *Susan B. Anthony: A Biography of a Singular Feminist* (New York: Ballantine Books, 1988); Ellen Carol DuBois, ed., *Elizabeth Cady Stanton, Susan B. Anthony: Correspondence, Writings, Speeches* (New York: Schocken Books, 1981), and Giddings, *When and Where I Enter.*

33. Logan probably never became aware of the disparaging tone and content of Anthony's letter to Emily Howland's niece. Her two articles about NACW activities appeared in the *Woman's Journal* on Jan. 26, 1901, and Jan. 17, 1903. Logan, or someone close to her, must have sent other "news" items about her to *Woman's Journal.* On July 4, 1903, for example, that paper reported that Logan had received an honorary master's degree from Atlanta University. Then, on Aug. 6, 1911, it acknowledged her contribution to a memorial fund honoring Susan B. Anthony. Logan to Howland, Mar. 19, 1906, EH Papers. In addition to her generally warm associations with both Terrell and Douglass, Anthony also had extended contacts and a friendly correspondence with

Wells-Barnett. I have assumed that Logan used these "initials only" bylines in the *Woman's Journal* so that she could more readily "pass" and could remain less readily identifiable as an African American at ostensibly segregated suffrage activities.

34. Logan to Howland, Dec. 1, 1901, EH Papers. I learned from my mother that *her* mother, my maternal grandmother, who also looked white, accompanied Adella Hunt Logan, my paternal grandmother, to segregated, all-white woman suffrage meetings in the early 1900s. Logan family members also revealed that they sometimes traveled in "whites only" railroad coaches. See Alexander, "How I Discovered My Grandmother." Like a number of other suffrage leaders, Carrie Chapman Catt was torn between a rather tolerant personal philosophy about race and the espousal of positions that she believed were more politically expedient. Catt stated, for example, "It is little wonder that the North is beginning to question the wisdom of the indiscriminate enfranchisement of the Negro" in *Woman's Journal*, Feb. 20, 1904; but less than a year earlier, on Apr. 25, 1903, in that same newspaper, she had responded to one of Belle Kearney's more racist tirades by arguing, "The Anglo-Saxon is the dominant race today, but things may change. The race that will be dominant through the ages is the one that proves itself the most worthy."

35. The existence of these volumes was revealed to me by Ann D. Gordon at the Susan B. Anthony Papers Project. *History of Woman Suffrage*, vol. 1, inscribed by Susan B. Anthony to Adella Hunt Logan, Feb. 15, 1902. Allen W. Jones and others at the Auburn University archives showed me the four books and provided information about the 1914 founding of the woman suffrage club at their institution.

36. *Tuskegee Student*, Aug. 24, 1894. *Woman's Journal*, Sept. 9, 1894, also reported that Howe spent a "day of visitation" at Tuskegee Institute.

37. *Tuskegee Student*, Mar. 28 and Apr. 4, 1903. As another indicator of Anthony's elitist views about African Americans, following this side trip to Tuskegee, she sent the school a small contribution earmarked for a program to teach its young women how to make brooms. A letter from Sylvanie Williams in the *Woman's Journal*, Apr. 18, 1903, cryptically mentions that although Williams herself could not attend, the NACW, in fact, *was* represented at the convention in New Orleans. Perhaps Logan also "passed" on that occasion in order to attend the meeting. Williams, however, did get to meet Susan B. Anthony that week when Anthony visited New Orleans's black Phillis Wheatley Club, as noted in Terborg-Penn, "Discrimination against Afro-American Women," 24. No evidence suggests that any African-American woman attended NAWSA's 1914 national convention in Nashville, Tennessee.

38. Allen, "Woman Suffrage in Alabama," 87–93, and Thomas, *New Woman in Alabama*, chaps. 6 and 7. NAWSA Convention Proceedings show that Logan became a life member in 1900. Bossie O'Brien Hundley, a white Alabama suffragist, obtained her life membership in 1913.

39. Programs from a number of conferences held by the Alabama Federation of Colored Women's Clubs, Southern Federation of Colored Women's Clubs, and Na-

tional Association of Colored Women, in MMW Papers; *Southern Workman* 11 (43) (1912): 534–35. Thomas, *New Woman in Alabama*, 87–88.

40. Logan, "Woman Suffrage," 488–89. This article also includes one surprising and, for Logan, inconsistent note. Although most of her writings support a broadly based and nondiscriminatory universal franchise, this particular piece reveals a degree of elitist bias as she expressed her frustration that "the native born Chinaman can vote in California but the late Mrs. [Leland] Stanford [the benefactor of the university bearing her name] could not."

41. Logan, "Colored Women as Voters," 213, and Terrell, "The Justice of Woman Suffrage," both reprinted in part 2 of this volume. Thomas, *New Woman in Alabama*, 87, provides an excellent analysis of the evolution of Logan's thinking about suffrage. It is significant that Logan, who was Booker T. Washington's next-door neighbor, contributed on several occasions to the NAACP's journal, *Crisis*, which was edited by Washington's most outspoken nemesis, W. E. B. Du Bois. There are few examples of such open apostasy within Washington's inner circle. Terrell, though a Washington friend, also managed to maintain an association with Du Bois. Wells-Barnett, on the other hand, moved more in the direction of the Du Bois camp (although they, too, had sharp differences) and became yet another thorn in Washington's side.

42. National Medical Association (NMA) Convention Program, Aug. 1912, BTW Papers. The NMA was founded in the 1890s when African-American medical practitioners were denied membership in the all-white American Medical Association (AMA). These practices of virtual racial exclusion by the AMA continued into the 1950s.

43. *Tuskegee Student*, Dec. 16, 1911, and Dec. 14, 1912, reported that Adella Hunt Logan was president of the Hospital Aid Society. NMA Convention Program, 1912, BTW Papers. Although a number of African-American women had entered the medical professions, none seems to have had any official duties at this particular NMA convention.

44. Ruth Logan was born in 1891 and had graduated with a degree in physical education from Boston's Sargent College in 1911. Her future husband, Dr. Eugene Percy Roberts, was a featured participant at this convention. NMA Convention Program, 1912, BTW Papers.

45. Logan to Howland, Jan. 24, 1898, EH Papers. Logan's daughter referred to in this letter was the same Ruth who organized the "suffragette parade" in 1912. After her mother's death, Ruth Logan married and moved to New York City where she became a lifelong reformer and activist in Republican party politics. See "Ruth Logan Roberts," in *Black Women in America*, 2: 986.

46. Logan, "Woman Suffrage," 488.

47. Booker T. Washington to Monroe Nathan Work, May 3, 1911, in Harlan and Smock, eds., *Booker T. Washington Papers*, 11: 126. Thomas, *New Woman in Alabama*, 202. Gilmore, "Gender and Jim Crow," suggests that the antisuffrage views of some

southern, middle-class, African-American men were grounded in their fears that black women who tried to vote would face the same dangers and indignities that black men had long encountered. Like W. E. B. Du Bois, however, many black women seem to have believed that white men would *not* greet them "with violence at the polls, since the justification for violence was protecting white women from sexual threats" (442, 444). Interview by the author with Bess Bolden Walcott, Dec. 1983.

48. Unlike Tennessee, the Alabama legislature did not ratify the Nineteenth Amendment. Walcott interview.

49. Gilmore, "Gender and Jim Crow," 412–15. Walcott did not name the three associates who went with her to register in 1920. It seems likely, however, that if either Washington or Moton—as prominent as they both were at Tuskegee—had been among them, she would have said so.

50. Logan to Howland, Jan. 24, 1898, EH Papers; Terborg-Penn, "Afro-Americans in Woman Suffrage," 319–22, and Giddings, *When and Where I Enter,* 162; Gilmore, "Gender and Jim Crow," 450. Gilmore asserts that black women, in great numbers, attempted to vote in 1920, especially in Georgia and Louisiana.

51. Wheeler, *New Women of the New South,* 100; Giddings, *When and Where I Enter,* 67, 165.

52. Giddings, *When and Where I Enter,* 308. See also "Dorothy Irene Height," in *Black Women in America,* 1: 552–54. Gilmore, "Gender and Jim Crow," chap. 8, "Finding the Fault Line of White Supremacy: Black Women and Ballots in 1920," provides a thorough analysis of the resistance to enfranchisement that black women encountered in North Carolina.

53. Jacqueline Jones, *Labor of Love, Labor of Sorrow: Black Women, Work and the Family, from Slavery to the Present* (New York: Random House, 1985), 276, 283–86; Giddings, *When and Where I Enter,* 277, 280, and Donna Langston, "The Women of Highlander," in *Black Women in United States History,* 16: 145–67; Thomas, *New Woman in Alabama,* 88. For more information about Cleaver, see "Kathleen Neal Cleaver," *Black Women in America,* 1: 252; on Parks, see "Rosa Parks," *Black Women in America,* 2: 907–9; on Robinson, see "Jo Ann Gibson Robinson," *Black Women in America,* 2: 988–89; on Nash, see "Diane Nash," *Black Women in America,* 2: 834–35, and on Clark, see "Septima Poinsette Clark," *Black Women in America,* 1: 249–52. For a good account of Tuskegeeites' participation in the Civil Rights movement of the 1950s and 1960s, see Robert J. Norrell, *Reaping the Whirlwind: The Civil Rights Movement in Tuskegee* (New York: Random House, 1986); see also James Forman, *Sammy Younge, Jr.: The First Black College Student to Die in the Black Liberation Movement* (New York: Grove Press, 1968), and Bernard Taper, *Gomillion versus Lightfoot: The Tuskegee Gerrymander Case* (New York: McGraw Hill, 1962). Taylor Branch, *Parting the Waters: America in the King Years, 1954–63* (New York: Simon and Schuster, 1988), interweaves a substantial amount of information about black women in the Civil Rights movement.

5

Beyond the Ballot:
The Radical Vision of the Antisuffragists

Anastatia Sims

"Victorious movements record their history," wrote Carrie Chapman Catt and Nettie Rogers Shuler in 1923; "vanquished ones rarely do." Thus Catt and Shuler, along with other veterans of the seventy-two-year campaign to win votes for women, produced numerous books and articles detailing their struggle, while most antisuffragists remained silent. Since the antis (as they were called) refused to speak for themselves in the aftermath of their defeat, historians have had to rely heavily on the unflattering portraits the victors painted of their opponents—accounts that emphasize adjectives like "sinister" and "unscrupulous" and "vile."[1]

The antis were the villains in the suffrage drama, and they played their part well. Their alliances with liquor manufacturers, railroad companies, and cotton mill owners linked them to political corruption, dishonest business practices, and exploitative labor policies. Their dire predictions that woman suffrage would destroy the home and family and, in the words of one opponent, "ring the death-knell of modern civilization," made them easy to ridicule at the time and sound downright absurd to modern ears. Their devotion to states' rights and white supremacy places them in the category of losers who, by current standards, deserved to lose. While acknowledging their significance, then, it is also tempting to treat them as narrow-minded reactionaries who were unable to envision a role for women that reached beyond the traditional boundaries of domesticity.[2]

But the antis cannot be dismissed so easily. An analysis of the arguments against suffrage in general, and against the federal amendment in particular, suggests an alternative interpretation. By 1920, opponents of the Nineteenth (or Susan B. Anthony) Amendment had a wider vision of its implications than some of its advocates. Unlike many white suffragists, who had come to regard the vote as the capstone of the women's rights movement, white antisuffragists, especially those in the South, saw it as the harbinger of more radical reforms. The Nineteenth Amendment, they believed, raised questions that extended far beyond the immediate issue of enfranchising women. They predicted that if it passed, it would unleash forces that would rip apart the fabric of racial and gender relations. The antis looked beyond the ballot to the potentially revolutionary consequences of votes for women.

Opposition to woman suffrage was born along with the suffrage movement itself. To many nineteenth-century Americans, the idea of women voting seemed ludicrous, and most people refused to take the early suffragists seriously. Opponents attempted to organize for the first time in Washington, D.C., in the early 1870s. As the suffrage movement gained momentum, the antis stepped up their activities. In 1911, female antis in the Northeast formed the National Association Opposed to Woman Suffrage (NAOWS). By 1916, it had branches in twenty-five states and claimed three hundred and fifty thousand members. Ad hoc committees, leagues, and associations for both men and women appeared in states where suffrage legislation was being considered. The antisuffrage organizations were never as large or as structured as the National American Woman Suffrage Association. Antisuffrage was less a cohesive movement than a loose coalition of forces with a common goal. But the antis succeeded in keeping their ideas in the public mind, and in setting the terms of the debate over votes for women.[3]

The antis assumed that the battle over woman suffrage was the opening round in a full-scale revolution in relations between the sexes. They recognized that the demand for the ballot challenged the distinction between public (masculine) and private (feminine) spheres that was the foundation of white, middle-class gender relations. As antisuffrage pamphleteer Emily Bissell explained, "The vote is part of man's work. Ballot-box, cartridge box, jury box, sentry box all go together in his part of life. Woman cannot step in and take the responsibilities and duties of voting without assuming his place very largely." If women were accepted as the equals of men in politics, they might also expect economic and social equality. They might reject domesticity and seek to enter "male" professions (as, in fact, some women were already doing). If they refused to accept male dominance in the public realm, women might question men's authority at home as well. The Reverend Albert Taylor Bledsoe, writing in the *Southern Review* in 1871, cited the example of ancient

Rome to demonstrate the consequences of women's rights. Quoting from the work of historian Edward Hartpole Lecky, Bledsoe argued that when Roman women won legal independence, "the principles of co-equal partnership" replaced "autocracy" in marriage. Later anti literature echoed the same theme. "Woman suffrage," wrote Isaac Lockhart Peebles in 1920, "wants the wife to be as much the ruler as the husband, if not the chief ruler."[4]

The antis opposed woman suffrage because they saw it as one plank in a wide-ranging feminist platform. Suffragists repelled the anti attack by retreating from feminism, at least in public. They called the anti charges that women would use public power to restructure private relationships absurd. Increasingly, the moderate suffragists who came to dominate the movement in the twentieth century insisted that they were content with their jobs as wives and mothers and wanted the ballot in order to fulfill their domestic duties more effectively. They hoped, as well, to impose "feminine" standards of purity, morality, and cooperation on a corrupt, competitive political system. Many suffragists believed the vote would enable women to apply their homemaking skills to "public housekeeping" in ways that would benefit women themselves and society as a whole. However, they did not expect enfranchisement to lead to a radical redefinition of gender roles. They argued, as Professor Jean Elshtain wrote in an essay published in 1982, that "Women would use the vote to change society, but the vote would not change women."[5]

While the antis predicted that political equality might enhance woman's power in the private sphere, they also feared (ironically) that it would diminish her status in public. Anticipating the arguments some former suffragists would use against the Equal Rights Amendment in the 1920s, the antis warned that legal and political equality would eradicate laws designed to protect women. Women would have to pay alimony and serve on juries. Legislation regulating the wages and hours of working women would be struck down. "To treat women exactly as men," wrote NAOWS president Josephine Jewell Dodge, "is to deny all the progress through evolution which has been made by an increasing specialization in function. Woman suffrage in its last analysis is a retrogressive movement."[6]

Although neither side would admit it, antis and suffragists grappled with the same dilemma: how could they assert women's equality with men while simultaneously celebrating the differences between the sexes? The antis portrayed themselves as the true champions of women's equality. Rejecting the popular notion that woman was "man's superior and not his equal," Dodge declared, "Many women are more intelligent, more moral than many men, but the morality and intelligence of women and men of the same opportunities and environment strike about the same average." Dodge and other anti-theorists accused suffragists of mistaking difference for inequality. "Sex equality does not mean identity of function," Annie Riley Hale wrote. She went on to defend the economic value of housework. "Material home comfort is a marketable commodity, which when furnished in hotels, clubs, and boarding houses is rated rather high," she asserted; "the fact that a woman is providing it for her own husband and children instead of the public does not in the least alter the economic side of it." Hale also criticized feminists for lionizing men and devaluing women: "The insane craving to imitate all his performances betrays a slavish admiration of the male creature that but ill accords with their [the feminists'] sometimes rancorous indictment of his selfishness and tyranny. It also betrays a contempt for woman and woman's work that is well-nigh pathological in its distorted sense of social values." Hale would doubtless have been astonished to learn that some radical feminists were making the same argument, chiding their sisters for judging themselves by male standards.[7]

While women in the antisuffrage movement affirmed female equality, they also believed that if women tried to compete with men they would only lose. After all, men made the rules and held the trumps. Moreover, women had already created a political role for themselves without the vote. The female voluntary associations that proliferated in the Progressive Era gave women a voice in public policy. Claiming to stand above politics, women's organizations lobbied with some success for a variety of reforms. Antis argued that if women entered the political fray as active participants, their influence would diminish. Describing woman suffrage as a "menace to social reform," Margaret C. Robinson maintained that suffrage "destroys the non-partisan power of women and gives them nothing worth having in its place." The vote would simply divide women into political parties, which would still be controlled by men. Better to hang onto the power and privileges they had, the antis reasoned, than to pursue elusive "rights" that might leave them only weaker and more dependent.[8]

The South was a stronghold of antisuffrage sentiment, and southern opponents made their own contributions to antisuffrage ideology. White southerners never forgot that the women's rights movement was an offspring of the abolitionist crusade. Long after the Civil War, some continued to regard the effort to enfranchise women as part of a Yankee plot to overthrow southern civilization. White southerners continued to cherish the ideal of the lady. They were slower than other Americans to accept *any* alteration in women's roles, and they were particularly distressed by women's increasing involvement in politics. Furthermore, woman suffrage was part of a package of Progressive reforms—including prohibition, regulation of child labor, and expanded social welfare programs—that many of the South's political and economic elite opposed. In a region that historically resisted change—particularly change imposed from the outside—antisuffrage propaganda found a receptive audience.[9]

In the South, more than in any other section of the nation, any change in women's status brought with it portents of social upheaval, for in the South ideas about gender were inextricably intertwined with ideas about race. The exaltation of white women went hand in hand with the degradation of African-American men. At one end of the South's racial spectrum was the lady, her unblemished white skin a visible sign of her purity. White men worshiped her as the symbol of all that was good in their civilization. At the opposite end of the scale was the lustful and strong African-American male. Whites saw him as a savage brute who must be controlled because he could not be tamed. White southern men, self-appointed guardians of the lady and all she represented, used the need to "protect" white women to justify slavery, lynching, disfranchisement, and segregation. The survival of the South's social hierarchy—and the white male dominance that went along with it—depended on everyone—male, female, white, black—accepting the place assigned by race, class, and gender. Any rebellion from any quarter could topple the entire structure. Many white southerners (male and female) feared that an expansion of power for white women would necessarily expand the power of African Americans.[10]

From Seneca Falls to the ratification of the Nineteenth Amendment, white southern ministers, politicians, educators, and editors admonished white southern women to refrain from adding their voices to the women's rights chorus that echoed from the North. They reminded women that feminine strength was moral and spiritual, not physical, and that they needed male protection and sustenance in order to survive. That message was hammered home to women during the turn-of-the-century white supremacy campaigns. Protecting the virtue of white womanhood became the rallying cry for white men seeking to disfranchise African Americans and enact segregation. Repeatedly, leaders of the Democratic party claimed that political equality led to social equality and that social equality, in its most base form, meant that African-American men would rape white women. White supremacist propaganda exaggerated reports of black men's assaults (verbal or physical) on white women and insinuated that such incidents were the inevitable result of black suffrage and office holding. To safeguard white women, then, white men must remove African-American men from politics.[11]

The glorification of white women at the expense of African-American men in the white supremacy campaigns of the 1890s and early 1900s had a lasting impact on woman suffrage in the South. White supremacist rhetoric portrayed white women as political symbols, the coveted prizes whose possession signified the dominance of the men of one race over those of the other. The maintenance of white male dominance under the guise of "protecting" white womanhood required the exclusion of African-American men from politics, and it mandated the exclusion of all women as well. For if African-American women could vote, they might open the polls to African-American men. And if white women could vote, if they became politically autonomous, they might no longer require the protection of white men, and the justification for black disfranchisement would evaporate. In the minds of southern antis, black rights and women's rights were inseparable. Woman suffrage, in their view, would inevitably subvert social order in the South.[12]

By the time the Nineteenth Amendment was submitted to the states in 1919, there was one more element that hardened southern resistance to woman suffrage: the process of economic development that was supposed to herald the coming of a New South. Beginning in the late 1800s, regional leaders tried to lure railroads and factories to the South. State legislatures granted concessions to railroad men and mill owners, arguing that these enterprises benefited all citizens. But some benefited more than others, and businessmen organized powerful lobbies whose tactics might not always bear careful scrutiny. Big business in the South, as in other parts of the country, was tainted with charges of political corruption. Moreover, some southern industries—cotton textiles in particular—owed their competitive advantage to their ability to employ cheap labor—that is, women and children—for long hours at low wages.

Long before they got the vote, southern women of both races in clubs, temperance societies, and civic leagues committed themselves to stamping out political corruption, exploitative labor practices, and immorality. They won some important victories. The Woman's Christian Temperance Union, for example, played a key role in prohibition campaigns throughout the South. Industrialists feared that women voters would be formidable adversaries. As the president of the Wholesale Brewers' Association declared in 1912: "We need not fear the churches; the men are voting the old tickets; we need not fear the ministers, for the most part they follow the men of the churches; we need not fear the YMCA; it does not do any aggressive work; but gentlemen, we need to fear the Woman's Christian Temperance Union and the ballot in the hands of women, therefore, gentlemen, fight woman suffrage." And fight they did.

"We now know," Ella Stewart reported in the *Annals of the American Academy of Political and Social Science* in 1914, "that the center and strength of the anti-suffrage army are the liquor traffic and its vicious allies." Distillers, mill owners, and railroad executives, armed with plenty of money and reinforced by powerful political friends, waged a covert war against woman suffrage.[13]

In the South, then, several forces combined to oppose woman suffrage: the code of chivalry that revered womanhood while it restricted the activities of real women; a hierarchy of race, gender, and class relations that regarded any change for any group as potentially revolutionary; and an influential and well-financed lobby determined to keep women out of politics. In the summer of 1920, all of these forces converged in Tennessee, in the final showdown over the ratification of the Nineteenth Amendment.

The antis' leading spokesperson in the 1920 campaign was Josephine Anderson Pearson, president of the Tennessee branch of the NAOWS and of the state's hastily formed chapter of the Southern Women's Rejection League (full name: Southern Women's League for the Rejection of the Susan B. Anthony Amendment). A teacher and school administrator from Monteagle, Tennessee, Pearson taught English and philosophy in colleges in South Carolina and Missouri before returning to Tennessee in 1914 to care for her aging parents. Her mother, Amanda Caroline Roscoe Pearson, opposed woman suffrage because of its abolitionist origins and, shortly before her death, made Josephine promise that she would fight the woman suffrage amendment should it ever come to Tennessee. Pearson first attracted the attention of Tennessee antisuffragists when she wrote a letter to the *Chattanooga Daily Times* denying that suffrage opponents were connected to the liquor lobby. In response, she received letters from "leading lawyers" of both political parties.[14]

One of the men who contacted Pearson was John J. Vertrees, a Nashville attorney, Democrat, and longtime foe of votes for women. He had begun speaking out against woman suffrage in 1887, when he suggested that the temperance movement harbored feminists, Republicans, and other "fanatics" bent on undermining social and political order in Tennessee. In 1916 Vertrees addressed the state Democratic convention at length on the evils of woman suffrage. The vote, he warned, was just a "milestone" along the road to radical feminist revolution. Suffragists were "determined to persist in creating a new womanhood"—a womanhood that would, he implied, prefer business and politics to domesticity. Vertrees's wife, Virginia, became the first president of the Tennessee Association Opposed to Woman Suffrage, formed a year later. When ill health forced Mrs. Vertrees to resign, she and her husband recruited Pearson to fill the office.[15]

In her unpublished memoirs, Pearson recalled that she was "virtually drafted" to lead the women's antisuffrage organization. She wanted to decline, she said, but a long-distance call summoned her to Nashville, where she was taken to dinner at the Vertrees home. Mr. and Mrs. Vertrees then persuaded her to accept the position. John Vertrees chose her, she remembered, for three reasons. First, she was a woman of "outstanding ability" who had some experience working with antisuffragists in Missouri. Second, she was a native Tennessean of good family. Finally, he told her, "You are too brainy—as well as tactful, to want to direct the strong alliance of the men constituents." From the standpoint of Vertrees and other male opponents of suffrage, Pearson represented the perfect choice to lead the fight in public. She was well-educated, articulate, and dedicated to the cause; she was also willing to submit to masculine authority.[16]

Pearson and Vertrees fought their first battle together in 1917, when the Tennessee legislature was considering a bill to give women the right to vote in municipal and presidential elections. The campaign to defeat the measure quickly got underway, "directed," as Pearson recalled, "by the fine brains of Tennessee's best statesmen." These "fine brains," it seemed, conceived a very limited role for their female allies. "It seemed never necessary for our Anti-Suffrage women to even climb the capitol steps," Pearson remembered. Those who did venture to climb the capitol steps found themselves at odds with their male patrons. "I have been guilty of insubordination," Sarah Bradford wrote to Pearson in February, "in going contrary to the opinion of Mr. Vertrees . . . I disobeyed to the extent of going to the Legislature, meeting the Senators, putting the literature on their desks, and writing in the paper. While he may have disapproved, I find the general public did not, but nevertheless it puts me out of the pale of his favor." Vertrees not only reprimanded Bradford himself, he also drafted a letter for Pearson to send to her, instructing Pearson to "put those frills and pleasant [*sic*] on it which you ladies usually do." Male antis were nothing if not consistent; they wanted to control the antisuffrage movement, just as they wished to continue to control politics.[17]

Vertrees and his male colleagues intended to be dominant but silent partners in the antisuffrage fight. Vertrees instructed Pearson to omit his name from public statements, and both he and his wife urged her to be guarded in her correspondence. "It is not best to *write* too much, as letters are sometimes *lost*," Virginia Vertrees cautioned. Pearson heeded her advice. Very little of her correspondence with Mr. and Mrs. Vertrees survives, and the letters that remain contain oblique references to "the interests which *we* have in common" and "our friends." When Pearson wrote her memoirs some years after the suffrage fight, she still refused to identify most of her allies by name.[18]

Vertrees had good reason to want to keep his name out of the public eye. He and other male antisuffragists no doubt understood that this should be women's war, and that opposition from women who didn't have rights and didn't want them would be much more effective than resistance from men reluctant to share their power. More important, the antis needed to dissociate themselves from liquor dealers, cotton manufacturers, railroads, and other vested interests (even though these interests were vested in the antisuffrage movement itself). John Vertrees was particularly vulnerable to suffragists' attacks on this count because liquor executives were among his clients. He always denied participation in the illicit activities of the liquor lobby. Indeed, he once confronted a man who accused him of representing the "whiskey ring" and forced him at gunpoint to retract the allegation. Antisuffrage pamphlets and newspapers persistently tried to refute suffragists' claims that railroad, liquor, and manufacturing interests were involved in the fight to keep the ballot out of women's hands. Josephine Pearson and many other female antis sincerely believed that their opponents fabricated these charges to discredit the antisuffrage movement. Despite evidence to the contrary, they seemed convinced that all of the men who joined with them were idealistic, honest, and concerned only with the welfare of women and of American society.[19]

Although their motives may have differed, antisuffragists were united in their determination to defeat the Nineteenth Amendment. By the summer of 1920, the amendment needed the approval of only one more state to become part of the Constitution. When Governor Albert H. Roberts of Tennessee called a special session of the legislature to consider ratification, antisuffragists from all over the United States focused their attention on Nashville.

The Tennessee campaign was a textbook example of antisuffrage arguments and tactics. The antis charged that enfranchisement would destroy homes and families. Broadsides depicted deserted homes, dejected husbands, and weeping children, and they taunted suffragists with slogans such as "The more a politician allows himself to be henpecked, the more henpecking we will have in politics" and "A vote for federal suffrage is a vote for organized female nagging forever." Conway Whittle Sams adopted the same theme in a pamphlet entitled "Why Men Should Vote Against Suffrage." Sams advised male readers to vote for woman suffrage only "if you admire the way women now consider themselves your moral superiors and wish to aid their aspirations to control you politically."[20]

Antis frequently linked suffragism with socialism, communism, anarchism, and other unsavory "-isms" and argued that the enfranchisement of women would violate the "natural" system of gender roles. The *Christian Science Monitor* reported that the Nineteenth Amendment's opponents in Tennessee accused suffragists of being "Bolshevik-minded" and of "having lost their grip on womanhood." In a pamphlet published by the Methodist Episcopal Church, South, Isaac Peebles insisted that woman suffrage "disregards God's order and ignores nature." Other antis cited biblical injunctions on man's superiority to woman to bolster their case against giving women the right to vote. Broadsides proclaimed that woman suffrage would "masculinize" women and "feminize" men. Women would lose the protection and courtesy guaranteed them under existing law and custom; men would lose their power and authority.[21]

Antis also predicted that the Nineteenth Amendment would destroy white supremacy and state sovereignty. Numerous pamphlets, leaflets, and broadsides compared the Nineteenth Amendment to the Fifteenth and warned that ratification would lead to another period of Reconstruction "horrors" when African-American men and "female carpetbaggers" would rule. Anti leaders informed white southerners that Congress had three "force bills" ready for adoption, bills similar to those used to enforce black male suffrage during Reconstruction. "The South is aware that it can expect no mercy if the amendment is ratified," declared Nina Pinckard, president of the Southern Women's Rejection League, in an open letter to Democratic presidential candidate James M. Cox.[22]

When antis evoked memories of Reconstruction, they reminded white southerners of an earlier time when chivalry had failed, and white men had been unable to protect white women. The historical analogy challenged white southern men to vindicate their honor. Using rhetoric reminiscent of the white supremacy campaigns of the 1890s, one pamphlet declared that "VICTORY is mostly a question of MANHOOD and MORALE . . . you can stop ANYTHING but death and taxes if enough REAL MEN say it shall not pass . . . The men who vote AGAINST RATIFICATION will go down in American history as the SAVIORS OF OUR FORM OF GOVERNMENT and the true DEFENDERS of womanhood, motherhood, the family and the state." Southern antis saw this battle as the Civil War all over again. The president of the Virginia Association Opposed to Woman Suffrage told Governor Roberts, "You *cannot* force upon the South even greater horrors than those of the Reconstruction period!" while a Richmond newspaper accused him of "asking Tennessee to commit political suicide and to murder in cold blood her sister states of the South."[23]

Antisuffrage propaganda implicitly—and sometimes explicitly—played on the sexual fears of whites of both sexes. Broadsides, leaflets, and pamphlets quoted feminists and African-American leaders who favored social equality

Nina Pinckard, a Confederate veteran, and Josephine Pearson at the Anti-ratification Headquarters, Hermitage Hotel, Nashville. The caption handwritten by Pearson on the original photograph reads: "'Truth Crushed to the Earth will rise again'—is illustrated in this lovely picture of Mrs. Jas. S. Pinckard, president general of the Southern Woman's League for the Rejection of the Susan B. Anthony Amendment, who as grand-niece of John C. Calhoun—unfurls the Confederate flag as emblematic of Southerners' States Rights fight for the defeat of the Federal Amendment; to her left sits the Veteran who 'fought and bled' for Tennessee's States Rights; standing to his left, holding the flag of the Union, is Miss Josephine A. Pearson, Pres. of the Tenn. Division of the Southern Women's Rejection League for the Rejection of the Susan B. Anthony Amendment, who led the fight in Tennessee which became the Battle Ground of the Nation, August 1920." From the Josephine A. Pearson Papers, Tennessee State Library and Archives, Nashville. Courtesy of the Tennessee Historical Society.

between the races, and concluded that woman suffrage would lead to interracial marriage. Again and again, southern antis declared that woman suffrage would result in the downfall of white supremacy, which, they implied, would leave white women vulnerable to assaults by African-American men. According to Anne Pleasant of Louisiana, "the passage of the Nineteenth Amendment would embolden both the negro [*sic*] man and the negro woman to give us even greater trouble than they are doing now." Antisuffrage organizations publicized the potential for "trouble" and hoped that racial anxieties would mobilize white southerners against the Nineteenth Amendment.[24]

While Pearson and the Southern Women's Rejection League circulated petitions and pamphlets, made speeches, and hosted receptions, male antisuffragists worked behind the scenes to secure the amendment's defeat. On July 30 the *Chattanooga Daily Times*, an antisuffrage newspaper, reported that "prominent lawyers and businessmen" had formed the Tennessee Constitutional League to lead the fight. The league was a subsidiary of the American Constitutional League, a national organization of men opposed to woman suffrage in general and to the federal amendment in particular.[25]

Who were these "prominent lawyers and businessmen"? Suffragists charged that they represented the united forces of the "whiskey lobby, manufacturers' lobby, and the railroad lobby." Across the nation, distillers, brewers, and factory owners (particularly those who employed large numbers of women and children) subsidized campaigns against state suffrage referenda and against the Susan B. Anthony Amendment, although they worked, for the most part, in secrecy. A Senate investigation of the United States Brewers' Association in 1918 revealed that the organization had actively tried to defeat woman suffrage in several states. In some states textile manufacturers joined with liquor interests. Walter Clark, chief justice of the North Carolina Supreme Court, believed that "the Whiskey Interests and the Cotton Mill owners of New England and the South" underwrote antisuffrage campaigns. Clark was one of the South's leading Progressive reformers, but his son David edited the *Southern Textile Bulletin*, a mouthpiece of the region's cotton industry.[26]

These forces had been evident on the Tennessee political scene for years, and it is likely that they were in Nashville in the summer of 1920. Prohibition had been the central issue of Tennessee politics during the first fifteen years of the twentieth century, and distillers and brewers had mobilized to protect their businesses. The Manufacturers' Association was also active in politics, opposing bills to regulate child labor, set minimum wages, and establish employers' responsibility for workers' safety on the job. Finally, the Louisville and Nashville Railroad had been involved in Tennessee politics since the 1880s. The

L&N's generosity in distributing free passes to legislators in 1913 (while the general assembly was considering a railroad bill) led to an Interstate Commerce Commission investigation in 1916. Woman suffrage—with its promise to deliver women's votes for the enforcement of prohibition, regulation of child labor, and reforms to end political corruption—threatened vital interests of all three of these powerful lobbies.[27]

Suffragists alleged that these groups "paid the bills" for the antis in 1920. Although the antis denied the charges, some of the men who led the fight against the Nineteenth Amendment in Tennessee were affiliated with the businesses that had opposed woman suffrage elsewhere. John Vertrees, for example, was among the founders of the Tennessee Constitutional League. So was Garnett Andrews, a textile executive described by one Tennessee historian as "one of the most prominent representatives of the knitting industry in the South." George A. Washington, along with his wife, Queenie Woods Washington, participated in the fight against suffrage; he was a director of the L&N.[28]

Then there was Edward Bushrod Stahlman, "the Major," publisher of the *Nashville Banner* and one of the most colorful (and powerful) figures in Tennessee politics. Stahlman had come to the United States from Germany before the Civil War. He got a job with the L&N in 1863 and worked his way up to a vice-presidency. In 1884 he led a successful campaign to abolish the state railroad commission, established only two years earlier. During that debate Stahlman not only presented the L&N's case to the general assembly, he also tried to curry favor with Nashville newspapers. His attempts failed. By the time the fight was over, all the papers in the capital city were hostile to the railroad, a situation that could weaken the L&N in future legislative contests. In 1885 Stahlman bought the *Banner*. He left the L&N in 1890 to become commissioner of the Southern Railway and Steamship Association, a post he held until 1895. After that, he devoted his attention to his family, the *Banner*, and Tennessee politics. Although he officially severed his ties with the railroad industry, his critics suspected that he continued to represent the L&N's interests in Nashville. In 1914 the *Nashville Tennessean* ran a cartoon with the caption: "Tennessee is governed by [Republican Governor Ben] Hooper; Hooper is manipulated by Stahlman; Stahlman is dominated by the L & N; find the real ruler of Tennessee." Stahlman dismissed the accusation as "a malicious lie." A few days later, a *Tennessean* editorial identified Stahlman as "the notorious crook and corrupt railroad lobbyist," and some people continued to regard the *Banner* publisher as an agent of the L&N. In the summer of 1920, Stahlman waffled on woman suffrage. Although he allowed Governor Roberts to name him to the Men's Ratification Committee in June, later he changed his mind. Through the pages of the *Banner* as well as in public addresses, Stahlman became an outspoken opponent of votes for women.[29]

Vertrees, Andrews, Washington, Stahlman, and the other influential men who fought the Nineteenth Amendment may have acted from conviction instead of, or in addition to, self-interest. Many antis sincerely believed that women had no place in politics and that enfranchising them would only create problems. But connections between prominent antis and liquor, textile, and railroad companies convinced suffragists that these men represented larger, more sinister interests. Events like Stahlman's change of heart persuaded pro-amendment forces that the antis were employing underhanded tactics.

The special session was scheduled to open on Monday, August 9. Lawmakers began arriving in Nashville on Saturday, and they, along with suffragists and antis, converged on the Hermitage Hotel. There were others at the Hermitage, too, "mysterious men" whom the suffragists did not recognize, but who clearly had a stake in the outcome of the vote. The night before the session was to open, suffragists observed these unidentified men escorting members of the legislature to a room on the eighth floor, a room where liquor flowed freely. By late in the evening, Carrie Chapman Catt recalled, "Legislators, both suffrage and antisuffrage men, were reeling through the hall in a state of advanced intoxication." Horrified, Catt asked officials to enforce Tennessee's prohibition law, only to be told that this was "the Tennessee way," and that "in Tennessee, whiskey and legislation go hand in hand."[30]

Catt and the suffragists may not have recognized the individual men they saw at the Hermitage, but they were convinced that the men were agents of the antis. Brewers, distillers, railroad men, and mill owners were working to defeat woman suffrage in Tennessee, just as they had done in other states. According to Catt, they operated "as one man," using liquor, loans, promises of high office, and "every other device which old hands at illicit politics could conceive or remember" to win converts to their cause. Whatever their methods, they were effective. Early in the summer, the suffragists had taken a poll to determine which legislators might be susceptible to bribes. One by one, every single man who had been identified as bribable switched his vote from the pro column to the anti list. Among the defectors was Seth Walker, speaker of the house, who earlier had supported suffrage and had promised to introduce the ratification resolution. Walker went on to lead the anti forces in what one observer described as "the most bitterly contested legislative fight that ever took place in our State."[31]

The legislature convened at noon on Monday, August 9. The senate was solidly prosuffrage. The ratification resolution was introduced on August 10 and referred to the committee on constitutional amendments the following day. On Friday, August 13, the committee recommended its adoption. "National woman's suffrage is at hand," the majority report stated; "it may be delayed but it cannot be defeated, and we covet for Tennessee the signal honor of being the thirty-sixth and last State necessary to consummate this great reform." That same day, the senate passed the resolution by a vote of twenty-five to four.[32]

After the senate approved the amendment, Walker delayed consideration in the house, hoping to round up enough votes to defeat it. Suffragists charged Walker and his allies with foul play. On August 12, a newspaper reported that "Nashville looks like a real oasis in the dry desert. Moonshine corn whiskey is flowing freely." Joe Hanover, a prosuffrage assemblyman from Memphis, accused "a certain newspaper connected with the opposition" of harassing his colleagues and threatening them with grim consequences if they voted for ratification. Walker and others made impassioned speeches on the house floor, while female antis—many of them wearing red roses, the antisuffrage emblem—watched from the galleries. On August 18, Walker could postpone no longer. With a crowd of spectators from both sides looking on, the Tennessee House voted on the Nineteenth Amendment—and approved it by only one vote.[33]

But the antis did not concede defeat. Walker tried a parliamentary maneuver to get the house to reconsider. When it became apparent that the suffragists would be able to hold on to their majority, thirty-eight antisuffrage representatives—the so-called "Red Rose Brigade"—fled to Alabama on an L&N train ("very suitably indeed in their choice of conveyance" was one suffragist's caustic comment). They hoped their absence would break the quorum and prevent further action on the amendment; it did not. On August 21, the house reconsidered the ratification resolution and again approved it.[34]

Meanwhile, antisuffrage organizations appealed to public opinion. On August 19 antis held a mass meeting "to save the South" at Ryman Auditorium; E. B. Stahlman was the featured speaker. Similar rallies were held throughout the state later in the month. Observers disagreed on the response to the meetings. "Indignation Spreads Over Whole State" declared a headline in the antisuffrage *Chattanooga Daily Times*, while the prosuffrage *Nashville Tennessean* reported "Little Interest Manifested in Mass Meetings." Antis throughout the nation condemned the Tennessee legislators who voted with the suffragists. Martin Lee Calhoun of Selma, Alabama, compared them to "assassins of the night who have stabbed the heart of the South and its traditions to the core."[35]

Even after U.S. Secretary of State Bainbridge Colby issued a proclamation certifying the addition of the Nineteenth Amendment to the United States Constitution on August 26, antis continued their efforts to prevent the amendment from taking effect. In September, Seth Walker led a delegation to Washington to persuade Colby that Tennessee's ratification was unconstitutional (the secretary was not convinced). Undaunted, Walker and his party moved on to Connecticut, where the legislature was considering ratification. There, as in Tennessee, too few men heeded their pleas. In mid-September Connecticut became the thirty-seventh state to approve the amendment. Still the antis refused to surrender. Rallying their forces one last time, female antisuffragists called on other women to use their new right to defeat the men who had voted for woman suffrage.[36]

The antis' campaign in the fall of 1920 produced mixed results. Harry Burn—the man who cast the deciding vote in favor of the Nineteenth Amendment in the Tennessee legislature, the man Josephine Pearson branded a "traitor to manhood's honor"—won his bid for reelection. But Governor A. H. Roberts lost. Roberts's position was already precarious because of his tax program and his hostility to organized labor; his support for woman suffrage sealed his political doom. Antis rejoiced over Roberts's downfall. "Election Returns Prove Strength of Anti-Suffragists" proclaimed the *Woman Patriot*, official newspaper of the National Association Opposed to Woman Suffrage. Female antis—women who had not wanted the vote in the first place—now boasted that they had used the franchise to drive their enemies from office.[37]

The antis' claim that they were responsible for Roberts's defeat highlights one of the underlying themes of the antisuffrage campaign: antisuffragists never underestimated the power of women. Male antisuffragists might talk of feminine frailty, irrationality, and emotionalism. Female antis might insist that women needed male protection or that they were above politics. But antisuffragists—male and female alike—agreed that women were a powerful force. As Ella Stewart explained, the strength of the opposition was "a high tribute to womanhood."[38]

Antis disagreed among themselves, however, over how suffrage would affect feminine power. Men feared that enfranchised women would use the vote to undermine existing political and economic structures and to challenge masculine authority throughout society. The prospect of a united bloc of female voters voting *against* child labor and *for* prohibition, *against* political corruption and *for* honest government, had wealthy, influential men running scared, willing to resort to extreme tactics to keep the ballot out of women's hands. Female antis, on the other hand, believed that the vote might actually *reduce* women's power and influence in the public arena. The vision of women using the vote as a stepping stone to step off the pedestal and compete with men repelled many intelligent, capable women who realized that votes alone would not ensure political equality.

Both men and women in the anti ranks acknowledged the symbolic potential of suffrage. They recognized that, for better or for worse, if women took on one "masculine" role they might also attempt to assume—or be forced to accept—rights, responsibilities, and privileges reserved to men in other areas as well. The antis knew—to return to Jean Elshtain's observation about the suffragists—that women could change society with the vote and that the vote *could* change women. Antis saw the power inherent in woman suffrage, and they fought long and hard to keep that power from being unleashed. Far from misunderstanding the implications of votes for women, the antis understood them all too well.

Notes

Portions of this article appeared previously in *Tennessee Historical Quarterly* 50 (Winter 1991): 203–25 and are reprinted with permission of the Tennessee Historical Society, War Memorial Building, Nashville, Tenn. The author wishes to thank the following for their comments on earlier drafts of this article: Elsa Barkley Brown, Alan Downs, Vernon Egger, Paul E. Fuller, Jacquelyn Dowd Hall, Lu Ann Jones, Harold C. Livesay, Carolyn Malone, and Mary Murphy.

1. Quotations are from Carrie Chapman Catt and Nettie Rogers Shuler, *Woman Suffrage and Politics: The Inner Story of the Suffrage Movement* (New York: Charles Scribner's Sons, 1923), 132. For examples of suffragists' descriptions of their adversaries, see ibid., 132–59, 271–78, 445–47; Carrie Chapman Catt to Mrs. John M. Kenny, June 29, 1920, and Carrie Chapman Catt to Mrs. Guilford Dudley, Mrs. George Fort Milton, Mrs. John M. Kenny, both in box 1, folder 6, Carrie Chapman Catt Papers, Tennessee State Library and Archives, Nashville, Tenn.; "Editorial Correspondence," newspaper clipping, *Chattanooga News*, Aug. 19, 1920, Harry T. Burn Scrapbook, Manuscripts Department, Special Collections, University of Tennessee Library, Knoxville.

2. Augusta Jane Evans, *St. Elmo* (New York: Grosset and Dunlap [1866]), 341.

3. For examples of early opposition to woman suffrage, see Aileen S. Kraditor, ed., *Up from the Pedestal: Selected Writings in the History of American Feminism* (Chicago: Quadrangle Books, 1968), 189–91. On antisuffrage organization and ideology, see Ida Husted Harper, ed., *History of Woman Suffrage* (New York: National American Woman Suffrage Association, 1922), 5: 678; Catt and Shuler, *Woman Suffrage and Politics*, 271; Eleanor Flexner, *Century of Struggle: The Women's Rights Movement in the United States* (New York: Atheneum, 1974), 294–305; Aileen S. Kraditor, *The Ideas of the Woman Suffrage Movement, 1890–1920* (New York: W. W. Norton and Company, 1981), 14–42; Jane Jerome Camhi, "Women Against Women: American Antisuffragism, 1880–1920," (Ph.D. diss., Tufts University, 1974); Susan E. Marshall, "In Defense of Separate Spheres: Class and Status Politics in the Antisuffrage Movement," *Social Forces* 65 (Dec. 1986): 327–51; Manuela Thurner, "'Better Citizens Without the Ballot': American Antisuffrage Women and Their Rationale During the Progressive Era," *Journal of Women's History* 5 (Spring 1993): 33–60.

4. Quotations are from Emily P. Bissell, "A Talk to Women on the Suffrage Question," pamphlet, box 1, folder 3, Josephine Anderson Pearson Papers, Tennessee State Library and Archives; Albert Taylor Bledsoe, "The Mission of Woman," *Southern Review* 9 (Oct. 1871): 924; Isaac Lockhart Peebles, "Is Woman Suffrage Right? The Question Answered" (Nashville, Dallas, Richmond: Publishing House of the Methodist Episcopal Church, South, 1920), 22, pamphlet, box 1, folder 3, Pearson Papers. See also "The 'New Woman' Experiment by One of Them," pamphlet, box 1, folder 5, Pearson Papers; John J. Vertrees, "An Address to the Men of Tennessee on Federal Suffrage," (Nashville: n.p., 1916), excerpt reprinted in part 3 of this volume; Marshall, "In Defense of Separate Spheres," 332–33; Ellen DuBois, "The Radicalism of the Woman Suffrage Movement: Toward a Reconstruction of Nineteenth-Century Feminism," *Feminist Studies* 3 (Fall 1975): 63–75; Kraditor, *Ideas of the Woman Suffrage Movement*, 21–28; Paula Baker, "The Domestication of Politics: Women and American Political Society, 1780–1920," *American Historical Review* 89 (June 1984): 620–47.

5. Jean Bethke Elshtain, "Aristotle, the Public-Private Split, and the Case of the Suffragists," in Jean Bethke Elshtain, ed., *The Family in Political Thought* (Amherst: University of Massachusetts Press, 1982), 62; Kraditor, *Ideas of the Woman Suffrage Movement*, 56–74; Nancy F. Cott, *The Grounding of Modern Feminism* (New Haven and London: Yale University Press, 1987), 29–30.

6. The Equal Rights Amendment, with a different wording, was first introduced in Congress in 1923. Mrs. Arthur M. Dodge, "Woman Suffrage Opposed to Woman's Rights" (New York: National Association Opposed to Woman Suffrage, n.d.; reprinted from *Annals of the American Academy of Political and Social Science*, Nov. 1914), 1, box 1, folder 3, Pearson Papers. See also "Why We Oppose Votes For Women," broadside, box 1, folder 4; "Votes for Women Means Jury Duty for Women," box 1, folder 5; "Equal Suffrage Results," box 1, folder 6; Amanda Caroline Pearson, "Woman Suffrage: A Resume," *Grundy County Times and Mountain Herald*, Apr. 27, 1916, 2, box 1, folder 6, all in Pearson Papers; "If They Can Vote, Will They Now Pay Alimony?" newspaper clipping, *Chattanooga Daily Times*, Sept. 5, 1920, Burn Scrapbook.

7. Dodge, "Woman Suffrage Opposed to Woman's Rights," 1; Annie Riley Hale, "Woman Suffrage Article on the Biological and Sociological Aspects of the Woman Question" (Washington, D.C.: Government Printing Office, 1917; 64th Congress, Second Session, document No. 692), 5, 7, box 1, folder 3, Pearson Papers. For similar arguments, see Joseph Gilpin Pyle, "Should Women Vote?" and Frances R. G. Gundry, "Feminism vs. The Woman Movement," both in box 1, folder 3, Pearson Papers. On the attitudes of suffragists and radical feminists, see Cott, *Grounding of Modern Feminism*, 29–30, 47–48.

8. Margaret C. Robinson, "Woman Suffrage A Menace to Social Reform" (N.p.: Women's Anti-suffrage Association of Massachusetts, n.d. Reprinted from *Cambridge Chronicle*, Oct. 16, 1915), pamphlet, box 1, folder 3, Pearson Papers. See also Dodge, "Woman Suffrage Opposed to Women's Rights," 5; "Why We Oppose Votes For

Women," broadside, box 1 folder 4; "The Woman's Protest Against Woman Suffrage," typescript, box 1, folder 9, all in Pearson Papers; Baker, "Domestication of Politics"; Estelle Freedman, "Separatism as Strategy: Female Institution Building and American Feminism," *Feminist Studies* 5 (1979): 512–29; Anastatia Sims, "Feminism and Femininity in the New South: White Women's Organizations in North Carolina, 1883–1930," (Ph.D. diss., University of North Carolina, 1985), chap. 6; Anne Firor Scott, *Natural Allies: Women's Associations in American History* (Urbana and Chicago: University of Illinois Press, 1991). Suffragists also recognized the hazards of getting involved in male-dominated political parties, as the nonpartisan stance of the National American Woman Suffrage Association demonstrated. In the 1920s, many women's organizations attempted to retain their nonpartisan influence by forming legislative councils to lobby for legislation of interest to women.

9. On antebellum southern attitudes toward feminism, see Dorothy Ann Gay, "The Tangled Skein of Romanticism and Violence in the Old South: The Southern Response to Abolitionism and Feminism, 1830–1861," (Ph.D. diss., University of North Carolina, 1975). For descriptions of the southern feminine ideal and postbellum attitudes toward women, see Anne Firor Scott, *The Southern Lady: From Pedestal to Politics, 1830–1930* (Chicago: University of Chicago Press, 1970). On the southern response to suffrage, see Elna Green, "Those Opposed: Southern Antisuffragism, 1890–1920," (Ph.D. diss., Tulane University, 1992); Marjorie Spruill Wheeler, *New Women of the New South: The Leaders of the Woman Suffrage Movement in the Southern States* (New York: Oxford University Press, 1993), 3–37; Donald G. Mathews and Jane Sherron De Hart, *Sex, Gender, and the Politics of ERA* (New York: Oxford University Press, 1990), 8–27, and Kraditor, *Ideas of the Woman Suffrage Movement*, 163–218.

10. Joel Williamson, *The Crucible of Race: Black-White Relations in the American South Since Emancipation* (New York: Oxford University Press, 1984); Wilbur J. Cash, *The Mind of the South* (New York: Vintage Books, 1941); Wheeler, *New Women of the New South*, 16–20; Jacquelyn Dowd Hall, *Revolt Against Chivalry: Jessie Daniel Ames and the Women's Campaign Against Lynching* (New York: Columbia University Press, 1979).

11. Wheeler, *New Women of the New South*, 6–9, 13–20; Williamson, *Crucible of Race*, 190–94; Mathews and De Hart, *Sex, Gender, and the Politics of ERA*, 6–8; Anastatia Sims, *The Power of Femininity in the New South: Women's Organizations in North Carolina, 1883–1930* (Columbia: University of South Carolina Press, forthcoming), chap. 1.

12. On the symbolic use of women in the white supremacy campaigns, see Wheeler, *New Women of the New South*, 16–20; Williamson, *Crucible of Race*, 190–94; Mathews and De Hart, *Sex, Gender, and the Politics of ERA*, 6–8; Sims, *Power of Femininity*, chap. 1. On the link between woman suffrage and black suffrage in southern minds see Elna C. Green, "Those Opposed: The Antisuffragists in North Carolina, 1900–1920," *North Carolina Historical Review* 67 (July 1990): 315–33; and Kraditor, *Ideas of the Woman Suffrage Movement*, 163–218. See below for examples of how the antis used the white supremacy argument in campaigns to defeat the federal amendment.

13. Quotations are from Catt and Shuler, *Woman Suffrage and Politics*, 154, and Ella S. Stewart, "Woman Suffrage and the Liquor Traffic," *Annals of the American Academy of Political and Social Science* 56 (Nov. 1914): 144. See also Catt and Shuler, *Woman Suffrage and Politics*, 132–59, 272–79; Wheeler, *New Women of the New South*, 10–13; Flexner, *Century of Struggle*, 296–305; David Morgan, *Suffragists and Democrats: The Politics of Woman Suffrage in America* (East Lansing: Michigan State University Press, 1972), 155–78.

14. "Biographical Sketch," finding aid, Pearson Papers; Josephine Pearson, "My Story!" typescript, 4–6, 9, box 1, folder 17, Pearson Papers. (See edited version of "My Story" reprinted in part 2 of this volume.)

15. Quotations are from Paul Isaac, *Prohibition and Politics: Turbulent Decades in Tennessee, 1885–1920* (Knoxville: University of Tennessee Press, 1965), 45–46, and Vertrees, "Address to the Men of Tennessee," 15, 18. See also A. Elizabeth Taylor, *The Woman Suffrage Movement in Tennessee* (New York: Bookman Associates, 1957), 80–82, 84–85, 110–11; Pearson, "My Story!" 9–11.

16. Pearson, "My Story!" 1, 11, 17.

17. Pearson, "My Story!" 16; Sarah P. Bradford to Josephine A. Pearson, Feb. 6, 1917, box 2, folder 12; John J. Vertrees to Josephine A. Pearson, Feb. 8, 1917, with letter to Bradford enclosed, box 1, folder 7; see also Sarah P. Bradford to Josephine A. Pearson, Feb. 13, 1917, box 2, folder 12, all in Pearson Papers.

18. Quotations are from Virginia Vertrees to Josephine A. Pearson, "Sunday," box 1, folder 7, and John J. Vertrees to Josephine A. Pearson, March 15, 1917, box 1, folder 7, Pearson Papers. See also John J. Vertrees to Josephine A. Pearson, Feb. 8, 1917; Virginia Vertrees to Josephine A. Pearson, "Friday afternoon," both in box 1, folder 7; Pearson, "My Story!" all in Pearson Papers.

19. Virginia Vertrees to Josephine Anderson Pearson, "Tuesday morning," box 1, folder 7, Pearson Papers. See also Mrs. Arthur M. Dodge, "Another Answer to the Only (?) Suffrage Argument," *The Woman's Protest Against Woman Suffrage* 9 (Sept. 1916): 3; "Another Suffrage Invention," *The Remonstrance Against Woman Suffrage* (Apr. 1916): 5; "WARNING!" broadside, box 1, folder 4, reprinted in part 3 of this volume; "Three Federal Suffrage Force Bills in Congress," press release from *Woman Patriot*, May 15, 1920, box 1, folder 14, both in Pearson Papers.

20. Quotations are from "America When Feminized," broadside, box 1, folder 4, Pearson Papers, reprinted in part 3 of this volume, and Conway Whittle Sams, "Some Reasons Why Men Should Oppose Suffrage," box 36, folder 1, A. H. Roberts Papers, Tennessee State Library and Archives. See also "The Antisuffrage Answer," "Home!" (reprinted in part 3), and "Why We Oppose Votes for Women," all in box 1, folder 4, Pearson Papers; Peebles, "Is Woman Suffrage Right?" 19.

21. Quotations are from "Winning the Vote in Tennessee," newspaper clipping, *Christian Science Monitor*, Sept. 4, 1920, Burn Scrapbook; Peebles, "Is Woman Suffrage Right?" 21; "America When Feminized." See also Bissell, "A Talk to Women on the Suffrage Issue," 5; "The Dark and Dangerous Side of Woman Suffrage," broadside; "The

Red Behind the Yellow: Socialism in the Wake of Suffrage," pamphlet; J. C. McQuiddy, "Woman Suffrage—Is It Right for Women to Vote and Hold Office?" pamphlet; all in box 1, folder 5, Pearson Papers; George Lowe to Governor A. H. Roberts, July 3, 1920, box 36, folder 1, Roberts Papers; "Declaration of Principles Of The Southern Women's League For The Rejection Of The Susan B. Anthony Amendment To The Constitution of the United States," box 4, folder 16, Collins D. Elliott Papers, Lizzie Elliott, Tennessee State Library and Archives, reprinted in part 3 of this volume; "The Menace of Allied Socialism and Feminism," *Woman Patriot* 4 (Sept. 11, 1920): 7. The *Woman Patriot* was the official newspaper of NAOWS. Its motto was "Dedicated to the Defense of Womanhood, Motherhood, the Family and the State AGAINST Suffragism, Feminism and Socialism," and it frequently printed articles connecting the women's movement with socialism and other radical movements; see Marshall, "In Defense of Separate Spheres," 333–36. On religious arguments against suffrage, see Kraditor, *Ideas of the Woman Suffrage Movement*, 14–18.

22. Quotations are from "Beware!" broadside, box 1, folder 4; and "Southern Women Appeal to Cox on States' Rights," press release for Thursday, July 19, 1920, box 1, folder 14, both in Pearson Papers. See also "That Deadly Parallel," broadside; "Can Anybody Terrorize Tennessee Manhood?" broadside; and "The New Negro and the Social Order," all in box 1, folder 4, Pearson Papers; "Woman Suffrage A Menace to the South: A Protest Against Its Imposition Through Federal Authority"; "Suffrage and the War: A Defense of the South"; "Suffragettes and Suffragettism," all in box 1, folder 3, Pearson Papers; "Miss Pearson's Open Letter to Governor Kilby," newspaper clipping, n.p., n.d.; "Says Fight is for States Rights," newspaper clipping, *Nashville Banner*, Aug. 7, 1920, both in box 1, folder 6, Pearson Papers; Josephine Pearson to "Dear Sir or Madam," July 9, 1920; Mrs. Morgan Brown to "Gentlemen of the General Assembly," Aug. 4, 1920, both in box 1, folder 7, Pearson Papers; "Three Federal Suffrage Force Bills in Congress"; "Declaration of Principles of the Southern Women's Rejection League"; George Stewart Brown to Governor A. H. Roberts, n.d., box 36, folder 8, Roberts Papers; Catt and Shuler, *Woman Suffrage and Politics*, 464; "Force Bills Certain If Suffrage Stands," *Woman Patriot* 4 (Oct. 2, 1920): 2; Green, "Those Opposed: Southern Antisuffragism, 1890–1920," chap. 4; Kraditor, *Ideas of the Woman Suffrage Movement*, 163–218. Some southern suffragists opposed the Nineteenth Amendment on states' rights grounds, and came to Nashville to assist antisuffragists during 1920; see Taylor, *Woman Suffrage Movement in Tennessee*, 110, and Paul E. Fuller, *Laura Clay and the Woman's Rights Movement* (Lexington: University Press of Kentucky, 1975).

23. Quotations are from "Can Anybody Terrorize Tennessee Manhood?"; Gilberta S. Whittle to Governor A. H. Roberts, July 24, [1920], box 26, folder 4, Roberts Papers, and "Tennessee and Suffrage," newspaper clipping, *Richmond News Leader*, n.d., box 36, folder 6, Roberts Papers. Antis had circulated similar literature in other southern states—see, for example, Elna Green's account of North Carolina, cited above—and NAWSA officers expected the same tactics to be used in Tennessee. See Carrie Chapman Catt to Mrs. John M. Kenny, June 29, 1920, box 1, folder 6, Catt Papers.

24. Quotation is from "Statement of Mrs. R. C. Pleasant, Leader of Anti-Federal Suffrage Ratification Forces of Louisiana," Burn Scrapbook. See also "The Negro and the New Social Order"; "Says Fight is for States' Rights"; "Questions for Mrs. Catt," broadside, box 1, folder 5, Pearson Papers, reprinted in part 3 of this volume; George Lowe to Governor A. H. Roberts, July 3, 1920; Gilberta S. Whittle to Governor A. H. Roberts, July 24, [1920]. On southern white fears of black sexuality, see Jacquelyn Dowd Hall, "'The Mind That Burns in Each Body': Women, Rape, and Racial Violence," in *Powers of Desire: The Politics of Sexuality*, ed. Ann Snitow, Christine Stansell, and Sharon Thompson (New York: Monthly Review Press, 1983), 328–49.

25. "Antisuffrage Faction Busy," newspaper clipping, *Chattanooga Daily Times*, July 30, 1920, box 2, folder 5, Catt Papers.

26. Quotations are from National American Woman Suffrage Association, *VICTORY: How Women Won It: A Centennial Symposium, 1840–1940* (New York: H. W. Wilson Company, 1940), 149, and Walter Clark to Henry Watterson, Apr. 12, 1919, in *The Papers of Walter Clark*, ed. Aubrey Lee Brooks and Hugh Talmage Lefler (Chapel Hill: University of North Carolina Press, 1950), 2: 396. See also *History of Woman Suffrage*, 6: 620; Catt and Shuler, *Woman Suffrage and Politics*, 135–38; Morgan, *Suffragists and Democrats*, 157–77; Camhi, "Women Against Women," 183–94.

27. Joe Michael Shahan, "Reform and Politics in Tennessee, 1906–1914," (Ph.D. diss., Vanderbilt University, 1981); Paul E. Isaac, *Prohibition and Politics;* Maury Klein, *History of the Louisville and Nashville Railroad* (New York: Macmillan Company, 1972), 388–94.

28. Catt and Shuler, *Woman Suffrage and Politics*, 446. Paul E. Isaac, historian of the prohibition movement in Tennessee, identified Vertrees as "an attorney for liquor concerns"; see Isaac, *Prohibition and Politics*, 46; John Trotwood Moore, *Tennessee: The Volunteer State 1769–1923* (Chicago, Nashville: S. J. Clarke Publishing Company, 1923), 4: 650–51; "Speaker Walker Lauded From Many States," *Woman Patriot* 4 (Aug. 28, 1920): 1. For examples of anti denials of connections between their movement and business, see "Yarn About The L & N In A Labor Paper," newspaper clipping, *Chattanooga Daily Times*, Sept. 5, 1920, Burn Scrapbook; "WARNING!" broadside, box 1, folder 4, Pearson Papers.

29. Will T. Hale and Dixon C. Merritt, *A History of Tennessee and Tennesseans: The Leaders and Representative Men in Commerce, Industry and Modern Activities* (Chicago and New York: Lewis Publishing Company, 1913), 5: 1401–2; Dumas Malone, ed., *Dictionary of American Biography* (New York: Charles Scribner's Sons, 1936), 9: 493–94; *National Cyclopedia of American Biography* (New York: James T. White and Company, 1898), 8: 224; Klein, *History of the Louisville and Nashville Railroad*, 376–78; "The Power Behind the Throne," newspaper clipping, *Nashville Tennessean*, July 11, 1914; newspaper clipping, *Nashville Banner*, July 11, 1914; "More Power Than A Good Governor Wants," newspaper clipping, *Nashville Tennessean*, July 15, 1914, all in box 1, folder 3, Edwin A. Price Scrapbook, Tennessee State Library and Archives; Catt and Shuler, *Woman Suffrage and Politics*, 443. Stahlman and *Tennessean* editor Luke

Lea had been bitter political enemies since the gubernatorial campaign of 1908, and each used the pages of his newspaper to try to discredit the other.

30. Quotations are from Catt and Shuler, *Woman Suffrage and Politics*, 442. See also "Antisuffrage Faction Busy," *Chattanooga Daily Times*, July 30, 1920, newspaper clipping, box 2, folder 5, Catt Papers; Marjorie Shuler, "Outside Influences Fight Suffrage in Tennessee," *Philadelphia Public Ledger*, Aug. 8, 1920, newspaper clipping, box 2, folder 4, Catt Papers; "Mrs. Catt Describes Long, Bitter Fight," newspaper clipping, n.p., Aug. 24, 1920, box 3, folder 2, Price Scrapbook; "Winning the Vote in Tennessee."

31. Catt and Shuler, *Woman Suffrage and Politics*, 445–46; Catherine T. Kenny to Carrie Chapman Catt, Sept. 10, 1920, box 1, folder 14, Catt Papers.

32. *House and Senate Journals of the Extraordinary Session of the Sixty-First General Assembly of the State of Tennessee* (Nashville: n.p., 1920), 254, 263, 292–96; quotation, 293.

33. Quotations are from *History of Woman Suffrage*, 6: 621n.; "Tennessee Likely To Vote Suffrage In Next Few Days," newspaper clipping, n.p., Aug. 12, 1920, box 2, folder 7, Catt Papers; Marjorie Shuler, "From the Tennessee Firing Line," *Woman Citizen* 5 (Aug. 28, 1920): 331. See also Catt and Shuler, *Woman Suffrage and Politics*, 422–61, and Taylor, *Woman Suffrage Movement in Tennessee*, 104–25.

34. Quotation is from Shuler, "From the Tennessee Firing Line," 334. See also "Suffragists Inspired With House Victory," newspaper clipping, *Chattanooga News*, Aug. 20, 1920, Burn Scrapbook; Pearson, "My Story!" n.p.; *History of Woman Suffrage*, 6: 624; Catt and Shuler, *Woman Suffrage and Politics*, 450–54; *House Journal*, 117–21.

35. "MASS MEETING *TONIGHT* TO SAVE THE SOUTH," broadside, box 1, folder 2, Catt Papers, reprinted in part 3 of this volume; "Indignation Spreads Over Whole State," *Chattanooga Daily Times*, Aug. 26, 1920; "Little Interest Manifested in Mass Meetings," *Nashville Tennessean*, Aug. 29, 1920; Martin Lee Calhoun, "God of Our Fathers Spare Us Yet!" *Woman Patriot* 4 (Sept. 11, 1920): 3. See also "Must Uphold Sovereign Will," newspaper clipping, n.p., n.d.; "Anti Meeting Proves Fizzle at Tullahoma," newspaper clipping, *Nashville Tennessean*, Aug. 30, 1920, both in box 1, folder 6, Pearson Papers; "The Truth About the Tennessee Campaign," *Woman Patriot* 4 (Sept. 11, 1920): 7.

36. *History of Woman Suffrage*, 6: 624–25; Catt and Shuler, *Woman Suffrage and Politics*, 454–60; "Anti-Suffrage Party Declares Bitter War," newspaper clipping, n.p., July 21, [1920], box 2, folder 4; Abby Crawford Milton to Carrie Chapman Catt, Sept. 1, 1920, box 1, folder 16; Catherine T. Kenny to Carrie Chapman Catt, Sept. 10, 1920, box 1, folder 16; Ellis Meredith to Carrie Chapman Catt, Oct. 5, 1920, box 1, folder 16, all in Catt Papers; A. H. Roberts to Carrie Chapman Catt, Sept. 13, 1920, box 1, folder 18, Catt Papers; "Tennessee Antis Wage Campaign Against Roberts," *Woman Patriot* 4 (Oct. 16, 1920): 1–2; "The Truth About the Tennessee Campaign," 6; "Governor Who Forced Ratification Defeated," *Woman Patriot* 4 (Nov. 13, 1920): 6. Walker based the unconstitutionality argument on a provision of the Tennessee constitution that prohibited the general assembly from ratifying an amendment that was submitted

after the legislature was elected. The legislature that met in 1920 had been elected in 1918; Congress submitted the Nineteenth Amendment to the states in 1919. Although the United States Supreme Court nullified that provision of the state constitution early in the summer of 1920, antis continued to argue that Tennessee's ratification was unconstitutional, and that lawmakers who voted for it had violated their oath to uphold the state constitution.

37. Pearson, "My Story!" 13; "Election Returns Prove Strength of Anti-Suffragists," *Woman Patriot* 4 (Nov. 6, 1920): 1; "Governors Who Forced Ratification Defeated," *Woman Patriot* 4 (Nov. 13, 1920): 6; Kenneth S. Braden, "The Wizard of Overton: Governor A. H. Roberts," *Tennessee Historical Quarterly* 43 (1984): 273–94; Gary W. Reichard, "The Defeat of Governor Roberts," *Tennessee Historical Quarterly* 30 (1971): 94–110.

38. Stewart, "Woman Suffrage and the Liquor Traffic," 146.

6

Woman Suffrage and the Gender Gap

Jean Bethke Elshtain

Virginia Woolf was sure that women and men did not speak the same language. Women, she believed, saw the world in ways formed by experiences that diverged from those of the dominant sex; women embodied an alternative consciousness. To some women—and to some feminists—Woolf's observations ring true, or at least seem plausible. To other women and feminists, her argument is a celebration of female marginality that leads into a "separate but equal" trap. This latter group is offended by—or at least troubled by—any suggestion that there may be real and important differences between the sexes and that it may not be desirable to eliminate all such differences, particularly if uniformity is achieved by calling on women to conform to male standards and roles.

This debate, which pervades women's studies and feminist politics, is essential background to a consideration of the story of woman suffrage and of the current "gender gap," as it is sometimes called. There is little doubt that a gender gap of some sort exists. We know, for example, that the majority of environmental activists are women. Even more startlingly, fully three-quarters of those active in the animal welfare movement are women. How does one account for this disparity? No consensus has been reached on the dimensions of the gender gap, its importance, or its potential for affecting public policy and political action. In the 1980 presidential election, leaders of national women's organizations pinned on women all their hope for the defeat of Ronald Reagan and a resurgence of social reform. That, of course, did not materialize as promised. In order to understand the playing out of the gender gap in 1980 and beyond, it is important to take a look back and to assay the hopes and fears embodied in the woman suffrage movement.

First, we do well to remind ourselves why suffrage is such a vital issue in a democratic society. Suffrage for individual citizens, like sovereignty for states, is the insignia of membership in a political society; it gives one political standing. In her essay for this volume, Marjorie Spruill Wheeler quotes one suffragist on "the dignity of citizenship." This dignity is tied to the vote. The indignity of watching others represent oneself fueled suffrage efforts. At the same time, suffrage did not bring about all that its most avid proponents promised. Adele Alexander cites "the fiery Ida B. Wells-Barnett" as querying, "Do you really believe the millennium is going to come when women get the vote?" Apparently, some suffragists did, just as the most optimistic, even utopian, feminist today predicts vast transformation should women gain greater political power and represent authentic women's interests in contrast to politics they find male dominated.

Let's take a closer look. Suffragists and their opponents expostulated at great length on the nature of woman and drew implications from whatever they presumed that nature to be to the political order. One group of early feminists argued that men and women were basically the same but were shaped and molded by their culture to different roles, behavioral patterns, and intellectual and emotional traits. These feminists believed most sex differences could be attributed to external factors. Males and females not only deserved equal rights because they were the same, but also women would become more like men once they were free.

A second group started with the assumption that women were innately different from men in emotional, mental, and spiritual attributes; therefore, granting women the vote or equality would not erase these characteristics. Feminists who began from the natural difference position argued that many "feminine traits" were the expression of women's unique qualities. Women deserved equal rights, including the vote, so that these qualities could be brought to bear on the social and political issues of the day. Thus, both groups of suffragists based their program for women on an assumption about woman's nature—either she deserved rights because she was basically the same as men, or she deserved them because she was different.

Mary Wollstonecraft's *The Vindication of the Rights of Woman* (1792) is an early defense of what might be called the sex neutrality thesis, the assumption that men and women are, or could be made to be, nearly identical. She agreed that women in her own day were frivolous creatures, but the source of their misery lay not in nature, but in a system of education that made them pitiful. She wanted women to acquire the "manly" virtues of moral courage and disinterestedness. True virtue, Wollstonecraft said, was reserved to men.[1] Sex differences would diminish if education were the same for both sexes. The only innate natural superiority the male enjoyed was his greater physical strength. But strength alone has nothing to do with either virtue or knowledge. Wollstonecraft clearly measures what woman may become by what man, who has liberty, ostensibly is.

Wollstonecraft recognized that many pleas for woman's differentness, including her moral superiority, were used to justify continued social, political, and economic inequality (although, as I will note below, the picture is rather more complex than this). Indeed, antisuffragists argued that *precisely because* she was a superior being—above the coarse, crude, intemperate affairs of man—woman should neither have nor desire rights that might carry her outside her anointed sphere. Not surprisingly, some feminists were driven to the contrary perspective that every observed difference, including physical strength, was the result of training and conditioning.

The justification for refusing to grant women equal rights on the basis of natural difference has been much explored by historians, sociologists, and political analysts. Early opponents of the suffrage cause argued that giving women the vote would be "ruthlessly tearing the angel elements from the homes of America, for the homes of the people of America are infinitely more valuable than any suffrage system."[2] This statement presents a dual conceptual rigidity: men are opposed to women and homes are set up in contradistinction to the suffrage system. One antisuffragist urges:

> Man assumed the direction of government and war, woman of the domestic and family affairs and the care and training of the child. . . . It has been so from the beginning, throughout the whole history of man, and it will continue to be so to the end, because it is in conformity to nature and its laws, and is sustained and confirmed by the experience or reason of six thousand years. . . . The domestic altar is a sacred flame where woman is the high and officiating priestess. . . . To keep her in that condition of purity, it is necessary that she should be separated from the exercise of suffrage and from all those stern and contaminating and demoralizing duties that devolve upon the hardier sex—man.[3]

The statement sets into crystal relief the rigidity of the idea that man and woman are different in essence; hence, they must have separate spheres of activity. Because politics is subsumed into man's sphere, it follows *a fortiori* that woman has nothing to do with politics. To the man alone, lie those "stern . . .

contaminated . . . demoralizing" duties. Indeed, this view of the appropriate range of male and female activities and identities was so firmly ensconced in the minds of most suffrage opponents, it is difficult to find an argument against suffrage couched in terms other than an elaboration of sex differences and natural spheres.

Arguments of this sort fell into disrepute very slowly. As late as 1919, in a last-ditch stand against suffrage, Senator Joseph Weldon Bailey of Texas and Henry A. Wise Wood, a civic leader, argued that giving the vote to women would actually cause women to become men. Predictably, social decay, moral deterioration, and the demise of the Republic would ensue, in that order.[4] Wood not only pointed out that women would cease to be womanly, but that male supporters of suffrage ("strong, masculine personalities") were inexplicably seeking to "demasculinize" government by diluting "with the qualities of the cow, the qualities of the bull upon which all the herd's safety must depend . . ."[5]

Well, this easily gets silly, but, of course, one cannot stop here, for there were suffragists who not only accepted male-female difference, but also sought women's rights in part because of them. As Adele Alexander points out, one of the strategies for achieving suffrage was to situate one's arguments within a form of what political theorists call "virtue theory" by speaking of "women's special mission," a mission that would be possible only once women possessed the self-sovereignty the vote would confer. One of the most famous of the women's rights proponents arguing from the difference perspective in the nineteenth century was Margaret Fuller. In 1845, she published her book *Woman in the Nineteenth Century*, which articulates the view that women are different from men and need freedom in order to assert their unique qualities. Fuller expressed an intensely felt notion of woman's "especial genius." Her protests against the status quo were enlivened by an assertion that "the electrical, the magnetic element in woman" was being denied expression.[6] She called the feminine aspect the site of love, beauty, and holiness. Men may share in this element, but women have far more of it.

Masculinity and femininity, for Fuller, were not absolute, pure, linear constructs, but qualities for which an individual tended more or less. "Woman's soul is shared with that of man, but modified in her as a woman . . . it flows, it breathes, it sings . . . that which is especially feminine blushes and blossoms the face of the earth, and pervades like air and water all this seeming solid globe, daily renewing and purifying its life. Such may be the especially feminine elements spoken of as Femality. But it is no more the order of nature that it should be incarnated pure in any form than that the masculine energy should exist unmingled with it in any form."[7] This is more transcendentalism than feminism, perhaps, with masculine and feminine powers tending toward Platonic perfection and efflorescent fullness of a vaguely defined natural sort.

Most reiterations of natural differences between men and women were bound up with woman's role as the bearer of values and the mainstay of familial and civic life. Much of the fear of the antis was that if women got the vote, they would forsake their traditional roles. Suffragists were forced to deny this contention by arguing that woman's traditional concerns were somehow natural and would not be repudiated if she were free to vote. This led suffragists into a complicated juggling act in which they tried, simultaneously, to embrace tradition and to force change. Thus, Elizabeth Cady Stanton, the movement's leading polemicist, advocated, at different times, the notion that men and women were fundamentally alike and the belief that they were inherently different. Perhaps Stanton was aware of the complexity of the position of many antis, including those women who opposed suffrage. As Anastatia Sims shows, many antis were more complicated than the picture of them as narrow-minded reactionaries tends to suggest. They feared that suffrage might, ironically, diminish women's public role by eclipsing difference. Antidifference feminists were criticized for "lionizing men and devaluing women." The worry was also that the nonpartisan power of women in the presuffrage era might diminish if women were to become partisans.

Small wonder, then, that Stanton sometimes denounced what she called the male element in civilization and, at other times, lifted up the male as that toward which women should aspire. She was quite capable of arguing that "the male element is a destructive force, stern, selfish, aggrandizing, loving war, violence, conquest, acquisition, breeding the material and world alike discord, disorder, disease, and death," even as she held up the male citizen as the apogee of what the vote (in Marjorie Spruill Wheeler's terms, "a badge of honor") would help women to attain. When Stanton got down to brass tacks philosophically, she embraced an ideal of almost perfect freedom, framed from the standpoint of a self she declares sovereign. She locates this ideal "in the great doctrine of Christianity," namely, "the right of individual conscience in judgment. You'll not find an ideal of the sovereign self in the Roman idea . . . that the individual was made for the state."[8] As a vision of the self alone, hers is a very selective appropriation of "the great doctrine of Christianity." Stanton, clearly, is one of the foremothers of contemporary individualism, but leave that to the side for now.

For Stanton, in this essay at least, the individual is preeminent, first and foremost. Deploying the Robinson Crusoe metaphor and describing women on their solitary islands, Stanton ranks the sovereign self as the central defining characteristic of all persons. After self-sovereignty comes citizenship, then the generic woman, and last what Stanton calls the "incidental relations of life, such as mother, wife, sister, daughter. . . ."[9] But such incidental social relations are not, for Stanton, essentially defining of the self. The self is prior to social arrangements. She speaks of the self-sovereignty of women and men and calls human beings solitary voyagers. We come into the world alone, we go out alone, we "walk alone," we realize "our awful solitude," life is a "march" and a "battle," and "we are all soldiers of the self and must fight for our own protection." In the tragedies "of human experience, each mortal stands alone." Ideally, she notes almost offhandedly, complete individual development is needed "for the general good." The exalted individual is one who exults in her own solitude.

This version of the suffragist project, of course, is very far removed from that tied to the so-called argument from expediency—one that Stanton also used at times—that women, once they achieved the vote, would use it, in Wheeler's words, "as a tool." At times, suffragists and their male supporters vied with each other in sanguine terms on the glorious future to be ushered in through woman suffrage. One male suffragist observed that politics would be nobler, the polls would become free from vulgarity, and casting the ballot would be invested with "a seriousness—I had almost said a sanctity—second only to religious observance."[10] In such suffragist writing, women were associated with morality, temperance, good order, religion, and charity.

Theodore Parker, a male suffragist and another of that group of New England Transcendentalists that included Margaret Fuller, cast a backward glance at human history and observed that things would have been much different had women exerted political control. "If the affairs of the nation had been under women's joint control, I doubt that we should have butchered the Indians with such exterminating savagery, that, in fifty years, we would have spent seven hundred millions of dollars for war, and now, in time of peace, sent twenty annual millions more into the same waste. I doubt that we should have spread slavery into nine new states, and made it national. I think the Fugitive Slave Bill would never have been an act. Women have some respect for the natural law of God."[11] This was heady brew, and many suffragists took it to heart. Yes, they said, women have their sphere, but that sphere cuts across all levels.

The following excerpts, from arguments for suffrage made in 1898, 1905, and 1910, respectively, echo one another in their categorization of women's unique nature and sphere. Note that women's interests are assumed to be of a piece. "Wherever the State touches the personal life of the infant, the child, the youth, or the aged, helpless, defective in mind, . . . there the State enters 'woman's peculiar sphere', her sphere of motherly succor and training . . ."[12]

> Does an intelligent interest in the education of a child render a woman less a mother? Does the housekeeping instinct of woman, manifested in a desire for clean streets, pure water, and unadulterated food, destroy her efficiency as a homemaker? Does a desire for an environment of moral and civic purity show a neglect for the highest good of the family?[13]
>
> Doubtless the home is woman's sphere; but the home includes all that pertains to it—city, politics, and taxes, laws relating to the protection of minors, municipal rottenness that may corrupt children, schools, and playgrounds, and museums that may educate.[14]

The hope was that if elected to public office, women would "far more effectively guard the morals of society and the sanitary conditions of cities."[15] There were suffragists who admitted that the vote for women would not cure all society's ills, but they believed that governments responsible to women would be more likely to conserve life and to conserve morals. Some even looked forward to the social triumph of the Golden Rule.

All of this was too much for the redoubtable socialist-anarchist, Emma Goldman. Goldman placed middle-class feminism within its larger social context. She adamantly rejected both universal suffrage as a political panacea and the notion of women's unique nature. Universal suffrage had become a "modern fetich" [*sic*]. Women had yet to realize "that suffrage is an evil, that it has only helped to enslave people, that it has closed their eyes that they may not see how craftily they are made to submit. Not only is suffrage a hoax, but American women believe they will purify politics." To Goldman, this was dangerous nonsense. Politics, in her view, was not susceptible to purification. The difference suffragists, by insisting on woman's virtue, served to magnify the mystification surrounding woman, who was always regarded either as an angel or a devil but never as merely human. Goldman condemned suffragists for their prudery and hypocrisy. Indeed, she herself falls into rigidity when she avers that woman is "essentially a purist . . . naturally bigoted and relentless in her effort to make others as good as she thinks they ought to be." (Goldman's ire had been roused by women in Idaho who had wanted to disenfranchise prostitutes.)

Feminist hypocrisy was evident, Goldman claimed, when women demanded the same rights as men, on the one hand, but still wanted men to behave toward them as if they were delicate creatures and ladies. The middle-class American woman "not only considers herself the equal of man, but his superior, especially in her purity, goodness and morality. Small wonder that the American suffragist claims for her vote the most miraculous power. In her exalted conceit, she does not see how truly enslaved she is, not so much by man as by her own silly notions and traditions."[16]

Despite volleys from the likes of the skeptical Ms. Goldman, many suffragists continued to press the notion that suffrage would help to eradicate social evil. The words of Reverend Florence Kollock, who spoke at a congressional hearing on woman suffrage in 1884 to the effect that if the moral power of women could be utilized through the ballot, suffering would be alleviated and social wrongs righted, continued to echo through the woman suffrage movement in the twentieth century.[17] Such arguments were not confined to American suffragists. Emmeline Pankhurst, the great British suffrage leader, believed that the evils of male civilization would never be removed until women got the vote. She found her own way to involvement in the quest for women's rights as a Poor Law guardian. She saw the vote in women's hands as a "desperate necessity" for the protection of women and babies. Once women won the vote, a golden era of reform would follow. "I am convinced that the enfranchised woman will find many ways in which to lessen, at least, the curse of poverty. Women have more practical ideas about relief, and especially prevention of dire poverty, than men display."[18]

Pankhurst justified the tactics of the Women's Political and Social Union militants on the grounds that women "care more about human life than men, and I think it is quite natural that we should, for we know what life costs."[19] She, therefore, defended destruction of property, and recklessness by suffragists with their own lives, but never condoned any tactic that would threaten the lives of others.

Jane Addams, the great American Progressive reformer, argued that suffrage for women was needed in building "that code of legislation which is alone sufficient to protect the home from the dangers incident to modern life." Woman, as the traditional housekeeper, was peculiarly suited to civic housekeeping, which Addams called "large scale housekeeping."[20] Woman's nurturing functions gave her capacities and sensibilities that were desperately needed by the larger society. Addams wrote movingly and at length of maternal affection and solicitude "in women's remembering heart" that she hoped would coalesce into a force for protection of all that was young and vulnerable. She believed women had a "profound imperative to preserve human life," which she traced back to the beginnings of human society when primitive women refused to share the nomadic life and forced men to adopt a fixed abode in which children might be better reared.[21]

Addams saw an unalterable cleavage between militarism and feminism. Militarism, to her, was both war and the argument that governments rest upon a base of physical force. "It would be absurd for women even to suggest equal rights in a world governed solely by physical force, and Feminism must necessarily assert the ultimate supremacy of moral agencies. Inevitably the two are in eternal opposition."[22]

As we approach the end of the twentieth century, how well have these high hopes held up? The record is mixed. What follows is a skeptical, but nonetheless hopeful, account of the fate and future of the gender gap.

It seems clear that stark opposites—either presenting men and women as exactly the same in identity and opinions, or claiming that men and women inhabit different universes—are both mistaken. It makes sense that there would be some differences in the political identities and interests of women. Of course, these identities and interests will vary depending upon region, ethnicity, race, and religion, as well as gender. Nevertheless, if it makes sense to talk about, say, "the union man" historically, it certainly makes sense to speak about "the mothering woman" or the playing out of a maternal imperative in politics. That is the imperative to which suffragists often repaired. Fewer contemporary feminists make this move, in part because they find a trap in evocations of maternity. But this places such analysts in a rather tricky position. Where do differences come from if they do not come from the varying experiences of women? The experience that most distinguishes male and female is not that of work any longer but that of primary mothering responsibility.

Let's take a closer look, returning to the 1980 presidential election. This was the first national election, since female suffrage, to show significantly different voting patterns between men and women. Political observers took immediate notice. Women's votes in 1980 largely followed party lines and showed little change from 1976: Jimmy Carter received 45 percent, Ronald Reagan, 47 percent. But men showed a significant shift to Reagan, and it was *this* change in male voting patterns that highlighted a gender gap. Male defections from Carter left him with only 36 percent of the total vote while Reagan won 55 percent. One could make the argument that it was the *men* whose 1980 voting behavior really should be explained.

But the gender gap discourse of the early 1980s inevitably focused on the attitudes of women. In August 1983, The *New York Times*, reporting on Gallup poll findings, notes that Reagan's job-performance rating had declined by 5 full percentage points in July and that the drop "was caused almost entirely by a loss of confidence on the part of women, among whom the President suffered an eight point decline from the June poll. Only 34% of women, as compared with 51% of men, approved of the way Reagan was handling his job."[23]

The seventeen-point spread could not be ignored. But the arresting question then and now is *why*. Why did so many women consistently give Reagan negative ratings? Nothing of that sort had ever shown up before in Gallup surveys of presidential approval. Some feminists insisted it was the president's stand on the Equal Rights Amendment and abortion that accounted for the gender gap. Others found that response too simple by far and hinted that something else was going on.

The correct answer seems to be "something else." On issues usually cited as explicitly feminist, especially abortion and the Equal Rights Amendment, there was little difference in the opinions of men and women. Indeed, from the beginning of public polling data on this subject, slightly more men than women favor abortion rights. Over time, the gap on abortion has narrowed, as more women have adopted a pro-choice position, bringing them closer to the view of men expressed from the start.

With respect to the ERA, a *New York Times*-CBS poll in 1983 (at the time, the ERA was still a hotly contested topic) found more men than women favoring the amendment. From the mid-1980s to the present, men and women have been about evenly divided on the ERA. My point is that pro-choice and ERA politics, central to the policies of the National Organization for Women, for example, do not explain the existence of a gender gap or the issues on which it is founded. In the words of social scientist Frances Fox Piven, "there is not much match . . . between the largely middle-class constituency of the women's movement and the cross-class constituency of the gap, or between the issues emphasized by the movement and the issues highlighted by the gap."[24] On which issues, then, is the gender gap based? It hinges on those questions and concerns that historically have been regarded as traditional female values—peace and social welfare. The gender gap extends a pattern established long before Ronald Reagan even dreamt of running for president.

From 1948 to the early 1970s, the main difference between women's attitudes and men's, as reflected consistently in public opinion surveys, focused on such issues as military conscription, the arms budget, and capital punishment. Kathleen Francovich, then director of surveys with CBS News, confirms that regardless of age, education, or socioeconomic status, a gender gap persists on issues involving resort to force, war, and aggression. If one eliminates the constellation of concerns linked to war and the willingness to use force, little remains of the gender gap. Francovich writes, "In the 1980 election, the difference in the way men and women cast their ballots could be entirely eliminated by controlling for willingness of men to be more aggressive in foreign policy, even at the risk of war."[25]

Peace, of course, has always been important as a woman's issue. There is a powerful tradition that assumes an affinity between women and nonviolence. Women have often assigned themselves a stake in preventing war. Admittedly, there is no dearth of examples of militarist mothers, of women who have goaded men into battle, and who have taunted men who refused to fight. Women have served as military wives, camp followers, and home front helpmeets supplying the material base for the pursuit of war.[26]

Nonetheless, the peace tradition continues to figure strongly in women's politics. One finds it, for example, in the disproportionate representation of women in peace movements, from the time of Jane Addams and the Women's Peace Party to the present. To be sure, women involved in such efforts have never been able to prevent war or to have a major impact on the sort of peace that followed, but it is noteworthy that even in wartime a significant number of women have been prepared to take a stand and endure a campaign of popular vilification.

World War I split the women's movement. After much debate, the National American Woman Suffrage Association endorsed the war effort. Addams and others were disaffected as a result of this endorsement. Similar divisions persist to this day. The question of women in military conscription, for example, sharply divided the National Organization for Women in the 1980s, but the NOW's version of "equal opportunity," cast in this issue as a "right to fight," held sway. In an *amicus* brief filed with the Supreme Court as part of a challenge to the requirement that only young men register for the draft, NOW argued that military participation is essential if women were to gain equality and first-class citizenship. Accepting compulsory military service as central to the concept of citizenship in a democracy, NOW spokeswomen contended that the all-male draft turned on "archaic notions of women's role" and that women would suffer "devastating long-term psychological and political repercussions" as a result of exclusion from the military.[27] Yet "archaic notions of women's role" appeared to figure significantly in women's commitment to peace and in contemporary women's politics across the board. As a rule, women have not identified themselves as the "expendable sex" that can be called upon to fight and die for a tribe or a nation. It is in their capacity as mothers and the protectors of vulnerable human life that women have insisted on condemning the use of violence.

Other issues that are associated with the gender gap—nuclear power, the reduction of social welfare benefits, capital punishment, environmental pollution, animal protection—are consistent with values associated with caring and protecting. These are the traditional "private" values of women, yet they are increasingly brought to bear on *public* issues and as public imperatives. Again, there are historic precedents, most notably among women reformers of the Progressive Era, such as Jane Addams, who saw politics as homemaking on a wider scale.

But tradition and precedent do not suffice to explain why women in the 1980s and into the 1990s continue to voice somewhat different views from men on a whole range of political issues. We can assume that women's values and modes of thinking are not biologically intrinsic to sex, but they must be rooted in *something*, and if an essential part of that something is women's traditional social identity, does it not follow that as women take on more and more "male roles" they will increasingly embrace more competitive values? This is a question that haunted the suffragists and continues to haunt feminists. Feminists are split on the answer. Indeed, they are divided as to whether the question should be asked at all, believing that any invocation of some moral good in "maternal thinking" may lock women into predetermined social roles.

Yet, the stubborn existence of a gender gap may indicate that the traditional attitudes of women are not entirely compatible with new identities. Women may become active public citizens on the basis of long-cherished "private" or religious values and, in the process, come to create a vision of public life that is more attentive to the needs of the vulnerable, the weak, the very young, and the very old. One can envision a gender gap evolving into a gender politics that forges new and creative coalitions knitting together women and men now divided by race, class, or their positions on such volatile issues as abortion. The gender politics I have in mind, then, would not essentialize male and female identity, but would permit and encourage women to express their deepest concerns without fear of being labeled reactionary because many of those concerns involve, and always have involved, children and families.

More recently, 1992 was widely proclaimed to be the "Year of the Woman." Of course, the election of 1988 *was* supposed to be the year women "delivered the president" by handing George Bush a resounding defeat. As things turned out, more women voted for Bush than voted for Michael Dukakis, and, most important, large numbers of men deserted the Democrats in favor of the Republicans.[28] In 1992, men returned to the Democratic fold and helped to hand Bill Clinton his victory. Women supported Clinton by 46 percent; 37 percent were for Bush, with Ross Perot garnering a healthy 17 percent.[29] But the Year of the Woman was primarily about women running for Congress. A pre-election poll showed that 61 percent of the electorate, when asked, said government would be better if women held office. On election day, forty-seven women were elected to the House of Representatives, up from twenty-eight, and four new women were elected to the Senate, tripling their number there from two to six.

The voters' view of women's political difference suggests that a "womanist" ideology has taken hold. I refer to the belief, discussed in this essay, that women care more about the quality of life, especially in the domestic arena, than do men. This is a position associated with the work of Carol Gilligan, especially her book *In a Different Voice* (Cambridge: Harvard University Press, 1982). This characteristic has always been a double-edged sword for feminism. On the one hand, many feminists assert that women will do better because they somehow are better; on the other hand, it is important for feminists to defeat stereotypes about gender, *including* the view that women are morally superior to men. Needless to say, these two positions cannot easily be squared with each other. Feminists at present tend to play either card, depending upon the context. When the issue is hiring women for traditionally male jobs, they claim gender is irrelevant. For the election, however, we heard a lot about how women would do things better because of qualities they possess *as women*.

Although hot-button issues such as abortion and sexual harassment tended to predominate as central concerns of feminist rhetoric during the campaign, when women were surveyed a different set of priorities emerged. Exit polls found that guaranteed health care was the runaway top issue for 86 percent of women surveyed; jobs and family issues followed in close order. Only 2 to 3 percent worried about rape or sexual violence. Far more (68 percent) were concerned about violent crime in their neighborhoods, in large part because of the danger crime poses for their children, who, in our besieged inner cities, are likely to become either recruits to gangs or victims of gang warfare.[30] All of this suggests a rather wide perception gap at present between the most visible feminist leaders and the vast majority of women, who, ironically, seem to be the primary leaders in the political gender gap.

What accounts for the perception gap? With all the data indicating enormous strides for women in the workplace, as the median pay for women as a percentage of that of men jumped sharply in the 1980s, women clearly want to cover those areas of greatest vulnerability—such as health care—for themselves and their children. This may indicate that women in the general population, by contrast to current national feminist leaders, have a far more realistic assessment of what the growing number of women in elective office can accomplish. Let us hope so. For the danger in proclaiming deliverance if women gain power is that cynicism will result when women do not effect miracles.

We need to know more about how men and women define politics, how they perceive the role of citizen, what issues they want to address, and what methods they deem appropriate. Perhaps the most important long-range effect of the gender gap will be an increase in our understanding of how political and social identities are formed. Women, for a change, are in the picture, speaking up and being heard, rather than being out-of-the-frame, silent spectators.

Notes

1. Mary Wollstonecraft, *A Vindication of the Rights of Woman*, ed. Charles W. Hagelman Jr. (1792; reprint, New York: W. W. Norton and Company, Inc., 1967), 33.

2. Elizabeth Cady Stanton, Susan B. Anthony, and Matilda Joslyn Gage, eds., *History of Woman Suffrage* (Rochester, N.Y.: Charles Mann, 1889), 1: 135.

3. Ibid., 145.

4. Ida Husted Harper, ed., *History of Woman Suffrage* (New York: J. J. Little and Ives Co., 1922), 5: 588.

5. Ibid., 585.

6. Margaret Fuller, *The Writings of Margaret Fuller*, ed. Mason Wade (New York: Viking Press, 1941), 168.

7. Ibid., 176.

8. "The Solitude of Self" is reprinted in Elizabeth Cady Stanton's autobiography, *Eighty Years and More* (New York: Schocken Books, 1971), 231. "The Solitude of Self" was also published privately by Doris M. Ladd and Jane Wilkins Pultz as a pamphlet in 1979.

9. Ibid.

10. Susan B. Anthony and Ida Husted Harper, eds., *History of Woman Suffrage* (Indianapolis: Hollenbeck Press, 1902), 4: 65

11. Stanton, Anthony, and Gage, *History of Woman Suffrage*, 1: 126.

12. Anthony and Harper, *History of Woman Suffrage*, 4: 308–9.

13. Harper, *History of Woman Suffrage*, 5: 125.

14. Eugene A. Hecker, *A Short History of Women's Rights* (New York: J. P. Putnam's Sons, 1919), 246.

15. Stanton, Anthony, and Gage, *History of Woman Suffrage*, 1: 19–20.

16. Emma Goldman, *The Traffic in Women and Other Essays in Feminism* (New York: Times Change Press, 1970), passim.

17. Anthony and Harper, *History of Woman Suffrage*, 4: 43.

18. Emmeline Pankhurst, *My Own Story* (New York: Hearst's International Library Company, 1914), 31.

19. Ibid., 240.

20. Cited in Aileen S. Kraditor, *The Ideas of the Woman Suffrage Movement, 1890–1920* (New York: Columbia University Press, 1965), 69–71.

21. Jane Addams, *Peace and Bread in Time of War* (New York: The MacMillan Company, 1922), 82–83.

22. Ibid., 7. Addams's interests went beyond civic housekeeping to the international sphere. She was instrumental in forming the Women's Peace Party in 1915 to fight for international amity and world law. Item 6 on the party's platform called for "the further humanizing of governments by the extension of suffrage to women." Women in the Women's Peace Party maintained that their roles as mothers gave them a vested interest in peace. The first annual meeting of the party was held in Washington in January 1916. During that year, mass meetings were held all over the country, and there were some 165 group memberships totaling some 40,000 women. The American Party was a section of the Women's International Committee for Permanent Peace, which had branches in fifteen countries. In 1919, an international congress of women condemned the Treaty of Versailles for violating the principles by which lasting peace might be secured on the grounds that Versailles sanctioned denial of self-determination, recognized the rights of victors for the spoils of war, and, particularly through its treatment of Germany and Austria, had created discords and animosities that would lead to future strife. They observed "by the financial and economic proposals, a hundred million people of this generation in the heart of Europe are condemned to poverty, disease, and despair which must result in the spread of hatred and anarchy within each nation" (Addams, *Peace and Bread in Time of War,* 163).

23. Cited in Jean Bethke Elshtain, "The Politics of Gender," *The Progressive* (Feb. 1984): 22–25; quotation, 22.

24. Ibid., 23.

25. Ibid.

26. For the full story, see Jean Bethke Elshtain, *Women and War* (New York: Basic Books, 1987).

27. Ibid., 24.

28. Paul J. Quirk, "The Election" in Michael Nelson, ed., *The Elections of 1988* (Washington, D.C.: CQ Press, 1989), 82.

29. Exit poll, *USA Today,* Nov. 4, 1992.

30. Gail McKnight, "Polls: Jobs First Worry for Women," *Nashville Tennessean,* Sept. 13, 1992.

PART 2

Documents

1

Colored Women as Voters

Adella Hunt Logan

From the *Crisis*, September 1912

Adella Hunt Logan (1863–1915) was born in Sparta, Georgia, to a free mulatto woman and a white planter.[1] She attended a local academy and became a teacher at sixteen. In 1881 she graduated from the "normal course" (teacher education) of Atlanta University, which later awarded her an honorary M.A. In 1883 she joined the faculty at Tuskegee Institute. In 1888 she married Warren Logan, who was a close friend and second-in-command to Booker T. Washington. They had nine children. Though her domestic tasks and official duties took much of her time, she played a major role in the creation of Tuskegee's model school and teacher training program.[2]

As Adele Logan Alexander described in part 1, essay 4, Logan was an active clubwoman and suffragist who was a life member of the NAWSA and published prosuffrage articles in both *The Woman's Journal* and the *Crisis*, including the article below. Many of the arguments presented here are similar to those often used by white suffragists, including the argument that woman's domestic skills are needed in politics, that women need the vote in their roles as mothers, and that women in the West have benefited from enfranchisement. But she also asserts that black women have a particular need for the vote to protect their children from some of the special hazards they face owing to discrimination and morally corrosive environments and to be able to demand adequate schools—and that where black women are given the opportunity, they serve society well. Moreover, unlike most white suffragists of her region, Logan calls for government by and for all the people—"even including the colored people."

Adella Hunt Logan. From the collection of Adele Logan Alexander.

More and more colored women are studying public questions and civics. As they gain information and have experience in their daily vocations and in their efforts for human betterment they are convinced, as many other women have long ago been convinced, that their efforts would be more telling if women had the vote.

The fashion of saying "I do not care to meddle with politics" is disappearing among the colored woman faster than most people think, for this same woman has learned that politics meddle constantly with her and hers.

Good women try always to do good housekeeping. Building inspectors, sanitary inspectors and food inspectors owe their positions to politics. Who then is so well informed as to how well these inspectors perform their duties as the women who live in inspected districts and inspected houses, and who buy food from inspected markets?

Adequate school facilities in city, village and plantation districts greatly concern the black mother. But without a vote she has no voice in educational legislation, and no power to see that her children secure their share of public-school funds.

Negro parents admit that their own children are not all angels, but they know that the environments which they are hopeless to regulate increase misdemeanor and crime. They know, too, that officers, as a rule, recognize few obligations to voteless citizens.

When colored juvenile delinquents are arraigned, few judges or juries feel bound to give them the clemency due to a neglected class. When sentence is pronounced on these mischievous youngsters, too often they are imprisoned with adult criminals and come out hardened and not helped by their punishment. When colored mothers ask for a reform school for a long time they receive no answer. They must wait while they besiege their legislature. Having no vote they need not be feared or heeded. The "right of petition" is good; but it is much better when well voted in.

Not only is the colored woman awake to reforms that may be hastened by good legislation and wise administration, but where she has the ballot she is reported as using it for the uplift of society and for the advancement of the state.

In California the colored woman bore her part creditably in the campaign for equal suffrage and also with commendable patriotism in the recent presidential nomination campaign.

The State of Washington, new with its votes-for-women law, has already had a colored woman juror. Why not? She is educated and wealthy and wants to protect the best interests in her state.

Colorado has never had a better school than her women have made. Judge Ben Lindsey is as popular with colored women voters as he is with white women voters. The juvenile court over which he presides gives the boys a square deal regardless of color. A majority of mothers and fathers can be counted on every time to support such an official.

Wyoming, Utah and Idaho, the other full suffrage states, have few colored women, but these few are not hurt by, but are being helped by, their voting privileges.

In the states that are now conducting woman suffrage campaigns the colored woman is as interested and probably as active as conditions warrant. This is notably true of Ohio and Kansas.

A number of colored women are active members of the National [American] Woman Suffrage Association. They are well informed and are diligent in the spread of propaganda. Women who see that they need the vote see also that the votes needs them. Colored women feel keenly that they may help in civic betterment, and that their broadened interests in matters of good government may arouse the colored brother, who for various reasons has become too indifferent to his duties of citizenship.

The suffrage map shows that six states have equal political rights for women and men, and that a much larger number have granted partial suffrage to women. In all these the colored woman is taking part, not as fully as she will when the question is less of an experiment, not as heartily as she will when her horizon broadens, but she bears her part.

This much, however, is true now: the colored American believes in equal justice to all, regardless of race, color, creed or sex, and longs for the day when the United States shall indeed have a government of the people, for the people and by the people—even including the colored people.

Notes

This article is reprinted with the permission of the *Crisis*.

1. See Adele Logan Alexander, *Ambiguous Lives: Free Women of Color in Rural Georgia, 1789–1879* (Fayetteville: University of Arkansas Press, 1991).

2. See Adele Logan Alexander, "Adella Hunt Logan, the Tuskegee Woman's Club, and African Americans in the Suffrage Movement," essay 4, above. Biographical information is from Adele Logan Alexander, "Adella Hunt Logan" in *Black Women in America: An Historical Encyclopedia*, ed. Darlene Clark Hine, Elsa Barkley Brown, and Rosalyn Terborg-Penn (Brooklyn: Carlson Publishing, Inc., 1993), 1: 729–31.

2

The Justice of Woman Suffrage

Mary Church Terrell

From the *Crisis*, September 1912

Mary Eliza Church Terrell (1863–1954) was born in Memphis, Tennessee, to former slaves who had become part of the city's black elite; her father, who made his fortune in real estate, has been called the South's first black millionaire. She attended high school and college at Oberlin, graduating in 1884. Defying the wishes of her father, who wanted her to lead the life of a "lady," Mary Church accepted teaching positions at Wilberforce University and at the M Street High School in Washington, D.C. Leaving teaching temporarily for a two-year European tour, she returned to her teaching position in Washington and married fellow educator Robert H. Terrell, who was subsequently appointed a federal judge.

Mary Church Terrell was one of the founders and the first president of the National Association of Colored Women (NACW), that had as its goal the elevation of the race through the elevation of its women. Though primarily a middle-class organization, the NACW was devoted to serving the less fortunate within the black community and to working for racial justice. An intellectual (who was fluent in three languages), Terrell promoted interracial understanding through education, and she wrote speeches, articles, and short stories on such topics as the peonage system, lynching, chain gangs, and the disfranchisement of African Americans. An active suffragist, she gave a major address to the NAWSA in 1898 in which she demanded that the organization fight for the enfranchisement of black women as well as white. She later picketed the White House with the National Woman's Party. Mary Church Terrell was a charter member of the NAACP and lived long enough to become active in the Civil Rights movement, helping to desegregate public accommodations in Washington, D.C., in the 1950s.[1]

In this eloquent and forceful essay, she argues in favor of woman suffrage, linking the issues of black and female suffrage, and expressing pride in the men of her race—especially Frederick Douglass—who were supporters of woman suffrage.

It is difficult to believe that any individual in the United States with one drop of African blood in his veins can oppose woman suffrage. It is queer and curious enough to hear an intelligent colored woman argue against granting suffrage to her sex, but for an intelligent colored man to oppose woman suffrage is the most preposterous and ridiculous thing in the world. What could be more absurd than to see one group of human beings who are denied rights which they are trying to secure for themselves working to prevent another group from obtaining the same rights? For the very arguments which are advanced against granting the right of suffrage to women are offered by those who have disfranchised colored men. If I were a colored man, and were unfortunate not to grasp the absurdity of opposing suffrage because of the sex of a human being, I should at least be consistent enough never to raise my voice against those who have disfranchised my brothers and myself on account of race. However, the intelligent colored man who opposes woman suffrage is very rare, indeed. While on a lecture tour recently I frequently discussed woman suffrage with the leading citizens in the communities in which I spoke. It was very gratifying, indeed, to see in the majority of instances these men stood right on the question of woman suffrage.

Frederick Douglass did many things of which I am proud, but there is nothing he ever did in his long and brilliant career in which I take keener pleasure and greater pride than I do in his ardent advocacy of equal political rights for women, and the effective service he rendered the cause of woman suffrage sixty years ago. When the resolution demanding equal political rights for women was introduced in the meeting held at Seneca Falls, N.Y., in 1848, Frederick Douglass was the only man in the convention courageous and broad minded enough to second the motion. It was largely due to Douglass's masterful arguments and matchless eloquence that the motion was carried, in spite of the opposition of its very distinguished and powerful foes. In his autobiography Douglass says: "Observing woman's agency, devotion and efficiency, gratitude for this high service early moved me to give favorable attention to the subject of what is called 'woman's rights' and caused me to be denominated a woman's rights man. I am glad to say," he adds, "that I have

Mary Church Terrell. From the Mary Church Terrell Papers, Library of Congress.

never been ashamed to be thus designated. I have been convinced of the wisdom of woman suffrage and I have never denied the faith."

To assign reasons in this day and time to prove that it is unjust to withhold from one-half of the human race rights and privileges freely accorded to the other half, which is neither more deserving nor more capable of exercising them, seems almost like a reflection upon the intelligence of those to whom they are represented. To argue the inalienability and the equality of human rights in the twentieth century in a country whose government was founded upon the eternal principles that all men are created free and equal, that governments get their just powers from the consent of the governed, seems like laying one's self open to the charge of anachronism. For 2,000 years, mankind has been breaking down the various barriers which interposed themselves between human beings and their perfect freedom to exercise all the faculties with which they have been divinely endowed. Even in monarchies old fetters, which formerly restricted freedom, dwarfed the intellect and doomed certain individuals to narrow, circumscribed spheres because of the mere accident of birth, are being loosed and broken one by one.

What a reproach it is to a government which owes its very existence to the loved freedom in the human heart that it should deprive any of its citizens of their sacred and cherished rights. The founders of this republic called heaven and earth to witness that it should be called a government of the people, for the people, and by the people; and yet the elective franchise is withheld from one-half of its citizens, many of whom are intelligent, virtuous and cultured, and unstintingly bestowed upon the other half, many of whom are illiterate, degraded and vicious, because by an unparalleled exhibition of lexicographical acrobatics the word "people" has been turned and twisted to mean all who are shrewd and wise enough to have themselves born boys instead of girls, and white instead of black.

But why grant women the suffrage when the majority do not want it, the remonstrants sometimes ask with innocent engaging seriousness. Simply because there are many people, men as well as women, who are so constructed as to be unable to ascertain by any process of reason what is the best thing for them to have or to do. Until the path is blazed by the pioneer, even some people who have superior intellects and moral courage dare not forge ahead. On the same principle and for just exactly the same reason that American women would reject suffrage, Chinese women, if they dared to express any opinion at all, would object to having the feet of their baby girls removed from the bandages which stunt their growth. East Indian women would scorn the preferred freedom of their American sisters as unnatural and vulgar and would die rather than have their harems abolished. Slaves sometimes prefer to bear the ills of bondage rather than accept the blessings of freedom, because their poor beclouded brains have been stunted and dwarfed by oppression so long that they cannot comprehend what liberty means and have no desire to enjoy it.

Notes

This document is reprinted with the permission of the *Crisis*.

1. Biographical information from Beverly Jones, "Mary Eliza Church Terrell," in *Black Women in America: An Historical Encyclopedia*, ed. Darlene Clark Hine, Elsa Barkley Brown, and Rosalyn Terborg-Penn (Brooklyn, N.Y.: Carlson Publishing, Inc., 1993), 2: 1157–59, and from Dorothy Sterling, "Mary Eliza Church Terrell," in *Notable American Women: The Modern Period*, ed. Barbara Sicherman and Carol Hurd Green (Cambridge, Mass.: Harvard University Press, 1980), 678–80.

3

Mary Johnston to the House of Governors

Mary Johnston

An Address Delivered under the auspices of the National American Woman Suffrage Association at the meeting of the House of Governors in Richmond, Virginia, December, 1912

Mary Johnston (1860–1936), the descendent of an aristocratic Virginia family, was already famous as a novelist when she "came out" for suffrage in 1909. The author of twenty-three novels, including the best-selling novel of 1900, *To Have and to Hold,* she was welcomed enthusiastically by suffragists all over the nation. Johnston was a valuable source of suffrage literature for the NAWSA, as well as an effective campaigner and orator in Virginia and throughout the South. After her January 1913 address to Tennessee legislators, the *Nashville Democrat* observed "that a young Southern woman of Miss Johnston's type, rearing, and environment should become an ardent advocate of equal suffrage is one of the most marked evidences of the growth of the sentiment. A speech from such a source before the Tennessee legislature twenty-five years ago would hardly have been conceivable."

Johnston was, however, more "radical" in her views than most southern suffragists. In the fall of 1913, she astonished her readers by publishing a suffrage novel, *Hagar,* a combination of intellectual autobiography, polemic, and fiction, that endorsed not only feminism but socialism and woman's economic autonomy. Such candor, however, was not typical for Johnston, who generally chose to conceal her relative radicalism in order more effectively to promote the cause that was dearer to her than all others—woman suffrage.

To the House of Governors

As this address to the House of Governors indicates, Johnston was usually quite conciliatory and traditional in her arguments, cultivating rather than berating, emphasizing a commonality of interest between suffragists and the legislators from whom they must win enfranchisement—the "kings" these elite white suffragists hoped to join as "queens." In another address, "*Noblesse Oblige*," given to the Virginia House of Delegates, for example, she demanded the vote on the grounds that her ancestors had helped establish the commonwealth, fight its wars, build its public works, etc. Yet, Johnston strongly disapproved of the racist tactics embraced by some southern suffragists and resigned as honorary vice-president of the Southern States Woman Suffrage Conference rather than be publicly associated with the racist "utterances" of its president, Kate Gordon.[1]

Your Excellencies: In standing here this morning we cannot but feel that we are in the house of our friends. Two years ago a suffrage petition, national in its scope, was presented to Congress, and on that petition appeared the signatures of sixteen Governors of States. Ten of your body are at this moment Governors of suffrage States—States in which the whole people rule, and not merely half the people; States which are in truth democracies; States in which men, the former electorate, have said to women, "Come here, where you belong, into the wider home which is the State! We are not afraid to trust you. We are tired of an ancient injustice, and, here and now, we formally put an end to it. Welcome, fellow citizens!" Ten of your honourable body are from those States. Others of you, we are convinced, see fully the signs of the time, and agree with the progress of enlightenment. You know that the day of woman's political freedom is fast rising in your own States; you know that that dawn can no more be stayed than can the rising of tomorrow's sun. You do not want to stay it; you believe it to be for the best. Therefore, we say again that we can but feel that we are in the house of friends.

Feeling this, your Excellencies, we wish to call your attention to a few significant facts and utterances, and, when that is done, to make the shortest of pleas, believing as we do that no long plea is necessary, but that we are talking to friends, well-wishers and helpers.

I wish to quote from three or four newspapers on the November election.

The Boston Herald has this to say: "Tuesday's decision of most far-reaching importance was the adoption by four States of a woman suffrage amendment to their constitutions. In the light of this decision, the common-sense thing for the country to do is to recognize woman suffrage as decreed by the spirit of the age, and to adjust itself accordingly."

Mary Johnston. Virginia State Library and Archives, Richmond, Virginia.

The New York Evening Journal says: "As important as any feature of this big election—more important by far than any feature in the long run—is the news that four more States have joined the ranks of those that give the vote to women."

The New York Evening Sun says: "The facts"—the suffrage victories and the increase in suffrage sentiment—"will have a decided influence upon all political parties, compelling them to stand for suffrage not only nationally but in their respective State platforms. This attitude was foreshadowed, even before the recent victory, by the fact that all political parties not only welcomed the aid of women, but vied with each other in appealing for their support. Never before were women urged into political service as during this campaign, and they are there to stay. No party can ever again afford to ignore them or to attempt a campaign without their moral and practical aid. To plead for the active support of disfranchised women and then deny them direct political power is too great an inconsistency for even modern politicians."

The New York Evening Post says: "The entrance of women into the national politics has justified itself in our country, as in Norway, Finland, New Zealand, Australia, and even China."

A monthly journal of wide circulation makes this remark: "In the press generally, regardless of party affiliations, these latest triumphs of the women's cause are recognized as earnests of yet more sweeping victories to come; yet the notes of ridicule, admonition or alarm, once so prevalent, are either absent or are lost in the general chorus of approval or of friendly interest."

Your Excellencies, I have just returned from the annual Convention of the National American Woman Suffrage Association, held this year in Philadelphia. Certainly no one in the city of Philadelphia, from Mayor Blankenburg, who, in a strong suffrage speech, declared that Pennsylvania women would be politically free in 1915, to the least unit in the enormous crowd that thronged Independence Square, or stood, five thousand in number, all one cold and windy afternoon around the Metropolitan Opera House, itself packed within, from floor to roof, while one noted speaker after another addressed them from improvised platforms—not a man or woman of those thousands, I am sure, but realized that a new era is here; that henceforth both halves of human society are to be reckoned with in the organization and government of society.

Your Excellencies, if there are two things in the world inextricably combined, they are men and women. Neither of us can live without the other. To tell the truth, neither of us wishes to live without the other. We talk of man in the abstract, and of woman in the abstract, and all the time there is no such thing as an abstract man or woman. It is a monster that doesn't exist. Men and women are concrete persons, here and now, human beings anchored and welded together. All men are the sons of women and all women are the daughters of men. Every man here was born of a woman and a man, and every woman here was born of a man and a woman, and we inherit equally from each. And that means, as any biologist will tell you, that we are each. Woman can not contemn man without contemning herself, and man cannot contemn woman without contemning himself. Man and woman, we are co-heirs, we are kings and queens—not kings with a queen-consort walking behind, but fellow sovereigns—Williams and Marys, Ferdinands and Isabellas!

That is our contention. That is what we stand here today to uphold. That is the heart of the woman movement. That is what, all over the world today, woman, awakened and struggling to her feet, is crying to her mate, is crying to the future!

What is at the root of the world-wide unrest among women? What is at the root of the Woman Movement? The oldest thing in the world is at the root of the Woman Movement. Evolution is at the root of the Woman Movement—growth, the divine yearning outward and onward and upward. Stop it? Still it? Stop the ocean with your hand; stop the wind with a straw; stay the great mind of the world with your plaintive "Day before yesterday was just the right weather!"

It did not come up in a night, the Woman Movement, and it is in no danger of perishing from view. It is here to stay and to grow. It is not the work of a few fanatics and faddists. It is a perfectly logical phenomenon, born out of the fullness of time and the larger mind of the world, evidencing itself in all the countries of the world and under the most diverse circumstances, participated in by members of every social stratum, by the rich and the poor, the learned and the unlearned, the young and the old. It is indestructible, it is moving on with an ever-increasing depth and velocity, and it is going to revolutionize the world. It has many sides—educational, economic, industrial, eugenic, political. In a thousand speeches we could only slightly touch the iridescent, many-angled Woman Movement. Today we are to speak, and that most briefly, only to its political aspect in our own country. Then, what are we asking, here in America, here in Virginia?

We are asking that a democracy be a democracy. We are asking that the government of this country be a government of the whole people, for the whole people, and by the whole people, and not a government of, for and by half the people. We are asking that we who live under the laws of a State—laws which we must obey and which affect our relation in life—may have something to do with the making of those laws. We are asking that we who pay a very considerable portion of the taxes of the State and of the country may have a voice in the apportionment of those taxes. We are asking that we who work may have a say as to the conditions which, even now, are largely under political control, and which, every year that we live, come more and more fully under that control. We are asking for the full responsibilities, duties and dignity of citizenship. We are asking for justice, for fair play, for a square deal. We are asking to be enfranchised.

Your Excellencies, our plea is a short and simple one. It is that, in your several States, you take the side of the eternal spirit of democracy, the eternal spirit of justice. It is that you do unto woman as, were you in woman's place, and woman in man's place, you would most assuredly and beyond the peradventure of a doubt have woman do unto you!

In a democracy the ballot is a symbol of human freedom and human responsibility. The ballot spells Political Liberty, and Political Liberty corresponds to a need of both halves of humanity. That gateway, Political Liberty, lies on our line of march, as it lay on yours. Our line of march does not end there—it goes on and on and on. But in order now to go on we must go through that gateway. A million cosmic forces have brought us full before it, and a million cosmic forces are going to draw us through it. What we ask of you today is that, in your several States and in your several ways, you do not obstruct those forces, but aid them. We ask that you range your personal weight and influence on the side of eternal justice, on the side of the evolutionary process. We ask that you give your help to the women of this country in their struggle for political independence.

And we thank your Excellencies for this hearing.

Notes

This document, printed in pamphlet form by the NAWSA and widely circulated, is published with the permission of Captain John W. Johnston, great-nephew of Mary Johnston.

1. This information is drawn from Marjorie Spruill Wheeler, *New Women of the New South: The Leaders of the Woman Suffrage Movement in the Southern States* (New York: Oxford University Press, 1993), quotations, 47, 102. Johnston is one of the eleven leaders featured in *New Women of the New South;* See also Marjorie Spruill Wheeler's introduction to a reprint edition of Johnston's *Hagar* (Charlottesville and London: University Press of Virginia, 1994).

4

The Southern Temperament as Related to Woman Suffrage

Anne Dallas Dudley

An Address Delivered at the "Dixie Night" Session of the National American Woman Suffrage Convention in Atlantic City, September 8, 1916

Anne Dallas Dudley (1876–1955) of Nashville was the best known (at least outside the state) of the Tennessee suffragists. The daughter of a wealthy industrialist, she was educated at Ward's Seminary and attended Price's College, both in Nashville. In 1902 she married Guilford Dudley, a prominent insurance executive and hardware dealer.

Elected president of the Nashville Equal Suffrage League when it first organized in 1911, Dudley served until 1915. She also served as president of the Tennessee Equal Suffrage Association, Inc., from 1915 until she gave up the position in 1917 to become Third Vice President of the National American Woman Suffrage Association. In this capacity she traveled extensively, aiding the cause in other states and regions and playing an active role in the ratification campaign.[1]

Aware that participation in "war work" not only helped the war effort but aided the suffrage cause, Dudley was actively involved in the Liberty Loan drives. She was appointed by the secretary of the treasury as a member of the National Woman's Liberty Loan Commission (1917–19) and was the state president of the Tennessee Woman's Liberty Loan Commission. A Democrat, Dudley was the first woman chair of the Association of Democratic State Committees in 1920 and a delegate-at-large to the Democratic National Convention in 1920.[2]

Like many of the white southern suffragists, Dudley presented her cause as unthreatening and in tune with prevailing values of her region, and she employed the traditional "weapons" of the Southern Lady—charm, flattery, and appeals to chivalry—as she tried to persuade the men of her region to share power. According to Anne Firor Scott in *The Southern Lady: From Pedestal to Politics*, northern suffragists were sometimes astonished and somewhat appalled by this "complimentary attitude" southern suffragists employed in speaking with southern legislators. When New Englander Maud Wood Park confessed to a co-worker her fears that "the men to whom it was addressed would think we had deliberately sent a honey-tongued charmer . . . to cajole them," the co-worker replied that "southern men were so accustomed to that sort of persiflage they would think a woman unfeminine if she failed to use it!"[3] Southern suffragists, at times, expressed repugnance for such tactics, but they were also aware that the only weapon they had for achieving "direct influence" was "indirect influence"—the power of persuasion.

Southern suffragists and their sympathizers in the press also fought the radical image of the woman suffrage movement by emphasizing the beauty, femininity, and domesticity of the movement's leaders, and Dudley, said to be a "legendary beauty," was a prime candidate for such stories. Tennessee newspapers proudly reported that when she assumed the dais to make a seconding speech at the 1920 Democratic National Convention in San Francisco, the band members broke into "Oh, You Beautiful Doll." Suffragists circulated photographs of Dudley reading to her two "attractive children."[4] In 1916, Dudley and her children led a suffrage parade from downtown Nashville to Centennial Park.[5]

In the speech below, a classic example of the "honey-tongued charm," Dudley outlines the initial aversion to and eventual embrace of woman suffrage by white southerners, emphasizing that "the Southern woman" would have nothing to do with a movement that smacked of "sex antagonism." She ridicules many of her male opponents, but hails the emergence of a new Southern Man: awake, unthreatened, willing to share responsibility with women, and ready to embark upon "a new knighthood, a new chivalry, when men will not only fight for women, but for the rights of women."

The awakening of Southern women to this great world question has been slow, because in order to grip the Southern heart a cause must have its glamour. That, you see, is our trouble—too much heart. The only business a Southern girl is ever taught or is born with a knowledge of is the business of hearts—the way to win them, the way to hold them, sometimes the way to destroy them, but more often the way to cherish them through life. So what had woman's suffrage to do with us? Our laws were bad, particularly those affecting women

Anne Dallas Dudley with her two children. Courtesy of the Tennessee Historical Society.

and children, but then our men were so much better than our laws, so why worry? The much-vaunted Southern chivalry was so real that it was almost impossible to convict a woman in court, and the Southern men so imbued with the idea of protecting women that the lawmakers would not permit a married woman to make a contract in her own name until two years ago.

Now, it seems to me that with us much of the opposition to woman suffrage is founded on the supposition that men and women are ideal creatures—that men are always going to protect women, and no woman is ever going to need protection against men.

We are a race of dreamers in the South, by choice and because of climactic conditions. Doing things makes no appeal to us as long as we can sit and think about them. That is why we are still doing the rough work of the world instead of turning out the finished product; sending our lumber to Eastern markets to receive the mark of the master craftsman; sending our cotton everywhere to be turned into the finest fabrics, and that is why we haven't already got woman suffrage throughout the South to-day.

A Change Came

As long as it was a question of woman's rights; as long as the fight had any appearance of being against man; as long as there seemed to be a vestige of sex antagonism, the Southern woman stood with her back turned squarely toward the cause. She wouldn't even turn around to look at it. She would have none of it at all. But when she awoke slowly to a social consciousness, when eyes and brain were at last free after a terrible reconstruction period, to look out upon the world as a whole; when she found particularly among the more fortunate classes that her leisure had come to mean laziness, when she realized that through the changed conditions of modern life so much of her work had been taken out of the home, leaving her to choose between following it into the world or remaining idle; when with a clearer vision she saw that man needed her help in governmental affairs, particularly where they touched her own interests, she said, "Oh, that is so different!"

Right about face, she turned, and she said to the Southern man. "I don't wish to usurp your place in government, but it is time I had my own. I don't complain of the way you have conducted your part of the business of government, but my part has been either badly managed, or not managed at all. In the past you have not shown yourself averse to accepting my help in very serious matters; my courage and fortitude and wisdom you have continually praised. Now that there is a closer connection between the government and the home than ever before in the history of the world, will you not let me help you?"

And he in turn has said—various things. Sometimes: "Oh, you want to help me, do you? Not to get in the way? Well, on the whole I see no objection to that." Sometimes when surpassingly truthful, he has said: "But you know, you'll try to reform us, and we don't want to be reformed. Why you'd take all the fun out of politics. What would we do if we couldn't drink and fight at a convention?" To which she might make reply, that there are plenty of other places, possibly more appropriate, for these delectable forms of amusement.

Some Southern Men

Then there is—yes, there is, even in the South—the gentle-mannered, sweet-tempered soul, who says: "Shucks, I don't take no stock in sich foolishness. My old 'oman, she raises children, chickens and hell, and that's enough for her." And there is, even in the South, the chivalrous gentleman who, when you have asked him to vote for your amendment, in order that we may all be free, with that glorious freedom which includes responsibility, will look at you and say: "I bet you left some dirty dishes on the table at home!" But, when you have, with truly heavenly patience, carefully explained to him that no good suffragist will permit dirt of any kind around her, not even dirty politicians, if he doesn't belong to the last-named class he may relent, and admit that perhaps women are needed in public housekeeping.

And we have, even in the South, the superior psychologist, the man who understands women so well, who knows perfectly why you are a suffragist, why you will deny yourself pretty frocks and put your jewels in the melting pot, or maybe give up a hard-earned vacation for the sake of the cause. It is because "you want to get your picture in the paper." And we have even in the South the man who considers that he has given you an irrefutable answer to all you may say about the desirability of a real democracy, about the injustice of class legislation and the inferior position given women in the eyes of the law, when he tells you a pathetic story of a child clutching tearfully at its mother's skirts, begging a story, or a cookie, and being pushed aside by a stern parent on the way to a suffrage meeting. Of course this same man, with characteristic logic, would feel that an impatient mother, bending over a washtub, and delivering a resounding smack to an annoying infant, was all that was sweet and womanly.

Other Southern Men

But, thank heaven, we have also in the South the man who has pointed the way to us, who has not been afraid to lead us, who has said to us, "The world needs its women; you must go where duty calls you. There is corruption to contend with, yes, but on you must rest the blame as well as on me. Who was it that taught me when my mind was soft and plastic? A woman. Who will teach the future citizen his duty to his country—not what he may take from it, but what he may give to it? A woman. And what do you know of citizenship? You must first learn before you can teach; and there is no education without participation. You must first act if you would know. Remember every nation stands where its women stand; and if we, as a nation, are to realize our ideals; if we are to go onward and upward, it must be together."

And so you see not only the Southern woman, but the Southern man is now awake, and present conditions strongly indicate that before another year has passed we will have some form of suffrage for the women of our state. I think our hope lies in the knowledge that Southern women have never sidestepped the fact that no matter how different the interests of men and women may seem, in the end, they are identical. I need not point you to stupid, lying statistics, to prove to you that we have fewer divorces in the South than in any other section of the country. We are not the temperament to sell our birthright for a "mess of facts"; but the feeling of oneness of aim is there, and if you think that is a poor foundation for our future achievements, you must remember that we are essentially an imaginative, romantic people and we have seen a vision—the vision of a time when a woman's home will be the whole wide world, and her children, all those whose feet are bare, and her sisters, all those who need a helping hand. A vision of a new knighthood, a new chivalry, when men will not only fight for women, but for the rights of women. You know the cynical French phrase, wherever there is trouble, "cherzez la femme." We do not accept it. We believe that wherever a man has reached the heights, there you may, indeed, look for the woman. There is in every woman's heart, for every man who has her affection, whether it is her father, her husband, or her son, the feeling Kipling understood so well, when he wrote "Mother Mine." So there is little to fear in the way of rivalry, and we look forward to the time when there will be a better, more complete understanding between men and women, when men will have more of tenderness and women more of courage; when each will lead and follow in turn; and the honor of both be increased thereby.

And you will not blame us if we keep steadily in mind the greater woman of the future, of whom Walt Whitman said: "I see her where she stands, less protected than ever, and yet more protected than ever." More protected because there will be less need of shielding her in a world that has been humanized by woman's untrammeled influence.

Notes

This speech is reprinted from a clipping from the *Nashville Banner* entitled "Suffrage in the South: Mrs. Guilford Dudley's Address Before National Convention: Southern Temperament: How It Has Affected the Point of View from Which Subject Has Been Approached: Rational Conclusions." The *Banner* printed it with the following noncommittal introduction: "The subject was treated in an original manner, and Mrs. Dudley showed that she had given it close thought and careful analysis." Clipping, n.d. Josephine A. Pearson Papers, Tennessee State Library and Archives.

1. On Dudley, see A. Elizabeth Taylor, *The Woman Suffrage Movement in Tennessee* (New York: Bookman Associates, 1957); Anastatia Sims, "'Powers That Pray and Powers That Prey': Tennessee and the Fight for Woman Suffrage," *Tennessee Historical Quarterly* (Winter 1991): 203–25, especially 206, 207.

2. Rose Long Gilmore, *Davidson County Women in the World War, 1914–1919* (Nashville: Foster and Parks, 1923), 354; Wilma Dykeman, *Tennessee Women: Past and Present*, ed. Carol Lynn Yellin (Memphis, Nashville: Tennessee Committee for the Humanities and Tennessee International Women's Decade Coordinating Committee, 1977), 5.

3. Anne Firor Scott, *The Southern Lady: From Pedestal to Politics* (Chicago: University of Chicago Press, 1970), 183–84.

4. See Sims, "Powers That Pray," 206, 222n. 19; Carol Lynn Yellin, "Countdown in Tennessee, 1920," *American Heritage* 30 (Dec. 1978): 12–35, especially 18–20.

5. Taylor, *The Woman Suffrage Movement in Tennessee*, 45.

5

"Telling the Country": The National Woman's Party in Tennessee, 1917

Inez Haynes Irwin

From Irwin's *The Story of the Woman's Party*, 1921

The National Woman's Party (originally the Congressional Union), was also called the "Woman's Party" or the NWP. Led by Alice Paul, it was much stronger in the North and West than in the South.[1] The group played an important role in the history of the movement by demanding that the suffrage movement focus once again on the federal rather than the state route to enfranchisement—to the dismay of the "states' rights" suffragists of the South. Most white southern suffragists, however, were quite willing to support the federal amendment after their attempts to win state suffrage amendments had failed. But the vast majority sided with the National American Woman Suffrage Association in its heated dispute with the so-called "militant" Woman's Party over strategy, partly because most of them were Democrats and knew that in their region most politicians were also.

In imitation of the methods of the British suffragettes, the "militant" suffragists insisted that the "party in power," the Democratic Party, adopt woman suffrage or face their opposition; indeed, they parted with the NAWSA over advocacy of this strategy, which conflicted with the NAWSA's long-standing policy of nonpartisanship. The NWP demanded that Democratic President Woodrow Wilson compel the Democrat-controlled Congress to approve the federal woman suffrage amendment. In 1916 they infuriated Democrats by calling upon women already enfranchised in the western states to oppose Democratic candidates—including President Wilson—then up for reelection. In 1917 they began picketing the White House.

Southern Democrats reacted strongly to these perceived insults to their hero and interpreted the demonstrations as acts of treason during wartime. When NWP representatives came to Tennessee as part of a nationwide speaking tour to explain the picketing to the public (and describe the arrest and imprisonment of the picketers), supporters of the president tried to stop them. Tennessee suffragist Sue Shelton White, until then unknown to the NWP, was appalled at the treatment of the suffragists and came to their aid. Closing up shop as a court reporter, she accompanied the organizers, drawing upon her considerable popularity with lawyers and politicians in the state to pave their way—and risking her own reputation in the process.[2]

Years later, Becky Reyher (Rebecca Hourwich in the text), the organizer who was proud to have "discovered" Sue White, recalled that White "reminded the audience that we had all been strangers at the gates once, and the South, with its great tradition of liberty-loving people owed us every courtesy and a friendly welcome. . . . She [White] was truly a great woman . . . [who] would do what she could for that she believed in, even when it meant adjusting her personal and business life to do it." Since White, unlike most of these suffrage leaders, "lived by what she earned, . . . her shutting up shop to help us was a real sacrifice. Her reward, as always, was the knowledge she had done right."[3]

White's association with the "militants," however, so scandalized members of the Tennessee Woman Suffrage Association and NAWSA President Carrie Chapman Catt that, in White's words, they practically forced her "into the bosom of the National Woman's Party."[4]

It is interesting to note that Maud Younger of California, the NWP orator sent to Tennessee, blamed Tennessee Senator Kenneth D. McKellar (later a strong supporter of ratification and Sue White's employer from 1920 to 1926) for the "persecution" of the NWP organizers in his state. Note also the strong support the NWP organizers received from organized labor.

. . . The country had not been kept misinformed or uninformed in regard to the treatment of the pickets. Of course, the press teemed with descriptions of their protests and its results. Again and again their activities pushed war news out of the preferred position on the front pages of the newspapers. Again and again they snatched the headlines from important personages and events. But despite flaming headlines, these newspaper accounts were inevitably brief and incomplete: sometimes unfair. The Woman's Party determined that the great rank and file, who might be careless or cautious of newspaper narration, should hear the whole extraordinary story. Picketing began in January, 1917. By the end of September, long before Alice Paul's arrest and through October and November, therefore, speakers were sent all over the United States. Alice Paul divided the States into four parts, twelve States each: Maud Younger went to the South; Mrs. Lawrence Lewis and Mabel Vernon to the Middle West; Anne Martin to the far West; Abby Scott Baker and Doris Stevens to the East. Ahead of them went the swift band of organizers who always so ably and intensively prepared the way for Woman's Party activity. . . .

The speakers had extraordinary experiences, especially those who went into the strongholds of the Democrats in the South. Again and again when they told about the jail conditions, and how white women were forced into association with the colored prisoners, were even compelled to paint the toilets used by the colored prisoners, men would rise in the audience and say, "There are a score of men here who'll go right up to Washington and burn that jail down." It has been said the Warden Zinkham received by mail so many threats against his life that he went armed.

From Headquarters, telegrams were sent to speakers as the situation grew at Washington, informing them as to the arrests, the actions of the police, sentences, et caetera [*sic*]. Often these telegrams would come in the midst of a speech. The speaker always read them to the audience. Once after Doris Stevens had read such a telegram, "Do you protest against this?" she demanded of her audience. "We do!" they yelled, rising as one man to their feet.

Suddenly while everything was apparently going smoothly, [drawing] audiences large, indignantly sympathetic, actively protestive, change came. Everywhere obstacles were put in the way of the speakers. That this was the result of concerted action on the part of the authorities was evident from the fact that within a few days four speakers in different parts of the country felt this blocking influence. . . .

Maud Younger's experiences in the South and West were so incredible in these days of free speech that it deserves a detailed narration.

She had passed through nine southern Democratic States. Every speech had been received enthusiastically, with sympathy, and without question. Suddenly the cry of "Treason," "Pro-German," was raised. She was to speak at Dallas, Texas, on Monday, November 18. But the organizer found she could not engage a hall nor even a room at the hotel in which Miss Younger could speak. The Mayor would not allow her to hold a street meeting. Miss Younger whose speeches are always the maximum of accuracy, informedness, feeling—coupled with a kind of diplomatic suavity—offered to submit her speech for censorship. They refused her even that. Finally on Monday morning a hall was found and engaged. The people who rented it canceled that engagement on Monday afternoon. The reporters flocked to see Miss Younger, who astutely said to them,

"Of course the President is not responsible for _____ etc, etc."—ad libitum—not responsible, in brief, for all the things she would have said in her speech. . . .

In Memphis, Miss Younger had the assistance of Sue White, who, not then a member of the Woman's Party, became subsequently one of its most active, able, and devoted workers. Miss White who is very well known in her State, had just gained great public approbation by registering fifty thousand women for war work. She fought hard and constantly to preserve Miss Younger's speaking schedule in the nine Tennessee towns. But it was impossible in many cases. Everywhere they were fought by the Bar Association and the so-called Home Defense Leagues; and often by civic officials. The Bar Association et caetera [*sic*] appointed a committee to go to all hotels, or meeting-places, to ask them not to rent rooms for Miss Younger's meetings, and to mayors to request them not to grant permits for street meetings. The Mayor of Brownsville, for instance, telephoned to the Mayor of Jackson: "I believe in one God, one Country, and one President; for God's sake keep those pickets from coming to Brownsville."

Fortunately, everywhere, as has almost invariably happened in the Suffrage movement, Labor came to their rescue.

In the towns where it was impossible to get a hall, Miss Younger did not stay to fight it out. First of all, she felt the situation had developed into a free speech fight between the people of these towns and their local governments. It was for them to make the fight. Moreover, she wanted as far as possible to keep to her schedule.

Sue White went on ahead to Jackson, which was her own home town, and appealed to the Judge for the use of the Court House. The Mayor said he could not legally prevent the meeting. Miss White opened the Court House and lighted it. In the meantime, the Chief of Police met Miss Younger in the Court House before the meeting began. He told her if she said anything against the President, he would arrest her. He came to the meeting that night, but left as soon as he discovered how harmless it was—harmless, that is, so far as the President was concerned. The audience unanimously passed a resolution asking the Mayor of Nashville, which was the next stop, to permit Miss Younger to speak.

However, when she got to Nashville, the Home Defense League had brought pressure on the local authorities and it was impossible for her to get a hall. The organizer had hired the ball-room of the hotel, had deposited twenty-five dollars for it; but the manager broke his contract, refused to allow them to use it, and refunded the money. The prosecuting attorney, months later, boasted, "I was the one that kept Miss Younger from speaking in Nashville."

The next two towns were Lebanon and Gallatin. In Lebanon, although they could get no hall, they were allowed to speak in the public square. Sue White introduced Miss Younger. It was a bitter cold day; but the weather was not colder than the audience at first. Gradually, however, that audience warmed up. When Miss Younger finished, they called, "We are all with you!" When the Suffragists reached Gallatin, they secured the schoolhouse. There was no time for any publicity, but Rebecca Hourwich hired a wagon and went about the town calling, "Come to the schoolhouse! Hear the White House pickets!"

In Knoxville, they met with the same hostility from the Bar Association. Their permit to speak in the town hall was revoked, and even the street was denied to them. Joy Young, thereupon, went to Labor. The local Labor leader, who was the editor of the Labor paper, saw at once that it was a free speech fight. He said that Labor would make the fight for the Suffragists. He also pointed out that though the Mayor was a Democrat, the Judge was a Republican. He went to the Judge and asked for the Court House. The Judge said that it was not within his power to grant the Court House; that three county officials, to whom, twelve years before, jurisdiction in this matter had been given, must decide the question. These county officials agreed to the proposition. Again the Bar Association interfered. All day long telephone pressure, pro and con, was brought to bear on these county officials. In the end it was decided to have a preliminary rehearsal of Miss Younger's speech.

At high noon, therefore, Maud Younger went to the Court House. The prosecuting attorney opened the proceedings by reading from a big book an unintelligible excerpt on sedition. Miss Younger then made her forceful, witty, and tactful speech. Of course they gave her the Court House. The prosecuting attorney said, "For an hour I argued against you with the Judge. Now, I don't see how he could possibly refuse." The Judge said, "You women have a very real grievance." Late as it was, Joy Young got out dodgers, inviting the town to the meeting and scattered them everywhere, and the afternoon papers carried the announcement.

That night at dinner, the editor of the Labor paper called. He told them that the Sheriff had suddenly put up the claim of jurisdiction over the county Court House taken from him twelve years ago and that he would be there with a band of armed deputies. "*But*," said the Labor leader, "*Labor will be there with eighty armed Union men to meet them*." Of course the two Woman's Party speakers did not know what would happen. But the only thing they did know was that they would hold the meeting as usual. So Maud Younger and Joy Young proceeded alone to the Court House. They both expected to be shot. The Sheriff with his deputies, instead of surrounding the building, went inside, holding the place against Suffrage attack. The Labor men stationed themselves in front of the door. The steps were filled with audience. Joy Young introduced the speaker. Maud Younger took up her position, and they held their meeting outside. Miss Younger always says: "The Sheriff had the Court House, but I had the audience."

At Chattanooga, Joy Young had explained the situation: The Mayor was with them; the Bar Association, the Chief of Police, the Sheriff were against them; so the Mayor with the assistance of Labor and the newspapers took up their fight. No hall was to be had, *and someone in the Bar Association instructed the Chief of Police to enter any private house and break up any meeting the Suffragists might hold; and the Sheriff to do the same in the country outside the city limits*. But Labor was not to be outwitted. They were holding a scheduled meeting in their own hall that night. Labor canceled that meeting and offered Maud Younger the hall free. They said they would like to see any police break up a meeting in *their* hall. All day long there was a stormy session of the Commissioners as to whether or not she might speak. But in the end she did speak.

Later, when Maud Younger returned to Washington [where she headed the National Woman's Party's Congressional Committee], she met Senator McKellar in the course of her lobbying activities. Of course, she was astute enough to know that orders for all this persecution had come from above. She referred quite frankly to his efforts to stop her in Tennessee. With equal frankness, Senator McKellar said: "I wasn't going to have you talking against the President in Tennessee."

Notes

Excerpt from Inez Haynes Irwin, *The Story of the Woman's Party* (New York: Harcourt, Brace, and Company, 1921), part 3, "1917," chap. 2, "Telling the Country," 292–98. Published here with permission of Harcourt, Brace, Inc. For a biographical sketch of Inez Haynes Gillmore Irwin, see *Notable American Women: The Modern Period*, ed. Barbara Sicherman and Carol Hurd Green (Cambridge: Harvard University Press, 1980), 368–70.

1. On the Woman's Party's activities in the South, see Sidney R. Bland, "Mad Women of the Cause: The National Woman's Party in the South," *Furman Studies* 26 (Dec. 1980): 82–91, and Bland, "Fighting the Odds: Militant Suffragists in South Carolina," *South Carolina Historical Magazine* 82 (Jan. 1981): 32–43.

2. This information on the NWP and Sue White is drawn from Marjorie Spruill Wheeler, *New Women of the New South: The Leaders of the Woman Suffrage Movement in the Southern States* (New York: Oxford University Press, 1993), 28, 76–77, and 170–71.

3. Becky Reyher to Florence Armstrong, Sept. 26, 1958, Sue Shelton White Papers, Schlesinger Library, Radcliffe.

4. Sue Shelton White to Carrie Chapman Catt, May 9, 1918, Sue Shelton White Papers, reprinted below as document 7.

6

"Burning the President's Words Again": A Demonstration at the White House, 1918

Inez Haynes Irwin

From Irwin's *The Story of the Woman's Party*, 1921

In December 1918, the National Woman's Party, appalled that Wilson had gone to the peace conference in Europe to "work for democracy" without securing the last few votes needed for congressional approval of the suffrage amendment, began a new round of demonstrations outside the White House in Lafayette Square. This time, Tennessee's Sue White was one of the NWP members who placed Wilson's words in the flames. She was not arrested for this incident, but she was later jailed for burning Wilson in effigy, and she was one of the NWP members who toured the nation aboard the "Prison Special" wearing replicas of their prison garb and inspiring sympathy for their cause.[1]

Many historians believe NWP demonstrations played a crucial role in converting a very reluctant Wilson into an active supporter of the federal amendment; the demonstrations were quite a political embarrassment for the president, particularly after word had gotten out, through the press and tours like Maud Younger's, about the arrests, forcible feedings, and grim prison conditions.[2] But the demonstrations such as the one described below infuriated the Democrats who thought Wilson was doing a great deal to secure woman suffrage, including giving up his former insistence on the enfranchisement of women through state action only. NAWSA loyalists feared the "militants" might alienate wavering politicians. In an article entitled "Sue White Joins Suffrage Pickets: Nashville Girl Will Bear Banner at White House," the *Nashville Tennessean* reported: "the militant tactics

> are regarded as particularly unfortunate at this time since Mr. Wilson has signally manifested his earnest support of the suffrage cause. . . . There is a prospect that instead of acquiring the two or three additional votes needed to pass the suffrage resolution in the Senate some of the votes already assured for the suffrage may be lost, as many members of Congress counted as friends of suffrage have expressed in strong terms their disapproval of the militant demonstrations."[3]

On December 16, a woman carrying an American flag, emerged from Headquarters. Behind her came a long line of women bearing purple, white, and gold banners. Behind them came fifteen women bearing lighted torches. Behind them came women—more women and more women and more women. Always a banner's length apart they marched and on they came . . . and on . . . and on . . . and on. . . . People who saw the demonstrations say that it seemed as though the colorful, slow-moving line would never come to an end. Witnesses say also that it was the most beautiful of all the Woman's Party demonstrations. They marched to the Lafayette Monument. Their leader, Mrs. Harvey Wiley, stopped in front of a burning cauldron which had been placed at the foot of the pedestal. The torch bearers formed a semi-circle about that cauldron. The women with the purple, white, and gold banners—who were the speakers—grouped themselves around the torch bearers.

Among these women were the State Chairman or a Woman's Party representative from almost all the forty-eight States; some of whom had come great distances to be present on this occasion. There were three hundred in all.

In the meantime, a huge crowd, which augmented steadily in numbers and excitement as the long line of Suffragists came on and on and on, formed a great, black, attentive mass, which hedged in the banner bearers, as the banner bearers hedged in the torch bearers. In that crowd were the National Democratic Chairman and many prominent Democratic politicians.

Dusk changed into darkness, and the flames from cauldron and torches mounted higher and higher.

After the Suffragists had assembled, there came a moment of quiet. Then Vida Milholland stepped forward and without accompaniment of any kind, sang with her characteristic spirit the *Woman's Marseillaise*. Immediately afterwards, Mrs. John Rogers opened the meeting, and introduced, one after another, nineteen speakers, each of whom, first reading them, dropped some words of President Wilson's on democracy into the flaming cauldron.

Mrs. John Rogers declared:

We hold this meeting to protest against the denial of liberty to American women. All over the world today we see surging and sweeping irresistibly on, the great tide of democracy, and women would be derelict to their duty if they did not see to it that it brings freedom to the women of this land.

England has enfranchised her women, Canada has enfranchised her women, Russia has enfranchised her women, the liberated nations of Central Europe are enfranchising their women. America must live up to her pretensions of democracy!

Our ceremony today is planned to call attention to the fact that the President has gone abroad to establish democracy in foreign lands when he has failed to establish democracy at home. We burn his words on liberty today, not in malice or anger, but in a spirit of reverence for truth.

This meeting is a message to President Wilson. We expect an answer. If it is more words, we will burn them again. The only answer the National Woman's Party will accept is the instant passage of the Amendment in the Senate.

Mrs. M. Toscan Bennett was the first speaker. She said:

It is because we are moved by a passion for democracy that we are here to protest against the President's forsaking the cause of freedom in America and appearing as a champion of freedom in the old world. We burn with shame and indignation that President Wilson should appear before the representatives of nations who have enfranchised their women, as chief spokesman for the right of self-government while American women are denied that right. We are held up to ridicule to the whole world.

We consign to the flames the words of the President which have inspired women of other nations to strive for their freedom while their author refuses to do what lies in his power to liberate the women of his own country. Meekly to submit to this dishonor to the nation would be treason to mankind.

Mr. President, the paper currency of liberty which you hand to women is worthless fuel until it is backed by the gold of action.

The Reverend Olympia Brown of Wisconsin, eighty-four years old, burned the latest words of President Wilson, his two speeches made on the first day of his visit to France. She said:

America has fought for France and the common cause of liberty. I have fought for liberty for seventy years and I protest against the President leaving our country with this old fight here unwon.

Mrs. John Winters Brannan burned the address made by President Wilson at the Metropolitan Opera House in opening the Fourth Liberty Loan Campaign, in which he justified women's protest when he said:

> We have been told it is unpatriotic to criticise public action. If it is, there is a deep disgrace resting upon the origin of this nation. We have forgotten the history of our country if we have forgotten how to object, how to resist, how to agitate when it is necessary to readjust matters.

Mary Ingham burned President Wilson's speech of the Fourth of July, 1914, in which he said:

> There is nothing in liberty unless it is translated into definite action in our own lives today.

Miss Ingham said:

> In the name of the women of Pennsylvania who are demanding action of the President, I consign these words to the flames.

Agnes Morey burned President Wilson's book, *The New Freedom*. She said:

> On today, the anniversary of the Boston Tea Party, in the name of the liberty-loving women of Massachusetts, I consign these words to the flames in protest against the exclusion of women from the Democratic program of this Administration.

Henrietta Briggs Wall burned President Wilson's address given at Independence Hall, July 4, 1919, when he said:

> Liberty does not consist in mere general declarations of the rights of man. It consists in the translation of these declarations into action.

Susan Frost, of South Carolina, burned President Wilson's last message to Congress in which he again spoke words without results.

Mrs. Townsend Scott burned his message to the Socialists in France which declared:

> The enemies of liberty from this time forth must be shut out.

Mrs. Eugene Shippen burned this message to Congress:

> This is a war for self-government among all the peoples of the world as against the arbitrary choices of self-constituted masters.

Sara Grogan burned another message to Congress dealing with liberty for other nations.

Clara Wold burned the message to Congress demanding self-government for Filipinos.

Jessie Adler burned the speech to the Chamber of Commerce of Columbus:

> I believe that democracy is the only thing that vitalizes the whole people.

Mrs. Percy Reed burned this message to Congress:

> Liberty is a fierce and intractable thing to which no bounds can be set and no bounds ought to be set.

Sue White burned the President's reply to President Poincaré of France.

Mary Sutherland burned the words:

> I believe the might of America is the sincere love of its people for the freedom of mankind.

Edith Phelps burned the Flag Day address.

Doris Stevens burned a statement to Democratic women before election:

> I have done everything I could do and shall continue to do everything in my power for the Federal Suffrage Amendment.

Dr. Caroline Spencer burned the words which President Wilson said when he laid a wreath on the tomb of Lafayette:

> . . . in memory of the great Lafayette—from a fellow servant of liberty.

Margaret Oakes burned the Suffrage message to the Senate:

> We shall deserve to be distrusted if we do not enfranchise our women.

Florence Bayard Hilles ended the meeting with a declaration that women would continue their struggle for freedom, and would burn the words of President Wilson even as he spoke them until he and his Party made these words good by granting political freedom to the women of America.

After the meeting was over, the long line marched back to Headquarters. A big, applauding crowd walked along with them.

Notes

From Irwin, *The Story of the Woman's Party,* part 4, "Victory," chap. 11, "Burning the President's Words Again," 386–90.

1. A. Elizabeth Taylor, *The Woman Suffrage Movement in Tennessee* (New York: Bookman Associates, 1957), 56, 57.

2. See, for example, Sally Hunter Graham, "Woodrow Wilson, Alice Paul, and the Woman Suffrage Movement," *Political Science Quarterly* 98 (Winter 1983–84): 665–79, and Christine Lunardini and Thomas Knock, "Woodrow Wilson and Woman Suffrage: A New Look," *Political Science Quarterly* 95 (Winter 1980–81): 655–71.

3. John D. Erwin, Washington Bureau, *Nashville Tennessean,* Aug. 11, 1918.

7

Correspondence between Sue Shelton White and Carrie Chapman Catt, 1918

The following correspondence is from the Sue Shelton White Papers at the Schlesinger Library, Radcliffe College. Significantly, these letters were exchanged between the president of the massive National American Woman Suffrage Association, Carrie Chapman Catt, and the humble recording secretary of a state association, Sue Shelton White. They illustrate the rivalry and the degree of distrust between the NAWSA and the NWP in 1918.

Sue Shelton White (1887–1943) was born in Henderson, Tennessee, the daughter of a lawyer/Methodist minister who died when she was nine. White's mother struggled to bring up Sue and her two siblings alone, until her death four years later. Sue was reared by an aunt. Unlike most of the southern suffrage leaders, Sue White needed to become self-supporting; she attended a "normal school," Georgia Robertson Christian College, and West Tennessee Business College in Dyer. She became a stenographer and then (in 1907) a court reporter in Jackson, Tennessee, a post that enabled her to make contacts among lawyers and politicians that would later prove to be quite fruitful.

At the age of twenty-six (1913), Sue White began serving the Tennessee suffragists as recording secretary. Despite her considerable talent and commitment to the cause, it is unlikely that she would have risen higher in the ranks of Tennessee's NAWSA-affiliated suffragists; the highest offices were occupied by older women, including Kate Burch Warner and Anne Dallas Dudley, who, like White, were extremely talented but were also wealthy and socially prominent.[1]

The exchange of letters began when Catt wrote to Kate Warner, Tennessee Woman Suffrage Association president, expressing concern that

White's "cooperation" with National Woman's Party organizers and her continued involvement in the NAWSA might lead to a breach of NAWSA security. White, who must have been astonished that the issue of her loyalty attracted the attention of the nation's most visible and powerful suffrage leader, seized the opportunity to communicate her unhappiness with the minor role Catt had assigned southern suffragists in her "Winning Plan." (See part 1, essay 2, above.)

After a full "confession" describing her aid to the National Woman's Party, White made it clear to Catt that her initial sympathy for the harassed NWP organizers had turned into serious interest in their organization *only* after White learned that the NAWSA was cutting back on support for state campaigns in the South. Catt denied that the NAWSA was turning its back on Tennessee suffragists, but urged White to "take a big view" of the suffrage situation and support the overall national strategy. And Catt insisted that the NAWSA's non-partisan policy and the NWP's "anti-party in power" policy were incompatible, and that White must "take your stand fair and square, one side or the other."

White was clearly torn between feelings of admiration and loyalty toward Tennessee's "regular" suffrage leaders and her distaste for their treatment of the National Woman's Party representatives—women whom White clearly admired. She would always try to cooperate with both organizations, but, of course, finally took her stand with the Woman's Party. Alice Paul, recognizing White's considerable ability, quickly elevated her to positions of prestige and authority, first as chair of the National Woman's Party in Tennessee (June 1918) and later as editor of its national paper, the *Suffragist* (1919).

Nashville, Tenn.
April 27, 1918

Mrs. Carrie Chapman Catt,
171 Madison Ave.,
New York.

My dear Mrs. Catt:

Mrs. [Kate Burch] Warner has shown me your letter of April 24th, and I think perhaps it is due her that I write you. I am always willing to "face the music" and answer for my own acts with as little embarrassment to my friends as is possible.

Let me say in the beginning that it was unnecessary for you to ask Mrs. Warner to remind me that the plans which were gone into at Indianapolis [NAWSA convention] were not to be given out to any member of the Woman's Party. I went to Indianapolis in the utmost good faith as a member

Sue Shelton White. From the Sue Shelton White Papers, The Schlesinger Library, Radcliffe College.

of the National Association and shall certainly respect the good faith in which I was received. However, after it developed that the southern states could not expect any assistance from the National for the Federal Amendment work, I became a great deal more interested in the work of the Woman's Party in the South. Up to that time, the "cooperation" I had given had hardly been worthy of the name, even though the word might have added to the interest of the news story in the Suffragist [the National Woman's Party newspaper].

In order that you may understand the position in which I was placed up to that time, and in explanation of the "cooperation" referred to, I shall give you a bit of history, since you say you do not know what my past history has been.

For the past five years I have been on the board of the Tennessee Equal Suffrage Association, Incorporated, and have done my part in the efforts to further the cause in this state. I did not see fit to accept any office in the amalgamated organization, and do not know that I would have been acceptable to all factions, but think I might have been.

Last November, Miss Maud Younger of California came to Tennessee. I was then living in Jackson, which was one of the first towns her advance agent made. Some one directed the advance agent to my office for the purpose of having an interview typed by a public stenographer who had a desk in my office. I engaged in some conversation with the suffrage organizer and of course was interested in her work. I had known of Miss Younger years ago in California. I thought very little more of the matter until a long distance message from Memphis a few days later, from which I learned that Miss Younger was being denied hearings upon the ground that she was "pro-German, disloyal, and un-American," all of which I recognized as a base political slander. I was appealed to, to do the only thing and the least thing that I could do under the circumstances, which was simply to state that while I did not subscribe to the policy of the Woman's Party and was not working with it, I did not regard either the party or Miss Younger as disloyal, pro-German, or un-American. The air got thick and I finally went to Memphis and saw with my own eyes a situation which was enough to alarm any one who holds American ideals dear. I then determined that if the same thing occurred throughout the state, I would have to join the pickets at the White House gates and take the consequences, not so much for equal suffrage as for freedom of speech, which is not only essential to our cause but to every other step in human progress.

I returned to Jackson and the following night introduced Miss Younger to an audience of several hundred of my towns-people, and without assuming responsibility for her politics, did assume responsibility for her loyalty. She was given a respectful hearing, made a good speech and undoubtedly removed a great deal of the prejudice against which all of us had been working on account of the picketing of the White House. The meeting passed a resolution commending the speaker and her message and wired it in to the Nashville papers. It was published in the Nashville Tennessean the following morning over my signature and the signatures of the Chief of Police and several prominent citizens of Jackson. I was then on the Board of the Tennessee Equal Suffrage Association, Incorporated. Rather than embarrass Mrs. [Anne Dallas] Dudley, I was willing to resign, but my place was difficult to fill and I continued.

In Nashville Miss Younger was again denied a hearing, and although the newspapers here were disposed to give her a squarer deal than they did in Memphis, an editorial appeared in the Nashville Tennessean, composed in the main of an interview given by Mrs. Dudley, which editorial opened with a personal reference to me. I do not remember the language of the editorial-interview, as I did not mind it very much. I know such words as "disloyalty" and "un-American" figured in it considerably. My friends resented it. I did not. I prefer to presume that my loyalty to my country is above reproach. I have refused to permit the incident to make any difference in my personal relations with Mrs. Dudley. I respect her and feel toward her in a way that nothing will ever change. I thought she was unjust to the National Woman's Party. I made every excuse I could think of for her to Miss Younger. It was all right for her to repudiate them, but the fact remained that she had been unjust and had gone further than it was necessary for her to go in repudiating them. In view of the personal reference to me, Miss Younger seemed to feel that I had been subjected to something very unpleasant on her account, and nothing that I could say has shaken her from a deep sense of appreciation. I tried to make it clear to her that I was not fighting for her or her party but simply because my idea of a square deal had been outraged; and that my interest went deeper than my regard for her or her party, when I saw, first hand, the political slander to which she was subjected and the flagrant violation of the American right to free speech. I was with her five days during her trip through the state, and the only apology I have is in behalf of my state, that such intolerance could have existed within its borders as to make it necessary for me to stay five days with one to whose policy I did not wish to commit myself.

Yet I think probably every corporate body holds within itself the germ of its own redemption. The re-action soon set it, and by the time Miss Younger had gotten hearings in three of the five towns she visited in West and Middle Tennessee, where I was with her, the situation had developed into a lively fight. She found more friends as the days passed, the most important being organized labor. Newspapers of Chattanooga and Knoxville, representing democrats, republicans and organized labor, began to give forth favorable editorial utterances upon free speech and the Federal Suffrage Amendment. In February of this year when the Publicity Chairman of the Tennessee Equal Suffrage Association, Incorporated, made her report, she told of one of the labor journals which had formerly favored the association having taken her severely to task because of the treatment the Tennessee suffragists "gave the pickets." One man who has had sufficient strength with organized labor to stand as a candidate for Governor wrote me he considered the position of those who would deny the hearings absolutely indefensible. So the re-action has gained strength and the day of redemption is at hand.

In all of my connection with the whole affair, I committed myself to nothing but the right of free speech, and always emphasized the point that I could not commit myself to their policy at that time. I do not suppose that any suffrage association, however conservative, would deny that right and hope to survive. The only one I know of whose head undertook to do so is now no more. I refer to the Tennessee Equal Suffrage Association, Incorporated.

You now have before you a full confession. It is but natural to suppose that from the conditions under which I was associated with Miss Younger during the five days I was with her, we should have parted very good friends, even if we were pursuing different policies. I can not question her devotion to the idea for which we strive. But whatever I have thought of her and the spirit of her party, its policy has been a different matter, and would doubtless have remained a different matter for all time to come except for the position of the southern democratic members of the Senate. I make no compromise with any one upon the suffrage issue. At the same time, I feel an interest in the Democratic party, and because of that and the further fact that I place my interest in the suffrage cause above my interest in any one suffrage organization, I am more inclined than I would have otherwise been to lend "cooperation" to the National Woman's Party, since it is working in the southern states and the National is not. If it is possible, I would like for some of the few votes yet needed to be votes of southern democrats. As improbable as it may seem, we can hope it is not impossible.

As to our Tennessee situation, you expect us to ratify at the next legislature, and when I promised we would do our best, I meant it with my whole heart. If Senator [John] Shields votes against the amendment, we can not expect, with any degree of assurance, that the Legislature will ratify. If the miracle should happen and he votes for the amendment, the fight will not be so hard. When you named us as a "fighting state," you put us in the trenches,—but we have no ammunition, except what our "allies" are lending us.

I beg your pardon for the length of this letter. Please hold me and me alone responsible for my own acts. Mrs. Warner and Mrs. Dudley are both splendid women who have the interest of suffrage very much at heart. They are worthy of your confidence. They both have mine. I did not go to Indianapolis as a spy. I went to gather what information I could for my own guidance, in helping to work out the Tennessee situation. I had no idea what would develop there. What did develop may influence my course, but I hardly think it will make me unmindful of the good faith I owe the National Association, not to give out is plans for Congressional work or ratification.

The organizer of the National Woman's Party who has been in the state for the past month holds her last meeting, I understand, in Knoxville tomorrow and then goes on to another southern state. It may be that they will send another out from Washington. If so, it will simply indicate that they recognize the need of waking up the south. If that is to be their policy, it is one to which almost any suffragist in Christendom could subscribe at this particular time.

Sincerely yours,

Sue S. White [signed]

[The following letter was written on NAWSA letterhead.]

May 6, 1918

Miss Sue White
Jackson, Tennessee

My dear Miss White:—

I am in receipt of your letter for which I thank you cordially. I regretted after the Indianapolis meeting that I had not said more emphatically that the plans agreed to there must not be made public; as these were alternate plans based upon going through Senate or not going through, it would be naturally unwise to give them out and further we have found that most people are very leaky and sometimes we have actually read in the papers confidential matter which we have sent to presidents. It is no reflection upon you therefore to warn you that the plans were not to be given out.

Thank you for "your confession." It probably was that history which led someone to raise the question of your loyalty to the National Association.

The National Association has been known to take a very definite stand concerning its relationship to the Woman's Party. This has been due entirely to the fact that the public is apt to think all suffragists as belonging to the same group. The Woman's Party has done very much to add to this confusion. We stand strictly and absolutely upon a non-partisan policy. Every victory which has been won in the United States has been won by our Association and has been won by that policy. We feel it is very necessary to keep it up to the end. The Woman's Party is not non-partisan but is anti-party in power, but as no party by [sic] the Democratic has been in since they came into existence or are likely to be in until we get through, it virtually amounts to an anti-democratic organization. Naturally they have alienated many democratic sympathizers and it has been very difficult to win them back. We have found that they have been untrustworthy and extremely disloyal to the old association which made conditions possible for their work. It is not necessary to discuss that point or to discuss them. We have avoided doing so. Those who like their policy must go with them and those who like the non-partisan policy should stay with us. It is impossible to be partisan and non-partisan at the same time. We have urged all our people when questions like this have arisen, to take their choice and have warned them that it was bad policy to give the public the impression that all suffragists were endorsing the things that the Woman's Party have done.

It is a very great pity that all suffragists cannot unite in tactics and follow the same plan, but since circumstances make that impossible, the only advantage there can possibly be in having two policies is to have them distinctly separate.

What benefit may have accrued from the Woman's Party activities, would have been lost absolutely if it had not been for the National Association's policy and organization which has smoothed matters over and won back many men who have been alienated. It will go hard in the state where there are two organizations and they do not agree as to the policy to be followed in reference to the state referendum. Of course you will understand that.

I wonder where you got the idea that the National was not going to help Tennessee. I thought it was made clear that the National was to help the "fighting states" above and beyond all else and that it was the plan to concentrate our aid on those states. Our policy has been not to expend money on states for which there was likely to be very little return in the Senate at this time, but take the outposts. The outposts are state referenda over which we had no responsibility. Michigan and Oklahoma submitted the question to the voters simply in response to the general increase in suffrage sentiment in their states and they did it in spite of the women. Now two policies are made possible. We can turn our backs upon those states, let our amendment go to defeat and thus stand the reaction which invariably follows, not only in those states but in the nation. But we can stand by the women in those states, bolster them up to carry on the campaign and thus win it and strengthen the ratification sentiment throughout the nation. That is what we are doing and we are putting thousands of dollars and all our organizers in the four states where campaigns are now on. We hope to carry them and if we do, ratification in Tennessee will be far more possible than it can be made by a few meetings at this time.

This is the period in which women everywhere must take a big view and try to consider all the data before making up their minds. The littleness of the view which our American states rights' plan has stimulated for a hundred years, is the greatest enemy of woman suffrage, of successful war activities and of everything else we wish to do as a nation.

I do not wish to influence you in your judgment. I only ask you to get the data and think the matter out to a conclusion and then take your stand fair and square, one side or the other.

Cordially yours,

Carrie Chapman Catt [signed]
President

Dictated but not read

May 9, 1918

Mrs. Carrie Chapman Catt,
171 Madison Ave.,
New York, N. Y.

My dear Mrs. Catt:

I appreciate more than I can tell you, the spirit of your letter.

Recently, Mrs. Samuel G. Shields of Knoxville has accepted the state chairmanship of the National Woman's Party in Tennessee. Mrs. Shields is a sister-in-law of Senator Shields and the widow of the former law-partner of Hon. Chas. T. Cates, who has announced as Senator Shields's opponent, and who is a good suffragist. For the present, although I ask you not to quote me, the organization of the National Woman's Party in Tennessee is hardly more than a paper organization. However, it is not a weak one on paper, and of course much depends on what happens in Washington during the next few days as to what shall be the policy of some of your Tennessee insurgents. A day has not passed during the past six weeks that at least one resolution and sometimes two or three were sent the Senator from meetings somewhere in the State. The regular organization has lagged a little in the work but the activities of the Woman's Party have spurred them forward a little during the past two weeks. Unfortunately, some of our women seemed to hold to the idea that "amalgamation" [of the two rival NAWSA affiliates in Tennessee] was the end of all effort and were resting a little too contentedly upon their laurels.

I do not think we had anything to lose with Senator Shields, but even if we had, I have seen to it that the work of the Woman's Party did not assume the aspect of a fight upon him. He knows I have had some connection with it and he knows that personally I feel very friendly toward him. The entrance of his sister-in-law in the field may have put another phase on it, in his mind, but the work has gone on in the same way. Mrs. Warner, I understand, has brought considerable influence to bear recently. The details of the work over the state have carried no evidence of whether it was done by friend or foe.

An effort was made in Nashville by a suffrage influence to block the work, which I think most unfortunate. The subject of the picketing of the White House was lugged in *by suffragists*, and the question of loyalty again raised *by suffragists*. Mrs. Dudley, herself, made no public statement this time. I do not think the Woman's Party would have undertaken even a paper organization except as it was forced upon them in this way. When put on the defensive they must defend, or look to some one to do it for them.

Of course, I am not the spokesman of the Woman's Party in Tennessee, but I told Mrs. Dudley some time ago that in my opinion it was simply a flank movement which could do no harm and might or might not do some good; that I did not think the Woman's Party expected anything more than a paper organization just now or wanted anything except the privilege of strengthening the public sentiment for the amendment. It is sometimes not altogether impolitic to sound a gentle warning, even to a U.S. Senator, and it may be that the senior member from Tennessee sees in the present situation a gentle warning that all will not be well for him in the future should the amendment get by without his vote.

At least, it has had the tendency to more firmly unite the forces of the National and set them to work. Sometimes an outside influence can do this when an inside influence can not. What shall be my own fate, I do not know. I have been the official "goat" of Tennessee suffragedom ever since I came into the work. I may be thrown by main strength and awkwardness into the bosom of the National Woman's Party. There I shall find a welcome, I am sure, but it remains to be felt, by me and me alone, whether or not my lot shall be an easy one. It may mean the greatest sacrifice I could make. So far, I can't say I have found any particular enjoyment from my association with them, although I have met some splendid young women and have suffered enough with them to greatly admire their courage and love their zeal.

Whatever course I shall take, I shall not forget the splendid efforts of those who have made all other work possible.

Sincerely yours,

[Sue Shelton White]

[The following letter was written on NAWSA letterhead to White, who was then serving a one-year term as executive secretary of the Tennessee Commission for the Blind. Here Catt responds magnanimously after White has accepted the chairmanship (in June 1918) of the Tennessee branch of the National Woman's Party.]

July 20, 1918

Miss Sue White
Commission for the Blind
Nashville, Tennessee

My dear Miss White:—

This is an acknowledgment of your letter of June 24th. There is no time for you and me to be bickering over nice points. The big battle is too hot and too important and demands of both of us too many duties to be wasting time that way.

I know you are doing the best you can and beyond that no one can make demands upon you. I know that you are able and strong and splendid and I beg of you to use all your influence and force at this time to bring together any discordant forces there may be in Tennessee and to help the big cause on.

I have mapped out a lively program for Mrs. Warner which I hope she will be able and willing to put through.

Yours cordially,

Carrie Chapman Catt [signed]
President

July 25, 1918

Mrs. Carrie Chapman Catt
171 Madison Ave.,
New York, N. Y.

My dear Mrs. Catt:

Your letter of the 10th makes me realize all the more how much I love the National Association. I have not wanted to leave it. We women are sometimes a little sentimental about the things we have mothered and the things that have mothered us. But I know that you understand that the highest loyalty I could ever give you, inside or outside of any organization, is loyalty to our cause. That I shall always give, in the best light that is mine.

I am willing to resign my membership in the National, although I do not know that it would be necessary, since the league of which I was a member in Jackson is now disbanded and I have never joined the organization in Nashville.

I have an organizer in the state now and have planned six weeks work for her. I am sending her to towns that have never been worked before, hoping to avoid confusion, friction, or duplication of effort.

Senator Shields has promised Mrs. Warner an audience, and the women of both organizations are ready to join the delegation. The Senator has not, however, set the date. Mrs. Warner has an abundance of faith in him, as she knows him quite well socially. I know him quite well also, but my acquaintance has been more political than social. There is sometimes a difference.

His statement to the voters yesterday claims that he has supported the administration in all things. He absolutely ignores the suffrage issue and says there are no public issues for him to discuss. His opponent, Governor [Tom C.] Rye, has declared for suffrage.

I wish there were some way to furnish Senator Shields with an issue, since he says he has none. Perhaps the President could do so, if the President really considers suffrage an issue. We understand he has written a letter.

In spite of every effort to curb my militant tendencies, my mind continued to revert to the suggestion of Abigail Adams to her John more than a hundred years ago, that the ladies might be constrained to foment a rebellion. Is a hundred years behind the times conservative enough?

Sincerely yours,

[Sue Shelton White]

Note

1. James P. Louis, "Sue Shelton White," *Notable American Women: A Biographical Dictionary*, ed. Edward T. James, et al. (Cambridge, Mass.: Harvard University Press, 1971), 3: 590–92; See also James P. Louis, "Sue Shelton White and the Woman Suffrage Movement, 1913–1920," *Tennessee Historical Quarterly* 22 (June 1963): 170–90; Marjorie Spruill Wheeler, *New Women of the New South: The Leaders of the Woman Suffrage Movement in the Southern States* (New York: Oxford University Press, 1993), 42–47, 52, 57, 61; and Elaine Showalter, ed., *These Modern Women: Autobiographical Essays from the Twenties* (Old Westbury, N.Y.: The Feminist Press, 1978), 45–52.

8

Strong Disapproval of Pickets Is Voiced: Tactics of Woman's Party Representatives Deplored by Mrs. Leslie Warner

Kate Burch Warner

Press Release, 1918

Katherine Burch Warner (1851–1923) of Nashville was born in Chattanooga. Her father, a colonel in the Confederate army, was one of Nathan Bedford Forrest's cavalry officers; after the war he was editor and publisher of the *Union and American* and later of the *Nashville American* and served as state comptroller of Tennessee and secretary of the United States Senate. Kate Burch graduated from Vassar and then completed a European tour before embarking upon a glittering "social career." In 1880, she married Leslie Warner, a pioneer in the iron industry in the South. Their three children all died early in their childhood.

Kate Warner was a prominent clubwoman, active in the Daughters of the American Revolution and the Centennial Club, among others, and was vice-president of the Tennessee Federation of Woman's Clubs. During World War I, she was the first vice-president of the Tennessee Woman's Council of National Defense and a member of the National Board of the Fatherless Children of France Society.[1] She was serving as president of the Nashville Equal Suffrage League when she had the opportunity to play a leading role in the reunification of the two statewide suffrage organizations. When the presidency of each of the suffrage associations became open at the same time, a campaign mounted for their union under Warner's leadership, and she announced she would accept a state presidency only of a unified suffrage movement. The groups merged in March 1918 as the Tennessee Woman Suffrage Association, with Warner as president. She later played an important role in the ratification campaign when she was appointed chair of the Ratification Committee by Governor A. H. Roberts. A gifted public speaker, Warner once addressed a crowd of twenty-five hundred people in Centennial Park.[2]

This statement, in which Warner attempts to disassociate the Tennessee Woman Suffrage Association from the National Woman's Party, is similar to many such statements issued by the leaders of NAWSA affiliates in southern states. National leaders of the NAWSA took pains to distance themselves from the activities of the "militants," believing they were hurting the cause. Southern suffragists, however, were particularly disturbed by the "militants," because they were so eager to avoid offending the Democrats, President Wilson was such a southern hero, and they were striving to avoid the taint of radicalism.[3] Warner also protested publicly in February 1919 when the "Suffrage Prison Special," the train carrying twenty-four of the women who had been arrested during the NWP's demonstrations—including Sue Shelton White—stopped in Chattanooga and conducted three street meetings and an evening rally.[4]

In order that there may be no misapprehension about the status of the Tennessee Woman's [*sic*] Suffrage Association, I wish to state that our organization belongs to the National Woman's [*sic*] Suffrage Association, of which Mrs. Carrie Chapman Catt is president.

We have no connection nor association with the picketers. They belong to the Militant or Woman's Party, of which Miss Alice Paul is president. We do not approve of their tactics and deplore most deeply their methods which have done incalculable harm to the suffrage cause.

Two weeks since they burned the President's message in La Fayette Square, Washington. All true suffragists resent deeply this base ingratitude and lamentable indignity to the head of our Nation and the staunch and splendid friend of woman's suffrage.

It is just as illogical and unfair to hold our party responsible for the misdeeds and misdemeanors of the picketers as it would be to hold the Democratic party responsible for the treason of the I.W.W. [Industrial Workers of the World].

Last winter, these same picketers flaunted banners in front of the White House which were insulting to the President. He looked over the heads of these misguided and mistaken women. He overlooked what he saw written on their banners.

He saw beyond them a great army of splendid determined women whose aim was the enfranchisement of their sex, whose aim was to better, to glorify, to uplift the mission of womanhood.

Then he wrote that letter to Congress, telling them the time had come for the emancipation of their women and the House heeded his words and voted aye on the side of right and justice and freedom and democracy. We are now pinning our faith to the Senate of the United States and to our own Tennessee Legislature. God grant to these American men the power to hear the call of democracy and to answer it.

Notes

From an unidentified newspaper clipping, n.d. [1918], Josephine Anderson Pearson Papers, Tennessee State Library and Archives, Nashville. Pearson wrote below the clipping, "Mrs. Warner once a guest in the home at Monteagle of Miss Pearson—before this Equal Suffrage 1920 Battle, we were friends."

1. This information on Warner's life is from Margaret Collier, *Biographies of Representative Women of the South 1861–1925* (3 vols., 1920–25), 3: 243–45.

2. A. Elizabeth Taylor, *The Woman Suffrage Movement in Tennessee* (New York: Bookman Associates, 1957), 45, 57, 68, 109.

3. Marjorie Spruill Wheeler, *New Women of the New South: The Leaders of the Woman Suffrage Movement in the Southern States* (New York: Oxford University Press, 1993), 74–77.

4. Taylor, *The Woman Suffrage Movement in Tennessee*, 56, 57.

9

An Address to the Men of Tennessee on Female Suffrage: An Antisuffrage Pamphlet, 1916

John J. Vertrees

John J. Vertrees, the leader of the male antisuffragists—and, according to the suffragists, leader of the antis of both sexes—published a lengthy pamphlet, excerpted here, addressed specifically to the men of Tennessee. That he addressed it to the men of the state was consistent with his view that woman suffrage was "not a question of what women want, but what they ought to have; and as men only now vote, it is a question for men alone to determine."

Unlike many of the antisuffrage broadsides prepared for quick digestion by the general public, this lengthy publication is clearly designed for the well-educated, leading men of the state. In it Vertrees asserts and defends a number of arguments for the exclusion of women from politics and insists that woman suffrage is just the "vanguard" for revolutionary feminism. He strongly implies that Tennessee "suffragettes" (in America, a term used pejoratively by antisuffragists) do not fully understand what female enfranchisement would mean, and concludes that repeal of "Nature's old Salic Law" excluding women from government would prove "supremely disastrous" for civilization.[1]

Vertrees was a Nashville attorney and Democratic politician, who, according to Anastatia Sims, had a number of liquor industry executives among his clients. As early as 1887 he suggested that the temperance movement, in Sims's words, "harbored feminists, Republicans, and other 'fanatics' bent on undermining social and political order in Tennessee." And he remained one of Tennessee's most vigorous opponents of both prohibition and woman suffrage for more than thirty years.[2]

Female Suffrage

To the Men of Tennessee:

I address you on the subject of female suffrage, and do so because it is apparent that Tennessee is on the Woman's Movement programme.

The last national platforms of both the Republican and the Democratic parties virtually declared for the *principle* of female suffrage, and that too in the face of the fact that several states, including great states like New York, Pennsylvania and Massachusetts had but recently rejected female suffrage at the polls. Why, it may be asked did these platform-makers do this? Twelve states, with ninety-one *electoral votes*, have woman suffrage. Delegations of women from these states representing equal suffrage associations infested the national conventions; and when the question of incorporating a female-suffrage plank in one of the platforms was under consideration, Senator Walsh (according to the Press) declared that "it is a simple question—whether you will incur the *enmity* of these women"—meaning the women of these twelve states. The platform declaration was made, and both Mr. Hughes and Mr. Wilson outran their platforms in their eagerness not to "incur the enmity of these women."

So, I cannot believe that the men of this Republic and of Tennessee really approve of female suffrage. Nor do I believe that the strident and conspicuous few now clamoring for the "rights," truly represent the womanhood of Tennessee.

I do not believe that the women of Tennessee *want* the ballot, but even if they do, the question which *men* must determine is not affected in the least. It is not a question of what women *want,* but what they *ought* to have; and as men only now vote, it is a question for men alone to determine. However, for that reason, and also because it is a question relating to those who are dearest to men, and for whom they labor and live, the decision should be made with an eye single to what is right, and *best*—not for women, not for men; but for *all;* for the men, women and children of Tennessee.

A great deal has been written and said, and well said, for female suffrage since this modern Woman's Movement began. While this Movement has the *same* object in all countries, its *declarations* are not only unlike in different countries, but they are dissimilar in different sections of the same country, notably in the United States.

In some countries they write and speak boldly of "self-realization in love," and "the spiritualizing of sex," and a "free personality" and "volitional motherhood," and declare that a "new race" of women is developing—"a type which has discarded the old ideal of physical and mental and moral dependence, and has substituted the idea of strength."

But the *suffragists* of the United States stress something else. They speak, and in an impressive way, of "equality" and of "rights." They contend that all persons are "created equal;" that "no human being can have any real rights unless all have the same;" that for the same work men and women should receive the same wage; that "taxation without representation is unjust;" that woman is man's "equal," and therefore should have equal rights; that she will "purify" politics, and the like. I admit that this is plausible, and, considered *apart*, more or less impressive; but catchy as this phrasing may be, there is *something else* which those who say these things studiously leave out of consideration—a *something else* which is undeniable, controlling, and determinative. The matter may be likened to what is known in criminal law as an *alibi*. The evidence adduced against an accused person on trial for crime may strongly tend to fix guilt upon him, but however inculpatory that evidence, of and in itself, may appear to be, it must crumble and fall before an *established alibi*.

That "something else" is *biological* and *governmental*. It consists of certain *facts* in respect of the *nature of government* and the *nature* of males and females.

II.

There are systems of organs in all living things. One of these is the *reproductive system*. It is not, like the *digestive* system, essential to the life of the *individual*, but it is absolutely essential to the life of the *race*. "Male and Female created he them."

It is often asserted that men and women are equal. Everybody knows that they are not. Everybody knows that in some respects they *are* equal and alike, but that in other respects they are *unequal* and *unlike*. . . .

In all the past, *political* institutions have been framed with regard to the differences and the inequalities of males and females, rather than those features wherein they are equal and alike; framed and builded upon the fundamental propositions that *government rests on force*, and that the race shall not perish from the earth. As a consequence *political* institutions in the past *assumed* that the stronger males should defend, and work, and that the weaker females should be mothers and perpetuate the race; that the males should discharge the duties of the field, and the females the duties of the home.

The modern Woman's Movement proposes to reverse all this. It proposes to change *political* institutions, and to frame them with respect to the *similarities* of the male and female, rather than with reference to the inequalities and differences as heretofore. It was aptly expressed by one of the leaders, when she said that the Woman's Movement "lays its *entire* stress on the spheres which are *common* to women and men, and demands an *independent* consideration of *each* case, *regardless of normal sex peculiarities*."

It will be observed that the New Woman is not demanding equal *civil* rights merely. The demand is for equal *political* rights—that our *political* institutions, based on normal sex differences, shall be reconstructed so as to ignore these differences and assume and affirm the *oneness* of males and females. This brings us to the proposition that,

III.

The inherent nature of government requires the elective franchise to be confined to males.

All human beings have certain natural rights—the right, as it has been expressed, to life, liberty and the pursuit of happiness. But these same rights relate to the *individual* life of the being, and one-half of these beings have *femaleness* as their "original endowment from nature." And when these male and female beings are not merely a few individuals but a multitude—many millions inhabiting the same country, they also have *relations* to one another. In this situation the individual cannot assert and exercise his "rights" without friction and conflict. Consequently, by the circumstances of their situation, these beings are *forced* and *driven* to seek shelter under, and to protect themselves with, some kind of *political* institution. *These political institutions are what men call governments.*

Government can be maintained only by *force*. Vicious persons will not respect the rights of others. The necessitous will depredate. Those made desperate by circumstances recognize no law but that of force. Good citizens sometimes become enraged. Rebellions arise. Civil wars break out. Foreign foes attack and invade. The honor of the nation must be maintained.

In fine, the only *guaranties* of good government and peace are "the ballot-box, the jury-box, the sentry-box, and the cartridge-box"—the soldier, the sheriff, the policeman and the gun. This is a *fact*, and on it rests this impregnable proposition:

Only those who can bear arms should have a voice in deciding questions which may lead to war, or in enacting laws which may require soldiers, sheriffs, posses [sic] *and policemen for their enforcement.*

This alone puts female suffrage altogether out of consideration.

The suffragists realize it, and seek to escape by pretending to believe that the days of war and force have *passed away*. In 1914 Mr. William Jennings Bryan declared for female suffrage, and to escape this proposition said:

> "The argument [that women should not vote because they can not bear arms] is seldom offered *now* for the reason that as civilization advances, laws are obeyed because they are an expression of the public opinion, not merely because they have power and lead behind them."

About the same time Mr. E. A. Hecker published a book entitled "A Short History of the Rights of Women," in which he assumed to take up and annihilate the . . . arguments against female suffrage. But among other things, he says:

> "A refutation of the *physiological objects to equal suffrage is*, however, not hard to find. Even in war, as it is practiced *today*, *physical force is of little* significance compared with *strategy*, which is a product of the intellect. . . ."

Mrs. Inez Haynes Gilman [*sic*, last name, Gillmore, and later Irwin], a prominent suffragette who writes for them, made this answer:

> "In the next place this objection to equal suffrage is absurd because war is gradually *disappearing* from the earth. . . . And in the last place the bullet isn't the ballot any longer; the ballot is the bullet."

The suffragists made these answers prior to 1914 because there had been a brief period of peace which had been *stuffed* with declamations about "altruism" and the "brotherhood of man," and "moral uplift" and—sob. But they had hardly persuaded themselves that the millennium had dawned, before the world was aflame with war. . . .

Mr. Edward D. Cope stated the matter admirably when, making answer to the question whether *government* is a function adapted to the female character, or within the scope of her natural powers, he said:

> "In endeavoring to answer the first question we are at once met by the undoubted fact that woman is physically incapable of carrying into execution any law she may enact. She cannot, therefore, be called on to serve in any executive capacity where law is to be executed on adults. Now service in the support of laws enacted by those who 'rule by the consent of the governed' is a *sine qua non* of the right to elect governors. It is a common necessity to which all of the male sex are, during most of their lives, liable to be called on to sustain. This consideration alone, it appears to me, puts the propriety of female suffrage out of the question. The situation is such that the sexes cannot take an equal share of governmental responsibilities even if they should desire to do so. Woman suffrage becomes government by women alone on every occasion where a measure is carried by the aid of woman's vote. If such a measure should be obnoxious to a majority of the men they could successfully defy a party composed of a minority of their own sex and a majority of the women. That this would

> be done that can be no question, for we have a parallel case in the attempt to carry into effect negro suffrage in some parts of the South. We know the history too well."

Some of the suffragettes, realizing the force of the proposition, boldly maintain that women *can* bear arms.

The Women [*sic*] Suffrage Party of New York held a meeting. The speeches delivered at that meeting were regarded as so powerful that they were published in a pamphlet entitled "Twenty-five Answers to Antis." One of the speakers, Mrs. Maud Nathan, said that

> "From the earliest days, women *have* proved themselves capable of taking up arms in defense of their country, when they have thought it necessary to do so."

After referring to some females who in the past had fought in wars as soldiers, the lady said:

> "It would seem that women like these would have no difficulty in defending their vote. However, in preference to smashing heads they smash windows."

Mrs. Carrie Chapman Catt expressed it in these words:

> "Superficial opposers of woman's political rights use the worn-out argument that women cannot fight. They *can* fight, and have proved it, but if *they* went to war, who would then support the nation?"

Undeniably some women, barren masculine individuals, can bear arms, just as there are some men who cannot. We must deal with both as *classes*, and not as if they were either husbandettes or masculettes. It is therefore no answer to suggest that old men cannot bear arms, and yet are permitted to vote. For these aged men, when young and capable, *stood ready* to bear arms, and many of them in fact did so. . . .

If then the time has not come when swords should be beaten into plowshares, and spears into pruning-hooks—and it has not: if government is based on force—and it is; if women cannot "bear arms"—and they cannot—our *political* institutions should preserve their ancient framework: should continue to recognize the differences and inequalities of *sex*. . . .

IV.

"Motherhood and Family"

We have seen that from a *governmental* and *political* point of view, women should not become electors.

There is another view in which female suffrage appears both harmful and unwise also, and that is the effect upon the woman and the family. If the race is to survive, women *must* bear children. In the nature of things motherhood must be her supreme function. It is the guaranty of the perpetuity of the race. Consequently if civilization is to be preserved, much less advanced, woman's *rights* and woman's *duties* must be such as *motherhood* requires. I am aware that the suffragettes repudiate this view. Dr. Anna Howard Shaw [M.D., ordained minister, and president of the NAWSA from 1904 to 1915] declared that she believed in woman suffrage "whether they will neglect their children, or never bear any children." And Mrs. Ittie K. Reno, of Nashville, says that "woman is something *higher than merely a mother*. She is an *individual,* with power to work out her own salvation. When women gain their rights, they will gain a new idea, as well as a new ideal, of life."

Upon the contrary, I would say that no woman can be higher than when she is a mother, and that her rights and duties should be such as motherhood requires. Anything which takes her abroad, whether it be business or politics, injures the race, the family, and her.

Up to about forty-five years of age, a woman's life is one of frequent and regular periods marked by mental and nervous irritability, when oftentimes even her mental equilibrium is disturbed. Students of such matters inform us that these periods lengthen as the race becomes civilized. Then there is pregnancy. The *profound* effect of that to which the women who at this time are so courageously doing men's work is known. Then there is infancy—years of constant nursing and attention.

Undeniably individual women *can* vote and can labor—*can* engage in politics and business: but the effect on the *race* forbids it. We are told by Mrs. Gertrude Atherton that the physicians and biologists of England even now are predicting a "lamentable physical future" for the women who at this time are so courageously doing men's work in English factories. . . . Of course I am not to be understood as intimating that in time of *national peril* every man, woman, and child should not do his best, be the ultimate consequences to the *individual* what they may. The proposition is that the *consequences* will certainly follow.

Dr. Kirch in "Sexual Life of Woman," stated the effect of woman's "emancipation" when he said:

"The woman who spends the whole day at a desk in the law courts, or in a house of assembly, may be a most honorable and most useful *individual*, but she is no longer a *woman*, she cannot be a *wife*, she cannot be a *mother*. In the conditions of our society the emancipation of women is in its very nature the *negation* of marriage."

. . . . Of course, the mere act of going to the polls and voting once a year is of little moment—a thing of minutes, or maybe an hour, but the right of suffrage would *put women in politics*, and that would not only take her without, but cause her to neglect the within—the home. In Kansas at the last November election there were 281 women candidates for state and county offices, while 120 were actually holding office at the time.

Female suffrage is a social, as well as a political problem. It involves not only the influence of women on politics, but the effect of politics on women—on the family and on the home. This will be referred to again.

Female suffrage is a racial and social poison because it tends to disintegrate the family life. It will affect men as well as women, for, as another has well said:

"The day in which you become our equals, civilly and politically, you will become our *rivals*. Take care then that the charm that constitutes your whole strength shall not be broken. For then, as we are incalculably the more vigorous and better equipped for the sciences and arts, your inferiority will appear and you will become truly oppressed."

Women are not built on the masculine plan. Sex makes men and women unlike and unequal. Their mental and moral characteristics are as different from those of men as are their physical differences. Their traits absolutely unfit them for government and for the enactment and enforcement of laws.

Women are far more emotional than men. This means that they lack judicial fairness.

Women are disposed to consider the *particular* case, and not to take the *long view* of things. This means that public policy, general rules, and precedents—the main considerations in just government, have little weight with them. . . .

To quote again from Mr. Cope:

"We find in man a greater *capacity* for rational processes. . . . In women we find that the deficiency of endurance of the rational faculty is associated with a general incapacity for mental strain, and, as her emotional nature is stronger, that strain is more severe than it is in man under similar circumstances. Hence the easy breakdown under stress, which is probably the most distinctive feature of the female mind. This peculiarity, when pronounced, becomes the hysterical temperament. But in all departments of mental action that depend on affection or emotion for their excellence, women is the superior of man; in those departments where affection should not enter, she is his inferior. . . ."

V.

"Citizenship" and "Human Right"

As already stated, many reasons are being advanced in support of female suffrage, but prominent and leading suffragettes concede that after all, the prosuffrage argument must be resolved to a very simple proposition. Mrs. Claude D. Sullivan, in an address at the State Fair at Nashville in September last, said that "a great French philosopher put into one sentence the *whole real argument* for equal suffrage when he said: 'Either no individual member of the human race has any real rights, or else *all* have the same.'" This was but a restatement of what Mrs. Florence Durant Evans of Chattanooga had previous[ly] stated. "Into this simple sentence Condorcet condensed the whole argument: 'Either no individual member of the human race has any real rights, or else *all have the same*.'"

Dr. Anna Howard Shaw, perhaps the most prominent of the suffragettes, thus expresses it:

> "Many women feel that the greatest good they can do with the ballot is to abolish commercialized vice, to prevent child labor, or to make effective their protests against war. This is perhaps true. We all agree that these evils must be abolished, and that women, unenfranchised, have not and will not be able to abolish them. But the evils themselves and the desire of women to right them do *not* constitute the *reason* women should be enfranchised. The reason would remain even though all the evils I have named, or could name, should be abolished at once. We, and the women who are to come after us, should have our political power to use in any way we think best. . . .
>
> "I am personally convinced that the enfranchisement of women should be considered from the standpoint of justice and logic alone. . . .
>
> "It seems to me very *unfortunate* that we suffragists would ever permit ourselves thus to *over-qualify* for the vote, which is exactly what we do when we prove, or attempt to prove, our fitness for the ballot, and our need of it, on any other ground than that of mere *citizenship*. We should say: 'The reason men are enfranchised is because *as citizens* they have a stake in government. The reason women should be enfranchised is because *as citizens* they have a stake in the government. *This is all there is to this question of woman suffrage*.' . . .

"The question is, Why should women, *as women*, be disfranchised? Or, in other words, Why should women not have the ballot on the same terms as men, no matter what these terms are now, or what they may be in the future?"

The fundamental proposition then on which the right of woman suffrage is based is that *all* persons are entitled to the *same* rights, because they are *human beings*; and because they are *citizens*, and, as such have "a stake in government."

The only inquiry, according to the much-lauded French philosopher, is—Is the demandant a human being?

Babes, felons, lunatics, and aliens within the state, all are human beings. Therefore, they are all entitled to vote the same as grown, rational, men. The very statement of the proposition is its own refutation. Even the States in which woman suffrage exists rejects this doctrine. They all have *classes* of human beings to whom suffrage is denied. This notion that the *individual* instead of the family, is the social unit, has also been seized upon by those who believe in social and racial equality.

In a book written by educated and leading men of the negro race entitled, "The Negro Problem," it is stated that "*the unit of society in a republic, is the individual*;" and in "The Negro," written by M.E.B. DuBois [*sic*, should be W. E. B. Du Bois], colored, editor of *The Crisis*, it is said that "a belief in humanity means a belief in colored men," and that the American Negroes are "today girding themselves to fight in the van of progress, not simply for their own rights as men, but for the ideals of the greater world in which they live; the *emancipation of women*, universal peace, democratic government, the *socialization* of wealth, and *human* brotherhood."

Miss Helen Keller, of whom everybody has heard, a zealous suffragette, in a letter to the "National Association for the Advancement of Colored People," published in *The Crisis*, urges all "to advance gladly towards out common heritage of life, liberty, and light, undivided by *race or color* or creed, united by the same heart that beats in the bosom of all."

Undeniably if the question is merely one of *individual* right, to be determined *apart*, regardless of all racial, political, and social considerations, the "common heritage of life, liberty, and light," cannot be divided by color or race.

The argument of "citizenship," which Dr. Shaw conceded to be all there is in the question of woman suffrage, is equally fallacious. The trouble is that Dr. Shaw and the suffragettes do not appear to understand what a "citizen" is, nor what the word "citizenship" means.

In this country government is bi-form. We have a Federal Government, and we have State Government. For the reason that there are *individual* or personal rights, and *political* rights, and a Federal Government and a State Government, the words "citizen" and "citizenship" have *several* meanings—a circumstance which seems to have altogether escaped the sagacity of Dr. Shaw.

Every Tennessean is a "citizen" of Tennessee. Every Tennessean, native-born or naturalized, is a "citizen" of the United States. Every such person has certain *civil* rights as a citizen of Tennessee, and certain other *civil* rights as a citizen of the United States. But the fact that a person is a "citizen" of the United States does *not* confer the right to vote. (21 Wall., 62.)

The women, children, aliens, infamous persons, and corporations of Tennessee, are all "citizens" of Tennessee, and as such have their *citizenship,* but they do not vote. The reason is that they are "citizens" in a personal and *civil* sense. But the *men* of Tennessee over twenty-one years of age, who are not aliens, and who have not been rendered infamous, *do* vote, because they are "citizens" in the *political* sense. *They* are the "people" in the *political* sense. As said by President Taft in a message relating to the State of Arizona:

> "In a popular government the laws are made by the people—not all the people, but by those supposed to be competent for the purpose, as males over twenty-one years of age, and not by all of them, but by a majority of them only."

So it is that those only who are "citizens" in the *political* sense, have the right to vote. It is not sufficient that they are "citizens" in a *civil* sense. . . .

It is for this reason that the Supreme Courts of Tennessee and the United States, indeed, all American courts, have agreed that suffrage, the right to vote, is a *political,* and not a natural right. In the past, when things were rough and mankind perpetually at war, men necessarily constituted the *governing* class because they were the fighting class. As the governing class it was of course for them to determine who, and what kind of persons, should from time to time be admitted to that class.

They everywhere decided that grown men only should vote. They decided that men under twenty-one years of age should not vote. They decided that "infamous" persons should not vote. They decided that insane persons should not vote. They decided that aliens, though residents, should not vote. They decided that women should not vote. Yet all these disfranchised persons are *citizens,* and have "a stake" in government. The only class whose disfranchisement is now claimed to be unjust is the female class. Even the suffragettes do not protest against the disfranchisement of minors, felons, and aliens. This, in effect, is an *admission* that considerations *apart* from personal or individual *right,* may be and indeed are, controlling.

VI.

Feminism and Suffrage

The modern Woman's Movement in those countries where it has most advanced, is known as "Feminism." In "Feminism in Germany and Scandinavia," Katherine Anthony says:

> "The *basic* idea of feminism, with which every other idea and every material achievement must square, is the *emancipation* of woman as a *personality*. . . .
>
> "When the whole tale of objective achievements has been completed, when the schools have been open to women, the dress fetish banished, state maternity insurance introduced, the legal protection of motherhood and childhood within marriage, *and outside* of it guaranteed, the economic independence of women assured, and their political enfranchisement accomplished—the sum of all these collateral victories will be more than needed to wipe out the psychological residue of subjection in the individual woman's soul. . . .
>
> "Freedom in love, freedom for love, that is what the dignity of the human race demands." (Elizabeth von Steinborn in "Sexual Position of Woman," Kirsch, 203.)

W. L. George says:

> "Personally I believe that the ultimate aim of Feminism is the suppression of marriage and the institution of free alliance. It may be that only thus can woman develop her own personality. . . ."

The suffragettes, particularly those in the Southern States, repudiate feminism, but for all that, it is worth while to know what Feminists understand to be the real relation between feminism and woman suffrage. According to Mrs. Beatrice Forbes-Robertson Hales, a prominent suffragist, female suffrage is "an *essential branch of the tree of feminism*."

Katherine Anthony declares that:

> "It is not placing the cart before the horse to say that the conquest of the *political franchise* and of economic rights is a valuable *means* towards the creation of a more *independent* state of mind in the individual woman. These things are mere *way-stations* in the process of her inner emancipation." (Feminism in Germany and Scandinavia) . . .

Mrs. Florence Durant Evans of the Chattanooga Equal Suffrage Association, made a "reply" to Mayor Littleton of Chattanooga in 1915, in which, among other things, she said:

> "In our estimation the cause is an altar to an *unknown* god, a pedestal waiting for a *hoped-for* statue. . . .

At the State Fair in Nashville in September last, Mrs. Claude D. Sullivan was introduced by Mrs. [Kate] Warner, and said:

> "A great French philosopher put into one sentence the whole real argument for equal suffrage when he said: 'Either no individual member of the human race has any real rights or else they all have the same. . . .'"

I do not wish to be understood as insisting that the Tennessee suffragettes, whose utterances have been quoted are feminists. Upon the contrary, I am quite sure that they would renounce female suffrage if they suspected it to be "an essential branch" of the tree of Feminism, the "vanguard" of Feminism—a mere "way-station" or "milestone" on the route. My proposition is that whatever *their* views of female suffrage may be, the Feminists as matter of fact, are right in their conception of what female suffrage *logically and inevitably* leads to.

VI.

The Suffrage States

The refining influence of woman, within her sphere, has long been realized and acknowledged. The suffragettes seize on this to justify the claim that female suffrage will "purify" politics. "Wherever woman has gone, in whatever walk of life" says Mrs. Leslie Warner [Kate Warner], president of the Nashville Equal Suffrage League, "she has always improved conditions, purified the atmosphere, and elevated morals. . . . We know the time has come when *we* must step into the *arena*, where we can give a helping hand . . . to the *purification* of civic affairs, and directing the education of the children."

I venture to think that woman has "purified the atmosphere and elevated morals" when she has *stayed*, and not when she has *gone*, and that when in her going she "steps into the arena," the result will be, not that men have been made better, but woman worse.

They have already entered the business and dramatic "arenas."

They have entered "the arena" of business. The stores, offices, shops and market places are full of them. Is business more *honest* than formerly?

They have almost taken the Stage. Has the stage become purer and less suggestive? . . .

They have been in the political "arena" in Colorado for twenty-three years. If, in those states and countries where female suffrage has long been established, politics has been "purified," or even improved, it might cause us to pause. *But no such result appears to have followed. . . .*

Dr. Helen L. Sumner was sent to Colorado by the Collegiate Equal Suffrage League of New York to investigate the workings of female suffrage in that state. The result of her inquiries is given in a book entitled "Equal Suffrage," published in 1909. She was a suffragette. Her conclusion was that the Colorado experiment *indicates* that equal suffrage is "a step in the direction of better citizenship, a more effective use of the ability of woman as an integral part of the race, and a closer understanding and comradeship between men and women." But notwithstanding this hopeful and vague generalization, Dr. Sumner admits and says:

> . . . The majority of persons who gave any reason for their belief that equal suffrage had had a good effect upon the selection of candidates spoke of the standard of *personal morality* as improved, but not a dozen even so much as *mentioned* the standard of ability, business honesty, and public honor. . . . The conclusion is therefore unavoidable that, while women have often caused men of clean *personal* lives, not connected with the saloon or gambling interests, to be nominated in preference to men of notorious immorality, equal suffrage has had *no effect whatever* upon the *other* qualities required of candidates for public office. . . . *Politics in Colorado are at least as corrupt as in other states. . . .*

Since this was written (1898) Colorado has had experiences which confirm what Dr. Sumner stated. The State found itself *unable* to cope with riot and disorder, and twice called on the United States for Federal troops—something which no man-suffrage state has ever done. . . .

Mrs. R. C. Campbell, of the Colorado State Board for the Care of Dependent Children:

> "We did believe, of course, in our hearts that women in public life would purify politics and would make for a higher moral and political standard. After twenty years we are forced to admit that human nature as displayed by women is not different from that displayed by men, and if the appeal had been made on the ground of uplift of politics it would have been disproved by the facts."

[Many other similar quotations are given and then Vertrees concludes:] So much for the influence of women on politics. The grave question of the effect of politics on woman still remains. Will it affect her character? Will it affect the social unit, the family? Time only can answer. It may be a question of generations. Time works quietly, almost imperceptibly, but very surely.

The more intelligent of those in the Woman's Movement are not unmindful of the fact that *this* question still remains. One of them has said:

"It is certainly conceivable that all the good which modern woman expects to realize from the liberty to determine her own destiny, may not outweigh those which the female sex had enjoyed in the capacity of gentlewoman. It is no less possible that the necessity for competition will tend, so far as the male element is concerned, again to ruin that refinement of instinct which manifests itself as chivalry; and, so far as the female element is concerned to destroy once more that cult of beauty, harmony, and physical and spiritual elevation from which the gentlewoman arose". . .

VII.

Conclusion

No longer ago than last year the Supreme Court of the United States said that:

"The *identity* of husband and wife is an ancient principle of our jurisprudence. It was neither accidental nor arbitrary, and worked in many instances for her protection. There has been, it is true, much relaxation of it, but in its retention, as in its origin, it is determined by their *intimate relation* and *unity* of interests, and this relation and unity may make it of *public* concern in many instances to *merge* their identify and give *dominance* to the husband. (239 U.S., 311)

The State of Oregon passed a law limiting the hours which females might be employed in any mechanical establishment, factory, or laundry. This act was assailed on the ground that it interfered with a woman's personal rights and was an unjust discrimination. Extracts from ninety reports of committees, bureaus of statistics, commissioners of hygiene and inspectors of factories, both in America and Europe, were given as evidence to the effect that long hours of labor were dangerous to women, primarily because of their special physical organization. The validity of the act was sustained by the Supreme Court of the United States in a unanimous opinion given by Mr. Justice Brewer. The Court said:

"That woman's physical structure and the performance of maternal functions place her at a disadvantage in the struggle for existence is obvious . . . by abundant testimony of the medical fraternity, continuance for a long time on her feet at work . . . tends to an injurious effect on the body, and as healthy mothers are essential to vigorous off-spring, the physical well-being of women becomes an object of public interest and care in order to preserve the strength and vigor of the race.

"Still again, history discloses the fact that woman has always been dependent upon man. He established control at the outset by superior physical strength, and this control in various forms, with diminishing intensity

> has continued to the present. . . . The two sexes differ in structure of body, in the functions to be performed by each, in the amount of physical strength, in the capacity for long-continued labor . . . the influence of vigorous health upon the future well-being of the race, the self-reliance which enables one to assert full rights, and in the capacity to maintain the struggle for subsistence. This difference justified a difference in legislation and upholds that which is designed to compensate for some of the burdens which rest upon her." (208 U.S., 422) [This was the famous *Muller* v. *Oregon*, upholding protective legislation for women.]

Mr. Brooks Adams, in delivering an introductory address in Quincy, Massachusetts, so admirably expressed what a real man feels and knows, that I conclude with his words:

> "From the remotest antiquity women have formed the cement or core of society, for women have represented the constant, and men the variable, principle in human relations. The man has been a farmer, or a hunter, or a shepherd, or a fisher, or a sailor, or a soldier, and to win a livelihood he has been forced to wander far. But he has always returned, hoping to find his wife and children safe at home. Thus the woman, by the law of her being, has incarnated the essence of the family, and the *family* has been the *cornerstone of the State*, the support of the church and the standard of morality. And to achieve her destiny the woman has sacrificed herself, just as the man, in moments of peril, has always given his life for the woman.
>
> "But to perform her office the woman has to divest herself of outside interests and to live at home. She could no more quit her family than the soldier could stray from his regiment, the sailor desert his ship, or the shepherd abandon his flock. For all obedience, all discipline, and all moral influence is rooted in unremitting personal supervision.
>
> "Most unhappily, as I conceive, I have seen during my lifetime, a growing tendency among the women of our blood to sneer at this supremest of human functions as though maternity, with its restraints and sacrifices, were a task below their genius. To me the spectacle is repellent, I may say shocking, for it is casting from the world its purest ideal and its highest source of happiness."

Do not the Supreme Court and Mr. Adams express the sentiments of Tennesseans, whether they be Republicans or Democrats? If so, they should realize that they should be vigilant to preserve their existing *political* institutions. . . .

Nothing, up to this time, has been suggested or revealed where the experiment has been made, to indicate that Nature's old Salic law can be repealed, or that the attempt to do so will not *eventually prove supremely disastrous*.

Notes

John J. Vertrees, "An Address to the Men of Tennessee on Female Suffrage," Nashville, Tennessee, 1916, pamphlet, Tennessee State Library and Archives.

1. Vertrees is correct that most Tennessee suffragists would not have referred to themselves as feminists in 1914. This term, now used generically to describe any advocate of women's rights, did not come into use in America until the 1910s and had a far more specific meaning. It was embraced by or used to describe a minority of women's rights advocates who were generally younger and more radical than most suffragists, and many of them were affiliated with the National Woman's Party: virtually all feminists were suffragists; only a few suffragists called themselves feminists. They adopted the term partly in order to differentiate themselves from the older, more conventional women's rights leaders, and were generally politically leftist. Most often found in large cities of the Northeast and influenced by contacts with feminists in Europe, they advocated major changes in the relationships between the sexes, including economic independence for women and free and open enjoyment of sexuality by women, and rejected the idea of woman's superior morality. Of the southern suffrage leaders I have studied, only Mary Johnston (who had spent considerable time in Europe) called herself a "feminist," though even she felt the need to qualify this by saying she was not "simply a feminist" but a "humanist" as well, and her views were generally more similar to those of the traditional woman's rights advocates in that she favored converting men to woman's "high" standard of sexual conduct and believed woman suffrage would inject morality into politics. For more information on the first American feminists and the history of the word "feminist," see Nancy F. Cott, *The Grounding of Modern Feminism* (New Haven: Yale University Press, 1987), especially 3–10. On Johnston, see Trudy J. Hanmer, "A Divine Discontent: Mary Johnston and Woman Suffrage in Virginia," (M.A. thesis, University of Virginia, 1972), ii.

2. See Anastatia Sims, part 1, essay 5 above: "Beyond the Ballot: The Radical Vision of the Antisuffragists," and "'Powers That Pray and Powers That Prey': Tennessee and the Fight for Woman Suffrage," *Tennessee Historical Quarterly* (Winter 1991): 203–25, especially 206.

10

President's Message: Retiring from Antisuffrage Leadership of Tennessee, September 30, 1920

Josephine Anderson Pearson

Josephine Anderson Pearson (1868–1944) was born near Gallatin in Sumner County, Tennessee. Her father, Reverend Phillip Anderson Pearson, was a minister; her mother, Amanda Caroline Roscoe Pearson, was profoundly antisuffrage. Josephine Pearson was educated at Gallatin Female College, Irving College in McMinnville, Tennessee (B.A. c. 1880), and Cumberland College in Lebanon, Tennessee (M.A. 1886). She also studied at Vanderbilt and the University of Missouri. She served as principal of McMinnville High School (1890–94) and Nashville College for Young Ladies (1895–97). Pearson taught English at Winthrop State Normal College for Women in Rock Hill, South Carolina (1897–99), and English and history at Higbee School in Memphis (1902–8). She was dean and chair of philosophy at Christian College in Columbia, Missouri (1909–14).

In 1914, Pearson returned to Tennessee—to Monteagle—owing to the failing health of her parents. Before her death in 1915, Amanda Pearson elicited a pledge from her daughter that she would fight woman suffrage in Tennessee if it should become necessary. As Anastatia Sims's essay above and documents 10 and 11 indicate, Josephine Pearson kept her promise—but clearly had antisuffrage convictions of her own as well.

Recruited by John J. Vertrees to replace his ailing wife, Virginia, as leader of the female antis, Pearson served as president of the Tennessee State Association Opposed to Woman Suffrage (1917–20), and, in 1920, president of the Southern Women's League for Rejection of the Susan B. Anthony Amendment. In later years she continued her career as an educator at Southern Seminary in Buena Vista, Virginia; March College in Staunton, Virginia; St. Agnes College for Women; and the Memphis Conservatory of Music.

Pearson's "President's Message," in which she resigned from the leadership of the antisuffragists in Tennessee, is extraordinary in that it proclaims and celebrates an antisuffrage victory. On September 30, 1920, the date of the letter, the antis were still hoping their court challenge to the Nineteenth Amendment would succeed; Pearson obviously believed—or chose to accept long enough to resign in triumph—the assurances of the antisuffrage men that they would prevail.

The letter is also remarkable in that it reveals Pearson's outrage against women's colleges and their (in Pearson's eyes) theoretical, impractical, and intolerant prosuffrage faculties; she was appalled that many professors were converting their impressionable young charges and influencing public school teachers who, said Pearson, looked up to college faculty and felt that they were "not Progressive" unless they were prosuffrage. As a college graduate and educator, she seemed to feel professionally isolated and bitter that her point of view was in eclipse among college women. She insisted that women's colleges were turning young women away from the home and motherhood, thus contributing to "national degeneration." "Motherhood," she said, was the "coronation of womanhood" and no "professional career ever attained" can "recompense the loss and love and companionship of home for the desolated spinster."

To Pearson, antisuffrage was a "religious fight," indeed a "Holy War" or "crusade" versus the suffragists and their leader (the "great outsider"), Carrie Chapman Catt, who would "level" the standards of southern women to those of men, and enfranchise African Americans. Still, in her "hour of victory," Pearson magnanimously forgave those friends who, forgetting their convictions, had made the mistake of becoming suffragists, and she urged her followers to be "patient" with them now that antisuffrage had triumphed. She offered her thanks to her faithful supporters, the antisuffrage women, and celebrated the heroics of the "Red Rose Brigade," before concluding: "Somehow I felt that we in Tennessee could not fail in this most crucial test of Southern rights and honor, when Tennessee became the pivotal battle-ground of the Nation! We are grateful that our valiant fight—no matter what the Courts decide—has saved the honor, the 'State's Rights' integrity, and the Constitutional record of Tennessee."

Josephine Anderson Pearson. Tennessee State Library and Archives. Courtesy of the Tennessee Historical Society.

PRESIDENT'S MESSAGE,
(Retiring from Anti-Suffrage Leadership of Tennessee)

Josephine A. Pearson

Monteagle, September 30, 1920

Faithful Associates of the Tennessee Division of the Southern Woman's League for the Rejection of the Susan B. Anthony Amendment:

For several years it has been my privilege, by my pen, in my class-room and on the platform, to give the best within me for the cause of Anti-Suffrage, in other states before the honored leadership of the women of my native state fell to me as successor to the lamented Mrs. John J. Vertrees, President [of] the Tennessee State Association Opposed to Woman Suffrage. This organization, by official action, was merged July 1920 into the Tennessee Division of the Southern Woman's League for the Rejection of the Susan B. Anthony Amendment, of which Mrs. Jas. S. Pinckard is President-General. This recent action I advised for the one distinctive purpose: to defeat ratification in Tennessee of the Federal Suffrage Amendment. Personally, I felt this name [of the League] alone, on paper, bears the hall-marks of the South and the latent sentiment in southern history of "States Rights"—the basic principle upon which the Democratic party has long rested. I felt this organization which embraces not only Anti-Suffragists but State Rights Suffragists opposed to the Federal Amendment, as well as those wishing to defend the Constitutional honor of Tennessee, is the most potent creation that we, as Tennessee women, could sustain for the one purpose of the battle versus the Federal Amendment.

My own convictions as opposed to Female Suffrage were the results of intensive investigation as "To the Wrongs and Perils of Woman Suffrage." For several years teaching and visiting at various University centers in the West, I made a study of the results of Equal Suffrage in the Western States, making trips over Colorado, Kansas, Wyoming, etc. collecting data as did my honorable opponent, Dr. Helen Sumner of New York, Suffragist from whose interesting book many of our most convincing Anti-Suffrage arguments are obtained. During this period, working under one of the greatest sociological authorities in America, Dr. Chas. Elwood, I read all available literature and histories of European and American Feminists, and studied the trend of the Feminist movement, of which Equal Suffrage is a component part. I heard most of the *noted* Suffrage leaders, meeting many, in this country. The broader my knowledge and actual observation and experience became, the deeper were my convictions that female suffrage, with its "Dark and dangerous side," is not a flower indigenous in the South! Through three campaigns I have been called to lead against "Votes for Women" in Tennessee since 1916. Despite the last five years of supreme personal bereavement [following the death of her mother], I have tried to give a consecrated *Service* to this cause; only few (including my long loyal co-laborer, Mrs. Morgan Brown, Executive Chairman) have known *Why* the burden has been so a part of my life. The consciousness, only, of the sacred vow to my Mother resting upon me, has made me brave in the stand against friends who have often upbraided me and also [has] given me courage and faith to enter into this last (1920) August Campaign! I felt it to be a "Holy War," as it were, a crusade in memory of my Mother for Southern Motherhood, through which her guiding spirit has led me all the way! Somehow, I felt that we in Tennessee could not fail in this most crucial test of Southern rights and honor, when Tennessee became the pivotal battleground of the Nation! We are grateful that our valiant fight—no matter what the Courts decide—has saved our honor, the "States Rights" integrity, and the *Constitutional record* of Tennessee.

To "our men" in Tennessee, to our distinguished legal advisors, to our own brave yeomanry of the State—"The Red Rose Brigade"—who fled to save us and returned to protect us—we justly give the glory of the victory; *for we* defeated Suffrage in Tennessee! We have proclaimed to the world that we will not, without protest, submit to the enforcement upon us of the lawless certification of an Amendment that all law-abiding peoples recognize was a pseudo-proclamation on false testimony! We believe that our Tennessee Manhood will take every step, honorable, to *strangle*, now and forever by the Courts, with a patriotic fervor, that brooks no dictatorship of any "man higher up," this Susan B. Anthony Amendment that, if ratified, would turn over the South to negro domination!

It is an open secret that I, personally, have suffered, professionally, [from the disapproval of] the "intolerant" for my long and unswerving steadfastness of purpose opposed to Equal Suffrage in the South! The professional world, so far, does not forgive or excuse one of its members who has not wanted "votes for women"! This almost pathetic intolerance first met in the West, served as one of the first convincing arguments to me of the inadvisability of women in politics! Here it becomes my unpleasant *duty*, certainly not for my own sake at this late date, but for the sake of Anti-Suffrage, to address to this organization a special section relative to the present attitude of the still opposing potent factor.

The teacher force, in this country upholding woman suffrage, whether organized or unorganized, bears the imprint of "The Modern Educator's Trust" for suffrage that sometimes seemed a reality, and I, at least, have on more than one occasion felt the fangs of this "octopus" upon me when positions of honor were offered and then suddenly withdrawn, with the honest explanation, that it was my position as a leader of Anti-Suffrage, that forced their attitude! Notice the rally of the West-Tennessee teachers to my state-opponent for Shelby! Also notice the public state-offices in Tennessee most generally held by the most partisan Suffragists, especially those supervising state and rural school departments, when the state and county taxes are being paid by 80% Antis, at a minimum reckoning. Some re-adjustment of all this should claim your attention. Notice also, a short time ago, the suffrage organizations in even some of our southern colleges for girls; many girls coming from the training of an anti-suffrage home became a member, often, just to keep from being unpopular, not only with girls but with her instructors. This, in the South, first claimed the attention of the late Mrs. John J. Vertrees, by complaints to her of Anti-leaders (in a sister-southern state), who had been importuned by the mothers of girl-students. I knew of a college for girls in the West, where certain inducements were offered to students to proclaim themselves for suffrage and to wear the "yellow ribbon," on occasions. There is a reason for this:

First: My experience in the literary world with distinguished men and women educators, gives me the right to say, truthfully, that nearly all college-bred men are *theorists*, very few vision practically; instead they see great economic, sociological and physiological problems all settled *on paper*, which often applied to real life evaporates "as the baseless fabric of a dream!" Even the *once* great teacher, President Woodrow Wilson, went before Congress with the plea that if it did not *give* the "Votes to Women" we could not, as an American Nation, win the World-War! All this type of men, with few exceptions, are for Woman Suffrage, even before any enter the political life and become "card-indexed" by the suffragists.

Permit me to refer, gratefully, to the recent conversion of such a dynamic force to our views as Prof. Gus Dyer of Vanderbilt University, who, in the past, has been such a splendid suffrage propagator in the student ranks of this section of the Educational World.

Second: The segregation sometimes too long, of women in our larger Colleges, away from the normal relations and intercourse of life, has too often suggested the cultivation of [a] *sex*-independence among teachers, that is not always wholesome in results. Too often the college atmosphere for women creates sex-dominance: that invariably leads to Woman Suffrage (the mildest form of feminism), then alas! to a sex-party [the] "Women's Party," political, today. By way of parenthesis, I am not sure that this *new* party formation spells any more serious menace to civilization than the picture, recently, of the great international suffrage leader, Mrs. Catt, marching through the streets of New York, with a negro woman on either side of her! Was she thus proclaiming her ideal of the supremacy of the negro-race that threatens the South, if Federal Suffrage should ever come to us?

By conclusion of the above first and second premises, we find much of the College leadership of women for women, has been augmented and led by the distinguished heads of colleges for women. Of course the smaller institutions must be educational satellites in thought and in action of the larger ones, all, alike not desiring to recall that these great colleges for women were founded many years before this country had a vote for women: (Mary Lyon, founder of the first college for women was opposed to Equal Suffrage). As the larger colleges and their instructors became prototypes for the smaller, so in turn city school-teachers and almost every little district school teacher has gotten the *germ* that she is not progressive unless she is for Woman Suffrage; still more amusing, she feels if you are fighting suffrage, you are fighting *women*, and (bless her dear soul) thinks "Votes for Women" is the panacea for every human ill! Like the old man in the mountains, who a few years ago, I heard speak; "If Billy Bryan gits 'lected, we'll git all the free-silver our whisky barrels can hold!" So, these *women's-right's-women*, think the vote will give them "all the rights" they want—even to enter into "the Kingdom come!"

One of the most popular American feminists, Miss Jane Addams, writing in the "Independent" exclaims: "The un-enfranchised woman of today stands outside of the *real* life of the world!" Think of what this means! The woman who may not vote, says this noted leader of women, "is outside of the real life of the world!" That is to say: practical life is real life; business life is real life; public office is real life! Almost anything is real life that goes outside the home. Conclusion: Home making women are not really living; is the[re] a sadder requiem for Woman Suffrage?! We trust that some of our best and valued suffrage friends will investigate further, go deeper into the feminist movement, and that honest research into causes and effects will later make them our comrades, like our own great "National President Opposed to Woman Suffrage," Miss Mary G. Kilbreath, succeeded by Mrs. Jas. Wordsworth of NY. Says a noted author: "I believe that the fancies and follies of woman suffrage or rather the woman's movement, is a movement towards *progressive* national degeneration and ultimate national suicide!" At any rate, the final test of the Woman's movement must succeed or fail according as it strengthens or weakens Woman's *motherhood*—physical, intellectual, spiritual! Take for example the recent apparent necessary upset condition of the women in the Tennessee

Capitol, through these hot August days, when we united to oppose the first "outsider" (Carrie Chapman Catt) who came into our state to attempt a "walkover sale" of it to her Federal Suffrage business; and draw your own conclusions what this "religious fight" (to us, for ultimate peace, quiet and conservation of *home*), would mean to our womanhood—if kept in perpetual motion every year! We could but rightfully rise, in the majesty of our instinctive rights to resent that attempted enforcement upon us of so-called "Enfranchisement," that means the leveling of Southern woman's standards to the equality of men, or to the "great outsider" herself, Mrs. Catt, proclaimer of *Equal Suffrage for negro women!* This so-called liberation of women in making their lives and their work approximate to the lives and the work of men, has been attained more by college leaders than any other set of women, far more than the lives of their wage-earning sisters in the stores and factories. [Their] innate instincts of womanhood causes them to shrink from the vortex of feminism, as was illustrated in the recent large number of young women in Nashville shops who were "Anti," and many voluntarily, during the campaign, wore the red rose, one even decorating thus her typewriter. Most of the best real business women of America, among whom are our own splendid associates: Mollie Claiborne, Willie Field, Louise Sloan, Julia Hindman, Mary Shackleford, Zella Armstrong, [and] Anne Rankin, editors and writers; Willie Bettie Newman, artist of international fame; and a host of others all over Tennessee who wrote me, offering their services, such as Eleanor Gilispie, Fayetteville; Mrs. Paty, popular proprietor of The King Hotel, Tullahoma, Mrs. Moore (?) of Harriman, who for twenty years, has successfully organized, owned, enlarged and operated great mining interests. All these [antisuffrage women] superbly challenge "Votes for Women" as an instrument for assistance in the great business world of men!

Facts are usually challenged, so I take them from the statistical publication of highest repute and unimpeachable integrity—the official Journal of the American Statistical Association.

First, it is proven that half of the college graduates do not marry at all. This conclusion is accepted by women leaders themselves, as indisputable. Miss M. Carey Thomas, president Bryn Mawr College, once my honored hostess, in the Educational Review says: "that 50 percent of college women marry and 40 percent bear and rear children—a gracious condescension to Nature and to Society," which should, in her opinion, save them from all criticisms.

Do you, women peers of my native state, surmise, that any sacrifices ever made, or ambitions of a professional career ever attained, have recompensed the loss and love and companionship of home for the desolated spinster, no matter if her life giv[ing] service is voluntary?

In way of my own Atonement I offer you this as my own conclusive evidence, in this message and as my personal tribute to the highest *Coronation of Women—Motherhood!*

I have given my life-work for what I have felt were the highest educational standards, ideals, progressively, for my sex. I do not believe that the object of woman's creation is merely to produce commodities and oddities, or to amass learning. I believe that the highest education for women is, to yet undergo radical scholastic and vocational changes; that real womanhood and her FAMILY may not perish from the Earth!

I ask you to take kindly these thoughts and suggestions and that you hold fast to the inheritances of our beloved Southland. Never let *die* its traditions of woman's protection against the Susan B. Anthony Amendment, which bears the name of a woman as *antipodal* in *birth and ideals to the South*, as are the poles of the *Universe!*

Thank God Anti-Suffrage is now popular in dear old Tennessee!

Educational revolutions and evolutions are sure to follow for the future Woman's welfare that the average suffrage-teacher, confined to her text-book and intolerant ideas, backed by no intelligent arguments, cannot possibly conceive.

Then I urge patience with these sisters and all our mistaken, to us, friends, whose convictions we trust may be *re-awakened!* Some of those in suffrage ranks are most dear to me. They have been true friends in many vicissitudes; some, as the loved contemporaries of my Mother, will never know *what* this campaign cost, my often—near "parting of the ways" [from] some I most cherish! Again, others, with the tents of their convictions pitched in the opposite camp, "have burning" for me still our mutual friendship! For the sake of these, all of them, I have never felt the *least bitterness*, during this the most desperate fight, I trust, you and I may ever be called to enter! Be this as it may, you, [antisuffrage] women of the Tennessee Division, have been wonderful coworkers! Never were the hours too long for your faithful service; never the days too hot, or the nights too dark or full, for you to not, at once, loyally respond to a call from Headquarters! We all now know something of the spirit that led "our boys" to fight in the trenches! They gave us the faith for this great moral battle in Tennessee history!

I am very tired and wary, even in the hour of victory; I feel I must soon, formally, ask you to accept my resignation as President of this distinguished body of women. I sadly need all relief from responsibility of the headship of management. I have kept the faith; the race for the time being is won! The results now pending in the courts may bring new complexities for administration; so this is my final official and retiring message!

Our Vice President, and *my successor,* Mrs. George A. Washington, is a woman of rare charm, sincerity, and is very "level-headed!" She has done, modestly, so much in her own home county of Robinson, along lines that will of themselves, give her prestige as a woman of ability to "Carry on" any *other woman's work for women in her native state!*

I commend her to you, with my heart's best blessings! That she and you will ever rally to the banner of "States Rights" for our beloved southland, I feel assured!

In conclusion, I ask that you be strong of heart, firm and determined in purpose, [and] judicious in every action, and may the "red rose"—talisman of the (1920) August victory in Tennessee, "ever on your bosom wave," emblem in your hearts of hope and faith and courage through future years!

(Signed) Josephine A. Pearson,
(Retiring President).

Miss Josephine A. Pearson, Southern writer and educator, having held the chair of Philosophy and History and served as associate head of colleges for women in Tennessee, South Carolina, and Missouri, also later in Virginia, has for the *last five years* led the anti-suffrage women of her native state. . . .

Note

This letter, part of which was printed in the *Chattanooga Times*, Oct. 31, 1920, is from a typescript in the Josephine Anderson Pearson Papers, Tennessee State Library and Archives, Nashville. It is reprinted here exactly as found except that a number of typographical errors have been corrected.

11

My Story: Of How and Why I Became an Antisuffrage Leader

Josephine Anderson Pearson

In the opening paragraphs of this fascinating memoir, Pearson described her goals in writing it: to "enshrine all the bitterness of the bitter periods" of what she called "the 1920 Bloody war of Women" and "the Verdun 1920," an "era in Tennessee history . . . so vital, that no one could live, actively, through it . . . without the sting of hurt," and to create a record of the "claimed but not constitutional nor honorable . . . passage in Tennessee of the Susan B. Anthony Amendment." She intended it to be a "Garden of Poesy," a dramatic rendering of her own motives and the actions of the antisuffragists, who attempted to prevent what was, to them, an error of monumental proportions. Inspired by a sense of obligation to these loyal friends who had given her guidance and support, nevertheless she acknowledged that, considering the bitterness of the conflict and the possible reactions to "My Story," she would like to see it "silently rest a little while longer in kindness and respect to those now gone!" "Possibly," she wrote, the document "may be for some historian to excavate for dissertations in the making!"

The memoir is dedicated to Pearson's mother, Amanda Caroline Roscoe Pearson, who, on her deathbed, elicited Pearson's famous pledge to oppose woman suffrage if and when it became an issue in Tennessee. One of Amanda Pearson's antisuffrage writings, an intriguing document in itself, is included within.

"My Story" has much to offer the student of the suffrage movement. Rarely have any of the participants on either side of this great political and social battle left such a detailed personal history of the development of their views. Pearson's memoir is particularly helpful in understanding her relationship with the male antis, especially John Vertrees, who, as Anastatia

Sims points out, selected Pearson to lead the women antis largely because she was too "brainy" and "tactful" to try to direct the actions of the men.[1]

Pearson's memoir is also quite interesting for its discussion of *class* in the southern suffrage movement. As she was well aware, Tennessee suffrage leaders had impeccable social credentials; but like her revered mother, Pearson considered support for suffrage to be beneath the dignity of any woman "to the manner born," a "plebeian" movement, instigated by the wrong kind of northern women such as Susan B. Anthony, of whom she spoke with contempt. Like Vertrees, and many southern antis, Pearson believed the elite, white southern women who became involved in the movement were simply misguided.

"My Story" also captures the sense of outrage and indignation shared by southern antis at President Woodrow Wilson's "face about"; their anger at all Tennessee men who supported ratification, especially Governor A. H. Roberts and Harry Burn; their reverence for the antisuffrage heroes of "The Red Rose Brigade"; and their belief that Tennessee's ratification of the Nineteenth Amendment was fraudulent and unconstitutional.

"My Story," as it appears here, is put together from several versions of the memoir, both handwritten and typed. Never published, it contained many spelling and punctuation errors that Pearson, I believe, would have been loathe to have in print, and which made the document quite difficult to read. I have taken the liberty of correcting these, and of omitting a few passages that were either incomprehensible, repetitive, or irrelevant to the story. Deletions are indicated by ellipses; words inserted for clarification are in brackets. I have taken care not to distort Pearson's meaning.

Readers of this version of "My Story"—or the original—should bear in mind, however, that Pearson wrote this document in 1939, nearly twenty years after the ratification of the Nineteenth Amendment, and five years before her death. Age and the passage of time had taken a toll on her memory. For example, she refers to her "three campaigns vs. federal suffrage . . . 1917 through August 1920," when in fact she fought two campaigns against state suffrage legislation in 1917 and 1919, and only one against the federal amendment in 1920. While her memoirs capture the spirit of the southern antisuffrage movement, specific facts cannot always be corroborated.

As a preliminary statement, I beg in justice to myself, to mention that this leadership was an honor not sought or coveted! But the surprising feature of My Story, so colorful, is—that now, in retirement, that as one grows older, at each year's sunset—"The South Winds of Memory" brush so many phases—recalled, that suffuses the Spirit with—serenity! Wistfully, I wander through the Winding Galleries of the Past—selecting the outstanding precious bits of Fading Tapestries!

One of the most cherished, and outstanding [memories] . . . *is My Story*, officially offered, of *How* and *Why*—I became an Anti-Suffrage Leader! . . .

My own record . . . [began with] the pressure in Memory of My Mother, Amanda Caroline (Roscoe) Pearson, [of] my vow, made as a daughter to her one week before she faded away! . . .

I was raised in an atmosphere of a cultured people, who respected Temperance! Many are the occasions, that as a child early and long accustomed to be called before the public in recitating, dramatics,—in the town of my girlhood, beautiful McMinnville, at the foot of Ben Lomond—I can well remember . . . bowing at the knees of some incognito inebriate (so assumed) while singing out my little soul to the words "Please do not Leave Me Tonight Dear Father" until the entire audience wept! When the Temperance War first strangely struck that section for organization, I was on "The Float of Yellow," and when we reached the church for the opening of the [temperance] convention, I was called on to pray for the cause! But later, when my frail mother was driven to see the great festooning of yellow cloth, that caught up several of the pictures of *Susan B. Anthony*, . . . my gentle, always poised Mother, quietly turned aside, remarking, "It would seem this occasion is one where the *Yellow* predominates the *White*—the Temperance insignia!" From that day to her death, my mother was in opposition to the encroaching stamp of Susan B. Anthony upon the South. [Anthony's] name became more and more objectionable to her aristocratic breeding, [since she opposed] the Abolitionist Leader! Her opposition was never harsh; just deadly positive! When in 1902 one of my former schoolmates [who] became a Temperance and Suffrage Leader (Carrie Lee Carter) of national reputation, was at Monteagle Assembly, she was invited as our guest during the period of her lectures. My Mother did not attend—no criticism, however! When this friend attempted, once, some instructions to my Mother, she was so surprisingly rebuked that pardon was asked!

When in 1909 I went to Missouri [where she became the dean and held a chair in philosophy at Christian College, affiliated with the University of Missouri, Columbia], the only prominent leaders who were for suffrage in Tennessee at that time [were] Mrs. Judge East and the far more able Mrs. Selina Holman, who had a magnetic personality! Personally, as always, upon new *soil*, I was open to convictions on Western questions [including] Co-Education, witnessed in a University Center of some 5000 or more students. . . . I had been wide-eyed, during the preceding year of travel in Old Mexico, New Mexico, and over to Yacatan [*sic*], etc. . . . [One] Thanksgiving, there was a notable Banquet, where sat the leading professors of the University of Missouri and myself, quite demure! As a stranger I was watching [and making] observations, when out of the brilliant repartee, came a challenge: "Miss Pearson, I presume you are too far from the South to be able to accept Equal Suffrage, now the predominant political issue in Missouri?" I accepted the challenge in words not (here) quite befitting to repeat; but for me, it resulted in a happy event. Instead of my becoming "taboo" for my outspoken response, I was the unexpected subject of congratulations from my opponent—later my friend [Dr. Charles Elwood?]. This led to my undertaking, during vacation periods, a certain amount of seminar work, going from first to last into several Western Suffrage States, to collect data, contacting the Suffragists themselves, personally and in clubs. Later, I was invited to make lectures, purely from an academic viewpoint, in the state of Missouri through two successful campaigns vs. Equal Suffrage! That led to my being rated an Anti Suffrage Leader! . . . All this [was prior] to the forthcoming Epidemic, destined to sweep America—floating from the North under the Banner of the Susan B. Anthony Amendment, 1920—and to Tennessee becoming, once again, as in The Sixties, the National Battle Ground!

During Commencement 1914 I was called from Columbia, Missouri, to the bedside of my mother, following the accident of her falling! I had not been informed—that for the last three years she had used her always graceful pen in articles sent to be published in the East—where a coterie of brilliant women had begun organizing, possibly first in conservative Boston, v. "Votes for Women"! . . . She had just finished the article I've incorporated.

WOMAN SUFFRAGE

A Resume.

Extracts from an article, written by Mrs. P.A. Pearson,
Monteagle Assembly Grounds, to her friends, which was published, first, a few months before her death, July 1915.

Dear Friends in Tennessee:—

I wish to relieve your minds of "the soft impeachment" that I am for Equal Suffrage. Following almost from the genesis of the movement . . . to its present crisis, I could say many things. . . . Up in a New England school from whence it became prominent, a few plebeian pupils working their way through school started the agitation from coarse natural audacity perhaps—which was repulsive to all femininity of finer mould, especially to the "Old South." It shows, however, what agitation will do. You see from this small beginning, before the war, over what a great stretch of country it has spread itself and how insidious in its effects into a section hitherto unsuspecting.

Boston has long considered herself "the hub of brains and talent" and New England literature has long held prestige by all lovers of book-lore. I have many dear northern friends and a niece living in Boston, whom I hope have not become inoculated with the virus of Equal Suffrage, so you see there is no prejudice of locality.

But back to the main point a-g-i-t-a-t-i-o-n, which . . . gives any cause zeal and notoriety and a rapid spread of influence in its behalf! Spiritualism, Daweism [Darwinism?], Eddyism, Mormonism, etc., are examples of it. The press ever alert in promulgating news, kept these unwholesome influences before the public, until each have, today, a fair following. It is said that any unique form of suicide brings a score of imitators in like self-murder, and the police understand that any new form of murder will, as soon as the newspapers have spread the story, reproduce itself in a dozen other attempts at assassination. So, Woman Suffrage is as a stone thrown into a river, sending out its innumerable circling waves, and . . . the press has kept up a constant agitation! But, alas! poor woman, your very first edition produced a damaging effect, when she influenced Adam her husband, to eat of the forbidden fruit. Now she is biting at the apple again, wanting the ballot which if granted will be through woman's persistency and man's submissiveness. I believe that if the feelings of most men were sounded and expressed, they would want their wives at home, and would not want them to become liable for jury duty, nor to be locked up all night, serving on a mixed jury especially when the children needed them at home! There are enough men to do men's work!

The gentleness and refinement of womanhood and the deference and chivalry [toward] womanhood are the two most important elements in nature, and the movement for women's political equality, if perfected, would destroy both. Womanly nature, biologically speaking, is unfit for politics, and if the public work is being ill done by men, the only remedy is to do it better, not shift the burden to weaker and already over-laden shoulders. But don't you see the trend of the movement? She [the suffragist] not only wants the silent vote, but she wants office. She wants to exploit herself, and I fear two-thirds of them would want to be "Speaker of the House."

And again woman must remember she could not make any "Jim Crow" distinction either against the sister-in-black! Many good women of the day are seeming to lose sight of the purpose of their Creator in the formation of the human race; that He made them male, and female and designed them for entirely different vocations in life, and neither ever can be fully at ease in the calling of the other.

God's purposes in the creation of woman are inimitable, and she should consider those purposes paramount to every other purpose. Then why does she clamor so frantically for the ballot, which if obtained, might prove her undoing, and destroy home, love and happiness?

I do think that little English woman, Miss [Sylvia] Pankhurst, from across the waters [England], a Militant Suffragist, too, who came a year or so ago [1912] to the United States, and included Nashville, was an imposition on America. But shame! thrice shame! that she was accorded all the courtesies and privileges as if she had been a whole delegation of authority to inspect the institutions of our land, and, acting as some great censor capable of instructing what is right, and rectifying the wrong, while her mother was back in England smashing windows and destroying property.

Now, my dear friends, I believe that woman's clamoring for the ballot, (equal rights) to be in direct conflict with divine teaching. You take from man this moral obligation, this sacred uplift, and in a measure you extract his highest ideals, and listen! [You] give him the softening of the brain, at least you minimize his influence, and in time make a weakling of him, and future sons of them all.

Gazing upon a Sistine Madonna has caused many a woman to realize in herself that glorious type of womanhood which has made possible our most sacred institutions; which has given to the world her Knight-hood; which has brought about her nation builders, her dreamers, her philosophers; and under whose tender guardianship patriots, heroes and martyrs have been molded.

So, dear woman of the southland, I would plead with you to be slow in giving up your sweet province the jurisdiction of home, keeping it immaculate and training your children in the way they should go. Your sweetest desire should be this ability, which means Eternal vigilance, the greatest allotment appointed to mortal. This is truly the coronation of your duty, and for woman to respond to the bugle call of the government is to leave her assigned work undone.

Amanda Caroline Pearson
(Mrs. P. A. Pearson)

[She had recently finished this article] . . . when I stepped, in the early evening into the Library, where sat my beloved parent. When [I was] as usual kissing her brow—she grasped my hand—showing me this her *last article*, saying: "Daughter, when I'm gone—if the Susan B. Anthony Amendment issue reaches Tennessee—promise me, you will take up the opposition, in My Memory!" I was, of course dazed! My father's glances gave me a kindly, awakening signal; and, I as I bent, again to impress the vow upon her forehead, I answered "Yes! God helping, I'll keep the faith, My Mother!"

Following my mother's death, I began to write, [to] *write volumes*, as it were; sometimes the entire night, I spent in writing, sending articles in all directions vs. "Feminism," "The Amendment," anything that could hold me true to my promise! I organized the women on the Mountain [Monteagle, Tennessee,] into a Chapter vs. Equal Suffrage—anything, [though] the desire to ever again be in politics [was] so utterly detested by me! I had all my life been a sincere student of Political (Science) Economy, growing up with such discussions with my father, and many exceptionally informed men, until I was once told by a noted scholar; "*You think as a man*"*!* I [had] taught, a simplified form of political science, correlated with Constitutional American History, while Principal of McMinnville High School [1890–94]. . . . But . . . this growing game of "Votes for Women"—[to] whom American men had granted every "Exaltation"—became a game I was unprepared to [comprehend]; with their [womens'] general lack of information, . . . they knew not how "To Count Their Blessings!" Personally I had been a believer in "Limited Suffrage" . . . (on the basis of real information, and [knowledge of] great issues); [I was] early influenced, likely, by my delight in reading of "The Women of the French Salon" . . . [about] those who, mentally, and personally attractive, could hold their own with a Beaconsfield. But the "Band Wagon Equal Suffrage Song," as an issue, started from the proletarian class calling for votes; [It] was an intellectual compromise, . . . [according to] my ideas of the intelligent American type of Woman.

So, "Go West Young Woman!" Meet these women in their Clubs, and I *did!* Listen to their expressions of dexterity of Men's (?) I did! Often the first amazement—amused me! Later came . . . a pure, calculating reasoning about all this imbibed experience. To transmit—How! Alas! To the Young Women I essayed to influence in College! As a teacher, I loved to believe I was receptive to the best, [was] broad in ideals! Then came the occasions to address audiences relative to "Feministic Impressions!" "The Good and Bad Approach," "The Negative and Positive Results," etc. until I became noted as an Anti-Suffrage Leader (through two campaigns) in Missouri! The better classes of the Univ. Fraternity Men were my staunch supporters, [though] few of the Professors, who generally are impracticable in their exhaustive rather than convincing reasoning! . . .

Not one of my family—on either side—stood with me on the Equal Suffrage Question—except Col. and Mrs. D. R. Roscoe. . . . A dear cousin—once a Sumner County belle—"Miss Betty Prince" (long the wife of Dr. A. H. Cousins of St. Louis) and her family (in which home for years I was an intimate) were all so incensed at my attitude . . . on the *Suffrage Issue* that it was tragic! One day, this very dear cousin said: "I hope to live to see the day that Missouri will elect you to the U.S. Senate—by the Suffrage Contingent!" [Pearson goes on to say her cousin did not live to see her actual triumphs, including being appointed on "a private mission of moment to meet some of the Nation's most brilliant Senators (and both occasions successful!)," a group of senators including two prominent antisuffragists, Senator Henry Cabot Lodge of Massachusetts and Senator John Sharp Williams of Mississippi, for whom she gave a dinner.]

As the World War began to grow, I . . . [noted] in the Tennessee papers, The Nashville, Memphis and Chattanooga *Times* . . . the names of prominent women in the State, who began to agitate Equal Suffrage in a business-like way, for, and opposed! The situation in Nashville became acute, when the Equal Suffrage faction proposed, that Women's Suffrage become a plank in "The Federation of Women's Clubs in Tennessee!" Heretofore, this had been taboo! I noted the Nashville women of great stamina, social position and influence, including Mrs. T. M. [Nannie] Steger, Mrs. Norman [Josephine Elliston] Farrell and a host of others, . . . appointed Mrs. John [Virginia] Vertrees, Chairman of an organization opposing this radical initiation! By invitation, Mrs. [Arthur M., Josephine] Dodge, National Pres. at that time of the Anti-Suffrage Association, New York [The National Association Opposed to Woman Suffrage], came to Nashville [1916]. I was cordially invited to be present, but graciously declined, stating I was in mourning for my mother, and now desired to give my entire time—when not writing—to my father's declining years. (My answer was respected).

Shortly after this "The Tenn. Federation of Women's Clubs" convened in Chattanooga. One morning, as usual, I walked to the N.C. and St. L. station—in view of our home and The Assembly Grounds to take The Chattanooga *Times* from the Agent. I walked along reading, slowly! The first column of the *Times* was given over to the Federation Gathering. [Then] I saw that in the Response of Welcome by Miss Earnestine Noe [was] the startling accusation that the "Anti-Suffragists were allied with the Whiskey Element and the Red Light Districts of America!" Immediately, my passivity of action was . . . [abandoned]! I handed the paper to my father saying, "Please read, hastily, I'm answering this challenge." Quite excited, my father urged, "Oh! no my Daughter! I beg you not to think of entering a newspaper controversy; it is bad enough between men, but a fearful thing between women—and most unthinkable for my daughter!" As I left him reading, I went to my desk and wrote out a reply to go down on the 11:00 a.m. train to Chattanooga. When I came out on the Veranda, my father ever gallant, arose. Then [he] placed his hands on my head, tenderly, and said, "Daughter you have my Blessing; you could not in honorable Memory to your Mother—as well as your own active pen of late, do otherwise than answer such untrue statements!" Before the next day's sundown—after my reply to Miss Noe had appeared in that Morning's Chattanooga *Times*—I was showered with letters [and] telegrams from leading lawyers—both of the Democratic and Republican parties in Tennessee, even [lawyers] in New York on the following day, offering me their support, etc. . . .

It all ended with Miss Noe's apology, published in The Chattanooga *Times,* and her personal apology to me! She gave as her authority some preacher in the North! Following all this came a lull—it did seem for a time—in Suffrage activities in Tennessee, at least in the open! Then, I began to note that . . . Mrs. James C. Bradford [Sara P. Bradford of Nashville], had espoused the Anti-Suffrage cause, having met a member of [the] Anti-Suffragists in the East. This did not interest me; I was heart-sick of suffrage—nausea! But, when Pres. Wilson (whom I had never admired—in spite of my parents' admiration and the loyalty of all my family . . . came out so strong in his statements "That Federal Suffrage was an issue to be settled by each state," *I was Delighted!* For the first time, I felt the sense of Allegiance. I had written extensively vs. "The Wilson Watching and Waiting Mexican Policy"; I did not—as one who has been close with the great, financially and politically, of Mexico—for a year think the President knew the conditions. . . . Again at that time I was "Was from Missouri" and for Champ Clark and "Hound-dog." Mr. Wilson was of half-southern inheritance, through his mother—(not his father). . . . [Pearson goes on to say she was on the faculty at Winthrop State Normal College for Women in Rock Hill, South Carolina (1897–99) with Wilson's aunt, Miss Woodrow, "a woman of real brains, but erratic and obstinate . . . yet a loyal friend of mine in emergencies."]

When the Tennessee Legislature met in Session, and the National Spotlight was first thrown on the Volunteer State as the likely *Leit Motif* for National Action; I, "In the Fastness of My Mountains" felt Tennessee was safe! Then—as a bolt out of the clear sky—came the message: "You are unanimously elected as President of The Tennessee State Association Opposed to Woman Suffrage," I replied; "Overcome with the honor, but impossible to accept." Then followed a long distance; urging me to at least come to Nashville. My father suggested that he thought that . . . [owing] to the memory of my mother [and] to this courtesy and the honor paid me, that I [should] go down to explain my position, and to assure these distinguished Tennesseans of my appreciation. I conceded to his advice, and I was met at the Nashville Union Station and driven to the residence of Mr. and Mrs. John Vertrees, where, on the night of my arrival, some were invited to meet me at dinner. Others, during the evening called, both women and men! By midnight, I had about been persuaded to accept this sacred honor, as Pres. opposing Federal Suffrage in Tennessee, feeling the assurance of the President's pronounced platform, and his expressed attitude that each State settle this question for itself, "Lest We Forget." I said to those assembled that my acceptance would depend [upon] . . . my conversation, next morning with my father, over the telephone! Mr. Vertrees assisted in this tentative acceptance; but I told him I desired, also, to consult a long, kind friend, [my friend] since my early childhood, Maj. E. C. Lewis [in McMinnville]. . . . Mr. Vertrees accompanied me to see Maj. Lewis. His reply was characteristic; "Go to it, damn it, and win!" His daughters, my dear friends, were suffragists! [Pearson then writes that, as her "swiftly-going pen now records so much that followed of so much personal bitterness," there is "some I could willfully expose" but more that she feels "the desire to make obscure 'at this hour of the day' in assembling these compilations." But she is particularly thankful for the "love and affection" of "possibly the favorite daughter of Maj. Lewis [unnamed]—as dear to me as a daughter—who blesses my last years, this 1939!"]

From now on I desire to confine "My Story" . . . [to the] strictly official! Speaking direct and simple to Tennessee Women and Men! [As] a woman who had awakened to the emergency of the issue at stake, and who held in sacred trust the honor accorded to her, in Three Campaigns v. Federal Suffrage in Tennessee through 1920. . . .[2]

It seems that Mrs. Jas. C. Bradford of Nashville, had before this occasion—on her own initiative—been active and cordial in extending invitations to some of the most noted members of The National Anti-Suffrage Association in New York to come to Nashville, to assist her in organizing a Nashville Chapter. This occurred simultaneously with . . . "The Inauguration of The President [Pearson] of The Tennessee State Association Opposed to Woman Suffrage."

This action was not approved by such leaders as Judge John Allison, and a host of others, as well as our constituents in the Tennessee Legislature, who felt it imperative—at this critical time—that only the Women of the State of Tennessee—should be in evidence to direct this pending campaign. [They believed] that suffrage as a Federal issue [should] be either enacted or rejected by the peoples of each state and its state leaders—as according to the expressed opinion of President Wilson—whose policy the Tennessee Legislature and the Tenn. Anti-Suffrage Constituents, were following! So when these noted women from the East—all unadvised, except by Mrs. Bradford, personally arrived, it gave rise to a very delicate situation that was delegated—a very unhappy task—to the President of the Tennessee State Association Opposed to Woman Suffrage. In this most embarrassed connection, as well as many other then pending emergencies at this time, I stay my pen from the run of "My

Story" to pay my living respects to this long, loyal [friend], Mrs. Morgan Brown, Secretary [of the Tennessee Association Opposed to Woman Suffrage].

Through Mrs. Brown, officially, and other leaders, it was gracefully arranged that these visitors be entertained as guests of the President-Elect—for dinner at the Country Club. Then and there, as gracefully as this occasion could command, so acute a contretemps (that taxed all the powers of any hostess) was . . . [honorably handled]. Be it said, that their understanding loyalty to the cause as well as . . . the amenities at stake [should be noted?]; they were *escorted*—with every due consideration—to the Union Station, and left on the late train that night for the East! Then—all seemed to be moving along all advisedly smooth—as politics goes—directed by fine brains of Tennessee's *best statesmen* and true, who were giving all their best efforts vs. Suffrage, as a Federal issue in Tennessee, compatible with the proclaimed policy, on this issue, by Pres. Wilson! It seemed never necessary for our Anti-Suffrage women to even climb the capitol steps—to the Senate and House of Representatives quarters—as the suffrage forces kept up a constant visitation. *Instead*, early at certain hours and occasions, on each desk was a leaflet [placed]—a cordial message of some kind (one of assurance of appreciation of co-operation, or a suggestion); each leaflet [was] printed with Greetings, or reminder of some especial exigency of that day. Frequently, members of the legislature were entertained in small groups for dinner at the Vertrees residence, giving ample occasion to discuss—in private with the Legislative Leaders—who were conducting the Forces in the Tennessee Legislature opposed to Federal Suffrage!

One morning there was sent to the Vertrees residence a telegram addressed [to] The Speaker of the Tennessee Senate, relayed, *immediately* to me, that was from Pres. Wilson to the Senate; that he advised for political expediency that Tennessee pass the Federal Amendment! Before Mrs. Vertrees and I could finish its reading Mr. Vertrees—getting from his own car—hastily rushed into his wife's room. Addressing me, he said, "Of course, Miss Pearson, you will send your instructions [on] how to answer the President to the Senate." Then he added, "I did not know that the Speaker expected to send this to you, at once!" I replied, "Mr. Vertrees I'm going in person before the Senate." Startled! He, with all his power of his masterful eloquence and logic, used every argument—including the fact that I had been so dignified—[that] not once [had I] gone myself or desired any of my constituents to go to the capitol—where the Suffrage forces had swarmed! Concluding—he impressed me with the arguments [that had prevailed] for my appointment to The Presidency of the Opposition to Federal Suffrage in Tennessee; chiefly;

1st. We desired a woman who had outstanding ability—and who had your remarkable experience in the study and knowledge of the attendant questions . . . [owing to your experience as] a leader of the Anti-Suffrage forces in Missouri, [and] as an Educator.

2nd. [That you were] A Native Tennessean to the manner born.

3rd. That you are too brainy—as well as tactful, to want to direct—the strong alliance of the men constituents, legal and professional—as well as the members of the Legislature!

All were these facts, or, statements that were made to me upon my induction into office as President. To all, I agreed; all I respected—as I did this gallant, brainy, legal light facing me, whom I respected as I did few men! Then, his wife spoke: "John let Miss Pearson alone! If she wants to go to the Senate, let her use her judgment to go! She did not want this office of President, it was forced upon her—we virtually 'drafted' her." All this time—I had stood silently white, with a resolution! For the first, and only time, clashing with the opinion and loyal protection of my legal advisor; also my host!

Immediately—as always—did this every inch a gentleman—bow—to his wife's wishes. Then—with a somewhat compromising bow to me, he said; "If *you must* go, you go as a lady, accompanied by a gentleman!" We each rode in quiet, restrained rage—almost; sitting side by side, on the rear seat of his car, not one word was spoken—until he escorted me up the flight of steps of the Capitol. When we reached the Senate Chamber door, as I was being met to go to the platform, (for I later learned that Mrs. Vertrees had phoned), were my steps stayed, as Mr. Vertrees leaned over to ask; "What are you going to say?" I replied, "I do not know!" (How often have I wondered, how hurt [and] anxious—really how must have suffered this strong man of heart and action of mind—in his mystified effort to try to comprehend what this recalcitrant woman whom he had trusted, had advised not to be hasty in action, etc. might be going to say, or do, possibly to ruin the well *laid plans, long conceived!*)[3]

I was led on to the platform—as in a daze—even while being applauded! I can scarce recall any of it at all—even the introduction—or the sensation I was (unhappily for poor anxious Mr. Vertrees) creating! Then stepping to the edge of the platform, holding up that fatal telegram, which I read in a ringing voice, I seemed to hear my voice touch the Capitol Dome! Concluded, I said, stronger, even louder: "President Wilson has overstepped [his] prerogative as President of the United States! Will you follow his advice?" I can never recall what, if anything, was said! I knew, only, that, two to one was that moment, in a shout, defeated Federal Suffrage in Tennessee! I was, after it was over, so dazed that I can scarcely recall how proud were the words of congratulations that reached my ears, as Mr. Vertrees—more proud than any—whisked me to his awaiting wife, who met me with welcome arms—so tenderly, so true! Then, "Home to My Mountains," that night once again, in the arms of my adoring father!

The World War waged on! Caring tenderly for my father, I did not need to go to Nashville—even to the funeral of that beloved, high-toned friend, the wife of Mr. Vertrees, whom I sincerely mourned! . . . [Pearson says in the years until the suffrage issue was again raised in Tennessee she took care of her father, and was active in an organization founded in her "father's library," "The Council of The Dixie Highway via. The Cumberland Divide," and served as leader of its auxiliary—"to please my father." She was also active in war work, Red Cross work, etc. She left her father only to give an October 1917 address, "to again, please him," the first "Woman's Address" before a National Good Roads Association meeting. At this time, she wrote, "it *seemed* that the Suffrage issue was *so secure in its defeat in Tennessee,* that I only went to Nashville once, as a formality of presentation, before its defeat, again, by the Tennessee Legislature!"]

Following my father's death, I attempted a new avocation for an Educator! The ravages attendant to securing the luxuries I had showered upon the declining years of my parents, [at] above normal cost during the World War, had depleted [what had been] a fair bank account in 1914. . . . [After that, it was necessary] to mortgage, at 10% interest, my *last piece of property* (of several *formerly owned*), to meet the expenses incumbent upon me for these years out of college, for I *spared nothing in the final care, attention,* and the burial of my parent! So, in 1920 I opened my large home to "Paying guests." I was just in the flush of this season's adventure—my house full of delightful friends—when on July 17 (?), the very hottest day I think I ever experienced, came the message, "Mrs. Catt arrived. Extra called session imminent by the Governor. Our forces are being notified to rally at once. Send orders—and come immediately," etc.

I left on the afternoon train, arriving in Nashville alone, unannounced . . . [I went] to [the] Hotel Hermitage, where I found orders were left—at my demand! I first, inquired the location of Mrs. Catt. Then I surprised the authorities at the desk by engaging the lowest-priced—an inside room—for myself, but [asking them] to set aside until further notified the large room on the Mezzanine floor [and] also the large Assembly Room on the 1st. floor. Going to that room—almost suffocating after coming down from the Mountains—I at once plunged into the bath, calling the office to line me up with New York! For hours, I stood in cool trickling water; that *seemed* like hiring a *spot in the suburbs of Hell* in which to pass the night! With the unfailing telephone in my hand, I had before midnight contacted through New York and Boston and Montgomery, Ala., the line up of many *rushing forces to Nashville!*

[Thus the anti-suffrage contingent was] there or were on the way, and by dawn [there was also] an assurance of money to be rushed from the United Efforts of our Women, East, North, and South. I had the feeling that this battle of Women vs. Women must be started with Women's funds; then we could be open to large benefits. After assurances from Women all over the land, we immediately merged "The Tennessee State Association Opposed to Woman Suffrage." [It had then, in] two sessions of the State Legislature, defeated honorably, and we felt, definitely, the issue . . . [of] Federal Suffrage in Tennessee, but for the action of a perfidious Governor, and [the] changed attitude of President Woodrow Wilson. . . . The organization now effectuated—by Women and Men—became a part of National History!

The women of Nashville who had left the city's heat (some far up in the East, some ready to sail to Europe), because of intense convictions entered their return, to join, [giving] generously of time and means in co-ordinated union of strength—upon arrival "to enter the fray!" Some Women and Men of Nashville, who had opposed [the antisuffragists, who supported suffrage if by state action], now joined wholeheartedly in this fight vs. the Federal Amendment all [their] forces. [Antisuffragists] from many states came to offer services; every conceivable loyalty was manifested in representation from 37 states, Mrs. Jas. Pinckard and Mrs. [Walter D.] Lamar leading our own forces from Ala. and Ga., while Laura Clay—who for 20 years had fought [for] Equal Suffrage—came at her own expense to remain the entire session—to fight Federal Suffrage [According to her biographer, Paul E. Fuller, Clay actually stayed only a few days[4]]; also in this line were the Misses [Kate and Jean] Gordon of New Orleans—and life-long suffragist and the brilliant wife of Gov. [Ruffin G. Pleasant] of La., [Anne Pleasant].

Our Eastern women from New York and Boston were a grand United force in all ways. Long had they led "Remain in Boston"—under Mrs. [Randolph] Frothingham; in New York following Mrs. Dodge was Mrs. Jas. Wordsworth—then Miss Kilbreath; and Mrs. Wiese in Baltimore, ad infinitum. . . . Reporters [came] from all the Eastern press, Chicago to Dallas, west to Denver—and all the Southern press [were] represented generously, waiting for daily, hourly interviews—which alone taxed the strength. No greater test of loyalty can be attributed to a once Noted Woman, the late Mrs. Van Leer Kirkman [Catherine], Pres. [of] the Woman's Board of the Tennessee Centennial, than when I urged her to let me place her own name in place of mine as President of the Tennessee Division; with her arm around me, with a tear in her eye she replied, "Listen—if you will just keep quiet about such an arrangement, (for I verily know nothing about all this), . . . I'll get out of the bath-tub, any hour, day or night, to come at your call!" Indeed it may be said [that] we each and all "Pass[ed] under the Rod of *Denial!*" . . .

The Great Bishop, Edward Thomson, D.D., L.L.D; of the Methodist Episcopal Church, in his delightful volumes "Oriental Missions," when he received in India, the news from the United States of the results of the War between the States, writes: "There is no telling what backwoods steps the world might have taken—if the Southern Rebellion had been *successful.*" I, myself, have often ventured the opinion, that, for long, there existed—in *certain classes in the North,* such exponents as Dr. Mary Walker who defied the Courts to *wear pants;* the writer Harriet Beecher Stowe, of "Uncle Tom's Cabin"; Dr. Anna Howard Shaw, who, in an address in Calif., *asked:* "What is The American Flag, but a piece of bunting?"; Mrs. Carrie Chapman Catt (Mrs. Tom Catt) [Catt's late husband's name was actually George William Catt]; Susan B. Anthony and others—(in certain *classes in the North*)—where this same Susan B. Anthony—the great "Abolitionist" and later leader of the suffrage forces, beginning in the North—all felt toward *Equal Suffrage* as did the great Bishop feel toward the Fall of the Confederacy!

Thus there arose from such leaders and classes—the origin of the Susan B. Anthony Amendment! Thus, we, representative women of the South arose, as did the representative women of Boston and the East and North, vs. (The Federal Suffrage) "Susan B. Anthony Amendment" which we declined to Digest without *Protest!*

Since 1920, I have been the guest in the elegant homes of a number of Eastern Women who came to Tennessee's assistance—several, including my House-Hostess Mrs. Randolph Frothingham of Boston! In 1926—there was a notable gathering in my honor at *Hotel Statler* with Mrs. Jas. Wordsworth Hostess, with several of the ladies who were in the group at Hotel Hermitage. Later that same season, I was as the guest at Poland Springs, Maine, again of Mrs. Frothingham. She and her Social Secretary assisted me in several compilations of "The Remonstrance Organizations," in the East *preceding 1920,* which I desire to file with ours of Tennessee. I had become, during my several sojourns in Boston to know that the *first promoters* of Suffrage of the East were, originally, (even as in 1920) of the type of Women, as Mrs. Catt, or Susan B. Anthony! The Remonstrance Women of Boston were the type that opposed Federal Suffrage in Tenn. I feel *this is due from my pen* as to the contact with class and type of Womanhood—that has the real discretion to be respected in any and all Sections! They often suggested to me the same old conservative type of families of the environs of Philadelphia and in Old Charleston, S. C!

The Mother of Mrs. Frothingham, the late Mrs. Anthony, whom I learned to love during my sojourn with them in Maine, at South Poland Hotel, was of that retired, quaint, sweet, conservative type of Women that reminded me of *My Mother*. She was raised in wealth [and] still quietly living in its environs. She was educated in Europe, which she knew well. Her fondness for literature—her tastes in general—all seemed to whisper memories that were linked in remembrance until *her death* a year later; the *class* of our own *Southern Women* of the *Old Regime!*

After my first night—spent in the bath-tub of Hotel Hermitage—all the authorities assembled had me moved to a private apt., in the N.W. corner 7th floor. Here I had private line connections; here, was showered on me all needed attentions; here,—where a friend on the opposing side (the late Mrs. Leslie Warner [Katherine Burch Warner] who had been a guest in my home) said, "If I can make Josephine Pearson mad—this fight will be over!" I valued this caution, and when I felt that suggestion stealing upon me I locked myself, for a spell, in room 718.

[Pearson now completely skips a sizable part of the ratification story, including both the Senate vote in favor of ratification and the dramatic House battle in which the ratification resolution carried by one vote until Speaker Walker changed his vote to "aye" in order to move to reconsider—and buy time for the antis. Pearson's story resumes with that night.]

From this high place [the Hermitage] in the dead of night came the ring from Headquarters! Stealthily I went by a side-stair to find our Leaders in the Legislature, were corralling our 27 men (all wore a Red Rose) in various hotels to be gotten off on the 3:00 a.m. train for Alabama, thus to break the quorum in the House next morning! The "Red Rose Brigade" stayed in Alabama three weeks, thus giving constituents in the Legislature time to go home for a rest—and to get instructions from the Home folks. I, also, took, a day's vacation up to the Mountain, . . . [before going] to meet the Red Rose Brigade at Cowan as warriors returning! During this waiting spell, so vital to our side [and] (so to the contrary [to] the Suffrage side), our Women still at the helm in Nashville sent these men all kind of nice things. And when a baby was born to one of the group, away from his home, that baby was remembered by our forces at headquarters who sent a layette with their compliments from its—"An-tis". . . .

My story—possibly too long in detail—yet withal so superficially told, of the years of tragic moment, must come to a close—with the utter helplessness of being unequal to discuss "The Burns Vote. . . ." The entire legislative procedure was so dishonored in Tennessee by this Episode that it . . . [would be] more dignified for a *woman* to ask that my Native State erase its false *ratification*—that had nothing valid about it—from the records as . . . for a *woman* to condescend to *outline* [the Burns story]!

That the compromised vote of the 19th Amendment was ratified by political corruption and, generally believed, bribery . . . will always be shrouded in doubt and uncertainty of some one or more man's dishonor! Also, that the Suffrage forces which could muster a quorum—because the Red Rose emigration to Alabama—they held a session just the same! They however admitted the validity of Mr. Walker's motion to reconsider—by taking it up and try[ing] to make it an illegal defeat. Then came the action of the Governor—already justly criticized for his lack of observance of the laws of the state, who had a Supreme Court judge summoned and without [a] hearing the injunction was dismissed! The illegal certificate of ratification was hurried to Washington with all possible haste, and to the shame of the Nation as well as the State, Sec'ty. Colby issued the proclamation from his *own house*—not from *his office!*

Thus will a vital political issue overshadow each name! The whole thing was an acknowledged National "fake"— that produced a Jubilee! Mr. Roberts [was] up to his neck in so many schemes to slip over the Amendment [that he] may well be called, as it was *my happy privilege* from a *platform*, "The Perfidious Governor of Tennessee!" That this act, together with the face about of the U. S. President . . . , may well, indeed, excuse a simple "Bobby Burns" (not of poetry); but we leave Blank his riotous escape, only to be "carried back home" (for his gymnastic defeat) in a private car! All of each circumstance also had its beginnings when the Members of the Tennessee Legislature were first made to forget their oaths that they had taken to support the *State Constitution! Shame* thrice *shame*; have I always bowed my head, in honest disgust?! No *woman's* pen could adequately trace the disgrace that marked Dear Tennessee! I leave it to some one, a man like . . . Dr. Gus Dyer, to equal the situation—*even if he can!* When I—go over the whole distasteful affair, I'm quite convinced that Hitler, hearing of this likely from afar, got the suggestion for his *first steps of his present power* from reading of this advertised feature of *state* and National Policy and Bravado—of such a degree of corruption in America! Having once known *Godly, classic Germany* (1900)—Last seeing it 1925—I sigh equally for *Germany*, as I blush to recall my state's (1920) policy, prototype of "Mein Kampf!"

President Wilson's face about, "for political emergency," [and] also other lesser possible mistakes, I've ever been grateful came after the death of my

Mother who admired him so! This, his *Perfidy* (I say the word with an understanding of its origin), I pray [will] ring down through the years, as long as *Tennessee is able to maintain the autonomy of its state hood. That this act* was a critical note bene for the then pivotal state of the Nation will ever remain to some, myself in particular, Unpardonable! For one so high in office! To me it has ever meant but one word—*Betrayal!*—to those who "entered the fray" believing his utterances were impeccable! . . . .

That memorable night, after the 1920 verdict stolen, I was not sorry for *defeat*. Ah! No! (I can be a good loser.) But [I was sorry] for the proclamation of a Stolen Verdict, [and I was] tired and heartsick to have fallen victim of Perfidy. I never in all the years before or since felt so empty a void in life, as Lost Ideals! [I felt] not defeat, but disgrace for my native state, and my country! There I was utterly alone [with] no one to whom I could confide. I had seen all my brave co-workers off for their distant homes! Those in the city, had their homes! Then there began to creep upon me a listlessness, not ever aroused—even after the venture up to my *mountain home!* I felt utterly impersonal! That I had done my best "To Keep the Faith!" That did not matter; yet *it* was very precious! But, that we men and women had to lose dishonorably—in defense of every compromise with the Nation's and the State's executive—embarrassed my self-respect, and it also *lost something* of *trust* never *quite restored!*

In the shadows of my yet unlighted room, I began to feel as I do tonight (the eve of my Mother's anniversary, April 6, 1939; she was born April 6, 1840) the encircling arms of my Mother; in her efforts to help me banish the empty void of something "Lost," never "found!" Then, turning over the mass of long preserved manuscripts, papers, letters—strange as a *dream of yesterday*—I find these appended pages, by my own pen; nineteen years ago, that night alone in my room, Hotel Hermitage, as well preserved, as clear to read, as if written to-day!

. . . "Dead, yet she speaketh!" This I do aver, more than any other one national utterance; [the fact] that the President did *not keep faith to his Southern Constituency* lost the Democratic Party leadership, 1920 to 1932—and justly so! When the President's selection for a successor was Mr. Cox, who left his home in the very face of a representative delegation of Women of Tennessee (even led by Mrs. George Washington and Mr. Frank Stahlman) whom Mr. Cox declined to meet for an interview (having before this granted a hearing from the Suffrage Delegation), his "*Bill of Rights*" to lead *Southern Democracy—was defeated!* In consequence, did the Anti-Suffrage forces of Tennessee, including its women, bind themselves to follow every available privilege to elect Mr. Harding, President, which was done!

"Home to My Mountains," long ill after *This Battle!* On the morning of The Election 1920, I went with some literature sent to me by Mrs. Washington to post at the polls at Monteagle. While doing—and excitement began to run high! Then the Patron of all Monteagle elections for the past [and] until this day, nervous [and] trembling came up to me saying: "You aint agoing to vote is you—you fit it too long and too hard! Tell us what you want voted and we'll vote for you!" I did and so always have I let this long loyal friend of my late father (Rev. P. A. Pearson), one who still "Who knows the law from 'Kiver to Kiver!'" to lead Grundy Co. politics—Esq. Wm. D. Bennett—[and] direct The Men of Grundy County to vote for

Josephine A. Pearson
April 20, 1939

Notes

"My Story" is in the Josephine A. Pearson Papers in the Tennessee State Library and Archives, Nashville, Tennessee.

1. See Anastatia Sims, "Beyond the Ballot: The Radical Vision of the Antisuffragists," part 1, essay 5, above; and "'Powers That Pray and Powers That Prey': Tennessee and the Fight for Woman Suffrage," *Tennessee Historical Quarterly* (Winter 1991): 203–25.

2. Pearson's reference here is to one of the other titles of "My Story" used in the various drafts of the manuscripts, "My Story: of the Three Campaigns vs. Federal Suffrage in Tennessee—1917 through August 1920!" This title is inappropriate as the campaigns before 1920 were against state suffrage measures. Indeed, on p. 233 and several pages that follow, Pearson describes events that occurred in 1917 as part of the campaign against the federal amendment when Congress did not submit the amendment to the states until June 1919.

3. Anastatia Sims doubts the authenticity of this story of Pearson's address to the Senate in defiance of Vertrees. She speculates that—*if* it occurred—it may be based on events that occurred in 1920.

4. See Paul E. Fuller, *Laura Clay and the Woman's Rights Movement*. (Lexington: University Press of Kentucky, 1975), 160.

12

Tennessee

Carrie Chapman Catt and Nettie Rogers Shuler

From *Woman Suffrage and Politics: The Inner Story of the Suffrage Movement*, 1923

Carrie Chapman Catt (1859–1947) was born in Wisconsin and grew up on a farm in Iowa. When her father objected to her going to college, she taught school until she could enter Iowa State College at Ames in 1877, supporting herself by working in the library and washing dishes. Graduating with a B.A. (1880), she put aside her goal of studying law in order to accept a position as a high school principal in Mason City. Within two years she rose to become superintendent of schools, quite unusual for the time. In 1885 she married Leo Chapman, editor of the *Mason City Republican*, and joined him at the paper as assistant editor. They moved to San Francisco, hoping to buy a paper there, but Chapman died suddenly, and she returned to Iowa. A talented orator, she went on the lecture circuit for a number of years.[1]

In 1887 Carrie Chapman joined the Iowa Woman Suffrage Association. She attended the historic 1890 convention in which the American Woman Suffrage Association and the National Woman Suffrage Association were reunited. The same year, she married George William Catt, a successful civil engineer and construction company president who encouraged her to devote time to suffrage work. They lived in Seattle and then settled in New York City. At Catt's urging, the NAWSA set up an Organization Committee (that she chaired) to manage its field operations,[2] including vigorous promotion of woman suffrage in the southern states.[3]

Carrie Chapman Catt was twice president of the National American Woman Suffrage Association. Susan B. Anthony chose Catt as her successor when she resigned from the presidency in 1900; she served until 1904, when forced to resign because of the failing health of her husband, who died a year later. She was very active in the New York state suffrage movement and chaired an impressive though unsuccessful state suffrage campaign in 1913–14. In 1915 she was elected to her second term as NAWSA president, succeeding Dr. Anna Howard Shaw. Catt acted quickly to reorganize and invigorate the organization, centralizing its operations, and putting into effect her famous "Winning Plan"—in brief, to work simultaneously for state and federal suffrage, and win enough state victories to assure the success of the federal amendment.[4]

Nettie Rogers Shuler (1862–1939), a prominent clubwoman and suffragist in New York state, worked with Catt in the state campaign and so impressed her that she made Shuler the NAWSA's corresponding secretary. Shuler served in that post throughout the remainder of the suffrage movement; Eleanor Flexner describes her as a woman of extraordinary talent and energy and as Catt's "alter ego." Shuler's daughter, Marjorie Shuler, later a prominent journalist, came to Tennessee and worked with Catt in the ratification campaign.[5]

As is indicated in this chapter from their 1923 book, *Woman Suffrage and Politics: The Inner Story of the Suffrage Movement*, Catt spent nearly two months in Tennessee, working with Tennessee suffragists to gain the thirty-sixth state. In this dramatic account, written soon after the events described, Catt and Shuler tell the incredible tale of the suffrage Armageddon as it deserves to be told, with insight and humor.

[By June 1920] . . . thirty-five states had ratified the suffrage amendment; eight had defeated ratification. The final decision therefore rested with the remaining five States that had not yet taken any action. These states were the Northern States of Connecticut and Vermont and the Southern States of North Carolina, Florida and Tennessee.

The poll of the Legislatures of North Carolina and Florida indicated an adverse majority so of course these States were expected to take adverse action, in accord with the remainder of the South. This limited the immediate prospect of the thirty-sixth ratification to Connecticut, Vermont, and Tennessee. None of the Legislatures of these States was in session, so none could ratify unless its Governor called a special session. Responsibility thus narrowed down to the Governors of the three States. Temporarily, the case of Tennessee was dismissed from consideration because of an amendment in its State constitution which read:

Carrie Chapman Catt. Courtesy of the State Historical Society of Iowa—Des Moines.

> "Article III, Section 32: No convention or general assembly of this State shall act upon any amendment of the constitution of the United States proposed by Congress to the several States, unless such convention or General Assembly shall have been elected after such amendment is submitted."

(Florida's constitution also contained this provision.)

This provision of the Tennessee constitution had stood unchallenged for half a century and was accepted as prohibiting a special session for the purpose of ratifying the Suffrage Amendment.

There was no longer any doubt of the ratification of the Amendment if it could be put before any one of the three Legislatures of Connecticut, Vermont, and Tennessee. All were favorable to ratification and the general sentiment in these States was not only very friendly, but the Republicans in the one-party Republican States of Connecticut and Vermont, and the Democrats in the one-party Democratic State of Tennessee, were pledged to aid ratification. Yet the presidential election of 1920 was coming nearer and nearer, with the women's chance to vote in it hanging upon a thirty-sixth ratification and that ratification hanging upon a special session. It was believed that the Governor of Tennessee [A. H. Roberts] could not call such a session. As has already been shown, the Governors of Connecticut [Marcus A. Holcomb], and Vermont [Percival W. Clement] would not. [Both Holcomb and Clement were antisuffrage and antiprohibition.[6]]

Feeling was tense and irritable throughout the country. Suffragists regarded the situation with the amazed irascibility of a plaintiff given a verdict by a jury but with the judgment mysteriously and suspiciously withheld. A more surprising manifestation came from hundreds, if not thousands, of women who had taken no part and had shown no especial interest in the campaign for suffrage, but who now developed a more raucous attitude toward the delay than the better disciplined suffragists. Women whose sympathies with the suffrage struggle had never been apparent, now, because the thirty-sixth State was not more speedily achieved, even went so far as to throw bitter invective at suffragists who had given the whole potentiality of their lives to the cause.

There were other causes of irritation. After the ratification of the thirty-fifth State on March 22, political leaders had concluded that there would be a thirty-sixth State and that millions of women would vote in November. The prediction had been widely heralded that these new voters might turn the scale in the coming election, and in consequence a hectic effort to enroll them in advance had been made by all parties. Suffragists, nonsuffragists and antisuffragists had been appointed to official posts and the first duty assigned them had been the organization of the coming women voters. Although hosts of women flocked to the organizing meetings, many declined to be organized as voters before they had attained that dignity. National chairmen of the political parties were harassed on the one hand by suffragists and their State party organizations, who entreated them to use every possible effort to find a thirty-sixth State; and on the other hand by women anti-suffragists and a powerful party minority, threatening a variety of disasters were that State found. Two considerations tipped the scale suffrageward, one that the politics of the thirty-sixth State might easily be a determining factor in the coming presidential election [ratification by a Republican-controlled state would help that party's chances and likewise for the Democrats]; the other that if there should be no thirty-sixth ratification each dominant party would be held blamable [*sic*] and the premature organization of women might prove a boomerang.

It was in the midst of this impasse that the Supreme Court handed down its decision [June 2, 1920 *George S. Hawke vs. Harvey C. Smith, Secretary of State of Ohio*, a case that removed various legal challenges antisuffragists had counted upon to complicate and confound the ratification process[7]]. It validated all the ratifications already effected, cleared the Amendment of legal doubt and emphasized the fact that completed ratification required the action of only a single State. Immediately a fresh campaign to persuade the two Northern Governors to action was begun, and the Republican party left no stone unturned to persuade them to call special sessions, but neither would budge. It left the Republicans, whose majorities in Congress had submitted the Amendment and whose proportions of the State ratifications was the larger, seemingly unable to deliver the thirty-sixth State.

Meanwhile Democratic hopes had turned slowly but steadily to Tennessee. Colonel Joseph H. Acklen, general counsel of the Tennessee Suffrage Association, on May 11, had published an opinion in the *Nashville Banner* declaring that should the Supreme Court of the United States hold that ratification of federal amendments may be accomplished only by the exact procedure outlined in the federal constitution, the Section 32 of Article III of the Tennessee constitution would be abrogated and a called session could legally ratify the suffrage Amendment. The opinion attracted little attention at the time but it convinced the women of the State auxiliary of the National Suffrage Association. (That auxiliary was now known as the Tennessee League of Women Voters [led by Abby Crawford Milton, whose husband George Fort Milton was editor of the *Chattanooga News* and an outspoken suffrage supporter[8]]. Its old title was the Tennessee Equal Suffrage Association.) [The NAWSA, at its February 1920 convention, had created the League of Women Voters and transferred its auxiliaries to the new organization, which had a board separate from the NAWSA.[9]] At their annual convention a week later, they [the Tennessee suffragists] discussed the situation and determined to be on watch. The decision clearly recognized and applied the principle that no State possessed the authority to alter or modify in any way whatsoever the method of amending the constitution, and Colonel Acklen urged the Tennessee League of Women Voters to agitate the question of a special session.

This the League lost no time in doing. Telegraphing to the headquarters of the National Suffrage Association for help, it turned its forces to the problem of converting the State press, the Governor and the Legislature to the idea that the Supreme Court decision had made ratification in Tennessee possible. Its first appeal was made to the State Democratic convention. The convention, with enthusiastic applause, carried a hearty resolution endorsing ratification of the Amendment and recommending a special session. Armed with this resolution, the women requested the Governor to call the Legislature. The National Suffrage Association added its request, but he gave them no encouragement.

> "There will be no extraordinary session of the sixty-first General Assembly," said he. . . . "I am forbidden by the constitution of Tennessee to call an extra session of the Legislature to act upon any amendment to the constitution of the United States. That matter is delegated to the succeeding General Assembly."

The agitation proceeded nevertheless. The *Tennessean*, the Chattanooga *News* and the Tennessee League of Women Voters were simultaneously taking a poll of the Legislature and from time to time publishing interviews with the legislators. On June 20 the Governor, still believing that Tennessee had no authority to ratify, again declined to call a session. The newspapers were timidly discussing the possibilities of the session, the suffragists alone being confident. It was then that the chairman of the Tennessee Ratification Committee wrote the National Suffrage Association:

> "Our only hope lies in Washington. In Tennessee all swear by Woodrow Wilson. No one here believes he has clay feet. The Democratic State Convention on the 8th of June exhausted every adjective in our voluminous Southern vocabulary to approve, praise and glorify his every word and deed. If he will but speak, Tennessee must yield."

Inspired by her faith, the entire State Board of the League of Women Voters, thirty-two women, signed a telegram to the President, urging him to ask Governor Roberts to call the session and assuring him that the Legislature would ratify if called. A copy of the telegram was sent to national suffrage headquarters and with it a plea for more help. Through its Washington representative, the National American Woman Suffrage Association secured the intercession of President Wilson, who asked the United States Department of Justice to render an opinion to the Tennessee Governor concerning the application of the Supreme Court decision to the constitution of Tennessee. This was done within an hour by Assistant Attorney-General [W. L.] Frierson, a citizen of Tennessee, and the following was made public by the White House in the afternoon, fifteen hours after the telegram had been sent from Nashville:

> "The ruling of the Supreme Court in the recent Ohio case, and the consideration which I gave to this question in preparing these cases for hearing, leaves no doubt in my mind that the power of the Legislature to ratify an amendment of the Federal Constitution is derived solely from the people of the United States through the Federal Constitution and not from the people through the Constitution of the State. The power thus derived cannot be taken away, limited or restrained in any way by the Constitution of a State. The provision of the Tennessee Constitution, if valid, would undoubtedly be a restriction upon that power.
>
> "If the people of a State through their Constitution can delay action on an amendment until after an election, there is no reason why they cannot delay it until after two elections, or five elections, or until the lapse of any period of time they may see fit, and thus practically nullify the article of the Federal Constitution providing for amendment."

On the same day President Wilson telegraphed Governor Roberts:

> "It would be a real service to the party and to the nation if it is possible for you, under the peculiar provision of your State Constitution, having in mind the recent decision of the Supreme Court in the Ohio case, to call a special session of the Legislature of Tennessee to consider the Suffrage Amendment. Allow me to urge this very earnestly."

Governor Roberts had no prejudices *per se* against a special session, for on March 11 he had announced that he would call a special session of the Legislature when and if the Amendment should be ratified by thirty-six other States, in order to preclude the possibility of contesting elections in which women had voted "without previous enactment of State laws relating to payment of poll tax and registration." With the proposal of the President, supported by the Frierson letter, a new light was thrown on the political scene. The next day, June 24, an elaborate opinion was handed by the Governor, at his request, by State Attorney-General Frank M. Thompson, which declared that ratification of the Suffrage Amendment by a special session would be legal.

The National American Woman Suffrage Association on June 25 gave to the public the opinion of Hon. Charles Evans Hughes, its counsel. In part it said:

> "The provision of the Constitution of Tennessee attempts to take away from any existing Legislature of that State the authority to ratify the Amendment as proposed by Congress for ratification of the Legislature, and to place this authority in a Legislature subsequently chosen. This, in my opinion, is beyond the power of the State. In the adoption of the Federal Constitution, the State assented to the method of ratification by the State Legislature without any such qualification and the State Legislature sitting as such after the amendment has been duly proposed by Congress has, in my judgment, full authority to ratify."

Chief Justice [Walter] Clark of the North Carolina Supreme Court [an avid supporter of woman suffrage] volunteered a similar opinion. The widely published opinions of these high legal authorities of both dominant parties instantaneously changed the direction of expectation throughout the nation. Democratic presidential candidates sent drastic telegrams to the Governor urging that Tennessee put an end to the uncertainty of the woman's vote. In response to combined entreaties, the Governor announced that he would call a session—whereupon a long-drawn breath of relief swept over the nation. Newspapers carried the news that the Democratic State of Tennessee had come forward as the gallant rescuer of the befogged Suffrage Amendment. Cartoonists discovered a wide diversity of humorous features with which to carry the same message [see part 3 below]; and Tennessee, "the perfect thirty-six," became the talk of the hour. Democrats were exultant; Republicans exceedingly generous.

The relief and joy in suffrage and political party headquarters were not, however, universal. The opposition had not given up hope and it now gathered its forces for the most terrific battle it had ever waged. That battle might have been a mere flurry had it not been for two unfortunate facts: First, the political situation within the State was the worst possible for united action on any measure, and second, the Tennessee League of Women Voters was ill-qualified at that particular date to take care of so serious a campaign.

Tennessee had been a Democratic State since the Civil War, although one-third of its Legislature was Republican. The Republicans came mainly from the eastern mountain regions which had remained loyal to the Union in the Civil War and loyal to the Republican party ever after. They were regarded by the majority with frigid tolerance and the only time that there were Republican victories in the State was when there were rifts in the Democratic forces. In one-party States the normal party antagonisms practically cease, but the instincts for division reappear as factions in the majority party. In Tennessee, these factions within the Democratic party were at each other's throats. Staid citizens anxiously shook their heads, remembering a similarly bitter occasion when a shocking murder had resulted from a factional political quarrel. The prevailing fear that a tragedy might ensue, or that the State might be thrown into the hands of the Republicans, tended to widen the breach as each group laid the responsibility for the gravity of the situation upon the other. A persistent rumor, untraceable to any definite source, ran through each faction to the effect that the Republicans, provided with unlimited funds, were making a deal with the leaders of the opposing factions. Suspicion, animosity and uncompromising hate possessed the entire State.

The Governor was a candidate to succeed himself against two rival candidates. A whispering campaign of scandal involving the Governor was traveling fast. Every person in the State was classified as for or against him. No neutrals were permitted and when workers sent by the National Suffrage Association entered the State they were regarded with suspicion, each side accusing them as favorable to its rival. The Governor, obviously indifferent in his own feelings toward the question of woman suffrage, now found it an exceedingly troublesome issue. His political opponents alternately charged that he did not intend to call the extraordinary session; or if he did, that he and his friends could be depended upon "to dish the Amendment." Whatever the harried Governor's personal impulse may have been, he was certainly much disturbed by these opposing conditions and weighed the question to call or not to call each day, with varying conclusions.

Many Tennessee women had been anxious to vote in the primaries on August 5, and might have done so had the session been called at once. The rival candidates' forces therefore scolded, threatened, ridiculed and dragooned the Governor in the effort to get him to call a special session; and were without doubt not a little moved in their anxiety for early action by the hope that the scandal afloat would drive the new women voters into their camp. On the other hand, the Governor's friends, recognizing the possibility, assured him daily that enfranchising the women before August 5 would be equivalent to putting a weapon in the hand of his enemy with which to slay him. So suffragists and the opponents to suffrage in State and nation watched, waited and grew wroth, while embittered Tennessee fought her way to and through the primaries.

Most unfortunately of all perhaps, some of the leading Democratic women suffragists of the State had yielded to urging from the men and become involved in the political quarrel, some being arrayed on the Governor's side, some on the other. Although the active and efficient chairman of the Ratification Committee of the State auxiliary to the National American Woman Suffrage Association [Catherine Kenny of Nashville] was strictly neutral, the Governor refused to deal with her on the ground that she belonged in the enemy camp. He appointed his own Committee of Women to work for ratification, with a former president of the Tennessee Suffrage Association [Kate Burch Warner] as its chairman.[10] Then he announced that he would call the special session for August 9, four days after the primaries.

Meanwhile the chairman of the Governor's Committee of Women [Warner] hurriedly began to organize and to take a poll of the Legislature. At the same time she appealed to the National Suffrage Association for official recognition of her committee. The Tennessee League of Women Voters had no objection to its one-time president, but she was not, at the moment, an officer. Other women were officers and responsible to their constituency for the success of ratification. These women found themselves in the curious position of having their official duty taken from them by the Governor. He had summarily waved aside the organization which had produced the conditions that made ratification possible. As the Equal Suffrage Association it had blazed the trail through the early gloom of Tennessee prejudice, and later had conducted without pause the agitation, education and organization which had so largely converted the State to the justice of woman suffrage. At the moment the local groups of the League, under the direction of their Congressional Chairmen, were engaged in getting the poll of the Legislature. It was the usual routine with all auxiliaries of the National Suffrage Association, the principle being applied that the legislator was responsible to his constituency, and that they alone should solicit his voting pledge. Without the League and its many connections, ratification was dubious.

The National Suffrage Association, dismayed at this unexpected tangle within its own forces, sent a representative [Marjorie Shuler] to reconnoitre. A call upon the Governor's staff confirmed the rumor that the chief executive was surrounded by a hostile group, who not only did not want the session called but would prevent it if they could. From both friends and foes of the Governor, it was learned that the session was considered doubtful. The Governor's tactical mistake in appointing an independent woman's committee was recognized by his enemies at its full value, and the *Tennessean*, the leading newspaper in Nashville, had a series of editorials and cartoons in readiness with which it intended to lampoon him in relentless fashion. Perceiving that such an attack would arouse the Governor's friends to urge the withdrawal of the promise of a session, the representative of the National American Woman Suffrage Association pleaded for delay in the publication. This was reluctantly granted. The Governor was campaigning afield but a doubty Leaguer, driving her own car, took the representative to the place of his next meeting. In a brief midnight interview she pleaded for a compromise which would enable the recognition of both committees by the National Suffrage Association and by the Governor. The plea was graciously granted and she returned to Nashville with the signed compromise in her pocket, at five o'clock in the morning, having motored all night. The *Tennessean* would not accept the agreement. Then further delay was begged until the president of the National Suffrage Association could reach Nashville. This plea, too, was granted and a hurry telegram was sent to New York. On June 15 the president of the Association, after a twelve hours' notice, started for Tennessee, expecting to remain less than a week. But it was not until the comedy-tragedy of the Tennessee ratification passed into history, more than two months later, that she was able to return.

The *Tennessean* reluctantly withheld its planned attack upon the Governor and in an interview with the chief executive on Sunday, August 18, between trains, the president of the National American Woman Suffrage Association assured him that the Association recognized that ratification would be accomplished only by his aid and the aid of his followers in the Legislature; that it was not interested in the local politics in any State; that it recognized the Governor's right to appoint any committee he chose but that it could not repudiate its own auxiliary. She pointed out that there were Republicans in the Legislature and also Democrats in the opposing faction. She undertook to guarantee that the officers of the League of Women Voters would neither work for nor against him but would give their undivided attention to ratification. From that moment the national suffrage president served as liaison officer between the Governor and the suffragists—and found the position most delicate and difficult.

The National Suffrage Association knew one thing that Tennessee did not know, and that was that the opposition meant to wage a desperate, and probably unscrupulous, battle to prevent ratification in the thirty-sixth State. It knew that every weak man would be set upon by powerful forces, and that every vulnerable spot in the campaign would be discovered and attacked. It knew that the chances of success depended upon preparedness to the "last buckle on the last strap." It was no easy task to arouse either men or women to comprehension of the dire need of the hour. All factions professed to stand for ratification. Both the National Democratic and the National Republican Committees had urged the Governor to call a special session and the Legislature to ratify. Both Democratic and Republican national platforms had confirmed this request. Both Democratic and Republican State conventions had urged a special session and ratification. The Legislature about to be called had extended presidential and municipal suffrage to women, and more than a majority of its members were pledged to ratification.

Suffrage men were inclined to pooh at any expression of doubt as to the result. Yet there was not long to wait before warnings against false security began to materialize. The opposition began its work with an old campaign device. In order that legislators might "save their faces" when they should repudiate their pledges, a plausible excuse must be found. Suddenly there appeared in the press and, directly after, in every street-corner conversation the remarkable claim that those legislators who voted for ratification would violate their oath of office. It was held that though ratification might be legal if secured by the Legislature called into special session for the purpose, that fact did not free men from their oath to uphold the State constitution as it read, even if it included an invalid provision!

Every wheel in the opposition machinery was set in motion to spread this idea and to fix it indelibly in the minds of Tennessee. The anti-suffrage press hammered it home in daily editorials. Anti-suffrage lawyers, surprisingly ignorant of the relation of the federal constitution to State constitutions, contributed further confusion to the situation by labored opinions on the inviolability of the oath of office. Men who had never been credited with political virtue came forward to warn legislators of the wickedness of voting for ratification under such circumstances. The Bar Association, in session, contained so many members who held this remarkable view that the friends of suffrage present did not introduce an intended resolution favoring ratification, lest it be rejected. With amazing docility, intelligent men fell into the trap and for three weeks this device of the opposition threatened defeat of the Amendment in the special session.

It was obviously the first duty of suffragists to destroy this legal contention. An invitation to address a luncheon of the Kiwanis Club of Nashville gave the president of the National Suffrage Association an opportunity to discuss it. An excerpt was published in all leading papers of the State and for the first time the answer to the claim, which had already gained widespread and distinguished support, was put squarely before the people of the State. She said:

> "Those who are urging that legislators who vote for ratification will be violating their oath to support the State constitution forget that every legislator takes an oath of loyalty to two constitutions. The oath is no more in support of one than of the other. In fact the obligation to take an oath to support the constitution comes from the federal constitution (Article VI, Section 3). The possibility of conflict between the two was foreseen and the federal constitution (Article V, Section 2) declares that to be the supreme law of the land, and 'the judges in every State shall be bound thereby, anything in the constitution or laws of any State to the contrary notwithstanding.' The legislator does not vote to nullify the Tennessee constitution when he votes to ratify the Federal Suffrage Amendment. Any part of a State constitution is already nullified when it conflicts with the federal constitution. His oath first supports the federal constitution, which is the supreme law of the land, and, second, such portions of the Tennessee constitution as are in agreement with the federal constitution, for all others, including the provision in question, would be held to be nullified and to all intents nonexistent should the question of their legality ever reach the Supreme Court."

Committees were hurriedly appointed in all chief towns and cities and suffragists were given instructions to visit all influential lawyers and secure either an opinion on the mooted point, or their signature to an opinion on the question: When a legislator takes a joint oath to support the federal and the State constitutions, does he violate his oath when voting in accord with the provisions of the federal constitution? As fast as these opinions were secured, they were printed by the favorable press. After a two weeks' vigorous campaign in this direction a large majority of the important lawyers of the State were publicly recorded against the assumption.

A tour of the chief cities of the congressional districts was next planned and a hurry call issued to the local groups in each district to send their leaders forward for conference with State and national officers of the National American Woman Suffrage Association. There were public meetings, newspaper interviews, talks with political leaders, and a private conference with workers at each point. At the conferences the poll of all legislators from the District was carefully reviewed, and arrangements were made for deputations of constituents, or a succession of them, if needed, to wait on every member not already pledged to vote favorably on ratification in the special session.

To every conference, the question was put: "Are there any known bribable legislators from your district?" Sometimes the entire group ejaculated a name in unison, so well established was some legislator's ill repute in this connection. The same question was put to all political leaders in private talk, and was often met by a surprised look of suspicion, to be quickly covered by an expression of canny determination not to reveal any names. However, further discussion usually secured the names. All such names were checked by a secret mark on the poll list. Several names were checked as bribable by eight different persons, each thoroughly acquainted with practical politics and each having given his opinion without the knowledge of the others.

The women of Tennessee, alarmed by the unexpected development of hostility, and now understanding the false grounds for their belief in prompt action, laid aside their political differences and worked together in a manner worthy of imitation by the men of the State. The Southern summer heat was merciless, and many legislators lived in remote villages or on farms miles from any town. Yet the women trailed these legislators, by train, by motor, by wagons and on foot, often in great discomfort, and frequently at considerable expense to themselves. They went without meals, were drenched in unexpected rains, and met with "tire troubles," yet no woman faltered and there was not a legislator who had not been visited by his women constituents before the Legislature met. In many instances, members were visited by deputations of men, or by joint delegations of men and women. Each day the poll was corrected in Nashville as the reports of interviews were received by wire and by mail. Each day the prospects were carefully estimated. Although several men under suspicion as bribable had signed pledges to vote for ratification they were never included in the private estimate. It was intended to make the poll so safe that it would not be endangered if the bribable fell from it.

The problem of arriving at an exact count of the ayes and nays was embarrassed by the fact that ten vacancies existed and by the further fact that there was a question of the eligibility of certain other members to serve at the special session, since they had been appointed to public office after the regular session.

Meanwhile the need of added political influence was not forgotten. The Democrats having announced that the National Committee would meet in Columbus on July 19 in connection with the ceremonies of notifying [Ohio] Governor [James M.] Cox of his nomination for the presidency, the National Suffrage Association appointed a committee of Democratic women to be present, under the leadership of a director of the Association who was also a proxy member of the Committee. This committee presented a memorial from the Association and made three definite requests. (1) A resolution of endorsement; (2) an expression from Mr. Cox; (3) the appointment of a representative of the Democratic Committee to go to Tennessee and North Carolina to work for ratification.

Representatives of the National Suffrage Association further advised the Democratic National Committee that suffragists were surfeited with resolutions and that what the women of the country desired was that the Democratic Committee should use its full power to bring about ratification in States like Tennessee and North Carolina and not content itself with mere adoption of a resolution.

All that was asked was done. The Committee resolved its hopes for Tennessee ratification, two Tennesseans were privately appointed as national representatives of the party to work for ratification, and Candidate Cox gave a frank and urgent request for Tennessee's ratification. At his own request two private conferences with the National Suffrage Association's committee were held and he agreed that he would come to Tennessee on his campaign trip if needed to urge ratification. As an additional expression he wired the president of the National Suffrage Association:

> "I am gratified over the news that you are to remain in Nashville for the ratification campaign. It gives me added reason for expressing confidence that the Tennessee Legislature will act favorably, which will greatly please the Democratic party."

The Republicans unexpectedly called their National Committee to meet at Marion [Ohio, home of Republican candidate Warren Harding] on July 21 in connection with their notification ceremonies. The National Suffrage Association thereupon hastily appointed a committee of Republican women, and provided it with a memorial similar to that sent to the Democratic Committee and instructed it to make the same requests. The Committee passed the following resolution:

> "Resolved, That it is the sense of the Executive Committee of the Republican National Committee that the Republican members of the Tennessee legislature should be and hereby are most earnestly urged to vote unanimously for ratification of the woman suffrage amendment in the special session of the Tennessee Legislature which is to be called, and the chairman of the Republican National Committee is hereby authorized to communicate this resolution to each Republican member of said Legislature."

This was wired to each Republican member of the Tennessee Legislature and confirmed by letter. The National Suffrage Association's Committee then called upon Mr. Harding, who declared that he was ready to throw the full weight of his influence for ratification, and the news was sent broadcast by the many correspondents then in Marion. Mr. Harding also wired the president of the National Suffrage Association and gave the message to the press himself:

> "I am exceedingly glad to learn that you are in Tennessee seeking to consummate the ratification of the equal suffrage amendment. If any of the Republican members of the Tennessee Assembly should seek my opinion as to their course, I would cordially recommend an immediate favorable action."

The opposition had been at work for several weeks upon a plan to defeat ratification by a solid Republican adverse vote, on the ground that should Tennessee ratify, "the Democrats would get the credit." The rumor of this had been persistent and disconcerting. The action of the National Republican Committee at Marion and the endorsement of Presidential Candidate Harding checked that effort, but did not eliminate it from the list of possibilities. Representative Fess, chairman of the National Republican Congressional Committee, now urged each Republican member of the Legislature by telegram to join in a solid vote for ratification. Several State Committeemen and Harding clubs wired the Republican chairman of Tennessee, H. H. Clements of Knoxville, urging a solid vote for ratification. He publicly announced that he did so urge the Republican members of the Legislature and added, "I feel safe in pledging every Republican member of the Senate and the House for the immediate ratification of the Amendment." Later the National Republican Committee sent a member, Mrs. Harriet Taylor Upton, to Nashville to join Republican legislators in the counter-campaign to secure a solid party vote for ratification. The combination of these influences secured nearly all the Republican votes for ratification; without them ratification would have failed.

Although the public announcement had been made a month before that the special session would be called for August 9, the official call was not issued until August 7. The ratification resolution went before the Legislature with the strongest political support it had had in any State or at any time. The preparations were complete. When, on July 25, the poll had shown a certain majority, the announcement had been given to the public, while deputations continued to visit the doubtful members and meetings were still held. A. L. Todd, presiding officer of the Senate, and Seth Walker, Speaker of the House, had agreed to introduce the resolution to ratify. Most of the best known lawyers of the State, including the Attorney-General, had given opinions not only upon the constitutionality of ratification by the Tennessee Legislature but upon the specific question as to whether men would violate their oath of office if they should vote for ratification, so that the argument which three weeks before had threatened to send the resolution to defeat had been largely eliminated from the field.

The League of Women Voters, the Governor's Committee of Women, the Democratic Woman's Committee and the Republican Woman's Committee had all been at last united under the leadership of Miss Charl Williams, Vice-Chairman of the Democratic National Committee. With all these influences on the side of ratification and with a majority of the Legislature pledged in writing to vote for ratification *in the special session* the prospects to onlookers seemed uninterestingly obvious, and the effort to accumulate further evidence of demand for the Tennessee ratification appeared to them a senseless waste of energy. Yet experienced suffragists faced the coming events with anxiety, and each congressional chairman to whose workers the legislator's pledges had been made was urged to be present when the Legislature met.

On Saturday evening, August 7, the great foyer of the Hermitage Hotel was packed with men and women bedecked with suffrage yellow and anti-suffrage red and the "War of the Roses" was on. The "anti" women had made an eleventh hour attempt to show numbers and had brought women from all parts of the country, especially from Southern States. All the women who had become familiar figures in anti-suffrage contests were there, and many more. Mysterious men in great numbers were there, taking an active part in the controversy, while in and out through this crowded "third house" moved the bewildered legislators.

That very day the ominous possibilities of the "invisible government" were made manifest. Seth Walker, Speaker of the House, who had willingly joined the Men's Ratification Committee and not only pledged his vote verbally and in writing to several persons but had accepted the invitation to introduce the resolution, sought out the president of the League of Women Voters and announced a change of mind. By evening it had become clear that he would assume the floor leadership against the Amendment. Before midnight, suffragists had other worries. During the evening groups of legislators under escort of strange men had left the foyer and gone to a room on the eighth floor. As the evening grew late legislators, both suffrage and anti-suffrage men, were reeling through the hall in a state of advanced intoxication—a sight no suffragists had before witnessed in the sixty years of suffrage struggle.

Sunday passed and Monday, August 9, came. The Legislature met at noon. The Governor's message recommending ratification was delivered and both Houses adjourned for the day. With nothing to do, members again accepted the invitation to the eighth floor, where a group of anti-suffrage men dispensed old Bourbon and moonshine whisky with lavish insistence. Tennessee had been a Prohibition State before the Eighteenth Amendment had been submitted, and the State had also ratified that amendment. Why was not the law enforced, asked the women. "Now see here," was the answer, "in Tennessee whisky and legislation go hand in hand, especially when controversial questions are urged." Denial of this traditional license when a great issue was at stake would be resented as an interference with established custom by suffragists and anti-suffragists—"This is the Tennessee way." Suffragists were plunged into helpless despair. Hour by hour suffrage men and women who went to the different hotels of the city to talk with the legislators came back to the Hermitage headquarters to report. And every report told the same story—the Legislature was drunk! "How many legislators?" was the abashed query. No one knew. "Are none sober?" was next asked. "Possibly," was the answer.

In agony of soul, suffragists went to bed in the early morning, but not to sleep. The members of the Tennessee Legislature, however, largely slept themselves sober during the night and hope revived.

Presiding Officer [A. L.] Todd introduced the resolution in the Senate on the tenth, according to agreement, and the entire Shelby County delegation introduced it in the House. At the request of the antis the Senate and House Committees to which the resolution had been referred granted a hearing on the evening of the twelfth. Meantime the opponents tested their strength in the House by introducing a resolution referring the Amendment to county conventions in order "to hear from the people." Suffrage legislators promptly tabled it by a vote of 50 to 37. The suffrage men also tabled another resolution declaring ratification of any amendment in that session to be in violation of the spirit of the State constitution.

One of the largest crowds ever assembled in the Capitol attended the suffrage hearing. The suffragists entrusted their side to a group of brilliant and distinguished Tennessee lawyers. The evening furnished the suffrage side with two disagreeable surprises. Major [Edward B.] Stahlman, of the Nashville *Banner*, who had faithfully promised support to suffragists at the Kiwanis Club, spoke for the antis. Later it was learned that he had assumed direction of the opposition body. His sudden change of position was regarded as another ominous sign.

The other incident that startled the suffragists was this: A man arose and read a letter from Presidential Candidate Harding:

> "I beg to acknowledge your esteemed favor of August 4th. Your letter is the first bit of information I have had concerning the provision in your State constitution. I have heard something about a constitutional inhibition against your Legislature acting upon the Federal Amendment, but I did not know of the explicit provision to which your letter makes reference. I quite agree with you that members of the General Assembly cannot ignore the State constitution.
>
> "Without having seen the document myself I should be reluctant to undertake to construe it.

> "I have felt for some time that it would be very fortunate if we could dispose of the Suffrage Amendment, and I have done what I could in a consistent way to bring about the consummation of ratification. I have tried throughout it all to avoid trespassing on the rights of State officials.
>
> "It has not seemed to me a proper thing for a candidate on the federal ticket to assume an undue authority in directing State officials as to the performance of their constitutional duties.
>
> "I did say and I still believe it would be a fortunate thing for Republicans to play their full part in bringing about ratification. I should be very unfair to you and should very much misrepresent my own convictions *if I urged you to vote for ratification when you hold to a very conscientious belief that there is a constitutional inhibition which prevents your doing so until after an election has been held.* (Italics ours.)
>
> "I hope I make myself reasonably clear on this subject, I do not want you to have any doubt about my beliefs in the desirability of completing the ratification but I am just as earnest about expressing myself in favor of fidelity to conscience in the performance of a public service."

Candidates Harding and Cox had both been fully informed of the alleged technical obstruction in the Tennessee constitution and of the campaign among the lawyers of the State to offset it. In the flood of impressions circling around a presidential candidate, the explanation had apparently slipped away in Mr. Harding's case, and the effect of this letter upon the campaign was to hand a cudgel to the opponents. It opened a way for the Republicans to creep out of their pledged obligations with a pose of extra conscientiousness and for a return of the argument which had been largely eliminated by intensive effort. To watching suffragists that letter came like a bolt from a blue sky, and again there was no sleep.

The anxiety was stilled for a time by the prompt and generous action of the Tennessee Senate. The Senate Committee met immediately after the hearing on the twelfth and voted to report the Amendment favorably by a vote of 8 to 2. The two dissenters made ready to present a minority report. Although the debate in the Senate on the thirteenth had been awaited with anxiety, only two speeches were made in opposition. One of these was so vituperative and vulgar that it not only aroused the fighting qualities of the friends of suffrage but called forth denunciation from the entire Senate. Many were the letters of apology sent to suffrage headquarters from prominent men on behalf of the State for this attack upon individual suffragists. Senator [C. C.] Collins, who had been brought from a sickbed to cast his vote for ratification, stood tremblingly clinging to his desk, as with shaking voice he eloquently defended women against the attack.

Senator [William] Monroe, who was carried on the anti poll, created a sensation when he announced that he had been reminded of the Fourteenth and Fifteenth Amendments and requested in that connection by Northern women antis to vote against the Amendment. "But," said he, "I am going to vote for ratification in order to give back to the North what the North gave to Tennessee when it ratified the Fourteenth and Fifteenth Amendments." Others for various reasons announced changes of attitude. The minority report was promptly rejected and ratification passed August 13, 25 ayes and 4 nays. To the outside world, watching, this result was an expected and normal action. To the suffragists on guard in Tennessee, it meant a reversal of the usual policy—the opposition had centered on the House instead of the Senate.

The political fate of the women of the nation now rested in the hands of a minority of a single legislative chamber. From day to day the House ominously postponed the date of the vote. Though the postponement meant that the pledged majority was still standing fast, in vain did the suffrage members try to get the resolution on the calendar. Meanwhile the male anti-suffrage lobby, from early morning of each day to the wee small hours of the next, threatened and cajoled the embattled sixty-two who had signed pledges. They were baited with whisky, tempted with offers of office, loans of money, and every other device which old hands at illicit politics could conceive or remember. An alleged attempt to kidnap a suffrage member was made. Various schemes were started to get rid of enough suffrage legislators to allow the opposition a chance to act, a favorite proposal being that men might conveniently get messages calling them home.

Engaged in this nefarious intrigue was what old-timers recognized as the former "whisky lobby" in full force, the one-time railroad lobby which was alleged to have directed Tennessee politics for years, and a newer manufacturer's lobby. All pretense was thrown aside and all three worked openly as one man, although who paid the bills the public never knew. Every day men dropped from the poll. In some cases the actual consideration was noised about. One man who had written nine letters in which he had declared that he would be on hand "to vote for woman suffrage until I am called up yonder" had fallen early. Before the end all men checked as bribable on the poll, taken before the Legislature met, fell from it.

The American Constitutional League, Everett P. Wheeler, president (formerly the Men's Anti-Suffrage League), formed a branch in Nashville, and its members, mainly politicians, joined in the bombardment of legislators friendly to suffrage. The Maryland Legislature sent a memorial, which was read at the opening of the Tennessee Legislature, urging rejection of ratification, and representatives of the Maryland League for State Defense (formerly the Men's Anti-Suffrage League of Maryland) joined the lobby. Women antis pressed the sharp point of Negro woman suffrage into Southern traditions; the men antis bore hard on the alleged illegalities of ratification by the Tennessee Legislature; all of them quoting Mr. Harding's sympathy with the oath-violating theory. Men and women, as organized anti-suffragists, issued daily press bulletins assuming the responsibility for the campaign of opposition, while, as usual, other men, whose presence in Nashville was unannounced to the outside world, were applying the "third degree" in a hotel bedroom.

The House Committee met on the evening of the sixteenth and reported favorably on the seventeenth. The vote on the resolution having been set for that day, the debate was opened by T. K. Riddick of Memphis (Shelby County), a distinguished lawyer who had allowed himself to be elected to a vacancy for the sole purpose of aiding ratification. Said he:

> "I have in my pocket the pledges of sixty-two members of this House which the people of Tennessee will have the opportunity to read. If those men fail to keep faith I shall go from this chamber ashamed of being a Democrat, ashamed of being a Tennessean."

Seth Walker in what the mountaineers called "a bearcat of a speech," saying that it had been charged that his change of attitude was due to a certain railroad which he named; this he resented, but he conspicuously failed to give an explanation of his strange *volte face* which was amazing the entire nation. The antis brought the debate to a close by a motion to adjourn, passed by a vote of 52 to 44. The previous tests had indicated that suffragists were in control of the House, but this one gave evidence that the position had been reversed. Suffrage anxiety had been intense.

That night the suffrage leaders with heavy hearts confessed their despair to each other. "There is one thing more we can do," said the president of the National Suffrage Association, "only one, we can pray."

In the interim representatives from a group of newspapers called upon the Governor and threatened to defeat him at the election if he did not "pull off his men." He stood firm. On the eighteenth the House was again packed and hundreds of would-be onlookers were turned away. The debate continued. "What is a greater crime than for interests, from New York to San Francisco, to send lobbyists here to break your pledges, or for certain newspapers connected with railroads to threaten you as they have been doing for the last ten days," demanded Joe Hanover, floor suffrage leader. L. D. Miller of Chattanooga closed with a ringing speech in which he said:

> "When the special interests made an attack on this Legislature in January they had a gang of lobbyists to put over their infamous bills. I recognize in the lobbies these same special interest servers. You have an opportunity on this occasion to rid this State of an incubus that has had its claws in this Legislature for fifty years. Let us show by our votes that the special interests are done in Tennessee."

The moment had become intensely dramatic; every onlooker knew that the fate of the question might depend upon a single vote. Of the ninety-nine elected members of the House, ninety-six were present. One had resigned and his place was vacant. The other two, both suffragists, were kept at home by serious family illness. Dr. J. Frank Griffin had hastened home from California to cast a suffrage vote. R. L. Dowlen, who had just undergone a serious operation, was brought from his bed to the capitol to vote for the resolution. Seth Walker, in a last effort to rally the weakening lines of the anti-ratificationists, at the end of the debate shouted in melodramatic manner, "The hour has come. The battle has been fought and won"—and moved to table the resolution. But the vote on tabling stood 48 to 48! The room rang with the cheers of the galleries. One more vote had been won for suffrage. The roll call showed that Banks Turner who was carried on the anti poll had dropped into the suffrage column. Unwilling to believe the roll-call, Mr. Walker demanded a second and it was taken. He left his Speaker's seat and, with arms thrown around Banks Turner, whispered insistent entreaties in his ears as the names were again called. Shivers ran down suffrage backs as Mr. Turner passed his call without response. Heads stretched forward and every eye centered on the legislator and the Speaker, while a breathless silence pervaded the room. The fans ceased to wave. Even the overpowering heat was forgotten. At the end of the roll-call Mr. Turner threw off the Speaker's arm, drew himself up proudly and shouted a defiant no. Cheers and shouts burst forth again and the galleries would accept no discipline from the chair. The vote still stood 48 to 48 against tabling.

A motion to ratify the Amendment was then made and the vote was taken in a tension that was well-nigh unbearable; 49 ayes, 47 nays. The House broke into an uproar, and the cheers of triumph that rang through the old legislative chamber were heard far down the street.

The second additional vote that had been won for suffrage was that of Harry Burn, a twenty-four-year-old Republican, who forthwith became a hero for suffragists and a traitor to their opponents. He had been placed on the suffrage poll as conditioned, for he had promised to vote on the resolution only if his vote should be necessary for ratification, otherwise he was going to vote against it, as he believed his constituents were opposed. From the vote on the motion to table he saw that his vote *was* necessary and so changed his attitude on the ratification motion.

Although 49 was a majority of 96, the number of members present and sufficient for legal ratification, Tennessee was accustomed to consider 50 the majority of 99, the total elected membership, as a "constitutional majority." Seth Walker, in order to move a reconsideration, changed his vote from no to aye, which made the final record 50 ayes to 46 nays, thus giving the constitutional majority.

Thus, by a freak of politics, the last vote needed by the Tennessee standard to enfranchise the women of a great nation was cast by a man who was clearly staking heavily to defeat it.

According to the printed rules of the House in Tennessee, a motion to reconsider any ordinary measure may be made by any person voting on the majority side, and that person controls the right to bring the motion up at any time within three days; no other person may bring it up. On each one of these three days the House met with full quorum present, but the Speaker did not bring up his motion to reconsider. The two suffrage absentees had returned and there were suffrage votes to spare. During that three days' period the opposition worked desperately. One suffrage member was called every half hour through two nights, each time with a different appeal to change his vote. Another was urged every half hour all night to come downtown to see an important man. A man who was laboring day and night in the midst of the anti forces to break the suffrage majority finally implored his daughter-in-law to renounce publicly the suffrage side and come out in opposition. With tears in his eye he entreated: "It will mean a great deal to you and your daughter in the future if this amendment is defeated."

Whereupon the spirited seventeen-year-old daughter, present at the interview, spoke for her mother: "Mother and I would rather live in poverty all the rest of our lives than get money by treachery to our sex. We will not desert the suffragists and we are not proud of the work you are doing." A man who was carried on the suffrage poll was reported by the suffrage men as wavering, and was boldly claimed by the opposition. A confession was secured by U. S. Senator McKellar that he had been offered a position under the Excise Commissioner for his vote. A telegram to the President of the United States brought prompt rebuke to the Commissioner, who left town at once. And the man ceased to waver. Young Harry Burn was the chief object of persecution. He was threatened with exposure of an alleged bribe if he did not remain out of the Legislature until the vote on reconsideration was over. Men declared they had affidavits to prove that he had been bribed by suffrage floor leader Hanover and the Governor's secretary between the vote on tabling and the vote on ratification. The presentation of affidavits disproved the charge. The efforts at intimidation led Mr. Burn to make a statement to the House:

> "I desire to resent in the name of honesty and justice the veiled intimation and accusation regarding my vote on the Suffrage Amendment as indicated in certain statements, and it is my sincere belief that those responsible for their existence know that there is not a scintilla of truth in them. I want to state that I changed my vote in favor of ratification first because I believe in full suffrage as a right; second, I believe we had a moral and legal right to ratify; third, I knew that a mother's advice is always safest for a boy to follow and my mother wanted me to vote for ratification; fourth, I appreciated the fact that an opportunity such as seldom comes to a mortal man to free seventeen million women from political slavery was mine; fifth; I desired that my party in both State and nation might say that it was a republican from the East mountains of Tennessee, the purest Anglo-Saxon section in the world, who made national woman suffrage possible at this date, not for personal glory but for the glory of his party."

A few hours later the president of the League of Women Voters received a telegram from Mrs. J. L. Burn, the young man's mother. The telegram read:

> "Woman was here to-day, claims to be wife of Governor of Louisiana, and secured an interview with me and tried by every means to get me to refute and say that the letter I sent to my son was false. The letter is authentic and was written by me and you can refute any statement that any party claims to have received from me. Any statement claiming to be from me is false. I stand squarely behind suffrage and request my son to stick to suffrage until the end. This woman was very insulting to me in my home, and I had a hard time to get her out of my home."

[The woman was probably Anne Pleasant, wife of Governor Ruffin G. Pleasant of Louisiana, who was in Tennessee working against ratification. The Pleasants favored woman suffrage, but by state action only, and Pleasant had tried to get the governors of thirteen southern states to form an alliance to prevent ratification. According to an antisuffrage press release, Anne Pleasant was "the daughter of Major General Ector, C.S.A., who had three horses shot from under him at the battle of Lookout Mountain."[11]]

An amusing indication of the state of suffrage nerves occurred when during this three-day period Harry Burn was reported as having left Nashville. His hotel said he had gone and the clerks did not know where. There was consternation again among the suffrage forces. Had he deserted after all? Had he been kidnapped? An hour later his name appeared upon the register of another hotel to which he had moved.

Men were found listening at the transoms of suffrage doors, a telegram between the receiving and operating telephone desk was stolen and given to the press. Men, who nobody seemed to know or what they represented, mysteriously appeared and joined the opposition forces. All day and all night suffrage lines were guarded. Suffrage women picketed the hotel floors where suspicious incidents had taken place and suffrage men polled the suffrage members every two hours during the day and watched over them at night.

On the 18th the opposition held a mass meeting where two things of note occurred. In a speech, Seth Walker confidently announced that three men had deserted the suffrage side and that in consequence the defeat of the Amendment was certain. The other incident was a letter from Presidential Candidate Cox surprisingly similar to that of Mr. Harding and dated on the same day. More doubt and confusion. Again the public did not know whether to believe that the two candidates were playing politics or were sincere in their desire to see the Amendment ratified, and the opposition made the most of the situation. Again the oath loyalty argument was revived and made to work. Could it be true that three men had deserted, suffragists asked. Faithful suffrage men did not sleep until they had sounded every pledged man, and when they found the sterling 49 still standing firm they recorded Seth Walker's claim as a political "bluff."

The vote on reconsideration was expected hourly on Friday, and the galleries were again packed. A manufacturer had given a holiday to his women employees and sent them red-rose bedecked to help fill the galleries and swell the anti numbers. It was clear that every vote might be needed. T. A. Dodson had received a message that his baby was dying and had just taken his train when it was discovered that his vote might prove crucial. A suffragist drove her motor on a flying trip to the station, taking two suffrage men with her. They reached the train just as it was moving out and the men promised the legislator a special train which would get him home as soon as the regular one if he would come back. He returned, remaining while needed, was given the special train, paid for by Newell Sanders, a Republican and ex-State Senator, and reached home to find the baby happily recovering. The hours passed, the suffrage voters were all there, but Mr. Walker, perceiving the futility of so doing, did not bring up his motion to reconsider. At the end of the session the suffrage majority carried a motion to meet on Saturday morning, the 21st. According to the custom, but not the printed rules of the

House, it was possible after the three days for any member to call up a motion to reconsider, and the suffrage members intended to bring it up on Saturday morning and vote it down.

The city of Nashville looked forward to another exciting session, but before Saturday's breakfast the news was all about town that 38 anti-ratification House members had ignominiously fled in the dead of night. They had gone in small groups to a station near Nashville where they boarded an L and N train which carried them across the border into Alabama. This move of last resort was intended to prevent any further action by destroying a quorum and to give time to anti-suffrage workers to break down a suffrage member.

The House met on Saturday morning with 50 suffrage men and 9 antis present and with women occupying the seats of the absentees. The anti-suffrage chaplain added a bit of irony to the situation when he prayed that "God's richest blessings be granted our absent ones." The suffrage garrison prepared to enjoy itself and harassed Speaker Walker by overturning every ruling and voting down every decision of the chair. Speaker Walker announced that an injunction against forwarding the certificate of ratification to Washington had been issued that morning by Judge [E. F.] Langford of the Supreme Court [actually, the Chancery Court at Nashville] and that the injunction had been served upon the Governor, the Secretary of State [Ike B. Stevens] and the Speaker of both Houses.[12] The ratificationists went on with the legislative program. The pending motion to reconsider was called up and voted down. The ratified Amendment was ordered returned to the Senate and it was returned. It was common knowledge that the Governor could not be enjoined by the laws of the State and lawyers now begged him to ignore the injunction and forward the certificate, but the Governor was noncommittal while neither the Attorney-General nor any of his assistants could be located! The Attorney-General's office mysteriously professed no knowledge of their whereabouts. After a two days' absence, however, Attorney-General Thompson emerged from his hiding place, brief in hand, supporting a plea which was heard by Judge [D. L.] Landsden, Chief Justice of the Supreme Court, on August 23. The plea was for a *writ of certiorari et supersedeas* and it was issued, thus dissolving the injunction of the lower court, and clearing the way for the Tennessee certificate to be sent to Washington.

During this time the Attorney-General issued two opinions which were seconded through the press by many other equally prominent lawyers throughout the State.

1. When a Legislature has taken favorable action on a federal amendment, it has exhausted its power to act and no motion to reconsider is applicable even for the limit of three days.

2. Had a motion to reconsider been applicable in the case of a federal suffrage amendment, that power was exhausted according to the printed rules of the House when the three days had passed; for no contrary custom of the House could be held to have legal value.

On Tuesday, August 24, at 10:17 A.M., Governor Roberts, in the presence of interested suffragists, signed the certificate and sent it by registered mail to the Secretary of State. It was delivered at 4 A.M. on the 26th, and was at once referred for examination to the Solicitor who had been sitting up all night in order to be on hand when it should arrive. An open threat to secure an injunction to prevent the issuance of the Proclamation certifying to the ratification of the Amendment had been continually made by the opposition. In July Justice Bailey of the District of Columbia Supreme Court had declined to issue such an injunction upon action brought by Charles S. Fairchild and the American Constitutional League. On August 25 Justice Seddons of the same court had refused the same application. The Secretary of State, Bainbridge Colby, however, took no chances and arose early on the morning of the 26th. At eight o'clock, without ceremony, he signed the Proclamation.

The group of workers of the National Suffrage Association, returning from Tennessee, arrived in Washington the morning the Proclamation was signed and found a great victory celebration awaiting them. In the evening, to a packed theatre audience, they told the story of the Tennessee campaign. The Secretary of State was there to represent the Administration, and on behalf of the nation congratulated the suffragists upon their freedom.

On August 27 the Tennessee suffrage group returned to New York city, the home of the national suffrage headquarters. The Governor of the State and representatives of the Republican and Democratic National Committees were at the station to welcome them and so were the "old guard" suffragists. With the 71st Regiment Band at the head and with the old familiar banners waving, they marched together for the last time to the Waldorf Astoria, where all made speeches of self-congratulation. Mrs. Harriet Taylor Upton, National Chairman of the Republican women, told how the Republicans carried Tennessee, and Miss Charl Williams, National Chairman of the Democratic women, told how the Democrats did it. Others told how resourceful and fearless the Tennessee women had been, how heroic were the faithful 49 in the midst of the whirlwind of opposition and how the victory was everybody's victory who had labored in the cause.

A hurry call had been sent to all the mayors of Tennessee, urging them to join the women's celebration by ordering the ringing of bells and blowing of whistles. And the whistles did blow and the bells did ring merrily and sincerely in most Tennessee towns, for the people in the main stood by the ratifying Legislature. From ocean to ocean, from "Canada to the Gulf," the celebrations continued. Meetings, processions, flag raisings, transformations from suffrage associations to Leagues of Women Voters were the order of the day for the month that followed. None was more significant than the draped flag over the tablet that marked the site of the chapel where the world's first woman's convention had been held in 1848, in Seneca Falls, New York; none more significant than the wreaths of flowers hung on the old building where the world's first woman's jury had sat in 1870 in Cheyenne, Wyoming.

Here the story of woman suffrage in the United States should appropriately end, but there was more to come—and come in Tennessee—before the long suffrage campaign was permitted to pass into history as a closed issue.

The Tennessee Legislature recessed from day to day, as there was no quorum. The call had included 132 bills as needing attention by the Legislature. The majority of the anti-ratificationists stubbornly remained in Alabama or at their homes and awaited the call of their masters. The ratification members, unwilling to remain in Nashville without a quorum, had gone home also. Anti-ratification mass meetings were still in progress and the speakers were defiantly threatening to undo ratification in the Courts. Meanwhile the Governor and the Sergeant-at-Arms were striving to get a quorum of the Legislature. It was publicly announced that on August 30 the "red rose brigade" would return. Four hours were spent on that day in an effort to secure the quorum of 66 members, but at no time could more than 63 be found. The filibusters had returned with "a great show of being ready for business." The full suffrage majority was not in Nashville and the ratificationists who were there feared to help compose the quorum lest some unfriendly act be passed. Ratification legislators, arrested and brought into the House, escaped by other doors while the 46 anti-ratificationists held their seats.

Finally it was announced that the ratificationists would all be in their seats on the 31st, whereupon the antis failed to appear, lest they could not muster a sufficient vote to overthrow the suffrage action of August 21. The scene had lost its attraction for both suffragists and anti-suffragists, who now deserted the balconies. Without the yellow and the red, the place looked lonesome. Even Mr. Walker absented himself on this date.

On September 11, however, the anti-ratificationists won the game of hide-and-seek and got control of the House, many suffrage men being absent. Amid shouts of glee, by a vote of 47 to 37, they passed a motion to expunge from the record all that had taken place on the 21st except the record that there had been no quorum. Mr. [T. K.] Riddick, on behalf of the ratificationists, contested every step with points of order. The entire controversy raged around the question of a quorum. By the rules of the Legislature two-thirds, 66, of the elected number constituted a quorum in the House. There was a quorum when the House ratified. There was a majority but not a quorum by Tennessee rules when the House voted down the motion to reconsider and returned the ratified Amendment to the Senate. Mr. Riddick contended that the authority for procedure was drawn from the federal constitution and that no rules of the House could supersede. He claimed that the authority for a quorum composed of a majority was drawn from parliamentary usage. In these views he was sustained by the Attorney-General whose opinion he quoted. The anti members refused to accept this interpretation. A resolution to reject the Suffrage Amendment as a substitute for the one to ratify, which the antis held to be pending on reconsideration, was voted on, 47 to 24, with 20 not voting. This rejection resolution was sent to the Senate with instructions that it be forwarded to the Governor. The suffrage House members now enjoined the Chief Clerk of the Senate from receiving it. On September 12, the Senate was in a turmoil of indignation as it discussed the resolution received from the House and resented "attempts to control its business." By a vote of 17 to 8 it refused to accept the resolution and returned that message, whereupon House members volubly informed Senators that if their resolution was not received there would be no passage by the House of the *per diem* for Senators nor other Senate legislation. The threats proved persuasive and on September 13, the Senate, having turned a somersault overnight, accepted the resolution by a vote of 21 to 4. Then the Senate forwarded the resolution of rejection to the Governor, who in turn sent it to the Secretary of State.

With the suffrage question thus disposed of to the satisfaction of each contending faction, the Legislature settled down to business, and remained in session until September 16, when it adjourned after passing—over the Governor's veto—the Appropriation Bill which gave to each member $100 extra for expenses incurred in remaining longer than the twenty days of the special session allowed by the constitution. Although the laws of the State of Tennessee declare desertion of a legislative post to be a felony, this law was not enforced and the fleeing opposition members of the House drew their *per diem* and extra allowances without protest!

On September 12 Speaker Walker and a group of anti men appeared in Washington to entreat the Secretary to withdraw the Proclamation. Failing in their mission, they went on to Connecticut with the avowed purpose of persuading the political group which had so stubbornly resisted all efforts to secure a special session in that State to continue that policy in order that the legality of the ratification of the Amendment might rest upon the case of Tennessee. They returned to Washington and again sought an interview with the Secretary of State in order to renew their appeal. Interviews in the press widely announced that they had not surrendered and would contest the ratification of Tennessee in the Courts.

The American Constitutional League (formerly the Men's Anti Woman Suffrage League) and the Maryland League for State Defense (formerly the Maryland Men's Anti-Suffrage Association) were still declaring through numerous press communications that ratification would be proved invalid. The women antis still continued their publicity service, announcing with frequency that litigation would be started not only to invalidate the Amendment but the entire presidential election.

None of the threatened litigation alarmed the nation, but it doubtless served to convince the political leaders that another State was desirable to make assurance doubly sure.

Governor Holcomb of Connecticut, although still unyielding, now called a special session to provide for registering women. When calling it he warned the legislators that they must confine themselves to the business contained in the call—and omitted the Suffrage Amendment from the list. No such restriction had been put on a Connecticut Legislature and the Governor himself had said, two years before, that he had no power to prevent the transaction of any business when once the Legislature had been called in special session. The members, a majority of whom had long been pledged to ratification, determined to show independence and to ratify.

As soon as the special session opened, Governor Holcomb appeared and asked that it adjourn without action, as it was his intention to issue another call to meet a week later to ratify the Amendment and to enact other necessary legislation. Both Houses refused, and by unanimous vote in the Senate and with only eleven voting in opposition in the House, ratified the Federal Suffrage Amendment, even though the Governor had failed to transmit the certified copy. In further defiance of the Governor they passed several bills, none of which was included in the call. They then adjourned until September 21.

When the Legislature again met, the Governor appeared and asked the members to ratify the Amendment. Many refused, as it seemed an acknowledgment that their former action was invalid, but reason conquered tempers and, as the Connecticut auxiliary to the National Suffrage Association strongly recommended a second action to make legality absolutely certain, the Amendment was again ratified. The same day, to placate the members who wished the first record to stand, a motion was made to reconsider and confirm the action of the first session. Thus terminated a continuous struggle of fifteen months to secure ratification from a Legislature which all that time had been ready to act favorably, and which finally ratified the Amendment not once but three times. The ratification of Connecticut stilled any restless questioning of the validity of Tennessee and forever established the Amendment as a part of the federal constitution.

Governor Clement of Vermont retired from office December 31, 1920, and was succeeded by Governor James Hartness. The Vermont Legislature met in regular session in January, 1921. The resolution to ratify the Federal Suffrage Amendment was read in the House for the third time on January 28 and passed, ayes 202 and nays 3. On February 8 it was passed unanimously by the Senate.

The threats of the Tennessee antis had died of inattention and the threatened invalidation of the Amendment had by now narrowed down to two cases. One—the Leser vs. Garnett case, claiming that thirty-six states had not legally ratified the Amendment, the ratifications of West Virginia, Missouri and Tennessee being cited as invalid—brought a decision from the Maryland Court of Common Pleas that thirty-six had duly ratified. The case was carried to the Court of Appeals (Maryland) where on June 28, 1921, the Judges affirmed the decision of the lower Court that these ratifications were valid. It was then appealed to the United States Supreme Court, where a decision sustaining the two prior opinions was handed down. The other, a similar contention, known as the Fairchild case, which had been pending in different form since July, 1920, was also dismissed by the Supreme Court of the United States. Thus all efforts to declare the Amendment invalid came to an end.

The final announcement of these decisions appeared in small paragraphs in obscure corners of the newspapers. Hardly anyone noted them. Woman suffrage was already everywhere recognized as an established fact.

Notes

"Tennessee," is chapter 30 of Carrie Chapman Catt and Nettie Rogers Shuler, *Woman Suffrage and Politics: The Inner Story of the Suffrage Movement* (Charles Scribner's Sons, 1923, 1926; reprint, Seattle: University of Washington Press, 1970), 422–61. Published here with permission of the University of Washington Press.

1. This biographical sketch is drawn from Eleanor Flexner, "Carrie Clinton Lane Chapman Catt," in *Notable American Women: A Biographical Dictionary,* ed. Edward T. James, Janet Wilson James, and Paul S. Boyer (Cambridge, Mass.: Harvard University Press, 1971), 1: 309–13.

2. Ibid.

3. Marjorie Spruill Wheeler, *New Women of the New South: The Leaders of the Woman Suffrage Movement in the Southern States* (New York: Oxford University Press, 1993), 48, 64, 116–19, 159–71.

4. Flexner, "Carrie Clinton Lane Chapman Catt," in *Notable American Women,* 1: 310–12.

5. See Flexner, "Nettie Rogers Shuler," in *Notable American Women,* 3: 287.

6. Catt and Shuler, *Woman Suffrage and Politics,* 399.

7. Ibid., chap. 29, "The Supreme Court Speaks," 414–21.

8. See Anastatia Sims, "'Powers That Pray and Powers That Prey': Tennessee and the Fight for Woman Suffrage," *Tennessee Historical Quarterly* (Winter 1991): 203–25, 207.

9. Catt and Shuler, *Woman Suffrage and Politics,* 381–86.

10. Abby Crawford Milton, president of the Tennessee League of Women Voters, had appointed Catherine Kenny as chair. Milton's husband, editor of the *Chattanooga News,* had endorsed Roberts's opponent in the Democratic primary, and Kenny was a friend of Luke Lea, publisher of the anti-Roberts *Nashville Tennessean.* Sims, "Powers That Pray," 211.

11. See Wheeler, *New Women of the New South,* 24, 33, 35, 47, 166, 168, 175; and Carol Lynn Yellin, "Countdown in Tennessee," *American Heritage* 30 (Dec. 1978): 27.

12. See A. Elizabeth Taylor, *The Woman Suffrage Movement in Tennessee* (New York: Bookman Associates, 1957), 121.

13

Women Owe Debt to Pioneers of 1848, Says Sue White

Sue Shelton White

From an Unidentified Newspaper Clipping, 1923

Life did not end in 1920 for the individuals involved in the suffrage battle; and as John J. Vertrees predicted and feared, the movement for women's rights did not end with the successful conclusion of the suffrage struggle. As Mary Johnston announced in her speech to the House of Governors, "the Woman Movement is here to stay and to grow."[1]

Sue Shelton White, only thirty-three in 1920, went to Washington as secretary to Senator Kenneth McKellar. She began to work toward a dream she had long deferred—becoming a lawyer. Attending classes at night, White earned her law degree from Washington College of Law in 1923. Still active in the National Woman's Party, she put her law degree to work immediately, studying discriminatory provisions in state legal codes and helping to design a "blanket bill" that would sweep away discrimination against women. The bill was unveiled to the public at Seneca Falls, New York, in ceremonies commemorating the beginning of the women's rights movement there seventy-five years earlier. This bill was, of course, the original version of the Equal Rights Amendment, which, at the instigation of the Woman's Party, was first introduced in Congress in 1923; they called it the "Lucretia Mott Amendment."

White returned to Tennessee in 1926 and briefly practiced law in Jackson before beginning a new stage of her career as a Democratic organizer. Though the stigma of association with the Woman's Party had earlier kept her out of the higher echelons of the state's Democratic Party, she broke with the NWP over its endorsement of Herbert Hoover in 1928. Working hard for Democratic nominee Al Smith, she was soon "discovered" again, this time by Molly Dewson, the famous Democratic Party leader. Before long, White was working with former governor of Wyoming Nellie Tayloe Ross, organizing Democratic women all over the country; when Ross went to Washington as vice-chairman of the Democratic National Committee, she took White with her as her executive assistant. Soon thereafter White was appointed Executive Secretary of the Women's Division of the Democratic Party. She later held several posts in the Roosevelt administration, including being a member of the legal staff of the Social Security Board.[2]

In this speech given in 1923 in "The Garden of the Gods," Colorado, Sue White celebrates the accomplishments of the women who began the women's rights movement seventy-five years earlier. Today we celebrate the accomplishments of Sue White and others, who won for women the right to vote seventy-five years ago. Her message to her audience is still relevant: that the battle for women's rights is not over until "not one of these little girls . . . will meet that curious, complex frustration of effort that other women have met in the attempt to be merely themselves."

Miss Sue White, militant suffragist from Tennessee, member of the national council of the National Woman's Party, was the principal speaker at yesterday's Equal Rights pageant in the Garden of the Gods. Her address, tho [*sic*] brief, was one of the chief factors in the success of the pageant, summarizing as it did, clearly and forcefully, the achievements and ambitions of the party.

Miss White's address reads:

Truth speaks with the same authority as generations come and go. Seventy-five years ago, women of a day that is gone arose to salute the truth calling from within their souls. Another generation has followed and another still, proud to affirm the right proclaimed by those who pioneered. Here we see today, not merely the women of yesterday. We see a brave allegiance to an ideal as young and fresh as it has ever been. It never can grow old. It has the vitality of life itself. It speaks the authority of truth.

Here in the fresh free air, in the lea of the mountain side, the sky above, the green earth beneath and mighty rocks for a background, abides the spirit of freedom. An elemental idea in an elemental setting. This is our temple and we come with reverence, remembering the deeds of those who had the vision and followed it. No one living today, man or woman, but has been benefitted by the pioneer women whom we honor here. Each of us here today owes the women of 1848 deep gratitude for bringing their cause to the great new, fearless west, where pioneer met pioneer, together in faith and courage.

As in the days following 1848, the west proved the most fertile field for the enfranchisement of women, so will it lead the way in carrying out the full program of equal rights, inaugurated at that time. In July of this year, at Seneca Falls, the National Woman's party voted to introduce into congress the Lucretia Mott amendment, demanding that men and women shall have equal rights in the United States and every place subject to its jurisdiction. In many states, laws are such that the husband owns his wife's earnings, controls her property, fixes her legal residence, has the superior rights to the care and custody of the child, and in various ways exercises dominion over her. Young women find themselves barred from educational institutions supported by public funds, and girls attempting to enter the professions find obstacles that their brothers do not find. Such a condition can not, must not, continue. It is inevitable that women shall take not only their lives into their own hands but that they shall share equally the responsibility of the lives that they ordain as the mothers of the race.

We have paused to trace the path of the early beginning, to test and to know the ground on which we stand, and now we face the climb ahead. If the Woman's party program is carried out—and it will be carried out—not one of these girls of all these little ones will meet that curious, complex frustration of effort that other women have met in the attempt to be merely themselves.

We have commemorated the first equal rights meeting held 75 years ago. We can not be content to memorialize and leave the work then begun unfinished. No higher honor can be paid a prophet than to make the vision come true. In this every one here can help by giving support to the campaign of the National Woman's party. How much do we value that which has been accomplished for women in the past 75 years? How precious to your little daughter is the heritage that is hers? How much do you desire that the yoke shall be entirely lifted? Women must be freed of their subjection whatever the cost. What you can give here today will measure the length of the next step to be taken and register your individual response to the appeal of women for unhampered lives.

Notes

Speech by Sue Shelton White, 1923. Clipping, n.d., from the Sue Shelton White Papers, Schlesinger Library, Radcliffe.

1. John J. Vertrees, "An Address to the Men of Tennessee on Female Suffrage," document 9 above; and "Mary Johnston to the House of Governors," document 3 above.

2. See Marjorie Spruill Wheeler, *New Women of the New South: The Leaders of the Woman Suffrage Movement in the Southern States* (New York: Oxford University Press, 1993), 61, 84–85, 195–97; see also James P. Louis, "Sue Shelton White," in *Notable American Women*, ed. Edward T. James, Janet Wilson James, and Paul S. Boyer (Cambridge, Mass.: Harvard University Press, 1971), 3: 590–92; Nancy F. Cott, *The Grounding of Modern Feminism* (New Haven: Yale University Press, 1987), 66–68.

PART 3

Broadsides and Cartoons

The Case for Woman Suffrage: Prosuffrage Broadsides and Cartoons

JUSTICE EQUALITY

Why Women Want to Vote

WOMEN ARE CITIZENS

AND WISH TO DO THEIR CIVIC DUTY

WORKING WOMEN need the ballot to regulate conditions under which they work.
Do working MEN think they can protect themselves without the right to vote?

HOUSEKEEPERS need the ballot to regulate the sanitary conditions under which they and their families must live.
Do MEN think they can get what is needed for their district unless they can vote for the men that will get it for them?

MOTHERS need the ballot to regulate the moral conditions under which their children must be brought up.
Do MEN think they can fight against vicious conditions that are threatening their children unless they can vote for the men that run the district?

TEACHERS need the ballot to secure just wages and to influence the management of the public schools.

BUSINESS WOMEN need the ballot to secure for themselves a fair opportunity in their business.
Do business MEN think they could protect themselves against adverse legislation without the right to vote?

TAX PAYING WOMEN need the ballot to protect their property.
Do not MEN know that "Taxation without representation" is tyranny?

ALL WOMEN need the ballot because they are concerned equally with men in good and bad government; and equally responsible for civic righteousness.

ALL MEN need women's help to build a better and juster government, and
WOMEN need **MEN** to help them secure their right to fulfill their civic duties.

EQUAL SUFFRAGE ASSOCIATION OF NORTH CAROLINA

RALEIGH

In this broadside, North Carolina suffragists affirm their right to vote in the name of *justice* and *equality*. They insist that women, whether in the work force or in the home, need the vote to protect their interests but also want to do their duty as citizens and aid in building a more just and effective government. North Carolina Collection, University of North Carolina at Chapel Hill Library.

THE SUFFRAGIST

I BELIEVE that it is my **inherent right** to express my opinion directly and effectively through the ballot.

I BELIEVE that it is not only my right but **my duty** to use my influence for the **betterment** of the world **in which I live** and that my influence depends on my personalty and the opportunity to express my character—an opportunity that the **ballot** will give me.

I BELIEVE that suffrage is the **quietest, easiest,** most **dignified** and **least conspicuous** way of exerting my influence in public affairs.

I BELIEVE it is **right and fair** that those who must obey the laws should have a voice in making them and that those who must pay taxes should have a vote as to the size of the tax and the way in which it should be spent.

I BELIEVE that it is just that those who are **governed** should have a voice in the **government** and I accept the doctrine that the government must derive its just power from the **consent** of the governed.

I BELIEVE that extending suffrage to women **increases** the proportion of **educated** and **native born voters** and that it increases the moral and law abiding vote very much while increasing the vicious and criminal vote very little—women form a **minority** of all **criminal classes** and a **majority** of all classes working for **human advancement.**

I BELIEVE that the **eight million women wage earners** of the United States should be allowed a voice in making the laws that so vitally affect their welfare.

I BELIEVE that **women of leisure** who are giving of their time, their talents and their money to serve the public welfare should be able to support their advice and their work by casting their ballots.

I BELIEVE that **busy housewives** and **professional women** are entitled to give public service in the same way in which busy men give it—by casting their votes.

....191....

I BELIEVE IN EQUAL SUFFRAGE FOR MEN AND WOMEN AND I HEREBY ENROLL MYSELF AS A MEMBER OF THE EQUAL SUFFRAGE LEAGUE.

....

....

....

HEADQUARTERS EQUAL SUFFRAGE LEAGUE OF VIRGINIA, RICHMOND, VA.
Commercial Building, Second Street between Broad and Grace.

Here Virginia suffragists state their beliefs while subtly answering many of the objections of the antisuffragists. They insist that voting is their "inherent right" and civic "duty," that woman suffrage would improve the electorate, and that woman suffrage would be the "quietest, easiest, most dignified and least conspicuous" way of exercising influence. Equal Suffrage League Collection, Organizational Records, Archives and Records Division, Virgina State Library and Archives, Richmond, Virginia.

Women in the Home

The place of the Woman is in the Home. But merely to stay in the Home is not enough. She must care for the health and welfare, moral as well as physical, of her family.

SHE is responsible for the cleanliness of the house.
SHE is responsible for the wholesomeness of the food.
SHE is responsible for the children's health.
SHE is responsible above all for their morals.
How far can the mother control these things?

She can clean her own rooms and care for her own plumbing and refuse, BUT if the building is unsanitary, the streets filthy, and the garbage allowed to accumulate, she cannot protect her children from the sickness that will result.

She can cook her food well, BUT if dealers are permitted to sell adulterated food, unclean milk, or short weight or measure, she cannot provide either wholesome or sufficient feeding for her family.

She can open her windows to give her children air, BUT if the air is laden with infection, she cannot protect her children from disease.

She can send her children out for exercise, BUT if the conditions on the streets are immoral and degrading, she cannot shield them from these dangers.

It is the government of the town or city that controls these things and the officials are controlled by the men who elect them.

Women do not elect these officials, yet we hold the women responsible for the results of—

Unclean Houses, Defective Sewerage, Unwholesome Food, Fire Risks, Danger of Infection, Immoral Influence on the Streets. If women are responsible for the results, let them have something to say as to what the conditions shall be. There is one simple way to do this. **GIVE THEM THE VOTE.**

Women are by nature and training housekeepers. Let them help in the city housekeeping. They will introduce an occasional spring cleaning.

VOTES FOR WOMEN

Equal Suffrage Association of North Carolina

RALEIGH.

This brochure, probably designed by the NAWSA, was reprinted and distributed by state suffrage associations in several southern states. It conveys one of the major arguments of the suffragists all over the nation: that woman suffrage, rather than taking woman away from the home, would enable her to better fulfill her traditional responsibilities. North Carolina Collection, University of North Carolina at Chapel Hill Library.

"Better Days Coming," June 20, 1914. This cartoon elicits sympathy for the poor struggling mother, who, implicitly, will be better able to care for her children when enfranchised. Carrie Chapman Catt Papers, Tennessee State Library and Archives, Courtesy of the Tennessee Historical Society.

This cartoonist implies that women, voting in the interest of "the home," would serve society far better than many men, whose purchased votes serve the interests of corrupt political "bosses." Carrie Chapman Catt Papers, Tennessee State Library and Archives, Courtesy of the Tennessee Historical Society.

Though some politicians insisted that women were too naive and ignorant of political realities to vote, this cartoon of August 1920 insists that woman's innocence was a blessing. Though she had been kept on a pedestal and out of politics, an enfranchised "American womanhood" would be a vast improvement over politicians who had been immersed in the mire of American politics, and who had no desire to have their world "cleaned up." Carrie Chapman Catt Papers, Tennessee State Library and Archives, Courtesy of the Tennessee Historical Society.

"The Real Battlefield," August 7, 1915, suggests that an enfranchised womanhood would take a dim view of war—like the war then devouring a generation of European men. Above the battlefield, where one man takes the life of another, two women appear to be making a pact to live in peace and preserve the lives of their children. Carrie Chapman Catt Papers, Tennessee State Library and Archives, Courtesy of the Tennessee Historical Society.

WHO SHARES THE COST OF WAR?

Who face death in order to give life to men? **WOMEN.**

Who love and work to rear the sons who then are killed in battle? **WOMEN.**

Who plant fields and harvest crops when all the able-bodied men are called to war? **WOMEN.**

Who keep shops and schools and work in factories while men are in the trenches? **WOMEN.**

Who nurse the wounded, feed the sick, support the helpless, brave all danger? **WOMEN.**

Who see their homes destroyed by shell and fire, their little ones made destitute, their daughters outraged? **WOMEN.**

Who are sent adrift, alone, no food, no hope, no shelter for the unborn child? **WOMEN.**

Who must suffer agony for every soldier killed? **WOMEN.**

Who are called upon to make sacrifiecs to pay the terrible tax of war? **WOMEN.**

¶ **Who dares say that war is not their business? In the name of Justice and Civilization give woman a voice in the government.**

Equal Suffrage League of Virginia
100 North Fourth Street,
RICHMOND, VA.

Many antisuffragists insisted that since women could not be soldiers they had no right to vote on matters of war and peace. This brochure insists that women pay a high price for war and have a right to a voice in government in the "name of *Justice* and *Civilization*." Equal Suffrage League Collection, Organizational Records, Archives and Records Division, Virgina State Library and Archives, Richmond, Virginia.

EQUAL SUFFRAGE AND THE NEGRO VOTE

The opponents of equal suffrage claim that the negro woman's vote will constitute a menace to white supremacy. This contention is altogether unfounded for the following reasons:

1. **BECAUSE** under the proposed amendment to the Constitution the same restrictions, which now apply to men must also apply to women and as these qualifications restrict the negro man's vote, it stands to reason that they will also restrict the negro woman's vote.

2. **BECAUSE** there are 191,000 more white women of voting age in Virginia than there are negro women of voting age, and white women outnumber negro men and women put together by 31,407. So the enfranchisement of Virginia women would increase white supremacy.

3. **BECAUSE** white supremacy would be further increased by the literacy test. The Constitution says, in reference to qualification of the voter that "unless physically unable, he make application in his own handwriting," and that he "prepare and deposit his ballot without aid." Illiteracy among negroes is 22 per cent. and among white people is only 8 per cent.

4 **BECAUSE** the Constitution says that the would-be voter shall pay a poll tax of one dollar and fifty cents "for three years next preceding that in which he offers to register." This qualification further increases the white supremacy, as there are comparatively few negroes who meet their money obligations three years in advance.

5. **BECAUSE** the Constitution further says that "the General Assembly may prescribe a property qualification of not exceeding two hundred and fifty dollars for voters in any county, city or town," etc. (See Article II, Sec. 30, Elective Franchise and Qualification for Office.) This is a provision to be used if needed, but it has never been needed anywhere in Virginia, for there is no county or city or town where negro men qualify in larger numbers than white men. They are shut out by the present restrictions. We are secure from negro domination now—then, even more.

EQUAL SUFFRAGE LEAGUE OF VIRGINIA,
Commercial Building, Richmond, Virginia.

White southern suffragists of the 1890s often insisted that the South should solve its "negro problem" by enfranchising white women rather than disfranchising black men and risking retribution by Congress. By 1910 this was a moot point as nearly all of the southern states had disfranchised black male voters with no sign that the federal government intended to intervene. In the second stage of the southern suffrage movement, roughly from 1909 to 1920, white suffragists were on the defensive on the race issue and denied its relevance to the "woman question." Like the Virginia suffragists who designed this flyer, most of them discussed race only when compelled to defend their cause against antisuffragists' claims that woman suffrage was a threat to the newly restored white supremacy. Equal Suffrage League Collection, Organizational Records, Archives and Records Division, Virgina State Library and Archives, Richmond, Virginia.

Woman Suffrage and White Supremacy in the South

The Federal Suffrage Amendment will not affect the negro situation in the South.

It sets aside no qualification for voting except the sex qualification. It simply eliminates the word "male". The same qualifications will apply to negro women as now apply to negro men. (See Constitution of North Carolina, Article 6, Section 4.)

The Census Report of the U. S. Government Tells the Story

1910—Population of North Carolina was upwards of	2,200,000
1920—At normal rate of increase population will now be upwards of	2,800,000
The rule is one adult male to every five persons, which gives us as adult males	560,000
There are fully as many adult females	560,000
Total adult males and females	1,120,000

As the ratio in North Carolina by the census is 70% white and 30% negro, it follows that the negro adults, male and female, are 336,000 and the white adults, male and female, are 784,000. One half (392,000) of these last are, of course, white females, making 56,000 more adult white women than the 336,000 negro men and negro women combined.

IF white domination is threatened in the South, it is, therefore, DOUBLY EXPEDIENT TO ENFRANCHISE THE WOMEN QUICKLY IN ORDER THAT IT BE PRESERVED.

U. S. Senator Simmons, who waged the successful fight for White Supremacy in North Carolina in 1898, advocates ratification of the Federal Suffrage Amendment by the Legislature of North Carolina.

The Democratic State Convention asked that the Legislature ratify this Amendment.

Woodrow Wilson urges every Democratic State to ratify.

Secretary of the Navy, Josephus Daniels is eager for North Carolina to ratify.

Chief Justice John M. Anderson, of Alabama, says: "This is the most important Amendment ever proposed to the Federal Constitution; indeed, more important than any original section of that instrument, as it seeks an interpretation of that part of the Bill of Rights which proclaims that all men are born equal by interpolating therein the word WOMAN".

Chief Justice Clark, of North Carolina, says: "No matter how bad a character a man has, if he can only keep out of the penitentiary and the insane asylum we permit him to vote and to take a share in the Government, but we are afraid to trust our mothers, wives, and daughters to give us the aid of their intelligence and clear insight".

Would these representative men of the South ask that a measure be passed which would endanger the civilization of the South?

EQUAL SUFFRAGE ASSOCIATION OF NORTH CAROLINA—RALEIGH

3

This brochure distributed by North Carolina suffragists invokes the authority of prominent Democrats (including Senator Furnifold Simmons, who had led the infamous white supremacy campaign of 1898) to counter claims that the proposed Nineteenth Amendment would destroy white dominance and "the civilization of the South." Indeed, they insisted that in a white-majority state like North Carolina, enfranchising women would actually serve the cause of white supremacy. North Carolina Collection, University of North Carolina at Chapel Hill Library.

Three Eminent Alabamians On Woman Suffrage

Hon. James Weatherly, One of the Ablest Constitutional Lawyers in the State Says:

Upon ratification of the suffrage amendment the women of the State will have the right to vote upon an equality with the men of the State, subject to the same limitations, conditions and requirements as our existing system imposes upon men.

The amendment will be self-executing to the extent of eliminating, of its own force, the disqualification of women, as women, and of automatically applying to women all those affirmative provisions, whereby men are admissible to the right of suffrage.

The qualifying clauses, as well as the disqualifying clauses, now relating to men, will apply equally to women, except the single disqualification of sex, and the entire mechanism of the present system under which men now vote will be equally available to women. Therefore, there need be no immediate or prospective revision of the present system, either by legislation or constitutional amendment.

Further, **the conclusions hereinabove announced are based on decisions of the United States Supreme Court** interpreting the effect on State suffrage systems of the Fifteenth Amendment to the Federal Constitution.

Must we deny our splendid womanhood the right and the privilege of sharing with us our burdens and of helping us work out a plan of salvation when they apply for their own political enfranchisement and their admission into the fold of democracy?

The slow centuries have brought to woman more and more of freedom and of individuality—along with the growth of democracy. Her complete enfranchisement is a postulate of democracy. We cannot resist it, if we would, and **our very necessities in this land of the South demand that we extend to her the rights, privileges and benefits**, as well as the burdens of which our State Constitution is the organic expression.

Dr. W. B. Crumpton, Secretary Emeritus of the Baptist Mission Board and President of the Alabama Anti-Saloon League, is quoted as follows:

For which of their many patriotic deeds will the Alabama solons punish them by refusing the ballot to women? Are the churches of Alabama worth anything to the State? The women are in the majority in every one of them. Could the churches and Sunday schools exist without them? Who are the teachers of our children? More than seventy-five per cent. of the teachers in Alabama schools are women, and they are the poorest paid servants of the people, excepting the preachers. Who fills our criminal courts and our prisons? Not the women, but the lordly men, who have the exclusive right to rule everything but themselves.

Many women own property and manage it, well—ofttimes far better than their husbands, now deceased. With all her property, her good management, her prompt payment of taxes and obedience to law, she has no right to vote even for a constable to protect her; or a school board, who will appoint the teachers of her children. Men of the Alabama Legislature, elected by your constituents to make laws for **all the people**, are you treating the women right?

Lastly, Brother Alabamian, let's remove the stigma on our women in having them classed with idiots and criminals, as being ineligible for service at the polls. Think of it! "From idiots, those convicted of crime, and women," the ballot is withheld. Shame on us if we allow our women to remain thus classified!

(Signed) W. B. CRUMPTON,
Gadsden, Alabama.

Ex-Governor B. B. Comer expresses the following sentiment:

One of the most far-reaching questions in the world today is the absolute, equal, free rights of women. The South, with its love, its admiration for woman, should strike hands with its sister States, its sister nations of the world to establish firmly this greatest democratic measure ever brought before the peoples of the world.

It would be just as serious a mistake for the leaders of the South to lead the Southern people as a section against this movement as it proved to be when they led them out of the Union as defenders of slavery. The enthrallment of our women should be broken. We of Alabama should give our women every right that we claim as our own. The association of the political right of woman and man should be on a basis of equal partnership, as is the marital relation.

Alabama will soon have an opportunity which comes not often in a lifetime, namely: to be among the first States to ratify the Susan B. Anthony amendment. Will Alabama prove reactionary, or will she join the sisterhood of advanced States and give our women the recognition that civilization demands?

Alabama Equal Suffrage Association

1818 Second Avenue 12 *Birmingham, Ala.*

Alabama suffragists similarly publicized the support of "eminent" men of their state. Here they feature a lawyer, a religious leader (and prohibitionist), and a former governor, who employed a broad range of arguments in favor of ratification. Equal Suffrage League Collection, Organizational Records, Archives and Records Division, Virgina State Library and Archives, Richmond, Virginia.

PRESIDENT WILSON IS WITH US!

"I intend to vote for woman suffrage in New Jersey because I believe that the time has come to extend that privilege and responsibility to the women of the State."

"I think that New Jersey will be greatly benefited by the change."
Statement made by President Wilson.

Do You Trust The President?

Then Stand With Him for Equal Suffrage!

President Wilson Says He will Vote for

EQUAL SUFFRAGE

In New Jersey October 19th.

DEMOCRATIC LEADERS FAVOR EQUAL SUFFRAGE

Vice-President Marshall, Secretary of the Treasury McAdoo, Secretary of the Interior Lane, Secretary of War Garrison, Secretary of the Navy Daniels, Secretary of Commerce Redfield, Secretary of Labor Wilson, Champ Clark, Speaker of the House, and William Jennings Bryan,

STATE HEADQUARTERS, RICHMOND, VA.

Commercial Building, Second Street, between Bro[illegible] Grace

Woodrow Wilson's conversion to woman suffrage, assiduously cultivated through quite different methods by the NAWSA and the NWP, was essential to the movement's success. Southern suffragists were particularly happy to claim him as an ally: born in Virginia and reared in Georgia and South Carolina, Wilson was celebrated by southerners as one of their own despite his many years in New Jersey and was regarded as a champion of states' rights. Equal Suffrage League Collection, Organizational Records, Archives and Records Division, Virgina State Library and Archives, Richmond, Virginia.

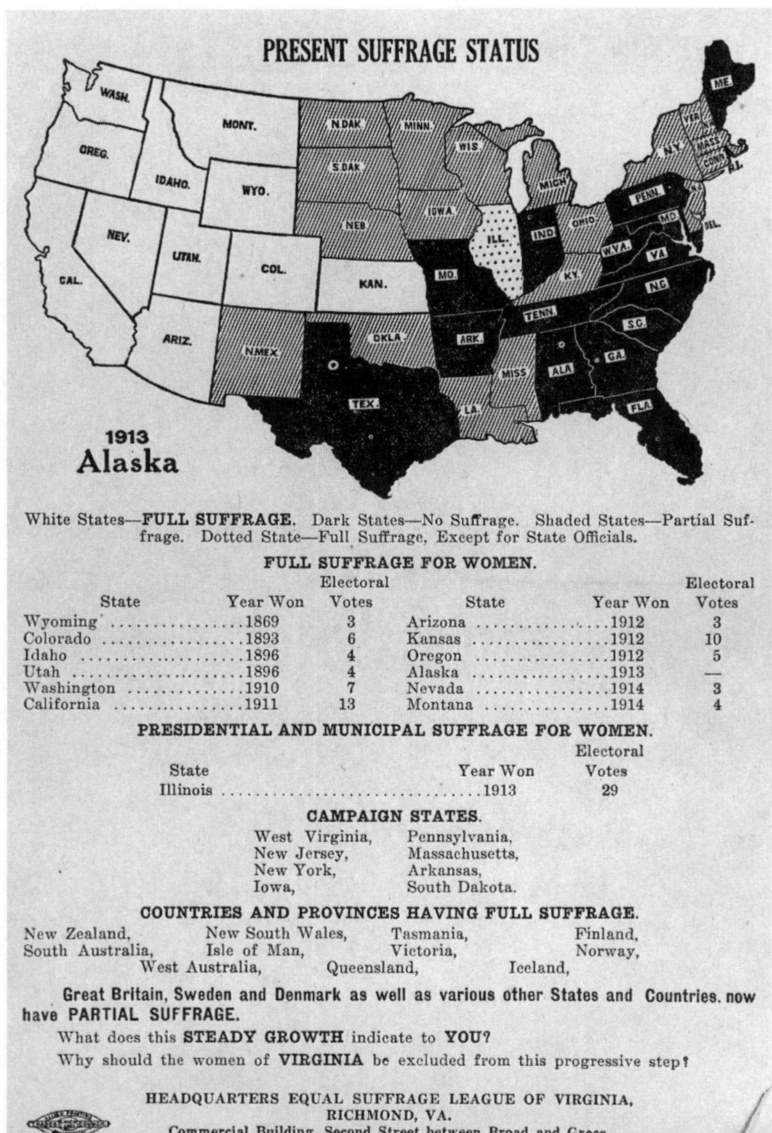

PRESENT SUFFRAGE STATUS

White States—**FULL SUFFRAGE.** Dark States—No Suffrage. Shaded States—Partial Suffrage. Dotted State—Full Suffrage, Except for State Officials.

FULL SUFFRAGE FOR WOMEN.

State	Year Won	Electoral Votes	State	Year Won	Electoral Votes
Wyoming	1869	3	Arizona	1912	3
Colorado	1893	6	Kansas	1912	10
Idaho	1896	4	Oregon	1912	5
Utah	1896	4	Alaska	1913	—
Washington	1910	7	Nevada	1914	3
California	1911	13	Montana	1914	4

PRESIDENTIAL AND MUNICIPAL SUFFRAGE FOR WOMEN.

State	Year Won	Electoral Votes
Illinois	1913	29

CAMPAIGN STATES.

West Virginia, New Jersey, New York, Iowa, Pennsylvania, Massachusetts, Arkansas, South Dakota.

COUNTRIES AND PROVINCES HAVING FULL SUFFRAGE.

New Zealand, South Australia, New South Wales, Isle of Man, Tasmania, Victoria, Finland, Norway, West Australia, Queensland, Iceland,

Great Britain, Sweden and Denmark as well as various other States and Countries. now have PARTIAL SUFFRAGE.

What does this **STEADY GROWTH** indicate to **YOU?**

Why should the women of **VIRGINIA** be excluded from this progressive step?

HEADQUARTERS EQUAL SUFFRAGE LEAGUE OF VIRGINIA,
RICHMOND, VA.
Commercial Building, Second Street between Broad and Grace.

Broadsides like this one circulated in Virginia suggested that woman suffrage was a positive and progressive movement already sweeping the globe and challenged legislators to enfranchise their "own" women. Equal Suffrage League Collection, Organizational Records, Archives and Records Division, Virgina State Library and Archives, Richmond, Virginia.

THE CHANGE IN THE STATUS OF WOMEN MAKES VOTES FOR WOMEN THE NEXT NATURAL STEP

The only reason for not enfranchising any class of people in a democracy is because they are mentally or morally incompetent to vote.

The reason why women are not enfranchised is because, when our Constitution was made a hundred and twenty-five years ago, women were considered mentally incompetent to vote.

One Hundred and Twenty-five Years Ago, girls were not admitted to the public grammar schools; women were not admitted to the colleges; women were not admitted to many of the trades and professions; married women could not own property; and married women did not own their own children.

During the Past Hundred and Twenty-five Years the Status of Women has Completely Changed.

At the Present Time, our high schools are graduating more girls than boys; forty thousand women are in our colleges; eight million women are working in the trades and professions; married women can own property; and, in sixteen states, married women are equal guardians of their children, with the father.

The mental competence of women is now recognized in all phases of social responsibility—except that of the franchise.

The time has come to change the political status of women and to make it accord with their present social, economic and intellectual status. This change has already been recognized.

Women Vote on Equal Terms with Men in: Isle of man, New Zealand, Australia, New South Wales, Finland, Iceland and Norway; in Colorado, Idaho, Utah, Wyoming, Washington, California, Arizona, Oregon, Kansas, and Alaska; and in Illinois for all except state officials. A woman suffrage amendment has passed the legislatures, and will be submitted to the voters of the following states in 1914: Montana, Nevada, North Dakota, South Dakota, and in Nebraska by Initiative.

Women Vote in Municipal Elections in: England, Scotland, Ireland, Denmark, and Sweden.

In three Southern states, Louisiana, Misssissippi and Kentucky, women have partial suffrage.

In Virginia women have no voice in the government. They cannot even serve on school boards. The State makes no provision for their higher education, nor as teachers do they receive from the State equal pay for equal work with men. Moreover, married women are not equal guardians of their children with the father. How much longer shall Virginia lag behind other states in according the dignity and power of citizenship to women?

EQUAL SUFFRAGE LEAGUE OF VIRGINIA

HEADQUARTERS:

Commercial Building, 2nd Street, Between Grace and Broad Streets

Richmond, Virginia

Send us your name for membership. No dues

Virginia suffragists insisted that woman's expanded social and economic role, the result of new ideas about woman's ability, all pointed to a new political role for woman. Equal Suffrage League Collection, Organizational Records, Archives and Records Division, Virgina State Library and Archives, Richmond, Virginia.

Stand by the Country

TO DEFEND THE NATION all its resources are needed. Women must be mobilized equally with men.

As a measure of Preparedness Give Women the Vote.

England has had to do it. The new franchise bill will give the vote to 6,000,000 women.

Canada has done it. Since the war began five big Canadian provinces have given women the vote.

France is going to do it. The Chamber of Deputies has announced that the municipal vote will be given at once to women.

Denmark did it in 1915; when threatened by war, she gave the vote to women.

Russia is basing her new government on universal suffrage.

THE UNITED STATES HAS BEGUN. Since January **North Dakota, Ohio, Indiana, Rhode Island, Michigan and Nebraska** have been added to the twelve woman suffrage states by giving the Presidential vote to Women. **Arkansas** has broken the ranks of the Solid South and given women primary suffrage.

Don't wait for the tragedies of War to prove that the Country belongs to **both men** and **women.**

It is **our Country** as well as yours. Give us the vote that we may **support** it **most effectively** in both **war and peace.**

NATIONAL WOMAN SUFFRAGE PUBLISHING COMPANY, INC.

171 Madison Avenue  **New York City**

During World War I, the National Woman Suffrage Publishing Company circulated this brochure insisting that limiting woman's ability to serve the nation weakened the war effort and pointing out that our allies were adopting woman suffrage. Equal Suffrage League Collection, Organizational Records, Archives and Records Division, Virgina State Library and Archives, Richmond, Virginia.

This political cartoon, which appeared in *The Texas Democrat*, portrays "Uncle Sam" wondering why American legislators kept him "with Mexico, Bulgaria, and Turkey" (where women were not enfranchised) when the newspaper revealed that Equal Suffrage had been adopted in England, Canada, Australia, New Zealand and that "practically all civilized nations [were] in line." The cartoonist appeals to the Democrats, who controlled Texas politics, to adhere to their prosuffrage party platform. Jane Y. McCallum Family Papers, Austin History Center, Austin Public Library.

The Case against Woman Suffrage: Antisuffrage Broadsides and Cartoons

In this antisuffrage cartoon circulated by the Massachusetts Association Opposed to the Further Extension of Suffrage to Women, a workman comes home from work to find his children alone, his table bare, and a note saying "Back Some Time This Evening" pinned to a suffrage poster. Josephine Pearson Papers, Tennessee State Library and Archives. Courtesy of the Tennessee Historical Society.

America When Femininized

The More a Politician Allows Himself to be Henpecked The More Henpecking We Will Have in Politics.

A Vote for Federal Suffrage is a Vote for Organized Female Nagging Forever.

"American pep which was the result of a masculine dominated country will soon be a thing of the past. With the collapse of the male ascendancy in this country we can look forward to a nation of degeneration. The suppression of sex will ultimately have its harvest in decadence, a phenomenon already beginning. The effect of the social revolution on American character will be to make "sissies" of American men—a process already well under way."—Dr. William J. Hickson, Chicago University.

WOMAN SUFFRAGE denatures both men and women; it masculinizes women and femininizes men. The history of ancient civilization has proven that a weakening of the man power of nations has been but a pre-runner of decadence in civilization.

Will you stand for this? Prove that you will not by voting to **Reject** the Federal Woman Suffrage Amendment to the Constitution of the United States.

SOUTHERN WOMAN'S LEAGUE FOR REJECTION OF THE SUSAN B. ANTHONY AMENDMENT

WE SERVE THAT OUR STATES MAY LIVE, AND LIVING, PRESERVE THE UNION

Brandon-Nashville

This cartoon shows the "Suffragist-Feminist Ideal Family Life," with the woman heading off to heed her country's call while telling her "Old Man" to tend the nest. Woman suffrage, says the cartoonist, will "denature" men and women and cause the "degeneration" of American society. Josephine Pearson Papers, Tennessee State Library and Archives. Courtesy of the Tennessee Historical Society.

THE "THREE IMMEDIATE WOMEN FRIENDS" OF THE ANTHONY FAMILY. SEE BIOGRAPHY OF SUSAN B. ANTHONY, PAGE 1435, BY MRS. IDA HUSTED HARPER.

CARRIE CHAPMAN CATT

The Rev. ANNA HOWARD SHAW

"Mrs. R. JEROME JEFFREY" (NEGRO)

From Left to Right: Carrie Chapman Catt; The Rev. Anna Howard Shaw; Mrs. R. Jerome Jeffery, Negro woman of Rochester, N. Y. Often "Guest in Anthony Home" with Mrs. Shaw and Mrs. Carrie Chapman Catt, President of National Woman Suffrage Association, to which all Southern Suffragettes belong.

"Suffrage Democracy Knows no Bias of Race, Color, Creed or Sex."—Carrie Chapman Catt.

Look not to Greece or Rome for heroes, nor to Jerusalem or Mecca for saints, but for all the higher virtues of heroism, let us WORSHIP the black man at our feet."—*Susan B. Anthony's Official History of Suffrage.*

Southern antisuffragists opposed woman suffrage by publicizing the early association between the antislavery and woman's rights movements, the continuing friendships between Susan B. Anthony and a number of black leaders, and northern suffragists' statements of support for the rights of African Americans. This is the first page of a pamphlet sent to Laura Clay by Alabama antis. Laura Clay Papers, Margaret I. King Library, University of Kentucky.

"WOMAN TO THE RESCUE!"
From "The Crisis" of May, 1916.

Southern white antisuffragists also *opposed* woman suffrage by pointing out that African Americans *supported* it. They reprinted this prosuffrage cartoon from the *Crisis* in an antisuffrage brochure. A black woman is using the federal constitution as a club with which to beat down "Jim Crow Law" and "Segregation." "Grand-Father Clause" has already fallen (ruled unconstitutional in 1915). Meanwhile, the black *man* runs away, saying, "I don't believe in agitating and fighting. My policy is to pursue the line of least resistance. To h___ with Citizenship Rights. I want money. I think the white folk will let me stay on my land as long as *I stay in my place*.—(Shades of WILMINGTON, N.C.) The good whites ain't responsible for bad administration of the law and lynching and peonage—let me think awhile, er—." Josephine Pearson Papers, Tennessee State Library and Archives. Courtesy of the Tennessee Historical Society.

Negro Women's Resolutions for Enforcement of Federal Suffrage Amendments

The National Association of Colored Women's Clubs in convention assembled at Tuskegee Institute, Alabama, July 12 to 16, 1920, offers the following recommendations:

Since it is evident that the women of the Nation are soon to be invested with the right of full franchise,

We recommend that the colored women give their close attention to the study of civics, to the laws of parliamentary usage and to the current political questions, both local and national, in order to fit themselves for the exercise of the franchise.

As Mrs. Mary B. Talbert, our retiring President, has been named as one of the ten women of America to go as delegate to the International Council of Women to be held in Norway in September next, we express our heartfelt appreciation for this representation given the women of our race. [Mrs. C. C. Catt, President National Suffrage Association, is one of the other nine delegates referred to above.]

We heartily commend the Urban League and the National Association of Colored People who are doing so much to bring about justice to the members of our proscribed race.

We wish to go on record as asking the instructors throughout this country, especially those in colored schools, to teach our boys and girls the lives of the great men and women of the race, who have thus far shaped, and are shaping our destinies.

We further recommend that wherever possible the local clubs coöperate with the teachers in building up good libraries in colored schools, and putting upon the shelves authentic publications from our best colored authors in literature, history, science and art.

We go on record as endorsing and urging the enforcement of the 18th Amendment to the Federal Constitution of the United States as interpreted in the Volstead Act.

And we also urge our National Congress to enforce the 14th and 15th Amendments to the Federal Constitution.

Since glaring headlines and detailed accounts in the press of crimes and misdemeanors committed by colored people tend to inflame the passions of the public against members of our race, culminating often in rioting and mob violence, we urge the press of the United States to refrain from thus perpetuating such propaganda against us.

We again make solemn protest against the continued prevalence of mob violence in the United States, and we pray for the enactment of a Federal statute against lynch law with severe penalties for the violation thereof and that such statute be enforced if need be, by the military power of this government.

We express our grateful appreciation to Dr. Robert R. Moton and his co-workers at Tuskegee Institute for the generous hospitality, courteous attentions and gracious kindness shown the National Association of Colored Women's Clubs while guests at the Institute during our 13th biennial convention and 25th anniversary.

Respectfully submitted,

Committee on Resolutions: Francis E. Keyser, H. A. Washington, Mary V. Parrish, Mary Church Terrell, S. Joe Brown, Alice Dunbar-Nelson

REPRINTED AND ISSUED BY

TENNESSEE DIVISION, SOUTHERN WOMAN'S REJECTION LEAGUE

HEADQUARTERS, HERMITAGE HOTEL, NASHVILLE, TENN.

[OVER]

This flyer, issued by the Tennessee Division of the Southern Woman's Rejection League, reprints a prosuffrage resolution adopted by the National Association of Colored Women's Clubs at a July 1920 convention at Tuskegee Institute. Josephine Pearson Papers, Tennessee State Library and Archives. Courtesy of the Tennessee Historical Society.

BEWARE!

MEN OF THE SOUTH: Heed not the song of the suffrage siren! Seal your ears against her vocal wiles! For, no matter how sweetly she may proclaim the advantages of female franchise,

REMEMBER that *woman suffrage* means a reopening of the entire *negro suffrage* question, loss of State rights, and another period of reconstruction horrors, which will introduce a set of female carpetbaggers as bad as their male prototypes of the sixties.

DO NOT JEOPARDIZE the present prosperity of your sovereign State, which was so dearly bought by the blood of your fathers and the tears of your mothers, by again raising an issue which has already been adjusted at so great a cost.

NOTHING can be gained by woman suffrage, and much may be lost.

(*Extracts from The Messenger*)

THE NEGRO
AND THE
NEW SOCIAL ORDER

A Reconstruction Program, Prepared by Chandler Owen and A. Philip Randolph (negroes),
Editors of *The Messenger*, March 10, 1919
THE MESSENGER PUBLISHING CO.
2305 SEVENTH AVENUE NEW YORK CITY

POLITICAL PROGRAM

Page 6: Political action must go hand in hand with industrial action. A class of people without the vote or the privilege of determining the kind of government under which they live has neither security of life nor property from which liberty proceeds.

In view of the foregoing, WE DEMAND the rigid enforcement of the Thirteenth, Fourteenth, and Fifteenth Amendments to the Constitution, which were primarily framed to give protection to negroes.

WE DEMAND the reduction of representation in the South upon the basis of actual voting population. The negro is not allowed to vote, which is in criminal violation of the Federal Constitution.

We condemn all property and educational tests for suffrage.

WE DEMAND *universal suffrage, without regard to race, color, sex, creed, or nationality.*

WOMAN SUFFRAGE

We favor the adoption of the Susan B. Anthony Amendment to the Constitution, granting suffrage to women, both white and colored.

("Suffrage democracy knows no bias of race, color, creed, or sex."—*Mrs. Carrie Chapman Catt.*)

SOCIAL EQUALITY

Page 9: *We favor "social equality" in every sense of the phrase.* WE DEMAND a new order based upon a society of equals. Evasions, pretexts, and excuses cannot explain away the fact that no genuine brotherhood can exist so long as the issue of social equality is not squarely met.

SOCIAL EQUALITY has grown out of the two cardinal and corollary principles of *identity of treatment* and *free interchangeability.*

INTERMARRIAGE

We now approach the American bugaboo—the question upon which the negroes and whites alike set up false theories in flagrant violation of the most fundamental principles of social evolution. *We refer to intermarriage between the whites and negroes.* WE FAVOR THE INTERMARRIAGE between any sane, grown persons who desire to marry, whatever their race or color. WE FAVOR THE INTERMARRIAGE OF WHITE MEN WITH COLORED WOMEN, AS WELL AS COLORED MEN WITH WHITE WOMEN, because there is no natural or instinctive aversion.

Race purity is both a myth and without any value.

WE, THEREFORE, DEMAND THE REPEAL OF ALL LAWS AGAINST INTERMARRIAGE AS BEING INIMICAL TO THE INTERESTS OF BOTH RACES. We further call attention to the fact that there is no desire to check the associations of white men with colored women, colored women with white men, nor to serve any interests of negro men. And inasmuch as no law requires any woman under any circumstances to marry a man whom she does not will or want to marry, *these laws narrow themselves down to the prevention of* WHITE WOMEN MARRYING COLORED MEN *whom they desire to marry.*

WE DEMAND as much intercourse—economic, political, and social—*as is possible between the races.*

"Women and negroes, being seven-twelfths of the people, are a majority; and, according to our republican theory, the rightful rulers of the Nation." (Official History Woman Suffrage, Vol. I., page 281.)

"We will see that Negro women in the South shall vote." (Ida Husted Harper, Editorial Chairman of the National American Woman Suffrage Association, in the New York Globe, November 4, 1918.)

Southern antisuffragists warned southern men to seal their ears to the sweet song of naive southern women asking for enfranchisement, for it would unleash upon the South "female carpetbaggers as bad as their male prototypes of the sixties." Josephine Pearson Papers, Tennessee State Library and Archives. Courtesy of the Tennessee Historical Society.

WARNING!

All persons who circulate the false and malicious charge that any of the noble women who compose the following undersigned organizations are "paid by liquor interests" WILL BE PROSECUTED TO THE FULL EXTENT OF THE LAW FOR CRIMINAL LIBEL OR PUBLIC SLANDER.

A certain suffragist at the Capitol yesterday, pointing out one of the beloved leaders of the Southern women who are waging the bravest possible battle for State Rights, said of her to a certain legislator:

"Don't talk to her. She is paid by the liquor interests."

Such false and malicious charges are an example of what woman suffrage means in action—cruel, unfair, dishonest and unscrupulous attempts to blast the reputation of every courageous woman who dares to disagree with the politically ambitious fraction who demand "votes for women" and "offices for women."

There is NOT A SINGLE ANTI-SUFFRAGE ASSOCIATION or Anti-Ratification Association which has received a cent from any liquor or brewery interest, or from persons formerly in such business. This charge, ALWAYS CIRCULATED whenever the suffragists feel themselves BEATEN IN A FAIR FIGHT, is founded only on the malice or ignorance of little minds which assume that the public can be fooled by repeated falsehood.

THE FACT is that the greatest anti-suffrage majority was polled in West Virginia, the dryest state in the Union, where prohibition carried by 90,000 and suffrage was defeated by 98,000 the following year. The greatest suffrage majority was polled in NEW YORK CITY while 10,000 saloons were in full operation. Anybody who wants to investigate this question SINCERELY is invited to inspect the real EVIDENCE at Anti-Ratification Headquarters, Hermitage Hotel, such as the appeal of SUSAN B. ANTHONY HERSELF to the United States Brewers' Association, begging them to indorse and assist in the adoption of the very amendment that bears her name and is now before the Tennessee Legislature.

But persons who insult, libel or slander noble women who, at great personal and financial sacrifices, represent only the solemn convictions of the vast majority of our people against woman suffrage, are going to learn that every available legal measure will be taken for the protection of our womanhood engaged in this battle for the Home, the Family and the State.

Southern Women's League for Rejection of the Susan B. Anthony Amendment

Judge John R. Tyson, General Counsel — Headquarters Hermitage Hotel

The National Association Opposed to Woman Suffrage

Hon. Everett P. Wheeler General Counsel — Headquarters Hermitage Hotel

There was considerable bitterness between the pro- and antisuffrage women lobbying the Tennessee legislature in 1920. This newspaper advertisement issued by the antisuffragists' lawyers warned suffragists against "libeling" antisuffrage women by charging that they were "paid by the liquor interests." Josephine Pearson Papers, Tennessee State Library and Archives. Courtesy of the Tennessee Historical Society.

Questions for Mrs. Catt

Which She has Strangely Failed to Answer although Published in the Chattanooga Times, July 24, and the Nashville Banner, July 25.

Why is the Suffrage Leader Silent?

"NASHVILLE, TENN., July 23, 1920.

"MRS. CARRIE CHAPMAN CATT,

"Hermitage Hotel, Nashville.

"MY DEAR MRS. CATT: Southern women abhor political combat for their sex. That is one of the reasons they deeply oppose the campaign of your organization to plunge women into perpetual political turmoil.

"We have no desire to make your campaign unpleasant, but we must insist at any cost that it be honest.

"You are quoted in a morning newspaper as saying: 'There is nothing in the past quarter of a century that would be so indicative of the traditions of the Old South as would the ratification of this amendment.'

"In view of this remarkable statement, I must ask you what your association meant when it passed a formal resolution, printed in the Crisis, official Negro organ, November, 1917, page 12, five months after that paper had endorsed the intermarriage of races, as follows:

" **'That all American men or women, white or black, shall share equally in the privileges of democracy.'**

"Again, what did you mean when, in a signed article in the same issue of that official Negro organ, you wrote:

" **'Suffrage democracy knows no bias of race, color, creed or sex.'**

"Again, what did you mean when, in a formal address before a convention of your association at Washington, Dec. 5, 1913, you declared:

" **'Our cause can wait no longer. If the constitution stands in our way, I say let us tear it to shreds and make a new one. We must train our guns on the South.'**

"Once more, when you wrote a letter to Senator Poindexter congratulating him on the introduction of a force bill to rob the South of its representation in Congress, were you under the impression that such a measure would be 'indicative of the traditions of the Old South?'

"In Tennessee, as you know, ratification cannot be accomplished without the violation of a solemn oath of office by every legislator who votes for your amendment. Even Northern newspapers that make no pretense of 'elevating the morals of politics,' such as the New York Journal of Commerce, strongly condemn this Tennessee proposition as a matter of plain perjury.

"Do you dare intimate, however indirectly, that the commission of perjury by public officers is 'indicative of the traditions of the Old South?'

"We intend to be as courteous to you as possible in any political campaign, but we must demand that the truth, the whole truth, and nothing but the truth, be stated in this matter of life or death to our beloved Southland.

"Very truly yours,

"MRS. JAMES S. PINCKARD,

"*President Southern Woman's League for the Rejection of the Susan B. Anthony Amendment.*"

ISSUED BY TENNESSEE DIVISION SOUTHERN WOMAN'S LEAGUE
FOR THE REJECTION OF THE SUSAN B. ANTHONY AMENDMENT
HEADQUARTERS, HERMITAGE HOTEL, NASHVILLE, TENN.

[OVER]

In this flyer, the president of the Southern Woman's League for the Rejection of the Susan B. Anthony Amendment makes public some of Catt's statements supporting equal rights for African Americans and portrays her as an enemy of the South. Josephine Pearson Papers, Tennessee State Library and Archives. Courtesy of the Tennessee Historical Society.

DECLARATION OF PRINCIPLES

OF THE SOUTHERN WOMEN'S LEAGUE FOR THE REJECTION OF THE PROPOSED SUSAN B. ANTHONY AMENDMENT TO THE CONSTITUTION OF THE UNITED STATES.

---

1. We believe in the political principle of Local Self Government and that **State Sovereignty is essential** to the Liberty, Happiness, True Progress, and Welfare of the American People.

2. **WE ARE UNALTERABLY OPPOSED TO THE ADOPTION OF THE SUSAN B. ANTHONY AMENDMENT TO THE CONSTITUTION OF THE UNITED STATES,** which Amendment will force the unrestricted ballot upon unwilling majorities in Southern States, and will place the control of the electorate outside the Sovereign State.

3. We deny the Justice of the Compulsory Regulation of the Electorate of our States by a **combination** of other States, who have no sympathetic understanding of our peculiar Social and Racial problems.

4. We oppose any measure that threatens the continuation of **Anglo-Saxon** domination of Social and Political affairs in each and evey State of the Union without strife and bloodshed which would inevitably follow an attempt to overthow it.

5. We oppose **SOCIALISM, BOLESHVISM, RADICALISM** and all the Social disorders that are now disturbing the world and are rapidly encroaching upon our own Republic, and believe that these disorders will be aided and multiplied and more effectually forced upon the Conservative States such as we represent, through the adoption of the Susan B. Anthony Amendment.

6. We declare that the REJECTION of the Susan B. Anthony Amendment to the Constitution of the United States, in **NO** way affects the rights of the several individual States, **TO SO AMEND THEIR CONSTITUTIONS,** as to enfranchise the women of those States, where a **majority** so elect; and to throw safeguards and limitations upon electoral qualifications as local conditions demand.

7. We believe that in its present form, we live under the fairest and most liberal Government in the world, and desire to see it perpetuated in order that generations coming after us may enjoy the same Liberty in the Pursuit of Happiness we have enjoyed; and to that end we pledge our most earnest and continued efforts in behalf of the **Rejection of the Susan B. Anthony Amendment to the Constitution of the United States,** and call upon **all true Americans** to join us in this fight.

This Declaration of Principles of the Southern Women's League for the Rejection of the Susan B. Anthony Amendment emphatically states their states' rights position and opposition to any measure that threatens "Anglo-Saxon domination." Josephine Pearson Papers, Tennessee State Library and Archives. Courtesy of the Tennessee Historical Society.

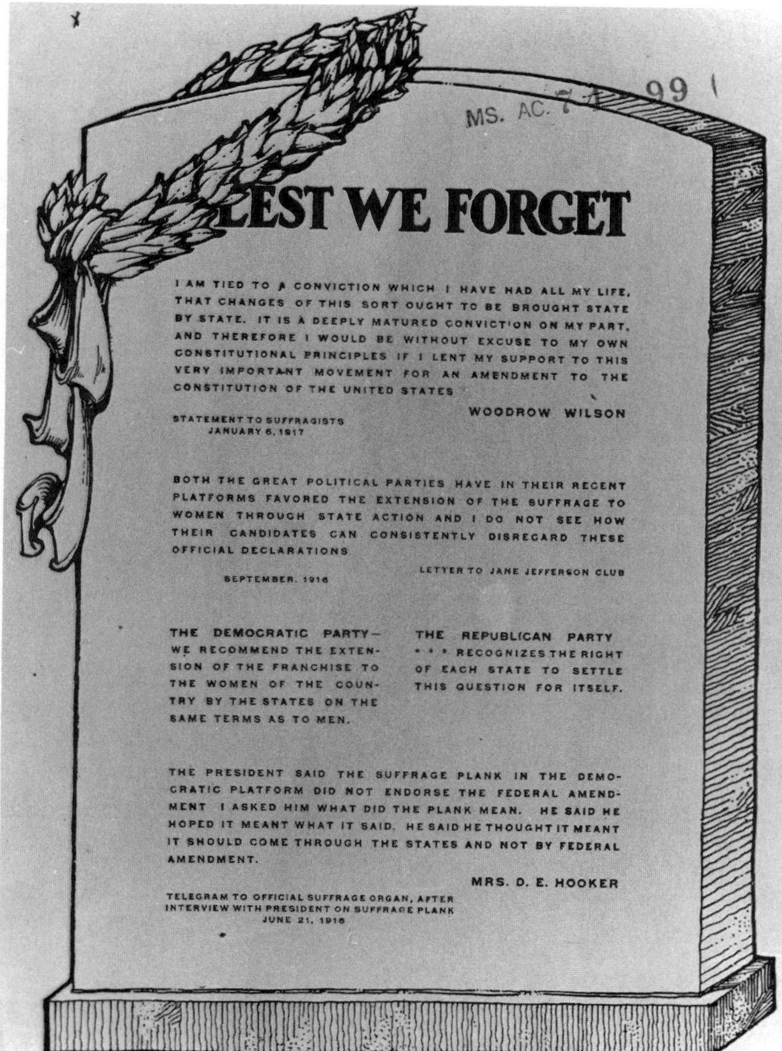

LEST WE FORGET

I AM TIED TO A CONVICTION WHICH I HAVE HAD ALL MY LIFE, THAT CHANGES OF THIS SORT OUGHT TO BE BROUGHT STATE BY STATE. IT IS A DEEPLY MATURED CONVICTION ON MY PART, AND THEREFORE I WOULD BE WITHOUT EXCUSE TO MY OWN CONSTITUTIONAL PRINCIPLES IF I LENT MY SUPPORT TO THIS VERY IMPORTANT MOVEMENT FOR AN AMENDMENT TO THE CONSTITUTION OF THE UNITED STATES

WOODROW WILSON

STATEMENT TO SUFFRAGISTS
JANUARY 6, 1917

BOTH THE GREAT POLITICAL PARTIES HAVE IN THEIR RECENT PLATFORMS FAVORED THE EXTENSION OF THE SUFFRAGE TO WOMEN THROUGH STATE ACTION AND I DO NOT SEE HOW THEIR CANDIDATES CAN CONSISTENTLY DISREGARD THESE OFFICIAL DECLARATIONS

SEPTEMBER, 1916

LETTER TO JANE JEFFERSON CLUB

THE DEMOCRATIC PARTY—WE RECOMMEND THE EXTENSION OF THE FRANCHISE TO THE WOMEN OF THE COUNTRY BY THE STATES ON THE SAME TERMS AS TO MEN.

THE REPUBLICAN PARTY * * * RECOGNIZES THE RIGHT OF EACH STATE TO SETTLE THIS QUESTION FOR ITSELF.

THE PRESIDENT SAID THE SUFFRAGE PLANK IN THE DEMOCRATIC PLATFORM DID NOT ENDORSE THE FEDERAL AMENDMENT I ASKED HIM WHAT DID THE PLANK MEAN. HE SAID HE HOPED IT MEANT WHAT IT SAID. HE SAID HE THOUGHT IT MEANT IT SHOULD COME THROUGH THE STATES AND NOT BY FEDERAL AMENDMENT.

MRS. D. E. HOOKER

TELEGRAM TO OFFICIAL SUFFRAGE ORGAN, AFTER
INTERVIEW WITH PRESIDENT ON SUFFRAGE PLANK
JUNE 21, 1916

Southern antisuffragists issued this broadside, reminding readers of President Woodrow Wilson's many statements supporting woman suffrage by *state action only*. Wilson's change of heart on the federal amendment and his active promotion of ratification infuriated southern antis who thereafter regarded him as a traitor to the South. Josephine Pearson Papers, Tennessee State Library and Archives. Courtesy of the Tennessee Historical Society.

The Federal Suffrage Amendment

WILL NEVER BE RATIFIED

IF THE PEOPLE OF TENNESSEE

GUARD THEIR RIGHTS

The Susan B. Anthony Federal Suffrage Amendment has NOT been ratified. The Tennessee Constitution PROHIBITS ratification of ANY Federal Amendment until the PEOPLE ELECT a NEW Legislature. ANY GOOD LAWYER who has ever heard of the Haire vs. Rice Case, 204 United States Reports, KNOWS that the attempted and so-called ratification by an illegal and insufficient PART of the present Tennessee Legislature (less than a legal quorum) was NULL AND VOID, ILLEGAL AND UNCONSTITUTIONAL.

NOBODY but the United States Supreme Court has a right to say that the Tennessee Constitution is in conflict with the United States Constitution. It is NOT IN CONFLICT, and CANNOT be in conflict, unless the UNITED STATES SUPREME COURT DECIDES THAT IT IS.

GOV. JAMES M. COX, Democratic Candidate for President, says: "Most lawyers to whom I have talked believe that it is not in conflict. It is a very good provision that ought to be in every State Constitution."

If it is NOT in conflict, then every attempt to EVADE and OVERRIDE the Constitution of Tennessee is plain LAWBREAKING and VIOLATION of their OATHS OF OFFICE by every official who solemnly swore, with God as a witness, to uphold the Constitution of Tennessee.

Such men ought to be IMPEACHED, as well as ENJOINED.

A man who deliberately CONSPIRES with lobbyists to break the SUPREME LAW of the State of Tennessee is in the same class with the BOOTLEGGER and the BOLSHEVIST. The PEOPLE must see to it that OFFICIAL LAWBREAKERS are dealt with BY THE COURTS, just as any OTHER LAWBREAKERS.

ABLE LAWYERS and Tennessee citizens have already ENJOINED officials who want to DEFY and OVERRIDE the CONSTITUTION and the PEOPLE OF TENNESSEE.

DO YOUR BIT, ORGANIZE MASS MEETINGS, Circulate Petitions, and we will UPHOLD the Constitutional Rights of the People.

During the ratification battle in Tennessee, antisuffragists fought against the momentum built up by the thirty-five previous ratifications. They repeatedly insisted that the federal suffrage amendment *could be stopped*. And they charged, quite forcefully here, that any legislator who voted for ratification acted in violation of his oath, because of certain provisions in the state constitution that they believed precluded ratification during this special session. Josephine Pearson Papers, Tennessee State Library and Archives. Courtesy of the Tennessee Historical Society.

Mass Meeting

TONIGHT

Ryman Auditorium

8 O'CLOCK

TO SAVE THE SOUTH

FROM THE SUSAN B. ANTHONY AMENDMENT
AND FEDERAL SUFFRAGE FORCE BILLS

Senator Oscar W. Underwood, of Alabama, and Ex-Gov. Ruffin G. Pleasant, of Louisiana, Have Been Invited to Speak

MAJ. E. B. STAHLMAN
MISS CHARLOTTE E. ROWE
HON. FRANK P. BOND
AND
PROF. GUS DYER
WILL SPEAK
MRS. THOMAS H. MALONE, JR.
WILL SING
JUDGE J. C. HIGGINS
WILL PRESIDE

EVERYBODY INVITED

Even after the Tennessee legislature adopted the ratification resolution, the antisuffragists fought on for weeks. They labored desperately to arouse public opinion against ratification through meetings such as this one at the Ryman Auditorium, later the home of the Grand Ole Opry. Carrie Chapman Catt Papers, Tennessee State Library and Archives. Courtesy of the Tennessee Historical Society.

The Nation Watches: Cartoonists' Depictions of the Ratification Struggle in Tennessee and the Victory of the Nineteenth Amendment, 1920

Cartoonists for newspapers all over the nation used the image of an elderly, distinguished-looking southern gentleman to represent Tennessee, sometimes calling him "Colonel Tennessee." In this cartoon from the August 9, 1920, *World*, "Suffrage," in classical attire, pleads with the legislator as he begins the special session. Carrie Chapman Catt Papers, Tennessee State Library and Archives. Courtesy of the Tennessee Historical Society.

This cartoon from one of the Nashville papers dated August 10, 1920, shows "Colonel Tennessee" chivalrously leaping over "Constitutional Technicalities" to help "suffrage" leap over "strong opposition" from the thirty-fifth to the thirty-sixth step, with the caption: "What does one care for a high fence and deep water, when such an opportunity presents itself?" Carrie Chapman Catt Papers, Tennessee State Library and Archives. Courtesy of the Tennessee Historical Society.

A Sacramento, California, paper shows "Woman Suffrage" sending presidential candidates James Cox and Warren Harding out to round up the thirty-sixth sheep, which she wants in the fold before November. Carrie Chapman Catt Papers, Tennessee State Library and Archives. Courtesy of the Tennessee Historical Society.

Here the ineffectual representatives of their parties, Cox and Harding, having failed to secure ratification from Louisiana (Democratic) and Vermont (Republican), urge the suffragist on to "Tennessee and Points South." She seems less than thrilled that they are leaving the task of securing the thirty-sixth state to her while "both [were] seeking her favor." Carrie Chapman Catt Papers, Tennessee State Library and Archives. Courtesy of the Tennessee Historical Society.

At times, suffragists felt that Cox and Harding were "cozying up" to antisuffragists even while "professing" and "declaring" their support for suffrage. Carrie Chapman Catt Papers, Tennessee State Library and Archives. Courtesy of the Tennessee Historical Society.

Most of the time Democrats and Republicans seemed to be singing the same song, courting the votes of women that they expected *would* be voting in the November 1920 presidential election. Here the donkey and the elephant sing a parody of a popular song in a cartoon distributed by the *Philadelphia Inquirer.* Carrie Chapman Catt Papers, Tennessee State Library and Archives. Courtesy of the Tennessee Historical Society.

A Rochester, New York, cartoonist represented "Colonel Tennessee" as occupying the "hot seat" between pro- and antisuffrage women vying for his favor during the special session. One Tennessee legislator actually wore a boutonniere made of both red and yellow roses, refused to yield to the pleading of either side, and remained neutral throughout the "War of the Roses." Carrie Chapman Catt Papers, Tennessee State Library and Archives. Courtesy of the Tennessee Historical Society.

When victory finally came, Colonel Tennessee is shown handing the ballot to a young suffragist, while the cartoonist reminds Americans of 1920 of the many women who fought for the victory but did not live to see it. Pictured are the shadowy images of Inez Milholland, Lillie Devereux Blake, Susan B. Anthony, Elizabeth Cady Stanton, Dr. Anna Howard Shaw, Eliza Tupper Wilkes, and Madame [Carolina M.] Severance. Carrie Chapman Catt Papers, Tennessee State Library and Archives. Courtesy of the Tennessee Historical Society.

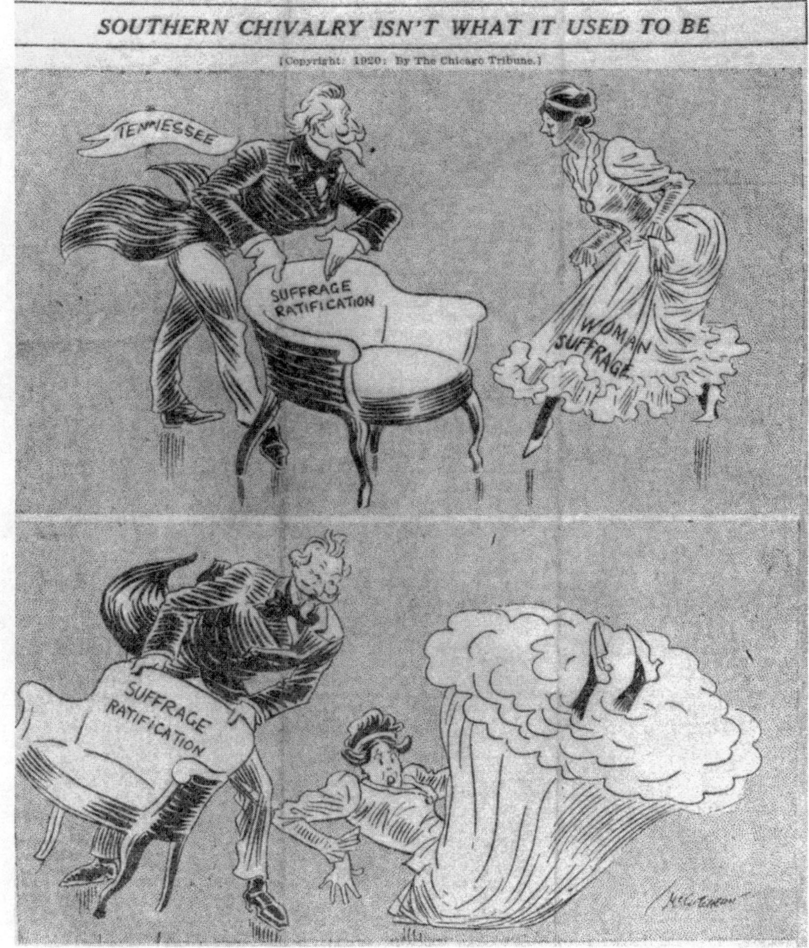

The *Chicago Tribune* viewed the "fight to the last-ditch" efforts of the Tennessee antisuffrage men to prevent ratification—even after Harry Burn's change of heart gave the ratification resolution a majority in the House—as decidedly *unchivalrous*. Carrie Chapman Catt Papers, Tennessee State Library and Archives. Courtesy of the Tennessee Historical Society.

"Thurlby," the cartoonist for the *Washington Times* (Seattle), presented the Tennessee antisuffragists as childish, giving women the vote and then taking it back. Carrie Chapman Catt Papers, Tennessee State Library and Archives. Courtesy of the Tennessee Historical Society.

Here "Uncle Sam" is joined by his "New Partner," as "Miss Columbia" enters carrying with her twelve million votes. He says, "WELL! HERE SHE COMES! I ALWAYS HAD TO LISTEN TO HER ADVICE—NOW I GUESS I GOT TO *TAKE* IT!" The suffragists, no doubt, would have said that was *precisely* the point, and the most important result of their victory; woman's *indirect influence* could be discounted and ignored, but *direct influence* exercised through the ballot could not be disregarded. Carrie Chapman Catt Papers, Tennessee State Library and Archives. Courtesy of the Tennessee Historical Society.

The cartoonist for the *Indianapolis News* posed to the newly enfranchised woman voter "THE QUESTION" that was on the minds of all Americans: "Whatcha goin' t' do with it." Carrie Chapman Catt Papers, Tennessee State Library and Archives. Courtesy of the Tennessee Historical Society.

Bibliography

Manuscript Collections and Interviews

Rachel Avery-Susan B. Anthony Papers. University of Rochester Archives, Rochester, N.Y.

Madeline McDowell Breckinridge Papers. In the Breckinridge Family Papers, Manuscript Division, Library of Congress, Washington, D.C.

Harry T. Burn Scrapbook. Manuscript Department, Special Collections, University of Tennessee Library, Knoxville, Tenn.

Carrie Chapman Catt Papers (#72–119). Tennessee State Library and Archives, Nashville, Tenn.

Laura Clay Papers. Special Collections and Archives, Margaret I. King Library, University of Kentucky, Lexington, Ky.

Otelia Carrington Cuningham Connor Papers (#3228). Southern Historical Collection, Wilson Library, University of North Carolina, Chapel Hill, N.C.

Collins D. Elliott-Lizzie Elliott Papers. Tennessee State Library and Archives, Nashville, Tenn.

Anne Dallas Dudley. Interview by A. Elizabeth Taylor, Jan. 16, 1943.

Rebecca Latimer Felton Papers. Special Collections Division, Hargrett Rare Book and Manuscript Library, University of Georgia, Athens, Ga.

Emily Howland Papers. Cornell University Archives, Ithaca, N.Y.

Judge Lucy Somerville Howorth. Interview by Constance Ashton Myers, June 20, 22, 23, 1975, Monteagle, Tennessee (#4007). Southern Oral History Collection, Southern Historical Collection, University of North Carolina, Chapel Hill, N.C.

———. Interview by Marjorie Spruill Wheeler, Mar. 15, 1983, Cleveland, Miss., and Mar. 6, 1984, Hattiesburg, Miss. Vol. 297, pt. II, 1983. The Mississippi Oral History Program of The University of Southern Mississippi.

Pattie Ruffner Jacobs Diaries. Property of Mr. and Mrs. John L. Hillhouse Jr., Birmingham, Ala.

Pattie Ruffner Jacobs Papers. Department of Archives and Manuscripts, Birmingham Public Library, Birmingham, Ala.

Mary Johnston Papers (#3588). Manuscripts Division, Special Collections Department, University of Virginia Library, Charlottesville, Va.

Belle Kearney Papers (#Z/778; Z/778.1). Mississippi Department of Archives and History, Jackson, Miss.

Winonah Bond Logan. Interviews by Adele Logan Alexander, 1983–90, Alexandria, Va.

Catherine Waugh McCulloch Papers. Schlesinger Library, Radcliffe College, Cambridge, Mass.

National American Woman Suffrage Association (NAWSA) Papers. Manuscripts Division, Library of Congress, Washington, D.C.

Josephine A. Pearson Papers (#74–99). Tennessee State Library and Archives, Nashville, Tenn.

Edwin A. Price Scrapbook. Tennessee State Library and Archives, Nashville, Tenn.

A. H. Roberts Papers. Tennessee State Library and Archives, Nashville, Tenn.

Somerville-Howorth Family Papers (Papers of Nellie Nugent Somerville and her daughter Lucy Somerville Howorth and their family). Schlesinger Library, Radcliffe College, Cambridge, Mass.

Mary Church Terrell Papers. Manuscript Division, Library of Congress, Washington, D.C.

Lila Hardaway Meade Valentine Papers (MSS1V2345a). Division of Manuscripts and Archives, Virginia Historical Society, Richmond, Va.

Virginia Suffrage Papers. Virginia State Library and Archives, Richmond, Va.

Bess Bolden Walcott. Interview by Adele Logan Alexander, Dec. 1983, Tuskegee, Ala.

Booker T. Washington Papers. Manuscript Division, Library of Congress, Washington, D.C.

Margaret Murray Washington Papers. Tuskegee University Library, Tuskegee, Ala.

White, Sue Shelton. Papers. Schlesinger Library, Radcliffe College, Cambridge, Mass.

Secondary Sources and Contemporary Accounts

Addams, Jane. *Peace and Bread in Time of War*. New York: The MacMillan Company, 1922.

Alexander, Adele Logan. "Grandmother, Grandfather, W. E. B. Du Bois and Booker T. Washington." *Crisis* (Feb. 1983): 8–11.

———. "How I Discovered My Grandmother, and the Truth about Black Women and the Suffrage Movement." Ms. (Nov. 1983): 29–33.

———. *Ambiguous Lives: Free Women of Color in Rural Georgia, 1789–1879*. Fayetteville: University of Arkansas Press, 1991.

Allen, Lee N. "The Woman Suffrage Movement in Alabama, 1910–1920." *Alabama Review* 11 (Apr. 1958): 83–99.

Ambrose, Andrew M. "Sister Reforms: An Examination of the Relationship Between the Tennessee Woman's Christian Temperance Union and the State Woman Suffrage Movement, 1890–1920." M.A. thesis, University of Tennessee, 1979.

Andolsen, Barbara Hilkert. *"Daughters of Jefferson, Daughters of Bootblacks": Racism and American Feminism*. Macon, Ga.: Mercer University Press, 1986.

Anthony, Susan B., and Ida Husted Harper, eds. *History of Woman Suffrage*, Vol. 4. Rochester, N.Y.: 1902.

Aptheker, Bettina. *Woman's Legacy: Essays on Race, Sex, and Class in American History*. Amherst: University of Massachusetts Press, 1982.

Arendale, Marirose. "Tennessee and Women's Rights." *Tennessee Historical Quarterly* 39 (Spring 1980): 62–78.

Baker, Paula. "The Domestication of Politics: Women and American Political Society, 1780–1920." *American Historical Review* 89 (June 1984): 620–47.

Banner, Lois W. *Elizabeth Cady Stanton: A Radical for Women's Rights*. Boston: Little, Brown and Co., 1980.

Barry, Kathleen. *Susan B. Anthony: A Biography of a Singular Feminist*. New York: New York University Press, 1988.

Beeton, Beverly. *Women Vote in the West: The Woman Suffrage Movement, 1869–1896*. New York: Garland Publishing, Inc., 1986.

Berkeley, Kathleen Christine. "'An Advocate for Her Sex': Feminism and Conservatism in the Post–Civil War South." *Tennessee Historical Quarterly* 43 (Winter 1984): 390–407.

Bird, Agnes Thornton. "Legal Status of Women in Tennessee, the First Seventy-five Years." *Tennessee Bar Journal* 15 (Feb. 1979).

Bland, Sidney R. "Mad Women of the Cause: The National Woman's Party in the South." *Furman Studies* 26 (Dec. 1980): 82–91.

———. "Fighting the Odds: Militant Suffragists in South Carolina." *South Carolina Historical Magazine* 82 (Jan. 1981): 32–43.

Bledsoe, Albert Taylor. "The Mission of Woman." *Southern Review* 9 (Oct. 1871): 923–42.

Bordin, Ruth. *Woman and Temperance: The Quest for Power and Liberty, 1873–1900*. Philadelphia: Temple University Press, 1981.

———. *Frances Willard: A Biography*. Chapel Hill: University of North Carolina Press, 1986.

Branch, Taylor. *Parting the Waters: America in the King Years, 1954–63*. New York: Simon and Schuster, 1988.

Breault, Judith Colucci. *The World of Emily Howland: Odyssey of a Humanitarian*. Millbrae, Calif.: Les Femmes, 1974.

Breckinridge, Sophonisba P. *Madeline McDowell Breckinridge: A Leader in the New South*. Chicago: University of Chicago Press, 1921.

Buechler, Steven. *The Transformation of the Woman Suffrage Movement: The Case of Illinois, 1850–1920*. New Brunswick, N.J.: Rutgers University Press, 1986.

Buhle, Mari Jo, and Paul Buhle, eds. *Concise History of Woman Suffrage: Selections from the Classic Work of Stanton, Anthony, Gage, and Harper*. Urbana: University of Illinois Press, 1978.

Camhi, Jane Jerome. "Women Against Women: American Antisuffragism, 1880–1920." Ph.D. diss., Tufts University, 1974.

Catt, Carrie Chapman, and Nettie Rogers Shuler. *Woman Suffrage and Politics: The Inner Story of the Suffrage Movement*. 1923. Reprint, Seattle: University of Washington Press, 1970.

Cott, Nancy F. *The Grounding of Modern Feminism*. New Haven: Yale University Press, 1987.

Dodge, Mrs. Arthur M. "Another Suffrage Invention." *The Remonstrance Against Woman Suffrage* (Apr. 1916): 5.

Doyle, Don. *New Men, New Cities, New South: Atlanta, Nashville, Charleston, Mobile, 1860–1910*. Chapel Hill: University of North Carolina Press, 1990.

DuBois, Ellen Carol. "The Radicalism of the Woman Suffrage Movement: Toward a Reconstruction of Nineteenth-Century Feminism." *Feminist Studies* 3 (Fall 1975): 63–75.

———. *Feminism and Suffrage: The Emergence of an Independent Women's Movement in America, 1848–1869*. Ithaca: Cornell University Press, 1978.

———. "Outgrowing the Compact of the Fathers: Equal Rights, Woman Suffrage, and the United States Constitution, 1820–1878." *Journal of American History* 74 (Dec. 1987): 836–62.

———. "Making Women's History: Activist Historians of Women's Rights, 1880–1940." *Radical History Review* 49 (Winter 1991): 61–84.

———., ed. *The Elizabeth Cady Stanton–Susan B. Anthony Reader*. Boston: Northeastern University Press, 1992.

Duniway, Abigail Scott. *Path Breaking: An Autobiographical History of the Equal Suffrage Movement in Pacific Coast States*. 1914. Reprint, New York: Schocken Books, 1971.

Elshtain, Jean Bethke. *Public Man, Private Woman: Women in Social and Political Thought*. Princeton, N.J.: Princeton University Press, 1981.

———. "Aristotle, The Public-Private Split, and the Case of the Suffragists." In *The Family in Political Thought*. Edited by Jean Bethke Elshtain, 51–65. Amherst: University of Massachusetts Press, 1982.

———. "The Politics of Gender." *The Progressive* (Feb. 1984): 22–25.

———. *Meditations on Modern Political Thought: Masculine/Feminine Themes from Luther to Arendt*. New York: Praeger, 1986.

———. *Women and War*. New York: Basic Books, 1987.

———. *Power Trips and Other Journeys: Essays in Feminism As Civil Discourse*. Madison, Wisc.: University of Wisconsin Press, 1991.

———. *But Was It Just?: Reflections on the Morality of the Persian Gulf War*. New York: Doubleday, 1992.

Elshtain, Jean Bethke, and Sheila Tobias, eds. *Women, Militarism, and War: Essays in History, Politics, and Social Theory*. Savage, Md.: Rowman and Littlefield, 1990.

Felton, Rebecca Latimer. *Country Life in Georgia in the Days of My Youth*. Atlanta, 1919.

———. *The Romantic Story of Georgia Women*. Atlanta, 1930.

Flexner, Eleanor. *Century of Struggle: The Woman's Rights Movement in the United States*. New York: Atheneum, 1974.

Floyd, Josephine Bone. "Rebecca Latimer Felton: Political Independent." *Georgia Historical Quarterly* 30 (Mar. 1946): 14–34.

———. "Rebecca Latimer Felton: Champion of Women's Rights." *Georgia Historical Quarterly* 30 (June 1946): 81–104.

Foner, Philip S. *Frederick Douglass on Women's Rights*. New York: Da Capo Press, 1992.

Ford, Linda G. *Iron-Jawed Angels: The Suffrage Militancy of the National Women's Party, 1912–1920*. Lanham, Md.: University Press of America, Inc., 1991.

Foster, Gaines M. *Ghosts of the Confederacy: Defeat, the Lost Cause, and the Emergence of the New South*. New York: Oxford University Press, 1987.

Fowler, Robert Booth. *Carrie Catt: Feminist Politician*. Boston: Northeastern University Press, 1986.

Frankel, Noralee, and Nancy S. Dye, eds. *Gender, Class, Race and Reform in the Progressive Era*. Lexington: University of Kentucky Press, 1991.

Franzen, Monika, and Nancy Ethiel. *Make Way! 200 Years of American Women in Cartoons*. Chicago: Chicago Review Press, 1988.

Freedman, Estelle. "Separatism as Strategy: Female Institution Building and American Feminism." *Feminist Studies* 5 (1979): 512–29.

Fuller, Margaret. *The Writings of Margaret Fuller*. Edited by Mason Wade. New York: Viking Press, 1941.

Fuller, Paul E. *Laura Clay and the Woman's Rights Movement*. Lexington: University Press of Kentucky, 1975.

———. "An Early Venture of Kentucky Women in Politics: The Breckinridge Congressional Campaign of 1894." *Filson Club History Quarterly* 63 (Apr. 1989): 224–42.

Gaston, Paul M. *The New South Creed: A Study in Southern Mythmaking*. Baton Rouge: Louisiana State University Press, 1970.

Gay, Dorothy Ann. "The Tangled Skein of Romanticism and Violence in the Old South: The Southern Response to Abolitionism and Feminism, 1830–1861." Ph.D. diss., University of North Carolina, 1975.

Giddings, Paula. *When and Where I Enter: The Impact of Black Women on Race and Sex in America*. New York: William Morrow and Company, 1984.

Gilley, B. H. "Kate Gordon and Louisiana Woman Suffrage." *Louisiana History* 24 (Summer 1983).

Gilmore, Glenda Elizabeth. "Gender and Jim Crow: Women and the Politics of White Supremacy in North Carolina, 1896–1920." Ph.D. diss., University of North Carolina, Chapel Hill, 1992.

Gluck, Sherna, ed. *From Parlor to Prison*. New York: Vintage Books, 1976.

Goldman, Emma. *The Traffic in Women*. New York: Times Change Press, 1970.

Goodrich, Gillian. "Romance and Reality: The Birmingham Suffragists, 1982–1920." *The Journal of the Birmingham Historical Society* 5 (Jan. 1978): 4–21.

Gordon, Ann D. "The Political Is the Personal: Two Autobiographies of Woman Suffragists." *American Women's Autobiography: Fea(s)ts of Memory*. Edited by Margo Culley, 111–27. Madison: University of Wisconsin Press, 1992.

Graham, Sara Hunter. "Woodrow Wilson, Alice Paul, and the Woman Suffrage Movement." *Political Science Quarterly* 4 (1983–84): 665–79.

———. "Woman Suffrage in Virginia: The Equal Suffrage League and Pressure Group Politics, 1909–1920." *The Virginia Magazine of History and Biography* 101 (Apr. 1993): 227–50.

Grantham, Dewey W. *Southern Progressivism: The Reconciliation of Progress and Tradition*. Knoxville: University of Tennessee Press, 1983.

Green, Elna C. "Those Opposed: The Antisuffragists in North Carolina, 1900–1920." *North Carolina Historical Review* 67 (July 1990): 315–33.

———. "Those Opposed: Southern Antisuffragism, 1890–1920." Ph.D. diss., Tulane University, 1992.

———. "The Rest of the Story: Kate Gordon and the Opposition to the Nineteenth Amendment in the South." *Louisiana History* 33 (Spring 1992): 171–89.

Griffith, Elisabeth. *In Her Own Right: The Life of Elizabeth Cady Stanton*. New York: Oxford University Press, 1985.

Grimes, Alan P. *The Puritan Ethic and Woman Suffrage*. New York: Oxford University Press, 1967.

Hale, Will T., and Dixon C. Merritt. *A History of Tennessee and Tennesseans: The Leaders and Representative Men in Commerce, Industry and Modern Activities*. Chicago and New York: Lewis Publishing Co., 1913.

Hall, Jacquelyn Dowd. *Revolt Against Chivalry: Jessie Daniel Ames and the Women's Campaign Against Lynching*. New York: Columbia University Press, 1979.

———. "'The Mind That Burns in Each Body': Women, Rape, and Racial Violence." In *Powers of Desire: The Politics of Sexuality*. Edited by Ann Snitow, Christine Stansell, and Sharon Thompson, 328–49. New York: Monthly Review Press, 1983.

Hanmer, Trudy J. "A Divine Discontent: Mary Johnston and Woman Suffrage in Virginia." M.A. thesis, University of Virginia, 1972.

Harlan, Louis R. *Booker T. Washington: The Making of a Black Leader, 1901–1915*. New York: Oxford University Press, 1972.

Harlan, Louis R., and Raymond W. Smock, eds. *The Booker T. Washington Papers*, Vol. 11. Urbana: University of Illinois Press, 1981.

Harley, Sharon, and Rosalyn Terborg-Penn. *The Afro-American Woman: Struggles and Images*. Port Washington, N.Y.: Kennikat Press, 1978.

Harper, Ida Husted, ed. *History of Woman Suffrage*. Vols. 5 and 6. New York: National American Woman Suffrage Association, 1922.

Hay, Melba Porter. "Madeline McDowell Breckinridge: Kentucky Suffragist and Progressive Reformer." Ph.D. diss., University of Kentucky, 1980.

Hays, Elinor R. *Morning Star: A Biography of Lucy Stone*. New York: Harcourt, Brace and World, 1961.

Hecker, Eugene A. *A Short History of Woman Suffrage*. New York: J. P. Putnam's Sons, 1919.

Hersh, Blanche Glassman. *The Slavery of Sex: Feminist-Abolitionists in America*. Urbana and Chicago: University of Illinois Press, 1978.

Hewitt, Nancy A., and Suzanne Lebsock, eds. *Visible Women: New Essays on American Activism*. Urbana: University of Illinois Press, 1993.

Hine, Darlene Clark, ed. *Black Women in United States History*. Brooklyn, N.Y.: Carlson Publishing, Inc., 1990.

Hine, Darlene Clark, Elsa Barkley Brown, and Rosalyn Terborg-Penn, eds. *Black Women in America: An Historical Encyclopedia*. Brooklyn, N.Y.: Carlson Publishing, Inc., 1993.

Holland, Patricia G., and Ann D. Gordon, eds. *Papers of Elizabeth Cady Stanton and Susan B. Anthony*. Wilmington, Del.: Scholarly Resources Inc., 1991. Microfilm edition.

House and Senate Journals of the Extraordinary Session of the Sixty-first General Assembly of the State of Tennessee. Nashville, Tenn., 1920.

Humphrey, Janet G. *A Texas Suffragist: Diaries and Writings of Jane Y. McCallum*. Austin: Ellen C. Temple, Publisher, 1988.

Irwin, Inez Haynes. *The Story of the Woman's Party*. New York: Harcourt, Brace, and Company, 1921.

Isaac, Paul E. *Prohibition and Politics: Turbulent Decades in Tennessee, 1885–1920*. Knoxville: University of Tennessee Press, 1965.

James, Edward T., and Janet Wilson James. *Notable American Women: A Biographical Dictionary*. Vols. 1–3. Cambridge: Harvard University Press, 1971.

Jemison, Marie Stokes. "Ladies Become Voters: Pattie Ruffner Jacobs and Women's Suffrage in Alabama." *Southern Exposure* 7 (Spring 1979): 48–59.

Johnson, Kenneth R. "Kate Gordon and the Woman Suffrage Movement in the South." *Journal of Southern History* 38 (Aug. 1972): 365–92.

Johnston, Mary. "The Woman's War." *Atlantic Monthly* (Apr. 1910).

———. *Hagar*. Edited with an Introduction by Marjorie Spruill Wheeler. Charlottesville: University Press of Virginia, 1994. First published in Boston by Houghton Mifflin, 1913.

Jones, Anne Goodwyn. *Tomorrow Is Another Day: The Woman Writer in the South, 1859–1936*. Baton Rouge: Louisiana State University Press, 1981.

Jones, Jacqueline. *Labor of Love, Labor of Sorrow: Black Women, Work and the Family, from Slavery to the Present*. New York: Random House, 1985.

Kearney, Belle. A *Slaveholder's Daughter*. Abbey Press, 1900. Reprint, New York: Negro Universities Press, 1969.

Kemp, Kathryn W. "Jean and Kate Gordon: New Orleans Social Reformers, 1898–1933." *Louisiana History* 24 (1983): 389–401.

Kerr, Andrea Moore. *Lucy Stone: Speaking Out for Equality*. New Brunswick, N.J.: Rutgers University Press, 1992.

Kimmel, Michael S., and Thomas E. Mosmiller, eds. *Against the Tide: Pro-Feminist Men in the United States 1776–1990*. Boston: Beacon Press, 1992.

Klein, Maury. *History of the Louisville and Nashville Railroad*. New York: Macmillan, 1972.

Kousser, J. Morgan. *The Shaping of Southern Politics: Suffrage Restriction and the Establishment of the One-Party South, 1880–1910*. New Haven: Yale University Press, 1974.

Kraditor, Aileen, "Tactical Problems of the Woman Suffrage Movement in the South." *Louisiana Studies* 5 (Winter 1966): 289–307.

———. *The Ideas of the Woman Suffrage Movement, 1890–1920*. New York: W. W. Norton and Company, 1981.

———, ed. *Up from the Pedestal: Selected Writings in the History of American Feminism*. Chicago: Quadrangle Books, 1968.

Lawson, Steven F. *Running for Freedom: Civil Rights and Black Politics in America Since 1941*. Philadelphia: Temple University Press, 1991.

Lebsock, Suzanne. "Woman Suffrage and White Supremacy: A Virginia Case Study." In Nancy A. Hewitt and Suzanne Lebsock, *Visible Women: New Essays on American Activism*. Urbana and Chicago: University of Illinois Press, 1993.

Lerner, Gerda. *The Grimké Sisters from South Carolina*. New York: Schocken Books, 1971.

Lindig, Carmen Meriwether. "The Woman's Movement in Louisiana, 1879–1920." Ph.D. diss., North Texas State University, 1983.

Link, William A. *The Changing Face of Southern Progressivism: Social Policy and Localism, 1880–1930*. Chapel Hill: University of North Carolina Press, 1992.

Logan, Adella Hunt. "Woman Suffrage." *The Colored American* (Sept. 1905).

———. "Colored Women as Voters." *Crisis* (Sept. 1912).

Louis, James P. "Sue Shelton White and the Woman Suffrage Movement, 1913–1920." *Tennessee Historical Quarterly* 22 (June 1963): 170–90.

Lunardini, Christine A. *From Equal Suffrage to Equal Rights: Alice Paul and the National Woman's Party, 1910–1928*. New York: New York University Press, 1986.

Lunardini, Christine A., and Thomas J. Knock. "Woodrow Wilson and Woman Suffrage: A New Look." *Political Science Quarterly* 95 (4) (1980–81): 655–71.

Marshall, Susan E. "In Defense of Separate Spheres: Class and Status Politics in the Antisuffrage Movement." *Social Forces* 65 (Dec. 1986): 327–51.

Mathews, Donald G., and Jane Sherron De Hart. *Sex, Gender, and the Politics of ERA*. New York: Oxford University Press, 1990.

Matthews, Glenna. *The Rise of Public Woman: Woman's Power and Woman's Place in the United States, 1630–1970*. New York: Schocken Books, 1971.

May, Antoinette. *Different Drummers: They Did What They Wanted*. Millbrae, Calif.: Les Femmes, 1976.

McArthur, Judith N. "Motherhood and Reform in the New South: Texas Women During the Progressive Era." Ph.D. diss., University of Texas, 1992.

McDowell, John Patrick. *The Social Gospel in the South: The Woman's Home Mission Movement in the Methodist Episcopal Church, South, 1886–1939*. Baton Rouge: Louisiana State University Press, 1982.

Melder, Keith. *Beginnings of Sisterhood: The American Women's Rights Movement 1800–1850*. New York: Schocken Books, 1977.

Merk, Lois Bannister. "Massachusetts in the Woman Suffrage Movement." Ph.D. diss., Harvard University, 1961.

Moore, John Trotwood. *Tennessee: The Volunteer State 1769–1923*. Chicago, Nashville: S. J. Clarke Publishing Company, 1923.

Morgan, David. *Suffragists and Democrats: The Politics of Woman Suffrage in America*. East Lansing: Michigan State University Press, 1972.

National American Woman Suffrage Association. *Proceedings of the Twenty-seventh Annual Convention of the National American Woman Suffrage Association . . . Held in Atlanta, Georgia, January 31–February 5, 1895*. Warren, Ohio: William R. Ritezel and Company, n.d.

National American Woman Suffrage Association Convention Proceedings, 1900. Schlesinger Library, Radcliffe College, Cambridge, Mass.

———. *VICTORY: How Women Won It: A Centennial Symposium, 1840–1940*. New York: H. W. Wilson Company, 1940.

Neverdon-Morton, Cynthia. "Self-Help Programs as Educative Activities of Black Women in the South, 1895–1925: Focus on Four Key Areas." *Journal of Negro Education* 51 (1982): 207–21.

———. *Afro-American Women of the South and the Advancement of the Race, 1895–1925*. Knoxville: University of Tennessee Press, 1989.

Norrell, Robert J. *Reaping the Whirlwind: The Civil Rights Movement in Tuskegee*. New York: Random House, 1986.

Pankhurst, Emmeline. *My Own Story*. New York: Hearst's International Library Company, 1914.

Papacristou, Judith. *Women Together: A History in Documents of the Women's Movement in the United States*. New York: Alfred A. Knopf, 1976.

Paulson, Ross Evans. *Women's Suffrage and Prohibition: A Comparative Study of Equality and Social Control*. Glenview, Ill.: Scott, Foresman and Co., 1973.

Quarles, Benjamin. "Frederick Douglass and the Woman's Rights Movement." *Journal of Negro History* 25 (Jan. 1940): 35–44.

Quirk, Paul J. "The Election." In *The Elections of 1988*. Edited by Michael Nelson. Washington, D.C.: CQ Press, 1989.

Robinson, Armstead L., and Patricia Sullivan, eds. *New Directions in Civil Rights Studies*. Charlottesville: University Press of Virginia, 1991.

Salem, Dorothy C. *To Better Our World: Black Women in Organized Reform, 1890–1920*. In Darlene Clark Hine, ed., *Black Women in United States History*. Brooklyn, N.Y.: Carlson Publishing, Inc., 1990.

Scott, Anne Firor. *The Southern Lady: From Pedestal to Politics, 1830–1930*. Chicago: University of Chicago Press, 1970.

———. *Natural Allies: Women's Associations in American History*. Urbana and Chicago: University of Illinois Press, 1991.

Scott, Anne F., and Andrew M. *One Half the People: The Fight for Woman Suffrage*. Philadelphia: J. B. Lippincott and Co., 1975.

Shahan, Joe Michael. "Reform and Politics in Tennessee, 1906–1914." Ph.D. diss., Vanderbilt University, 1981.

Shaw, Anna Howard, with Elizabeth Garver Jordan. *Story of a Pioneer*. New York: Harper and Bros., 1915.

Sheldon, Charlotte Jean. "Woman Suffrage and Virginia Politics, 1909–1920." M.A. thesis, University of Virginia, 1969.

Sheppard, Alice. *Cartooning for Suffrage*. Albuquerque: University of New Mexico Press, 1993.

Showalter, Elaine, ed. *These Modern Women: Autobiographical Essays from the Twenties*. Old Westbury, N.Y.: The Feminist Press, 1978.

Sicherman, Barbara, and Carol Hurd Green. *Notable American Women: The Modern Period*. Cambridge: Harvard University Press, 1980.

Sims, Anastatia. "'Powers That Pray and Powers That Prey': Tennessee and the Fight for Woman Suffrage." *Tennessee Historical Quarterly* (Winter 1991): 203–25.

Spiers, Patricia L. "The Woman Suffrage Movement in New Orleans," M.A. thesis, Southeastern Louisiana College, 1965.

Stanton, Elizabeth Cady. *Eighty Years and More: Reminiscences, 1815–1897*. New York: Shocken Books, 1971.

Stanton, Elizabeth Cady, Susan B. Anthony, and Ida Husted Harper, eds. *History of Woman Suffrage*. 6 vols. Rochester, N.Y., 1881–1922. Reprint, New York: Arno Press, 1969.

Sterling, Dorothy. *Ahead of Her Time: Abby Kelley and the Politics of Antislavery*. New York: W. W. Norton and Company, 1991.

Stevens, Doris. *Jailed for Freedom*. New York: Liveright, 1920.

Stewart, Ella S. "Woman Suffrage and the Liquor Traffic." *Annals of the American Academy of Political and Social Science* 56 (Nov. 1914): 143–52.

Strom, Sharon Hartman. "Leadership and Tactics in the American Suffrage Movement: A New Perspective from Massachusetts." *Journal of American History* 62 (1975): 296–315.

Taper, Bernard. *Gomillion versus Lightfoot: The Tuskegee Gerrymander Case*. New York: McGraw Hill, 1962.

Taylor, A. Elizabeth. "The Origin of the Woman Suffrage Movement in Georgia." *Georgia Historical Quarterly* 28 (June 1944): 63–79.

———. "The Woman Suffrage Movement in Texas." *The Journal of Southern History* 17 (May 1951): 194–215.

———. "The Woman Suffrage Movement in Arkansas." *Arkansas Historical Quarterly* 15 (Spring 1956): 17–52.

———. *The Woman Suffrage Movement in Tennessee*. New York: Bookman Associates, 1957.

———. "The Woman Suffrage Movement in Florida." *Florida Historical Quarterly* 36 (July 1957): 42–60.

———. "Revival and Development of the Woman Suffrage Movement in Georgia." *Georgia Historical Quarterly* 42 (Dec. 1958): 339–54.

———. "The Last Phase of the Woman Suffrage Movement in Georgia." *Georgia Historical Quarterly* 43 (Mar. 1959): 11–28.

———. "The Woman Suffrage Movement in North Carolina." *North Carolina Historical Review* 38 (Jan. and Apr. 1961): 45–62 and 173–89.

———. "The Woman Suffrage Movement in Mississippi." *Journal of Mississippi History* 30 (Feb. 1968): 1–34.

———. "South Carolina and the Enfranchisement of Women: The Early Years." *South Carolina Historical Magazine* 77 (Apr. 1976): 115-126.

———. "South Carolina and the Enfranchisement of Women: The Later Years." *South Carolina Historical Magazine* 80 (Oct. 1979): 298-310.

———. "Woman Suffrage Activities in Atlanta." *Atlanta Historical Journal* 23 (Winter 1979–1980): 45-54.

Taylor, Lloyd C., Jr. "Lila Meade Valentine: The FFV as Reformer." *Virginia Magazine of History and Biography* 70 (Oct. 1962): 471–87.

Tennessee *House Journal*, 1915, 1917, 1919, Called Session, 1920.

Tennessee *Senate Journal*, 1915, 1917, 1919, Called Session, 1920.

Terborg-Penn, Rosalyn. "Nineteenth Century Black Women and Woman Suffrage." *Potomac Review* 7 (1977): 13–24.

———. "Afro-Americans in the Struggle for Woman Suffrage." Ph.D. dissertation, Howard University, 1978.

———. "Discrimination against Afro-American Women in the Woman's Movement, 1830–1920." In *The Afro-American Woman: Struggles and Images*. Rosalyn Terborg-Penn and Sharon Harley, eds. Port Washington, N.Y.: Kennikat Press, 1978.

Terrell, Mary Church. "Woman Suffrage and the 15th Amendment." *Crisis* (Sept. 1915).

Thomas, Mary Martha. *The New Woman in Alabama: Social Reforms and Suffrage, 1890–1920*. Tuscaloosa: University of Alabama Press, 1992.

———, ed. *Stepping Out of the Shadows: Alabama Women, 1819–1990*. Tuscaloosa: University of Alabama Press, 1995.

Thurner, Manuela. "'Better Citizens Without the Ballot': American AntiSuffrage Women and Their Rationale During the Progressive Era." *Journal of Women's History* 5 (Spring 1993): 33–60.

Van Voris, Jacqueline. *Carrie Chapman Catt: A Public Life*. New York: The Feminist Press, 1987.

Vertrees, John J. "An Address to the Men of Tennessee on Federal Suffrage." Nashville, 1916.

Walker, S. Jay. "Frederick Douglass and Woman Suffrage." *Black Scholar* 14 (1983): 18–23.

Welch, Richard E., Jr. *George Frisbie Hoar and the Half-Breed Republicans*. Cambridge: Harvard University Press, 1971.

Wells-Barnett, Ida B. "How Enfranchisement Stops Lynching." *Original Rights Magazine*, June 1910.

Wheeler, Marjorie Spruill. "Mary Johnston, Suffragist." *The Virginia Magazine of History and Biography* 100 (Jan. 1992): 99–118.

———. *New Women of the New South: The Leaders of the Woman Suffrage Movement in the Southern States*. New York: Oxford University Press, 1993.

———. Introduction to *Hagar*, by Mary Johnston. First published 1913. Charlottesville: University Press of Virginia, 1994.

———, ed. *One Woman, One Vote: Rediscovering the Woman Suffrage Movement*. Troutdale, Ore.: NewSage Press, 1995.

Whites, LeeAnn. "Rebecca Latimer Felton and the Problem of 'Protection' in the New South." In *Visible Women: Essays in Honor of Anne Firor Scott*. Edited by Nancy Hewitt and Suzanne Lebsock. Urbana: University of Illinois Press, 1993.

Williamson, Joel. *The Crucible of Race: Black-White Relations in the American South Since Emancipation*. New York: Oxford University Press, 1984.

Wilson, Charles Reagan. *Baptized in Blood: The Religion of the Lost Cause, 1865–1920*. Athens: University of Georgia Press, 1980.

Winegarten, Ruth, and Judith N. McArthur, eds. *Citizens at Last: The Woman Suffrage Movement in Texas*. Austin, Tex.: Ellen C. Temple, Publisher, 1987.

Wollstonecraft, Mary. *A Vindication of the Rights of Woman*. Edited by Charles W. Hagelman Jr. New York: W. W. Norton and Company, Inc., 1972.

Yellin, Carol Lynn. "Countdown in Tennessee." *American Heritage* 30 (1978): 12–23, 26–35.

Yellin, Jean Fagan. "DuBois' *Crisis* and Woman's Suffrage," *Massachusetts Review* 14 (Spring 1973): 365–75.

———. *Women & Sisters: The Antislavery Feminists in American Culture*. New Haven: Yale University Press, 1989.

Zimmerman, Loretta Ellen. "Alice Paul and the National Woman's Party, 1912–1920." Ph.D. diss., Tulane University, 1964.

Newspapers

Chattanooga News, Nov. 10, 1914.

Memphis Commercial, May 19, 1889.

Memphis Commercial-Appeal, Apr. 25, 1900; Dec. 21, 1906.

Nashville American, May 12, 13, 1897.

Nashville Banner, July 24, 1920.

Nashville Tennessean, Jan. 20, 1917; Feb. 2, 1917; Aug. 6, 1920; Aug. 25, 1920; Aug. 27, 1920; Sept. 1, 1920; Sept. 5, 1920; and Sept. 13, 1992.

Revolution, selected issues.

Richmond News-Leader, Sept. 24, 1936.

Suffragist, 1916–1920.

Tuskegee Student, selected issues.

Woman Citizen, 1917–1920.

Woman Patriot, 1918–1920.

Woman's Journal, selected issues.

Contributors

ADELE LOGAN ALEXANDER graduated from Radcliffe College where she majored in architecture and urban planning. She held a number of positions in government and in business (as well as serving on the District of Columbia's Board of Higher Education) before the discovery of her grandmother, Adella Hunt Logan's, amazing suffrage career led her to an interest in history. She has recently completed her Ph.D. in American history at Howard University. She lectured in African-American and women's history at the University of Maryland, College Park, Howard University, and Washington's Trinity College, and is a visiting professor of history at George Washington University. Her book *Ambiguous Lives: Free Women of Color in Rural Georgia, 1789–1879*, 1991, won a 1992 Gustavus Meyer award. She has also contributed chapters to several other books and published articles in *Ms.*, *Washingtonian*, *The Washington Post*, *Woman's Review of Books*, and *American Visions*. She is presently compiling and editing a collection of essays about women in the orbit of Booker T. Washington.

JEAN BETHKE ELSHTAIN is Laura Spelman Rockefeller Professor of Social and Political Ethics in the Divinity School, the University of Chicago. Previously, she was Centennial Professor of Political Science at Vanderbilt University. Among her many scholarly publications are *Democracy on Trial* 1994; *Power Trips and Other Journeys: Essays in Feminism as Civic Discourse*, 1990; *Rebuilding the Nest: A New Commitment to the American Family*, 1990; *Women, Militarism, and the Arms Race* (co-editor with Sheila Tobias), 1990; *Meditations on Modern Political Thought: Masculine/Feminine Themes Luther to Arendt*, 1986;

Women and War, 1987; *The Family in Political Thought* (editor), 1982; and *Public Man, Private Woman: Women in Social and Political Thought*, 1981. She is currently working on a biography of Jane Addams. She has also published more than a hundred articles or chapters in books and essays, and she serves on the editorial board of numerous journals. Previously on the faculties of the University of Massachusetts, Amherst, Northeastern University, and Colorado State University, she has been a visiting professor at Yale, Oberlin, and Smith College. She received her Ph.D. from Brandeis University.

ANN D. GORDON is an associate research professor of history at Rutgers University in New Brunswick. She co-edited the comprehensive *Papers of Elizabeth Cady Stanton and Susan B. Anthony*, microfilm edition, 1991, 1992, with Patricia G. Holland, and is now editing the multivolume *Selected Papers of Stanton and Anthony*. A list of her articles on women's history includes "Afterword" in Elizabeth Cady Stanton, *Eighty Years and More*, 1993; "The Political Is the Personal: Two Autobiographies of Woman Suffragists" in *American Women's Autobiography: Fea(s)ts of Memory*, edited by Margo Culley, 1992; "The Young Ladies Academy of Philadelphia" in *Women of America: A History*, edited by Carol Ruth Berkin and Mary Beth Norton, 1979; and the pioneering "Women in American Society: An Historical Introduction," co-authored with Mari Jo Buhle and Nancy Schrom Dye, first published in *Radical America* in 1971. In 1992 she authored *Using the Nation's Documentary Heritage: The Report of the Historical Documents Study* for the National Historical Publications and Records Commission and the American Council of Learned Societies. She has published *The College of Philadelphia, 1749–1779: Impact of an Institution*, 1989, and is co-editor of the forthcoming collection, *To Be a Citizen: African-American Women and Political Action*. She received her Ph.D. from the University of Wisconsin—Madison.

ANASTATIA SIMS is an associate professor of history at Georgia Southern University. She has also taught at Vanderbilt University, Virginia Polytechnic Institute and State University, North Carolina State University, and Indiana University, South Bend. Her publications include an award-winning essay on the woman suffrage movement in Tennessee, "'Powers That Pray and Powers That Prey': Tennessee and the Fight for Woman Suffrage," *Tennessee Historical Quarterly*, 1991, as well as "The Sword of the Spirit: The WCTU in North Carolina, 1883–1933," *North Carolina Historical Review*, 1987; "Sisterhoods of Service: Women's Clubs and Methodist Women's Missionary Societies in North Carolina, 1890–1930," in the book *Women in New Worlds: Historical*

Perspectives on the Wesleyan Tradition, volume 2, 1982. She has contributed to *Women's History in the United States: A Handbook* and *Dictionary of North Carolina Biography*. Sims was a Rockefeller Humanist-in-Residence at the Duke-UNC Center for Research on Women. She is the author of *The Power of Femininity in the New South: Women and Politics in North Carolina, 1883–1930*, forthcoming. She received her Ph.D. from the University of North Carolina, Chapel Hill.

A. ELIZABETH TAYLOR, pioneering scholar in the field of southern women's history, died in October 1993. At that time she was Professor Emerita, Texas Woman's University. Educated at the University of Georgia, the University of North Carolina at Chapel Hill, and Vanderbilt University—from which she received her Ph.D.—she taught briefly at Judson College in Marion, Alabama, before spending most of her career on the faculty of Texas Woman's University. In 1981 she retired to her native Columbus, Georgia. Her publications include *The Woman Suffrage Movement in Tennessee*, first published in 1957 and reissued in 1987. She also published sixteen scholarly articles on the woman suffrage movement in southern states. Her essay on the woman suffrage movement in Texas is highlighted in *Citizens at Last: The Woman Suffrage Movement in Texas*, edited by Ruthe Winegarten and Judith N. McArthur. She contributed to the *Encyclopedia of Southern History*, the *Encyclopedia of Southern Culture*, and the *Historical Dictionary of the Progressive Era, 1890–1920*, and wrote biographical sketches for *Notable American Women* and the *Dictionary of Georgia Biography*. Upon her retirement, the Southern Association for Women Historians named one of their major prizes in her honor, a prize for the most outstanding article on women's history.

MARJORIE SPRUILL WHEELER is an associate professor of history at the University of Southern Mississippi. She is the author of *New Women of the New South: The Leaders of the Woman Suffrage Movement in the Southern States*, 1993; editor of a reprint edition of Mary Johnston's 1913 suffrage novel *Hagar*, 1994; and editor of an anthology on the woman suffrage movement, *One Woman, One Vote: Rediscovering the Woman Suffrage Movement*, 1995. It is a companion volume to the documentary *One Woman, One Vote*, produced by the Educational Film Center for PBS. Wheeler is also the author of several articles, including "Mary Johnston: Suffragist," in the *Virginia Magazine of History and Biography*, 1992; "Feminism and Antifeminism in the South," *Encyclopedia of Southern Culture*; and an overview of the history of the suffrage movement, "One Woman, One Vote," in *Humanities*, the journal of the National Endowment for the Humanities Vol. 1 (Jan./Feb. 1995). She serves as president of the Southern Association for Women Historians in 1995–96. She received her Ph.D. from the University of Virginia.

Index